Marilyn Monroe & Joe DiMaggio - Love In Japan, Korea & Beyond

Marilyn Monroe & Joe DiMaggio - Love In Japan, Korea & Beyond

Jennifer Jean Miller

J.J. Avenue Productions
New Jersey, 2016

Marilyn Monroe & Joe DiMaggio - Love In Japan, Korea & Beyond

Copyright © 2016 Jennifer Jean Miller, First Edition © 2014

All rights reserved. No part of this book may be used or reproduced by any means, graphic, electronic, or mechanical, including photocopying, recording, taping or by any information storage retrieval system without the written permission of the author.

Cover design by Jennifer Jean Miller, with photo from the author's collection.

All photos within this book are from the author's collection of original photos, negatives, or press photos, unless otherwise noted, and appropriate credits, when known, are cited with photos.

Updated Edition - ISBN: 978-0-9914291-0-3

For Marilyn and Joe with Love.

Contents

Acknowledgements...Page 9
Preface..Page 12
Chapter One – Before Their Love..Page 15
Chapter Two – Love and Marriage...Page 50
Chapter Three – Love in Japan and Korea...Page 74
Chapter Four – True Love Never Dies...Page 99
Chapter Five – True Love Comes to the Rescue...................................Page 127
Chapter Six – Love Beyond Life...Page 162
Bibliography..Page 192
Author Biography..Page 200

Acknowledgements

I thank God above for the purpose He has instilled in my heart, of which I am still learning what it may be. I thank Him for all the blessings He provides to me, second by second of every day.

I offer my sincerest gratitude to all those who supported me through this project, most especially to Jason, Christopher, Amanda and Jadin, who have been here for me with their loving encouragement. You are all so special to me and provide the fire to the little engine that could…meaning me…without your love, I know that this project could not have been possible. You have my greatest love in return always and thanks for being you. I thank God for all of you.

For my father, Joel, who has been my technical guru and spent time with me scanning my one-of-a-kind slides. I am grateful for his support and love during this project and my writing and photography endeavors overall.

For my family -- parents (Mom, John, Joel and Flor), siblings (Erik, John, Becky, Gina and Aleja), aunts (Donna, Ronnie, Dolores), uncles (Neil and David), niece (Alaina), cousins (David, Becky, Salley, Wendy, Ted, Mark, Tara, Alex, Samantha, Tommy, Michael and family, Allan and Paula, Janice and family, Barbara and family and so on), "in-laws," present and future (especially Mecca, Kristie, Karen, Bill and members of my future extended family that I have yet to be introduced to) -- thank you for enriching my life in all the ways that you do…I love you all.

In memory of my dear "Nana" Jean Miller, I thank her for being the spark in my writing career, when years ago I was led after a prayer to submit a writing sample, which was a tribute biography about her. I know she had wanted to be a reporter, a dream potentially fulfilled as a police stenographer. While she was not on a news beat, each day when I type in my byline "Jennifer Jean Miller," her name is within, thus she has a byline too. I love you Nana and thank you for touching my heart for our quarter century here together on earth and…forever.

I also thank a few longtime friends, Stephanie Slick, Lauren Dermody and Cristina Norcross. They are ladies who I have known since girlhood and have been encouragers throughout various circumstances. Thank you all for believing in me. I have enjoyed our correspondences and chats online and off and I would like to acknowledge you all with special thanks and love. Also to friends I have not known as long, Kevin Morris and Julie Hanes, who are both wonderful friends who I have met on Facebook, thank you for reaching out to me like you do and being here for me.

And a friend "in real life" and on Facebook who I've enjoyed late night chats with as well as time in person enjoying coffee and camaraderie in our local diners, the talented Sara Hudock. She is the photographer who captured my image for this book's headshot used in my bio. As a photographer too and one who owns unpublished images that are featured here, I understand the special role a photographer plays in cementing a person forever in time, thanks to their talents. I give that shout out to Sara who is amazingly gifted and give her and her business One Red Tree Photography a plug too.

To Tom Russo and Hap Rowan, who both offered me their knowledge of baseball, and Tom, Hap and also George Graham, who have given me the encouragement to become even more independent with my various writing projects, thank you for all for believing in me and my potential in my writing and business endeavors.

To Bill Truran, Cristina Norcross and Max Zimmer for their support they offered to me, one writer to another penning my first book, I look forward to continuing to inspire one another in our book projects. Thank you to Bill for the introduction to Pauline and Georgie Riggio. Pauline gladly shared with me their memories of meeting Joe, and relatives who had, as well as their photos of Joe playing ball in his military years. I am of course also very grateful to Pauline and Georgie for their generosity in allowing me to use their photos.

Speaking of writers, I am grateful to the reporters who worked on my team when I was their editor, especially Jennifer Fratangelo, Alley Shubert and Jane Primerano, for all your support and encouragement. I feel blessed to have had the opportunity to work with the three of you and also Nisha Kash, who worked with me as a marketing consultant and has believed in me and my projects and endeavors.

I am grateful to the unknown military heroes who captured photos of both Marilyn and Joe. Thank you for watching over us and serving our nation as you did. This book is in tribute to you too. We all enjoy freedoms today because of your sacrifices.

For Tammie Horsfield, John Drake and the staff at the Sussex County Chamber of Commerce, our local businesses and their leaders are blessed to have your support, and I believe, with your encouragement and mentorship, my various projects received an extra boost, which I thank you for. I know you view this as services you provide and your "job," I still would like to extend my thanks for doing such a stellar job at that job.

For my "Marilyn friends," especially Ted Stampfer, Christine Krogull, Eric Woodard, Peter Gonzalez, Heidi Hanson, Jill Adams, Lauren Dermody, Jennifer Peña, Michelle Leiby, Michelle Morgan, Keira Dazi, Holly Bevan and Andreea Pittei, your friendships, kind words, knowledge we have exchanged over the years about Marilyn and other subjects, and overall support for me and my children, has meant more to me than you will ever know.

To my family and friends, including those on Facebook who have been absolute virtual angels, I thank you for always cheering me on. There are so many of you to name, who have offered kind words, and have taken the time to watch my back along the way, online and offline...I am grateful for what you have done for me. There are so many to mention, who have always been there...

I am truly humbled and blessed to have you in my life...and am thankful to you all. Please forgive me if there is a name I have not specifically named here...please know you are most importantly close in my heart and I so appreciate you!

Preface

It was a match made in media heaven, between the King of Baseball and Queen of Hollywood, often coined by the press as "Mr. and Mrs. America."

For Marilyn Monroe and Joe DiMaggio it was a union on paper that would only last nine months beginning sixty years ago on January 14, 1954 -- nearly one of those months in that three-quarters of 1954 was spent overseas in Japan and Korea.

There was a preamble, however, to this legal binding in the form of their courtship, which endured just shy of two years prior to their marriage.

As a postscript to their marital love story, in spite of their separate paths, Marilyn and Joe eventually connected again. Joe remained Marilyn's champion and suitor in shining armor until and beyond her untimely death.

In addition, 2014 marks a special time in the legacy of Joe DiMaggio. This year, Joe DiMaggio would have celebrated his 100th Birthday on November 25. A century ago, a baby blessed the planet with his presence. He would achieve such greatness in the sports world, that even more than seventy years after he achieved an incredible personal record known as "The Streak," it still remains unbroken.

This story focuses most of all on the eternal bond between Marilyn Monroe and Joe DiMaggio. It is one of the most fabled and poignant love stories of all time. Their relationship could be stormy, yet there existed an enduring tie and devotion that is otherworldly.

Marilyn and Joe were so opposite in many ways, yet so alike. Not even Joe was able to save her from the emotional captors who took her hostage. As astute in some matters, the Jolter, as he was sometimes nicknamed, was even fooled. He was not able to see the crash course Marilyn was on with particular individuals, as he was possibly careening on one of his own.

As a lifetime fan of Marilyn's, I began acquiring my collection of original Marilyn Monroe photos in 2009. There have been particular focuses for me during my relic gathering and one of them has been her relationship with Joe DiMaggio. One of the highlights of her life, as she was known to phrase it, was her voyage to the Far East with Joe. More specifically, one of the most extraordinarily special times in her earthly existence was her four-day excursion to Korea to entertain the troops.

Since this was a period of such elation for Marilyn, it has been important to me to capture it through my collection. The photos I have acquired from this segment of her life are press photos, as well as original one-of-kind photos, some never before published and taken by soldiers who chronicled portions of her visit.

Although Marilyn knew very little about baseball, the sports world was the catalyst for bringing the couple together, and had been the focal point for their trip overseas. However, as passionate as the Japanese were and are for baseball, they additionally were -- and still are -- for Marilyn Monroe. In many ways, the frenzy over Marilyn overpowered the initial mission for the trip, which was to kick off Japan's 1954 baseball season.

This book touches on the respective and phenomenal careers of both Marilyn Monroe and Joe DiMaggio, in each of their worlds. It especially highlights and celebrates the sixtieth anniversary of the nearly one-month period of their lives during their nine-month marriage that they took the trip to Japan, and she to Korea. This was a time especially pivotal for Marilyn Monroe both personally and professionally. And amazingly and sadly, in slightly over eight years following this milestone, Marilyn would earn her angel wings.

This book also features very special photos from my collection -- some never seen or published until now -- sixty years following the time they were first captured by photographers witnessing Marilyn's historic performances in Korea. There are other special treats in this book from my collection, including some pieces of memorabilia for both Marilyn and Joe.

Today, both Joe DiMaggio and Marilyn Monroe remain stars on this earth, as much as they do so in heaven.

This book weaves in elements about baseball, entertainment, the military, the tragedies of stardom, and above all, the love Marilyn and Joe shared.

This biography also dispels some of the myths surrounding Marilyn's death, including removing the Kennedy brothers from the equation, parties that Joe himself believed responsible for his love's passing. Had Joe seen the truth, perhaps Marilyn's true killers would have never remained at large.

As an author, seasoned researcher and genealogist, I have done my best to recreate their lives step by step. There are some conflicting accounts that exist and those are addressed in this book. I have sorted through a lot of folklore as well -- some sources I have discarded altogether and not referenced them if I do not believe their accounts to be valid. I will be addressing these tales further in depth in the future.

As a journalist by trade, I have attempted to remain as neutral as possible however, with my adoration for Marilyn as well as acting as press representative for the Marilyn Monroe Family website and Facebook Page run by Marilyn's second cousin Jason Kennedy (not related to RFK and JFK), it is obvious where my loyalties lie. After having witnessed Marilyn's memory be taken advantage of over the years by parties who never held the right (some who continue to assert they do), it has been upsetting to me. When I discuss those who snuffed that right from her, as well as those who snuffed out Marilyn period, my protective nature over her naturally shines through in those sections of the book.

This book came to life in 2014, when it was first published, and then updated two years following in 2016, after the release of my book with Jason, *Marilyn Monroe Unveiled: A Family History*. Upon learning details of Marilyn's ancestry that previous "reputable" biographers had suppressed, regurgitated or confounded with their own spins, as a journalist I realized it was my duty to provide proper updates for the readers that may required updating this book. Most biographers have not performed their journalistic due diligence and done the same, and I pray one day they do, in order to put these myths to bed that have suffocated Marilyn's legacy for over 50 years, and even while she still walked the earth. On a personal note as well, in addition to defending Marilyn's legacy as I have naturally since childhood, Jason Kennedy and I married in July 2015. As her second cousin by marriage (plus a very distant blood relation genealogically, which is a whole other story), it is my love and duty, to share Marilyn's story with accuracy.

While I share this account, I will digress at times and share back stories that happened during the lifetimes of both Marilyn and Joe, as well as stories that have emerged after both of their deaths. It is important for the reader to learn of these insights in this book, as they both relate to the full picture overall of both of these stars' lives and deaths, together and separately, and are intertwined together.

I have also grown to know and adore Joe DiMaggio more, especially through this project, and have sifted through fact and fiction, omitting particular sources, which are not always trustworthy and accurate. I have especially dissected some of the incidents in the countering books, *Joe DiMaggio: The Hero's Life*, and *DiMaggio: Setting The Record Straight*, which turned into a flame war between an author and Joe's friend and attorney (the author has, along with several others, accused the attorney/friend of catapulting from Joe's fame and earnings). I have in the process, become further protective of the memory of the man who strove to protect Marilyn. In addition to acting as one manager of Marilyn's profile on a popular genealogy site, I additionally have been given authority to oversee Joe's.

While I acknowledge the flaws in both of these wonderful human beings, Marilyn and Joe, and the hurdles they encountered along the way -- which, admittedly we all have flaws and hurdles so they are no different than us everyday people -- I hope I have done so with the utmost love and respect for these two enduring legends.

This book is dedicated by its author to the memories of Marilyn Monroe and Joe DiMaggio, each one of them legends in their own right, with the greatest amount of love and reverence for the legacies they have both left all of us with here.

Thank you both for inspiring so many of us.

With Gratitude and Much Love,
Jennifer Jean Miller
February 2014 and 2016

Chapter One - Before Their Love

For two respective legends, their lives and rises to fame have become tales told and retold over the years, in the worlds of entertainment and sports. Both are the stuff that the dreams of many following them, have been made of.

Norma Jeane Mortenson, best known as Marilyn Monroe, and Joseph Paul DiMaggio (the ethnic Italian version of his name was "Giuseppe Paolo"), most recognized by the world as Joe DiMaggio, were born twelve years and about 375 miles apart from one another. She entered the world in Los Angeles and he in Martinez California, slightly Northeast of San Francisco.

Marilyn and Joe walking on the beach in Florida, 1961
Image from a negative in the author's collection.

Norma Jeane Mortenson was born to Gladys Monroe on June 1, 1926 in the charity ward of the Los Angeles General Hospital. Her paternal line is currently unknown, though legally her father was Martin Edward Mortensen (Gladys misspelled his last name on the birth certificate with a "son" at the end of the surname, rather than a "sen," as it is correctly written). Martin Edward Mortensen was technically still Gladys Monroe's husband, though she was separated from him at this time (the divorce was finalized in 1928). "Monroe," was Gladys's maiden name.

On Norma Jeane's birth certificate, her father's occupation was also listed as a "baker." With Gladys potentially utilizing a play on words "Baker" however, was Gladys's married name from her first marriage and a last name that Norma Jeane also used during her childhood. She was sometimes also known as "Norma Jean Baker," dropping the "e" in her middle name.

She potentially used the name "Baker," it is said, for cohesion between she and her half-siblings from her mother's first marriage. There were also the concerns of discrimination she faced in those days, without knowing exactly who her father was. The third scenario that has been presented was that her mother's friend Grace started registering Norma Jeane under that last name, to keep the child hidden from the man legally listed as the father on her birth certificate, Martin Edward Mortensen.

Gladys's family line arrived in California, with originations from the central part of the United States. Her grandparents, Tilford and Charlotty Virginia "Jennie" Nance Hogan, made their way to Missouri, where the narrative stated Tilford toiled his life away as an itinerant farmer. Although Tilford slaved himself, the family was said to have remained impoverished. This is fiction, not fact.

Tilford and Jennie had five children, Dora, Della, William, Myrtle and James. Tilford reportedly taught himself to read and write, and in his fleeting spare moments, savored reading classic literature. This was typical in this day and age when teachers were itinerant. Like his great-granddaughter Norma Jeane, who he would never meet, Tilford was self-educated (though she remained in school until tenth grade) and enjoyed a lifelong relationship with books.

The narrative of Marilyn's life has always stated that Jennie tired of life with Tilford, and they divorced by 1882. To the contrary though we know they divorced, newspaper reports show that after eldest daughter Dora married first husband Louis Milton Andros, she returned to visit her parents in Missouri for four months in 1891. Tilford and Jennie did divorce, and she eventually moved to Kansas City, while Tilford remained in Linn County. The author explores Marilyn's family history with co-author Jason Edward Kennedy (Tilford's second great-grandson) in the 2016 book, *Marilyn Monroe Unveiled: A Family History*.

Though Tilford would remarry, in 1933 and in the midst of the Great Depression, he committed suicide at eighty-two years old. His wife Emma fainted as she found her husband swinging from a rope draped over a wooden beam in the barn. His death notice specified that Tilford held "imaginary financial worries."

Many erroneously stigmatize Marilyn's family tree as having been subject to a history of insanity and mental illness, commencing with Tilford's self-inflicted death. However, Tilford was a man who the records show built a prosperous and diverse life branching into farming, business, politics, real estate, philanthropy and other arenas. Eventually, when he died at almost eighty-three years, his health was failing him and he had fears during the financially devastating times in United States history, when deaths from suicide were at a premium.

A long line of Marilyn Monroe biographers have defamed her family line, indicating a troubling history, when instead some of her family members were truly individuals who crashed into brushes of misfortune.

What is known of William, Myrtle and James is they each lived normal and fairly stable existences with their respective families. Della on the other hand lived like her famous granddaughter, with a more colorful and abbreviated life. Sister Dora also had a very unique life journey that is explored in depth in *Marilyn Monroe Unveiled: A Family History*.

Otis Elmer Monroe reportedly swept Della off of her feet. Otis loved to paint for enjoyment, but also did so for a vocation. Once Della and Otis married, they headed outside of the country to Mexico for work, where Otis was slated to paint houses. Instead of houses, Otis became a supervisor for the Mexican National Railway and during his employ, painted railway cars and supervised Mexican workers.

Della passed the time by befriending the women in the town, and aiding the locals as a midwife and mentor.

Tables turned in 1902, and Della turned to her Mexican girlfriends, who acted as her midwife at the birth of her daughter, Gladys Pearl Monroe.

Otis and Della found opportunity in Los Angeles, where son Marion Otis Elmer Monroe was born. Otis's work evolved to painting "red line" trolleys for the Pacific Electric Railway. The Monroe family began planting their roots, living in a one-bedroom bungalow to commence their implantation in Los Angeles.

Their happiness was short-lived, as Otis supposedly developed migraines, moodiness, fits of rage alternating with tearful bouts, seizures, trembling of the hands and feet and finally paralysis. Gladys was reportedly frightened by the changes in her father, and stayed with neighbors.

Otis became a statistic in 1909, as one of thousands of patients at the San Bernardino County California State Hospital at Patton, where he spent nine months in a hospital bed. He was diagnosed with general paresis, a neuropsychiatric condition affecting the brain as a result of non-sexual syphilis. He instead contracted syphilis from unsanitary working conditions in Mexico.

The narrative expresses that his family mistakenly believed that Otis died from insanity because of the impact on his brain, which was never the case. Della, it was said, often told strangers that Otis passed from paint poisoning to conceal the stigma. But newspaper reports following his death showed that Otis was a beloved member of the community and there should have been no shame over his death.

Della, only thirty-three years old, fended for herself as a single parent, engaging in a couple of violent subsequent marriages laced with drama. While in Venice near California's City of Santa Monica, Della believed her luck changed when she met Charles Grainger. Charles worked as a driller with Shell Oil, and Della was head over heels in love with the man. Some have written that Della never married Charles, yet in some documentation, including her passport application, she was able to attest to government officials that she had planned to visit Borneo where her husband was working.

Della started a new life, and some biographers have reported she sent Marion to live with relatives in San Diego, and urged Gladys to marry. While Gladys did marry no evidence has surfaced that Marion lived in San Diego with relatives.

It is often speculated a man named Charles Stanley Gifford, a beau following Gladys's separation from second husband Martin Edward Mortensen, may have possibly been Norma Jeane's father. Both would assert later in their lives, that they had fathered Marilyn.

Norma Jeane had initially been told her father perished in a motorcycle accident, however this was erroneous information given to Gladys about a man with the same name. Marilyn continued to tell this story to biographers, perhaps with the shame of illegitimacy hanging over her head. Or maybe, this is what she truly believed to be accurate. The genuine Martin Edward Mortensen that Gladys had been married to, often known to his friends as "Eddie," died in February of 1981, with not only news clippings of Marilyn found in his apartment, also her birth certificate and records from his divorce with Gladys.

Lore has governed that Marilyn was born an "illegitimate" child. On paper however, she was not. If Martin Edward Mortensen was in fact her father, then that also negates the illegitimacy factor. If she was truly the love child of the relationship between her mother and Charles Stanley Gifford, that would change the story.

According to relatives of Martin Edward Mortensen, he did attempt to reach out to his daughter, who technically she could be referred to, as she was his child on legal documents. Marilyn allegedly spoke with him several times, apparently rebuffing Eddie. If this was the case, it could have been caused by disbelief on Marilyn's end, as she had always been told that he was died in the motorcycle crash.

On the other hand, Marilyn did pursue Charles Stanley Gifford -- a decision that was said to end each time she did, in heartbreak. He reportedly told Marilyn to stay away, after she had reached out to him.

For Gladys, her marriage to Martin Edward Mortensen was not her first go-round, nor would it be her last. Her first was the one Della encouraged her into when she was fifteen years old in 1917, which ended in divorce after a violent relationship. Following ugly divorce proceedings, her ex-husband Jasper Baker kidnapped their son and daughter, Robert Kermit (aka "Jackie") and Berniece, driving the two small children away from her custody back to his native State of Kentucky during one of his permitted weekend visits. Gladys followed him there, only to be emotionally beaten down. She returned to California after a stint in Kentucky, without her two first born.

As a single parent, Gladys plugged away on the fringes of the film industry, working in its dark crevices as a negative cutter. Her daughter Norma Jeane, in spite of the many tales of woe that have often been disseminated about her, did not go without, and first lived with a family in the Los Angeles suburb of Hawthorne named the Bolenders, who were paid to care of her for the first seven years of her life. The Bolenders were not just some strangers off the street either -- they were neighbors and fellow church parishioners of Della's, who recommended on her way out the door to Borneo that Gladys enlist their help in caring for Norma Jeane while she was at work. Gladys actually lived there with Norma Jeane on the weekends, and on the 1930 census, mother and daughter were both listed in the Bolender household as "boarders."

Many a careless biographer has written of Gladys abandoning her daughter and walking away. On the contrary, Gladys was a responsible mother. She never missed a payment of $25 to the Bolenders for Norma Jeane's monthly care expenses. She held a stable employ as a supervisor of other negative cutters, even leading her flock out of the film lab when the place caught fire. Once when Norma Jeane was very young, Gladys was so determined to work while co-workers were striking, she was one of two women the press reported to have climbed over a fence to enter into her workplace.

Gladys took a two-month maternity leave when Norma Jeane was a newborn, staying in the Bolender's back room with her infant daughter. When Norma Jeane was also a small child Gladys took off two weeks from work, after she learned Norma Jeane picked up whooping cough from Lester, one of the Bolender children. Gladys spent that time lovingly doting on her daughter, applying cool compresses to her head to quell her skyrocketing fever and constantly changing her sweat-soaked pajamas. Gladys spent those weeks in the same cycle, and passed the time rocking her ill child to sleep. A mother, who was said to abandon her child, would not have ever made such a concerted effort to care for her.

Money was tight but little Norma Jeane was still beautifully attired. Gladys would purchase fabric and Ida Bolender, the matriarch of the household where she stayed, was crafty with her Singer sewing machine. Ida would fashion cute dresses for the girl. Norma Jeane's hair fell into ringlets when it was curled, which were often pulled back with an oversized bow, as most little girls of the 1930s wore their hair.

Gladys bought her daughter her first bathing suit -- a horizontal striped one-piece -- the garment that would be the accessory for the first beach pictures of a toddler Norma Jeane.

Norma Jeane participated regularly in extracurricular activities. Ida arranged for piano lessons, and she and Albert Wayne carted the children of their home to church each Sunday. Some have said that movies were forbidden, as they were believed to be "sinful" in the eyes of the Christian couple and only particular radio programs were permitted at the Bolender home. But this is fallacy as the Bolenders' other children have said their lives were only filled with love, not judgment. And in spite of propaganda later spread about the Bolenders, they never judged Marilyn's choice of a career in film. The children also had plenty of books and toys to keep them occupied -- as well as their imaginations -- as they invented games together in the backyard.

Of course, there was school -- and along the way, Norma Jeane was enrolled at several because of her moves. She was a student beginning at age four at the Hawthorne Community Sunday School, and then spent some of her elementary school years in Hawthorne at the Ballona Street School (later known as Washington Elementary).

Norma Jeane had her first stage appearance in these early years at the Hollywood Bowl in 1932, during the annual Children's Cross performance at Easter Sunrise Services. The children traditionally wear black robes at the ceremonial concert and then each unveils a white one at the end to signify Christ's resurrection. Norma Jeane allegedly forgot to remove her robe in sync with the other children and in adulthood said the Bolenders supposedly reprimanded her harshly for it. In Marilyn's later life, this incident was harped upon as a "sinful time" in Norma Jeane's formative years, one that analysts and the acting theorist she hired explored with her and diagnosed that she harbored shame over. Yet most definitely if this affront happened to Norma Jeane, those who emotionally held Marilyn Monroe captive in adulthood for their own means and motives, ameliorated the level of pain and impact that it actually held in Marilyn's later life. Psychiatrists that she enlisted overanalyzed many incidents in her earlier life, simply in order for them to keep Marilyn emotionally dependent on them. Arthur Miller, her third husband, also cited the incident at the Hollywood Bowl in his book *Timebends* -- Arthur is another suspect in the later emotional destruction of Marilyn Monroe.

After Marilyn's death, a distraught Ida Bolender penned a letter to Marilyn's sister Berniece. She mailed a news clipping of Norma Jeane with it, where Norma Jeane was attired in a dress that she had sewn. The picture, which was supposedly taken by Della, is now a famous picture of Marilyn as a toddler and featured in this book.

"It has almost broken my heart to read the terrible stories that have been written about her early childhood," Ida wrote, "when I know personally they are so untrue."

Writer Corey Levitan later chased down Marilyn's years in Hawthorne for a story, in which he interviewed Nancy Jeffrey, one of the Bolender adopted siblings.

"People like to make things sensational," she said, "because when she was moved around later, they want to make it sound like it was all awful, but it wasn't. She was happy in our home."

Nancy also reiterated, "We were never poor. Everybody always had clothes and there was always food on the table."

Albert Wayne Bolender, Norma Jeane's foster father who she liked to call "Daddy" (when toddler Norma Jeane would call Ida "Mama," she would inform her that the "lady with the red hair," meaning Gladys, was her mother and she was "Aunt Ida."), worked at the post office and he and wife Ida cared for several small children in their home. Lester was one boy they adopted. He was often referred to as Norma Jeane's "twin," as both were fair-skinned, blue-eyed and towheads. Lester was about two months younger than his "sister." Norma Jeane and Lester palled around, played games on the Hawthorne streets and walked to and from school together. With Norma Jeane's dog Tippy, they were a happy trio. The little dog obediently waited each day for the children like clockwork in front of their school when they wrapped up classes for the day.

None of the other children in the Bolender home had a dog, which alone is something that shows Marilyn Monroe's childhood was not a horrendously deprived one as has often been painted. Not to say, she did not endure struggles or heartbreak. One of the sad moments involved Tippy, who was shot by a neighbor annoyed that the dog tore through the neighborhood on a nightly basis. Norma Jeane was devastated, yet she was not alone in her sadness -- the Bolenders grieved with the young lady and Gladys as well. Gladys was there with Norma Jeane to oversee the burial of her beloved pet.

Gladys's emotional health began to stagger from the responsibilities of single-parenthood, combined with the passing of Della, who died in 1927 from a bout of malaria she contracted while traveling in Borneo. The malaria, as Otis's syphilis had, made Della's moods irregular. She began suffering from delusions, even envisioning that her own parents Tilford and Jennie had reconciled and were planning a visit to Hawthorne together. Gladys often stayed with Della in those final days to care for her declining mother.

Before Della became ill, she shared some enjoyable interactions with her young granddaughter Norma Jeane. She adored the child, though there exists an erroneous account of Della (who is sometimes replaced with Gladys in the story) having made an attempt to suffocate Norma Jeane with a pillow. This story has circulated for more than half a century. At the time of the occurrence, Norma Jeane who was only slightly over a year old, was the only one who could vouch for this incident and said that she fended off the attack. This was another false memory implanted in Marilyn's mind as an adult by the Freudians therapists who emotionally subdued her through their memory digging sessions.

Della on the other hand, doted on her granddaughter. She was freely permitted to take Norma Jeane to her own home next door for visits. Once Della actually walked in on Ida Bolender (per a story from Ida) who had admittedly just administered a spanking to young Norma Jeane for tossing a bowl of cereal onto the floor. Della verbally reamed Norma Jeane's caretaker for slapping her grandchild. If Della were ever a threat to Norma Jeane, she would have never been allowed to regularly enjoy visits with her, if ever at all.

The rumor of Della having been inherently "crazy" was further ignited when she inexplicably began banging on the Bolenders' front door one morning, breaking a pane of glass and cutting her hand. The police were called and Della was carted to the hospital for treatment on August 4, 1927 -- thirty-five years later on that date her famous granddaughter would mysteriously die. Della's body gave out to heart failure at the Norwalk Sanitarium on August 23 of that year from "myocarditis" or swelling of the heart. "Manic depressive psychosis" was listed as a contributory cause of death.

Viral, bacterial and parasitic factors can trigger myocarditis. Malaria is caused by the parasite "plasmodium," which can spark respiratory issues. Della struggled with malaria in her last days. Cerebral malaria could have caused Della's delusionary behavior, a byproduct as malaria progresses. Her accompanying high fevers, another symptom with malaria, most definitely contributed to her hallucinations -- a family history of mental illness has since inaccurately become an underlying cause of her demise.

In 1933 Norma Jeane moved back with her mother after Gladys purchased a home in Hollywood. Gladys had plans to retrieve Jackie and Berniece (some have said Gladys was unaware of Jackie's death also the same year). It was a time of adjustment for Norma Jeane, who had previously lived somewhat sheltered in the realm of religion in the Bolender home. Life was freer at Gladys's home. Gladys's best friend Grace McKee (later Goddard) stopped by regularly to socialize and enjoy meals with Gladys and Norma Jeane. An English family in the movie industry leased most of Gladys's residence and that helped to pay for the bulk of the mortgage, while Gladys and Norma Jeane lived in one of the rooms in the home.

However, as hard times befell Gladys in early 1934 both financially and after learning of the suicide of her grandfather Tilford, she suffered an emotional breakdown. Gladys ended up in the mental health system with long-term hospitalization until one of her releases from hospital care in 1945.

Norma Jeane learned of Gladys's hospitalization, after returning from a day at the Selma Street School. The Atkinsons, the name of the English family who resided in the home, informed her that Gladys had fallen ill. Grace stopped by daily after Gladys was hospitalized, and helped to tend to Norma Jeane with the Atkinsons.

Norma Jeane stayed with family and friends of her mother's while Gladys was hospitalized. Gladys's friends Harvey and Elsie Giffen also looked after Norma Jeane. The Giffens had children the same age as Norma Jeane and offered to adopt her. Gladys exerted her parental rights though she remained hospitalized and refused that offer. She later rejected others like it -- she never wished to give up her daughter.

Grace McKee handled Gladys's finances with court supervision and continued looking after Norma Jeane, while constantly advising the court of Norma Jeane's whereabouts and expenses for her care. If Norma Jeane was not staying with her, Grace made provisions for the child.

Marilyn's second cousin Jason Kennedy had learned from stories passed down through his family, about their concern for Norma Jeane. His great-grandfather, Norma Jeane's great-uncle and Della's brother William, who lived nearby with his wife Clara and their children, proposed to Gladys that they could help with Norma Jeane. Gladys thanked her uncle, yet said she did not wish to place an extra burden on his family -- he had six children of his own already.

In her later break from hospitalization, Gladys lived with Norma Jeane and Grace's Aunt Ana. Prior to that and after her release from medical care, she resided in Oregon with her Aunt Dora, who was then about seventy years old. In those years back in the real world, Gladys also held down stints of employment along the way. Later, Gladys was conned into marrying a bigamist named John Eley. This third husband, who died in 1952, later made attempts to extort money from Marilyn, claiming he needed it for her mother's care.

Gladys was admitted to the Rockhaven Sanitarium in 1953 -- she would stay there beyond Marilyn's death and in 1967 was released into Berniece's care. Inez Melson, Marilyn's business manager, became Gladys's legal guardian around 1959.

New York attorney Larry Cusack handled Gladys's legal affairs between 1980 and 1984, the year that she died. His son Lawrence X. Cusack would be accused of and later jailed for creating forged documents, suggesting JFK gave hush money to Marilyn for Gladys's care. The claim was that JFK asked Marilyn to remain mum about her relationship with him, as well as dealings the President was purported to have with mobster Sam Giancana -- all details that Lawrence X. Cusack the son, was found to have doctored. His lies have defamed the reputations of the American movie legend and U.S. President.

At the end of Gladys's life, she lived independently in a retirement community in Florida, years away from the mental health system.

In those earlier days when Gladys was first admitted, as it can sometimes be today, the mental health system implemented "poke and hope" and "trial and error" type of approaches in their care of patients. No psychiatric medication is foolproof and known how it will react in a patient's body, there are many factors that drive it. It was worse in those days when medications and procedures were in the "trial" phase. Sometimes it is necessary to shift through options in psychiatric care until ones that work are found. Yet in those days, not enough was known about what patients were being doled out.

Gladys suffered a violent reaction to medication that a doctor had prescribed for her just prior to her incarceration in the mental health system. Rather than discontinuing the medicine, writer Ted Schwarz who authored the book *Marilyn Revealed: The Ambitious Life of an Icon*, rightly pointed out that the doctor instead increased Gladys's dosage -- an action that worsened her symptoms.

That author studied Gladys's condition as well, analyzing that she suffered from seasonal affective disorder from working in cooped up dark conditions as a film cutter. That, combined with her erratic sleep and poor diet, impacted her health.

The mental health community diagnosed Gladys as schizophrenic, which this author believes was erroneous and a cookie cutter conclusion for many experiencing emotional upset in that day and age. They additionally reviewed her "history" of a father, mother and grandfather who were thought to be mentally unstable. With their verdict of "schizophrenia," Gladys's mind received a death sentence. Schizophrenics were filled up with seizure-inducing medications and electroconvulsive therapy (ECT) in those pioneering years. Gladys was one of those patients administered ECT in times when it was not fully known how, when and if to dose this type of a treatment to a patient. ECT fried Gladys's brain, rendering her incapacitated when she was simply battling the blues to begin with.

One event that was a catalyst in strengthening the "Gladys is hearing voices" theory was when Martin Edward Mortensen, her second ex-husband who was very much alive, tracked Gladys down in Norwalk Hospital. Norwalk was one facility where she lived and where Della had died. When Gladys learned that he was living and sought her out, she plotted an escape. Following her attempted breakout, Gladys was further subdued and then transferred to Agnews State Hospital, a higher security facility.

In addition to this, Norma Jeane lived with the whispers in her ear from early childhood that she hailed from an emotionally disturbed line, which had a devastating effect on the path of her life, especially her final seven years of existence on this earth.

Throughout her childhood Norma Jeane lived with family and friends, as well as a stint in the Los Angeles Orphans Home Society from 1935 through 1936. Norma Jeane stayed in this facility until the guardianship process could be resolved through the courts, permitting Grace to become Norma Jeane's legal guardian. Many careless biographers have indicated that Grace dumped Norma Jeane there because she had fallen for Erwin "Doc" Goddard -- this was far from the case. Grace was not happy with the idea at all, and visited Norma Jeane on a regular basis. Grace would take Norma Jeane out for lunch, to have her hair done, to the movies and more. She stayed in habitual contact with those in administrative positions of the home.

Many fables have emerged as well, of her days at the orphanage. The stories and dollar amounts she earned have changed over the years, as have the tales told of the types of chores Norma Jeane was said to have performed, from scrubbing toilets all day and being paid pennies a week to wash hundreds of dishes. The institution however, had employed workers who tended to these tasks. As personnel at the facility would later point out, if Marilyn had been washing dishes all day every day, she would have never been able to attend school or partake in other activities. Those who stayed at the home with Norma Jeane later attested that the people who worked at and ran the home were very kind and loving. The children were showered with attention as well as parties throughout the year -- one neighboring movie studio often hosted the festivities. There was a playground at the home and games and activities that the children could occupy their free time with.

This author is not denying that a transfer to an orphanage was indeed a traumatic experience in the early life of Marilyn Monroe. Her days there however have been blown out of proportion and doctored with shades of *Cinderella*, *Annie*, and *Oliver Twist*.

Norma Jeane had wrongly been portrayed as a waif, and Marilyn was further painted as one by the Hollywood machine, as well as those who emotionally sought reasons to "keep" her (these were the individuals who benefitted off of her will).

Norma Jeane's stay in the orphanage was a necessary step in the process for Grace to achieve guardianship. At the same time, it could have been easily avoided. The truth of the matter is that on court papers, Gladys and Grace lied that Norma Jeane had no other family, in order to appoint Grace as the child's legal guardian. Norma Jeane had a legal father and extended family throughout the Los Angeles area. Geographically, her Aunt Olive Monroe lived in the area -- Norma Jeane stayed in Olive's mother's home for a period after the orphanage. There was also great-uncle William and his family.

Grace's relatives also took part in caring for Norma Jeane. Aunt Ana Lower, the Atchinsons, and the Knebelcamps, were parties Norma Jeane spent parts of her latter childhood with, in addition to Grace.

Perhaps, Gladys only had her heart set on Grace caring for Norma Jeane, as the one who was also appointed to look after her own affairs.

It has often been said that Norma Jeane was shuttled from foster home to foster home, often tallying at twelve or thirteen, where she had been physically, emotionally and sexually abused. However, the reality is that she lived in a total of approximately a half a dozen residences with people she knew, before her first marriage. Norma Jeane's whereabouts in her early years are well documented through court paperwork.

Some of her alleged foster parents, who have been regurgitated in books and stories, have been nameless and faceless -- those who were not nameless, like the Bolenders, were often wrongly smeared and painted as abusive in her tales of her early life to elevate her story to a rag-to-riches Cinderella caliber. In actuality, those that Norma Jeane lived with all cared deeply for her.

There are several players in her youth that have been tagged as sexual abusers, such as a man who was purportedly a boarder in one place that she stayed, "Mr. Kimmel," as well as her cousin Jack and foster father Doc Goddard.

"Mr. Kimmel" has never been fully identified and the tales vary about Jack. Norma Jeane continued to live with Jack and family (Olive's son) although an incident supposedly occurred between the two teens. Jack's sister claimed to witness Norma Jeane bathing obsessively afterward. Norma Jeane was known anyway to be fastidious in her hygiene, obsessively washing her face up to fifteen times daily to prevent blemishes. In Marilyn's 1962 address book, now in the hands of a collector, there was a listing for "Jack Monroe," the cousin said to have committed such a brutal and violating act.

Norma Jeane additionally after she married her first husband Jim, would write to Grace asking her to convey love to "Daddy" aka "Doc," one of the other accused. Bebe Goddard, a foster sister of Norma Jeane's, and Doc's biological daughter, said her father never laid an inappropriate finger on Norma Jeane. Instead Bebe recounted that Norma Jeane borrowed painful stories of abuse from Bebe, who suffered terribly in her childhood.

As another sad result of the circulating tales of abuse committed against young Norma Jeane, the surviving extended relatives of Marilyn Monroe on the Hogan and Monroe sides, though not her sister Berniece or niece Mona, have been subject to attacks by several members of online fan clubs, who snootily began asking them when they also made their ways onto online forums, "Where have you been the last fifty years? You abused Marilyn! You must now be looking to make money off of Marilyn!"

Twelve years before Norma Jeane was born, Joe made his way into the world. Joe, whose one-hundredth birthday is being recognized throughout 2014, was born on November 25, 1914 to Giuseppe and Rosalie DiMaggio, the eighth of nine children, and the fourth of five sons. His parents were native Sicilians, having immigrated to the United States in 1898. The names of the children in the order of their births were: Nellie, Mamie (sometimes referred to as "Mae"), Tom, Marie, Michael (aka "Mike"), Frances, Vince, Joe and Dominic (aka "Dom").

A fisherman by trade, Giuseppe encouraged his boys to follow in his footsteps. By the time Joe reached one year of age, his parents relocated to the North Beach area of San Francisco, a section of the city teeming with Italians. Joe's brothers, Tom and Michael, joined the family business -- Michael later drowned after a fall from his boat.

They lived in a rickety four-room home near the Fisherman's Wharf, with a rent that tallied to $25 per month.

Giuseppe struggled as a fisherman, stuck in a financial predicament as a hardworking man supporting a family of eleven. He could not afford a larger boat to compete in the open sea for decent fish. Salmon and crab, considered the jewels of the sea, were accessible in those waters and yielded more cash. With a smaller boat, Giuseppe was relegated to the Bay, where he would not have access to the more lucrative catches.

"We had some really rough times," Joe once said. "After all, a man doesn't raise nine kids, a hard working man at that, and have an easy time of it."

Nellie and Tom, the two oldest of the girls and boys, always had new clothes. The rest of the children sported hand-me-downs. This is in a stark contrast to Norma Jeane, who although claims reign that she was mistreated, was always dressed by Grace in decent and new clothing. Receipts that Grace submitted to the court documented those purchases.

Joe ended up an impeccable dresser as an adult, believed to have spawned from his days of wearing patched clothes and shoes lined with cardboard bottoms to counter for their excessive wear.

Although they were poor, love ruled above all in the DiMaggio household.

"The DiMaggios were a tightly knit clan," wrote author Robin Moore, "and love was the glue which kept them so close, so unified in their purpose, so devoted to each other and to each other's welfare and well-being."

Giuseppe had a critical nature though and particularly referred to his namesake as "lazy" and a "good-for-nothing," because he preferred not to fish.

A well-preserved matchbook from the author's memorabilia collection, from the DiMaggio family restaurant, all matches still intact. Photo courtesy of the author.

Joe passed the days of his early youth in a nearby lot where milk deliverers parked their horse-drawn wagons. Joe attributed his weak stomach from cleaning the boat. Joe did in fact suffer from gastro issues. Giuseppe did not buy his claims of queasiness, and simply deduced his son was slothful. Giuseppe's tune would obviously change later when his son bore his success via a pinstripe uniform.

"Bueno per niente!" or "Good for nothing!" Giuseppe often bellowed about Joe in Italian and English.

"No good for the house! No good for the boats! No good for nothing! Only for the street, good! Only for to play ball!" Giuseppe ranted daily.

Dario Lodigiani who debuted as a player for the Philadelphia Athletics then wrapped up his career with the Chicago White Sox as an infielder, grew up with Joe. He lived up the hill from the Yankee Clipper's boyhood home. The boys attended Francisco Junior High School together and played on the same playground frequently between their two homes.

"He was a quiet kid," Dario said of Joe. "Never said too much. But he was a good athlete, no matter what sport we played."

Joe played for money in those days too, usually "winner takes all." In that game, each boy tossed in a nickel or dime and the winner would walk away with the pot. Joe was frequently the winner.

Joe was also a champ at cards, especially when he and his pal Niggy Fo rigged the deck.

The sports Joe played varied from touch football to basketball to tennis to Piggy on a Bounce, a game played with a stick and a rubber ball.

"He was a heckuva tennis player," Dario marveled.

Dario said that Joe's baseball game was of course, impressive even in those early days. Friends nicknamed Joe "Coscilunghi," the Sicilian word for "Long-legs."

"You could tell there was a pretty good ball player, he looked like he was gliding," Dario had observed. "He was that kind of a ball player. His brother Dominic was the same way. They both played like they were floating."

It was here on these early fields of dreams in the sandy area by the wharf where the milk wagons parked, where Joe's passion for baseball began. It was an act of improvisation in those days, with a broken oar repurposed as a bat and black tape packed into a substitute ball shape, which the players would pummel into the stratosphere to the best of their abilities with their creatively-fashioned bat.

For a time, Joe took a break from playing ball and resorted to selling newspapers. Father told son it was an ideal job for the boy, as Joe told in his later memoirs, "since it consisted merely of standing still and shouting," skills that the older DiMaggio inferred his son excelled at already.

Dominic, Dario said, was the one who did the yelling while shy Joe did the standing. When the brothers brought home monies to help their household including $1.06 after a day of hawking papers, Giuseppe approved.

Dario sold newspapers with Joe, who he recalled peddled papers for the *San Francisco Call-Bulletin*.

At that age Joe had already started his nearly lifelong love affair with cigarettes and often rolled his own in those days.

"What the heck are you smoking those cigarettes for?" Dario questioned, noting Joe had not yet learned to smoke them and instead simply burned them.

"It makes you look good," Joe fired back.

His brothers Vince, two years his senior, and Dominic, three years his junior, also played on those sandlots. Vince became a shortstop with the Boston Bees, Cincinnati Reds, Pittsburgh Pirates, Philadelphia Phillies and New York (later San Francisco) Giants. Dominic, also known as "Dom" and nicknamed "The Little Professor" because of his stockier build and the spectacles he wore on and off the field, was a center fielder for the duration of his career with the Boston Red Sox. Out of the DiMaggio baseball dynasty, it was Joe who would exhibit the greatest gifts and fame for his command of the game.

Vince was not like his two older brothers, who held the old world ideals of their father. Those traditions were steeped in routine. Tom and Mike followed into their papa's footsteps, dutifully walking into the fishing industry. Vince embraced American notions of dreaming, and grabbing for the brass ring.

When his father forbade Vince, who had become the family rebel, from playing ball professionally, Vince warned his father that he would be ready to pursue his goal no matter what stubborn Giuseppe mandated. Since Vince was underage he required parental consent to play, which Giuseppe refused. Vince lied about his age and signed his contract for the Lumber Leagues of Northern California.

Vince ruffled his pop's feathers further by announcing he planned to marry. First play ball, and then marry? A good Sicilian son was first expected to support the family by working in the industry that had kept them afloat for so many years. Vince refused to break off the engagement and Giuseppe cut him off.

It was Joe that Giuseppe pursued next as the ray of hope to make it big in the fishing industry and he planned to force the issue. Rosalie however, could see what was coming around the pike for her eighth child from his dictatorial father, and told Giuseppe, "Il é bonu, Lasce sta'," which in Sicilian translates to, "He's a good boy, leave him alone."

"Joe's gonna do fine," she predicted.

Vince delivered $1,500 into his father's hands at the start of his ball career. Giuseppe questioned how Vince could have acquired the money outside of stealing it. Once Vince convinced Giuseppe that baseball was his solution, Vince was invited back into the home.

"If Vince can get that kind of money for playing baseball, I can too," Joe decided.

By age eighteen, Joe was already on his way. The road to that success was not always an easy one.

Joe worked his way through the ranks, playing baseball through Hancock Grammar School and into junior high school. He joined the Boys' Club League as a shortstop at age fourteen, and dropped out from Galileo High School after two years.

Like Joe, Marilyn Monroe still known as Norma Jeane, also dropped out of high school at Los Angeles's University High School (having previously attended Van Nuys High School). This was in her sophomore year, just before her sixteenth birthday. It was a decision that stunned her schoolmates and teachers. While her future husband Joe made his own educational decision to cease his high school studies, she was still enjoying her childhood. She made the same choice herself a little over a decade later in 1942 to marry a family friend James Dougherty, a local man who was five years her senior.

It has been debated if Marilyn Monroe married James (nicknamed "Jim" or "Jimmie" as she penned his name in letters to her guardian Grace Goddard) for love or because of Grace's relocation to West Virginia with her husband Doc. That move left Norma Jeane an unattended minor, ward of the court and thus, a potential returnee to the orphanage. Gladys forbade that Norma Jeane leave California. Some have surmised the marriage was not arranged and the couple truly had feelings for one another while others said the orphanage was a hurdle because of Grace's departure. Some have said marriage was as an alternative suggested by Grace and Jim's mother, to the naive Jimmie. Then employed at Lockheed, Jim agreed to the union proposing Norma Jeane could reside with his mother when the call arose for him to serve in the military. Many times in her life, Marilyn contended that she never loved Jim -- her letters to Grace during her marriage painted a different picture. In either case, Norma Jeane could marry legally at age sixteen though she was technically not considered an emancipated adult until the age of twenty-one, when she was first able to make her own legal decisions without a countersignature.

Joe left school for other reasons. He lived, in some ways, a typical city boyhood at the turn of the twentieth century. He and his buddies would cause mischief at times for example, by swiping wares from the local man selling pies from his truck, then reselling them to raise cash for movie tickets. The boys carried the scam further by only purchasing a ticket or two, and then sneaking a group of about ten kids in through a side door of the theater.

School was not their center of attention. Joe was not a juvenile delinquent despite some of the antics. He was not a stellar student either and focused on athletics instead. However his grades were acceptable enough to be pushed up to the next grade levels. Yet he and his best friend Frank Venezia, both quiet boys, hardly knew what was happening in class once they arrived to Galileo High School, not having applied themselves in the previous grade levels.

Joe was a silent kid in school, also because he was so painfully shy and petrified to speak up. At home he learned some Sicilian though he did not speak it well, which was a point his siblings grilled him about openly. Behind the scenes the DiMaggio sisters gossiped about the eighth child in the lineup and surmised that Joe was simply "slow" in terms of his intelligence level.

After Joe's Italian teacher, who was a more upper crust Italian who looked down on Sicilians, kicked him out of class for no apparent reason other than his own personal prejudice towards Sicilians, Joe resolved not to return to school. He feigned that his father needed help on the boat, which was true. Joe did not suddenly love fishing overnight when he quit high school. Instead of fishing he played hooky and Frank soon joined him.

Each day Joe and Frank would pretend to head to class and spent the day instead exploring the city. Like clockwork at the end of the school day Joe returned home, as if he spent the entire day with his nose in his books.

The charade continued for several months until one day when a letter arrived home and Joe faced the wrath of and caught a beating from Mike and Tom. Tom accompanied Joe for a meeting with the principal -- the pair waited for nearly two hours -- the principal stood them up.

"They don't want me," Joe told his brother since the principal was a no-show.

Tom did not disagree and the two left. Joe's school career officially ended that day, though he would be bestowed with honorary college degrees in his later life.

While Marilyn Monroe was still a schoolgirl and not yet a housewife, Joe DiMaggio was gaining momentum on the ball field. First with the Boys' Club League, which evolved into a private club funded by a neighborhood olive oil dealer. He slugged two homers in their championship game for which he received his first financial award after the game -- two gold baseballs and two orders for merchandise at $8 a pop.

Although Joe assured Tom he would attend a "continuation class" which provided equivalency education to dropouts, Joe never attended. He and Frank instead took up odd jobs. Among them, Joe stacked wooden crates at Pacific Box for a week, and then tried out a local orange juice plant for a month, another job he despised. Unbelievably, Joe worked in a cannery, which must have surely been nauseating for a boy who was sick to his stomach from the aroma of fishing. Even in his later life, Joe squeezed lemon juice over his tuna salad to lessen the odor.

The monotony of quirky employment ended when Joe was picked up by the minor leagues. At age seventeen in 1932 he was added to the roster of the San Francisco Seals, part of the Pacific Coast Leagues, a team his brother Vince was already a member of.

From there, more early rewards came. Joe first played with a semi-pro club before the Pacific Coast Leagues in the Class A League on the Sunset Produce Team, transitioning from third baseman to shortstop and batting an impressive .632 over eighteen games. Joe garnered a pair of featherweight baseball shoes for his achievements.

The rival team, the Mission Red A's, offered Joe a tryout and $150 a month. Joe held off on the offer waiting to speak to Tom for advice.

It was Vince who intervened on Joe's behalf, a move that promoted Joe to the bigger leagues instead with the Seals. The team's shortstop and one of its outfielders left a few days before the end of the season, creating a void in three games at the end of the season.

"My kid brother can play short," Vince volunteered.

Joe subbed in for the Saturday game and Sunday doubleheader. There he made it to bat nine times and hit a .222 average. After that weekend he received an invitation from the club's manager and president to report to training school in the spring of 1933. At age eighteen he was signed for $225 a month, not a paltry sum at about $4,043 a month by today's standards.

Dario Lodigiani watched Joe play shortstop in those days.

"He was kind of erratic at shortstop," Dario observed. "But when they put him in the outfield, boy, he became an outstanding player."

Although Giuseppe could barely read English, he would head out early to purchase the newspaper to review the sports scores. In those days the San Francisco papers butchered Joe's last name. When Giuseppe read the name "J. DeMaggio" or "De Maggio" he would recognize his son's achievements. When Joe earned more than one run, it would warrant waking Rosalie to share the newsworthy tidbits with her.

Joe enjoyed a strong tenure with the Seals though he battled a bum knee from a car accident. Yet as the persistent athlete recovered and while his knee was confined to an aluminum splint, his ears were ringing with the news that the Yankees wished to recruit the wonder player. However the trick knee cost Joe more trouble and his batting average and attendance on the field slipped. The issue nonetheless, did not dim the Yanks' interest in the emerging superstar.

He was on his way to the Yankees as a rookie in 1935 with a .398 batting average.

Joe received medical clearance in Los Angeles in 1934 and the Yankees contracted him for their 1936 roster. Though wistful while saying goodbye to Seal Park and friends such as his manager Lefty O'Doul, Joe was grateful to head to the team he dreamed of.

As he would state in 1949 during the latter part of his career on Joe DiMaggio Day, "I want to thank the good Lord for making me a Yankee."

Marilyn Monroe did not know much about sports though she was athletic, earning her own recognition for the high jump at the Lankershim School, where she was a student when she lived with her aunt Olive (Norma Jeane was a student at the Vine Street School in Hollywood, when she lived at the orphanage). She did play ball on the fields at the orphanage and in her later teens and early twenties took to keeping in shape by weight training with barbells and jogging. Although Joe climbed the ranks in sports as she grew up, she was unaware of the greatness he had achieved until they actually first met in 1952.

Joe DiMaggio was assigned the number five to the back of his Yankee jersey, following his stint as number nine as a rookie. His number lined up in succession to Babe Ruth (number three) and Lou Gehrig (number four). In his first season with the Yanks in 1936, Joe earned $8,500 for his Yankee freshman season (close to $143,000 today). At first, Joe would play left field then right, and lastly was placed in center field, where he would remain until his retirement.

Joe initially brought his offer from the Yankees to Lefty O'Doul for a second opinion. Lefty, in turn recruited famous outfielder Ty Cobb, who helped to instill in Joe the fine art of bargaining. Ty, who finished his last game with the Philadelphia Athletics while Joe was still a schoolboy, knew how to squeeze the most from a contract. He helped Joe to craft a letter to the Yankees, rejecting their initial offer of $5,625 -- Joe's Seals' salary, was almost equivalent to that first offer. The second offer of $6,500 Ty also told him to kick back, and helped him to pen another letter. The last offer of $8,500 headed Joe's way, which he accepted.

After Joe returned home with monies he earned his rookie year, it meant a future for his struggling family. He was able to help Mike upgrade his boat, and secured him one for salmon fishing in the winters and another for crabbing in the summers. The open waters were no longer off limits to any of the DiMaggios. Tom was now vice-president of the Crab Fisherman's Association. Tom and Joe then toyed with the idea of opening a family restaurant too.

When Joe arrived to New York's Penn Station to start playing in the Bronx, it was unbeknownst to him that the New York papers were already abuzz about his arrival for weeks in advance. DiMaggio fever had hit the Big Apple and the moment he stepped from the train to the platform, a young boy was at his heels asking Joe for his first autograph.

On his way to Yankee Stadium even in those days he was a man of few words. Joe appeared cool, and hardly spoke to teammates Tony Lazzeri and Frankie Crosetti who fetched him from the train.

His only utterances on the ride happened when the pair asked him if he could take a turn at driving.

"I don't drive," Joe replied.

In his inaugural year Joe helped his team to snag the pennant by September 9, an unheard of feat. He also wowed President Franklin Delano Roosevelt and an audience in excess of 43,000 spectators with a .346 hitting average in a game against the Giants, as well as sweeping in for a legendary catch in center field.

Joe told his friend and attorney Morris Engelberg in his later life, that President Roosevelt waved his hat at Joe at the end of the game. Joe was nervous and excited as the President complimented him with a "good game."

Overall that year, he held a .323 batting average, scored 125 home runs and was an integral player who helped his team to snag both the American League Pennant and World Championship.

His fame soared quickly. Joe would report in his memoirs *Lucky to Be a Yankee*, "Precisely four weeks after I broke into the Yankee lineup, I needed a police escort to get out of Yankee Stadium."

Joe's parents were now able to dine and stay at lush venues, plus receive preferential seating at World Series Games in New York.

The 1937 season equipped Joe with the opportunity to purchase a large home for his family with all new furniture and accessories. The family left everything behind in their four-room domicile in the previous neighborhood and moved to Beach Street. This would remain the family home until it was determined uninhabitable following the 1989 earthquake. Joe and Tom also opened Joe DiMaggio's Grotto, the family restaurant.

With 167 home runs and a .346 batting average, in 1937, baseball was still his number one passion above all.

There was a particularly graceful demeanor for which Joe became known. Infielder and teammate Jerry Coleman said that Joe always looked elegant and dignified as he entered the club, dressed in a blue suit, shirt and tie.

"He always knew who he was and what he represented," Jerry said.

Jerry said that Joe conveyed a particular style with his uniform that separated him from the rest, with his cap angled just right, his jersey perfectly tucked in and his pants lower than how most wore them.

"He carried himself with a lot of elegance at all times," sportscaster Bryant Gumbel said about the champ following Joe's death.

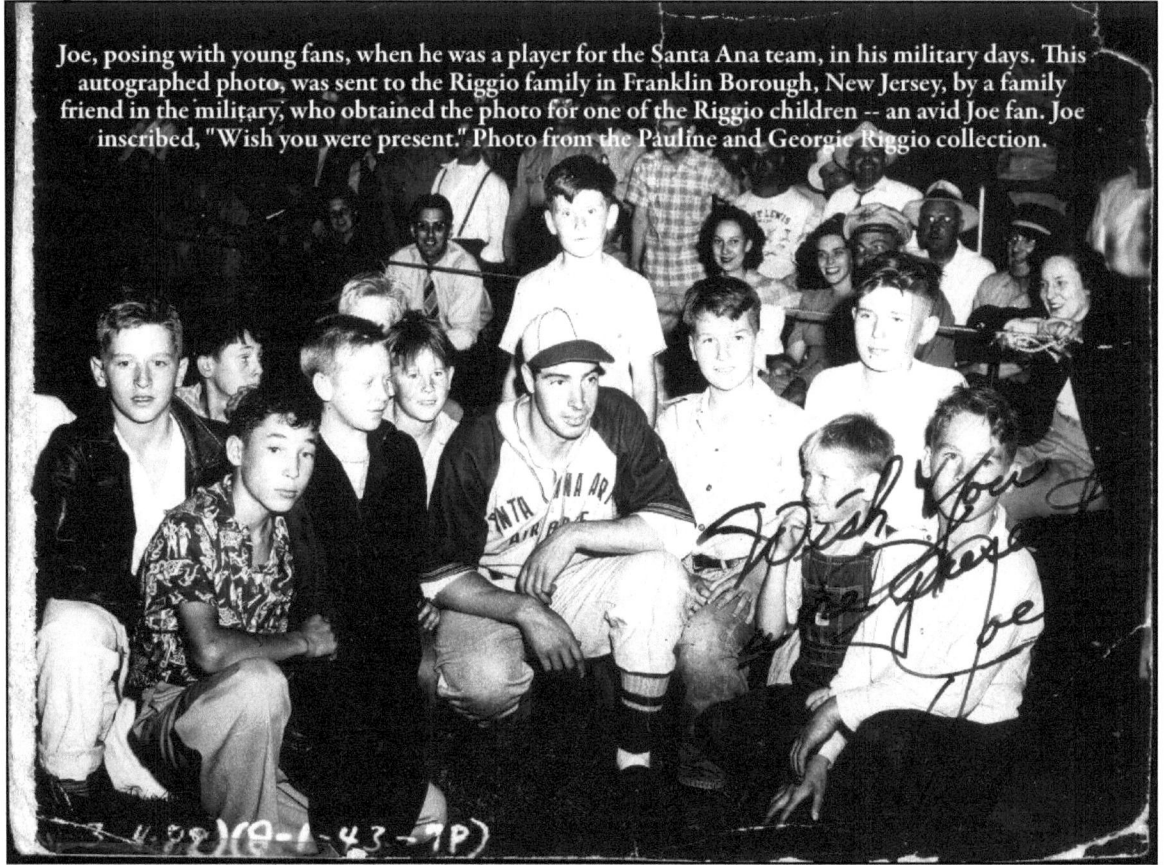

Joe, posing with young fans, when he was a player for the Santa Ana team, in his military days. This autographed photo, was sent to the Riggio family in Franklin Borough, New Jersey, by a family friend in the military, who obtained the photo for one of the Riggio children -- an avid Joe fan. Joe inscribed, "Wish you were present." Photo from the Pauline and Georgie Riggio collection.

"He was always a gentleman, always had a very special style, class and dignity," said Rudolph Giuliani, then the Mayor of New York, when he spoke at Joe's memorial service. "Joe DiMaggio ultimately transcended the Yankees and New York to become a symbol of America."

Phil Rizzuto was one player and a friend, who watched Joe in admiration. He joined the ranks of the Yankees with Joe, in the same year that Joe accomplished "The Streak."

"He shaved with such distinction," Phil laughed, as he told a group at a memorial service for Joe in 1999, about even how Joe made ordinary tasks extraordinary. "It was beautiful to watch. Now it might be a little flaky to say that. But he was perfect in everything he did."

He never spewed out tobacco as many baseball players did and some still do, which to Joe reflected sloppiness -- he chewed gum instead.

"You know when you dress like a champion, you feel like a champion," Joe told legendary Boston Celtics basketball coach, Red Auerbach. "If you act like a champion, you're more apt to be a champion."

"If you could get a whole team to look and act the way DiMaggio did," Red said, "you'd have a helluva club on your hands."

Unlike his Boston Red Sox contemporary Ted Williams, who was known to spit at fans, speak profanely and throw bats, Joe always held together a calm exterior, even with a constant whirlwind spinning out of control inside his soul. Joe was naturally a passionate individual and extremely sensitive, a dichotomy that he kept in check, putting forth publicly his unruffled demeanor instead.

Newsday Sports reporter Marty Noble wrote of Joe, "Even his teammates thought DiMaggio wouldn't let you look inside. It has been suggested that his pristine image exists at least partially because he hid his true self away. In his generation, privacy was more treasured and the media less aggressive. The right to know wasn't exercised so much, and rarely was abused.

When asked why he publicly never lost his cool Joe said, "I can't. It wouldn't look right."

Joe kept an even keel no matter what was happening on the field, and even if he hit a home run he never displayed his excitement.

"He was the same every inning of ever game," teammate Bobby Brown shared.

Jerry commented about Joe's presence on the field, which he described as "imperial."

"He knew what to do and how to do it," he said. "He knew how to act. He was absolutely incredible."

Yogi Berra was another one touched by Joe DiMaggio. In his autobiography *When You Come To A Fork In The Road, Take It!* Yogi devoted an entire chapter in his book to the wisdom he learned from Joe. Having been raised by an Italian family, left high school before graduation and wrestled intensely during contract negotiations just like his teammate, Yogi expressed how he related to Joe.

"DiMag never showed emotion," Yogi wrote. "Nobody made you feel prouder to be a Yankee. He made no excuses. People thought because of his coolness, he was arrogant -- he wasn't. He was a serious and proud man, proud of his ability, proud to be a Yankee. He expected to win, and he knew the team depended on him. He'd play hurt, and expected you to do the same. If he saw something he didn't like, he'd give you the glare, or say it in a way you'd never forget."

Joe distanced himself from his teammates, though Yogi noted, not in a snobby way. He was simply a leader, who was quiet and spent time alone in the locker room, often seen sitting crossed-legged, while smoking a cigarette, and sipping on a cup of coffee delivered by the clubhouse man. When the team was on the road, Joe hardly dined with the Yankees and took room service within the solitude of his hotel room.

Yogi remembers Joe reaming him following a doubleheader game. Though the date is not specified it was most likely in 1948. Yogi said in his book he did not play the second game and Gus Zernial subbed for him as backup (though Gus is not shown to have played with the Yankees). Joe broke his locker room silence to deliver a tongue lashing to the twenty-three-year-old player. The substitute player's performance was less than exemplary and Joe who normally kept profanities to himself, then verbalized his displeasure to Yogi, who was in his second year with the Yankees.

"That's when Joe wanted me to know that being a Yankee, being a professional, was deadly serious business," Yogi said.

Joe told him that a "twenty-three-year-old kid should play both ends of a doubleheader."

Yogi never skipped out on another doubleheader in his career.

Though Joe was hard to approach, he demonstrated his care in various ways. Yogi said that during his rookie year in 1946 Joe often treated him to breakfast because Yogi was not yet earning the type of salary Joe took home. In turn, Yogi paid it forward through this example and ended up bringing rookies to his family's home for dinner in New Jersey.

"Joe helped make you feel that being a Yankee was special," said Yogi.

Yogi recognized Joe's price of fame.

"A lot's been said and written about DiMag, especially about his personal life," he wrote. "It was sort of sad he was alone a lot, he wanted his privacy -- he didn't have close family or friends. But I know what he meant to his teammates on the Yankees. Sure, he was kind of hard to get to know. But after he got to know you, he was a heck of a nice guy. We'd talk baseball for hours in the clubhouse or on the train -- he always was encouraging to us. He had a tremendous hold on people."

By nature, Joe DiMaggio was a private person, in spite of his superhero status in "The House That Ruth Built." He was very reserved and never garish. Marilyn Monroe was leery of meeting for their first date, fearful that she would encounter an ostentatious spectacle, typical of what she thought the sports world personified. She was pleasantly surprised to be introduced to a sophisticated, well-dressed man, with a slight amount of grey in his hair, and she likened his appearance to that of a steel magnate.

However, Joe was not an easy nut to crack. He could be mercurial by nature, and mercenary in his business dealings. In his early years and especially with his spouses, he had tendencies to be mean-spirited, obsessive, insanely jealous, controlling, insensitive, gruff and emotionally distant.

In the same vein, there was a soft spot in his heart that he developed for Marilyn mixed within the moments of his insane rage. As time marched on, he mellowed and their love further blossomed.

Before there was Marilyn though, Joe would receive his first bite of gossip column fodder treatment, preceding his marriage to first wife Dorothy Arnold.

Although Joe resented the hypocrisies of Tinseltown, especially blaming the Kennedys as well as players in the Hollywood Dream Factory as the accomplices in Marilyn's death, Joe was actually cast in one Hollywood minor speaking part and holds one movie credit on IMDb in the role of himself in *Manhattan Merry-Go-Round* (though credited as "Joe Di Maggio"). He had many television appearances over his career including *The Joe DiMaggio Show* and also his own radio show. IMDb does not currently account for his two known television gigs, in which he endorsed Mr. Coffee and The Bowery Savings Bank in commercials.

During his career, Joe had numerous endorsements under his belt, a way for ballplayers to earn some extra money in the days before signing events garnered them a sweet income. In fact, some writers have commented that ball players of days gone by would most likely shudder to know that today's athletes typically charge for their autographs. In those days, their signatures were given away liberally, whereas it has now become an extra cash stream. Joe was always enthusiastic in moneymaking anyway. Chesterfield and Camel Cigarettes, Avon Toiletries, Louisville Slugger, Wheaties and Champ Lighters, were among some of the products Joe lent his image to in those nostalgic years for a financial return.

Joe (left) stands at attention during the National Anthem, when he was a player in his military days.
Photo from the Pauline and Georgie Riggio Collection.

A Republic Pictures production released about two weeks after Joe's twenty-third birthday in 1937, the film would eventually earn a Best Art Direction Academy Award nomination. Joe said in his early memoirs he turned down the offer to appear in a vaudeville series because of his appearance in *Manhattan Merry-Go-Round*, which convinced him that he "wasn't an actor." Joe, the boy who had been afraid to utter a peep, truly still was -- his brief appearance required twelve retakes for his three lines in the film. While he was there, the showgirls from the picture fussed over and flirted with the baseball star. It was on the set where we met an extra by the name of Dorothy Arnold, then age nineteen, who was cast as a dancer.

Dorothy, who had been from the Midwest and previously known as Dorothy Arnoldine Olson, had no idea who Joe was when he requested to meet her. Even when he was legendary, Marilyn would echo the same confession when Joe begged for an introduction to the sex symbol.

Joe took cues from his friend, pitcher Vernon "Lefty" Gomez, who was a sharp-dressed fellow off the field and married showgirl June O'Dea. Having a showgirl was the right thing for a baseball hero in those days. Having a looker on his arm was a change for the blushing boy who would sprint in the other direction when his sisters' friends would come to their home for an afternoon.

Dorothy created a buzz when she entered the stadium. Perfect curls sat atop her head, she dressed in fancy dresses and elegant hats, and her face was flawlessly painted in all the right places with dark lips and brows framing her visage. Spectators stopped by for a signature from Joe's girl, who unlike her man, sometimes wore a puss for pictures. When she was photographed among Joe's friends and family, she was typically the most attractive-looking girl in the crowd. Marilyn would later eclipse and outrank Dorothy -- her following was one way beyond what Dorothy could ever attract -- there was especially no comparison when Marilyn visited Yankee Stadium in 1952.

Dorothy was pretty though commonplace when compared to Marilyn. Once Joe laid eyes on Marilyn, his heart never turned back. He also had a very difficult time locating a "replacement" for her, not only because of her outer beauty yet more importantly, the sweet spirit he truly fell in love with.

For Dorothy, Joe was a breath of fresh of air, with men in Hollywood having attempted to make her their plaything. Joe, on the other hand, was gentlemanly and chivalrous. Though his friends supposedly took him along to brothels a few times in his early days with the Yankees, Joe by nature was not a playboy. Instead, Joe was bashful, a trait which appealed to her. Dorothy was an extrovert and socialite and was intrigued by Joe's coy demeanor.

Dorothy had her sights set on success and outwardly appeared to have it all together. Inwardly she was a mess. She always sought to be the center of attention and engaged in strange antics to do so. If she failed in her attempt for notice, she turned huffy.

Dorothy was bulimic before bulimia was an understood concept. Some daughters of Joe's friends in Newark New Jersey caught Dorothy hugging the porcelain goddess, a purge that followed a dinner they all shared together.

Dorothy never achieved the heights with her stint in Hollywood that Marilyn attained. Dorothy's résumé consisted of mostly uncredited roles in 1937 and 1938. In 1939, she gained some recognition in Bela Lugosi's *The Phantom Creeps*, as well as the film *The House of Fear*.

Then a "tween" becoming a teen in the age rank, Norma Jeane was a movie aficionado. Although movie going was a banned activity in the Bolender home where she resided in Hawthorne (listening to radio programs such as *The Green Hornet* was permitted), Gladys and Grace liberally brought the child to the well-known cinemas, such as Grauman's Chinese Theatre. Trips to the movies happened when Gladys would spend time with Norma Jeane on the weekends when she lived with the Bolenders and especially after Norma Jeane moved in with Gladys. Norma Jeane's foster sister Bebe was another friend she frequented the movies with. The girls spent summer afternoons following trips to the movie houses at local soda shops, for burgers and other treats.

Gladys and Grace worshipped the movie idols of the day, including Norma Talmadge and Jean Harlow, instilling their love of the cinema in Norma Jeane. It was natural for these two women to gravitate towards movie magic as one of their primary interests, with their vocations in the industry. It has been rumored over the years that Marilyn's first legal name (she did not officially change her name to Marilyn Monroe until 1956) was a combination from the two stars (which is unlikely since Jean Harlow had not officially changed her name to her screen name until after Norma Jeane's birth). Gladys countered this myth and told Berniece that she named Norma Jeane after a girl she was a nanny for while she lived in Kentucky (Gladys worked nearby to where son "Jackie" was hospitalized. The boy suffered many health woes, including problems with his leg and the loss of his eye from a firecracker. He would later develop tuberculosis of the bone in his leg, which stressed his kidneys to the point they failed. Then at home his father catheterized him to drain his kidneys instead of transporting the child back to the hospital. Jackie died shortly afterward at age fifteen).

Gladys would later become a devout Christian Scientist and intermittently shun the film world from her life, at times showing disdain for Marilyn's career choice.

Perhaps in Norma Jeane's many afternoons at the Los Angeles movie palaces where she would pass the time away, she may have watched her future love onscreen in his cameo part in *Manhattan Merry-Go-Round* or watched Dorothy Arnold with her mouth agape as a damsel in distress in *The Phantom Creeps*.

While he started to build a future with Dorothy, Joe missed his 1938 opening game because of a contractual dispute. The financial aspect of the institution always presented a bone of contention between Joe and his ball club, now holding out for an increase to $40,000 from the Yanks. However, the brass would not bend and Joe relented and returned two weeks into the season, greeted by boos from the fans.

While Joe had hoped to snag the $40,000, a counteroffer of $17,000 was thrown back his way.

When Joe learned that Lou Gehrig was not even earning what he sought, his reply was, "Then Mr. Gehrig is badly underpaid."

When Joe consented to $25,000, the fans booed their prodigy upon his return.

The booing did not deter Joe from wrestling the Yanks for a greater salary each year.

While many Yankee devotees still struggled to make ends meet as a result of the Depression and scrounged for money to purchase their tickets, they were disappointed when they could not watch the team's prodigal son play. Joe's quest for the almighty dollar often offended fans, including in 1941, a monumental time in his career, when he was absent frequently because of injuries and salary gripes.

Joe wrote in his memoirs, "My impending marriage with Dorothy was creating quite a stir on the sports pages, of all places, and there were almost one-hundred rumored elopements. We had made our plans, however, to be married in San Francisco in mid-November."

With Marilyn's meteoric rise to fame already in motion when Joe and Marilyn would meet in 1952, the touch in the papers about his marriage to Dorothy the same year he earned his enduring nickname "The Yankee Clipper," would provide Joe with a brief introduction to the whims and wiles of the pop culture press. However, in spite of this and compounded with his own fame and established relationship with sports writers, Joe was far from ready or thrilled about the overwhelming and unprecedented attention Marilyn naturally magnetized.

His wedding to Dorothy took over the City of San Francisco the day the couple married on November 19, 1939.

Before Dino Restelli became an outfielder for the Pittsburgh Pirates (he played for the Pirates from 1949 through 1951, his last game a few months before Joe retired) like Joe he also grew up in San Francisco. He and Joe shared some commonalities -- they were both children of Italian immigrants and each served in the Army during World War II. Dino was additionally a notable player who once batted with the San Francisco Seals.

Dino was among the thousands of spectators who waited outside the church for Dorothy and Joe's grand exit. He and a friend had another vantage point along the scaffolding above the church entrance. The pals moved slightly just as the newly married Joe and Dorothy emerged, knocking some dust onto them from the structure.

"Joe kind of looked up and laughed," Dino said. "He saw the two of us up there."

The crowd was so massive that the bridesmaids were unable to navigate through to the church entrance and arrived a half hour late. Brother Vince and his family also had difficulties bypassing the crowds, arriving into the ceremony through a side door.

A woman in the heap of people fainted and police with clubs needed to push a path through for ambulance attendants to reach her.

The crowd on the wedding day was too overwhelming for Joe who in spite of being a beloved baseball hero often crushed by masses of fans, preferred the quiet. Dorothy, on the other hand, soaked up the attention she was receiving as the bride of Joe DiMaggio. They invited 800 guests to the family restaurant for the buffet and celebration. Joe simply wanted to cut the cake and leave, which he insisted be brought out right away -- Dorothy cut her finger on the knife during the rush. Though the two would not specify where their honeymoon was, Dorothy was spotted behind the wheel with Joe in the rumble seat of their car, annoyed and not saying a word to her.

It was this same year that *LIFE* magazine profiled Joe in a way, which focused almost discriminatorily on his Italian heritage. He was portrayed as if he arrived off the boat and headed right for Yankee Stadium. The writers obviously took some creative license to pen Joe's bio.

"Although he learned Italian first, Joe, now twenty-four, speaks English without an accent, and is otherwise well adapted to most U.S. mores," was how he was introduced. "Instead of olive oil, or smelly bear grease, he keeps his hair slick with water. He never reeks of garlic and prefers Chicken Chow Mein to spaghetti. Unlike many ball players, he does not chew tobacco. His favorite pastimes are listening to the radio and going to the movies. His favorite radio star is Bing Crosby, whom he calls, 'Bingaroo.' His favorite movies last year were: *Jesse James, They Made Me a Criminal,* and *In Old Chicago.* His favorite star is Gloria Stuart."

Dorothy quit Hollywood as Joe had asked her to do, returning to television for one episode of *The Lone Wolf* in 1954, long after their divorce. In 1957, she appeared on television for one episode each of *The Adventures of Jim Bowie* and *Dragnet*, as well as holding a minor role in the film *Lizzie*. Her last film role was in the 1958 film *Fräulein,* an appearance that would pale in comparison to her rival and successor for Joe's heart, Marilyn Monroe.

Joe was late to spring training in 1941, fighting to achieve $35,000, an amount that did not thrill him with three unsigned contracts under his belt before that number was reached.

Then, the slump struck him. Joe was still a favorite with the fans, voted by the Boys Athletic League a player of even greater magnitude than Babe Ruth. Afterward, Joe would show the fans that year how he was victor, a man who reached for his goals, and achieved them. He had a beautiful wife waiting for him at home, and would become a parent for his first and only time that year too.

Joe's teammates would bust his chops that they had never seen him smile as widely as he did in his Camel cigarette ads.

"I've smoked Camels for eight years," Joe vouched in one ad. "They have the mildness that counts with me."

He was turning twenty-seven that year, which meant he began puffing on Camels in his late teens.

Even Dorothy would light his cigarettes for him, as a way to show how she doted on her husband.

"I find Camels easy on the throat -- milder in every way," Joe said. "And they've got the flavor that hits the spot every time. You bet I like Camels!"

In 1941, Joe was apparently enjoying Camels even more than he publicized in his ad, as he tended to indulge more liberally in his tobacco when he was nervous or in a foul mood.

Before there was "The Streak," a streak of another kind existed. It was Joe's batting slump.

Joe's friend and teammate, right fielder Tommy Henrich, aka "The Clutch," described the phenomenon that, "When Joe wasn't hitting, then he was a human chimney."

As Joe attempted to reconcile the reasons for the slump in his swing, he swigged down more coffee and inhaled more Camels.

It was a rough season for the Yankees, with only eighty-eight games the year prior, and landing in third place. Morale was down for the fans as well, but the Yankees have held an enduring legacy, even in those times, as the "comeback kids."

Joe took his ups and downs even closer to heart, as a determined perfectionist who sought to please his fans, he carried an immense pressure on his shoulders. Even in Red Sox enemy territory, he was also revered for what an Italian-American son of an immigrant fisherman could accomplish. His story was already legendary and he was viewed as a figure in idol worship, which placed a burden in his heart adjacent to the glory.

He confessed to teammate Lefty Gomez, "Sometimes, it's only when I sleep that I don't feel thousands of eyes staring at me. And that's only if those eyes don't follow me into my dreams."

Joe held a top hitting spot in the league in 1939 (.381) and 1940 (.352), though in his memoirs he noted the slump's start during the 1940 season, which he credited Dorothy to having been the one who unlocked the door to the reason for his temporary decline.

A matchbook, from the author's memorabilia collection, with matches still fully intact, from Joe DiMaggio's family restaurant. Photo courtesy of the author.

Dorothy obsessed about baseball, learning all she could about the game, entering into their relationship clueless about the sport.

"I noticed what's wrong with your hitting," she told him, after having sat in the same seat day after day, observing from the same angle. "The number on your shirt is in a different position. You're not swinging the way you used to."

Although initially expecting a prosaic, irrelevant and illogical commentary from Dorothy, Joe was impressed with her observation and took note. Afterward, Joe made a slight adjustment to his stance and was back on track.

His elegance, ease and efficiency at the bat would crescendo to the record known as "The Streak," beginning on May 15, 1941. Within that time through July 17, Joe would achieve a fifty-six game hitting streak. His record has remained unbroken more than seventy years later, with Pete Rose slightly closing in on it with forty-four games in 1978.

What commenced as an ordinary hit on May 15, bloomed into hit after consecutive hit by Joe as the season progressed. With his batting average, now up to .408, with fifteen home runs and fifty-five RBI's as other feathers under his cap, the nation's attention was focused on Joe.

That day, Joe almost prophetically poured out to sportswriter Dan Daniel, "I just have to keep believing things are going to get better tomorrow. Tomorrow is what sustains me."

There are fifty-five ball players in the history of the game, who have achieved a hitting streak in excess of thirty games or more, with Joe at the top of the list.

Pete Rose played for the Cincinnati Reds and was a versatile career ballplayer, a switch hitter who also played both infield and outfield. Pete Rose's hitting streak was still unable to touch Willie Keeler's, a right fielder that achieved his record with the Baltimore Orioles over the 1896 and 1897 seasons. Pete Rose technically tied the Willy Keeler record -- in one season (1896), Willie hit forty-four times. Yet, it is not an exact match, as Willie Keeler still exceeded Pete Rose by his one hit achieved in 1897, which was tacked on to his season-ending 1896 streak.

The press took notice quickly of "The Streak" as it was in formation. Over a month into "The Streak," Joe played in a doubleheader game versus the Washington Senators. Not only did the Yanks defeat the Senators in both games, 9 to 4 and then 7 to 5, Joe surpassed the forty-one hit record of George Sisler, who had been the Cleveland Browns first baseman -- a milestone that had been achieved nineteen years prior in 1922.

As the country kept its eyes turned to Joe in excitement, Joe outwardly held onto his quintessentially cool exterior.

Joe did not want to jinx himself, as he started to achieve hit after hit through the month of May and June.

"I'm not thinking about it," Joe remarked calmly to the press when asked seven games prior to reaching the George Sisler record. "It would be a nice record to have beside your name, but I'm not going to worry about it. I'll either break it or I won't. Now if I wasn't hitting and was in a hitless slump, then I'd have something to worry about."

It was on June 20 that Joe and the fans began to surmise that perhaps this "streak" was record-worthy.

Joe said in 1986 of his achievement, "I didn't make a big deal about it in '41, until I felt like I was swinging the bat well enough to really so something about it. That was around the thirty-third game, when I got four hits and the baseball started looking like a beach ball to me then, and for the next couple of weeks. That's when people really started asking me about it, too. Until then, they seemed to have other things on their mind."

Joe's popularity began to strengthen and blossom with even greater brute force, also at another big sporting event that he showed up to, dressed to the nines, the Billy Conn and Joe Louis fight, another fascination that year.

About Joe's appearance at the fight, ticket broker and friend George Solotaire who attended with him said, "He [Joe] nearly started a riot. There were so many people asking for his autograph that he had almost as many cops around him as the fighters did."

"The Streak" was something Joe would own and placed him in a special rank and class in baseball history.

Tommy Henrich said, "Joe tried to downplay 'The Streak,' almost from the moment people started talking about it. But I think he knew that this was his chance to do something so amazing that other guys would be chasing him forever."

Once Joe was caught in "The Streak" it was glory, yet there was an anxiety forming, as it was a performance that required consistent maintenance.

Lefty Gomez witnessed firsthand as one of Joe's closest friends. He watched Joe chain smoke his Camels and leave his room service dinners half eaten, as his stomach fluttered from the stress of "The Streak."

Lefty said, "All of the craziness, and the son of gun always came to the park, got his hits, and helped us win baseball games. I've yet to meet the man who could go through what he went through and produce what he produced."

Third baseman for the Cleveland Indians Ken Keltner and Joe would have a brush with one another in games seventeen and eighteen. Ken was one person attempting to knock Joe's tower down, and did so by the fifty-sixth game. One of Joe's balls brushed against and off of Ken's glove during one of these games, something for which Ken made a mental note about for following games.

"One more inch," Joe told him as they crossed paths between innings during the double header, "and I start all over tomorrow."

By game thirty-three, it was Joe against Joe from now on in a class all his own, which confirmed his slump was a distant memory. He was proceeding onward to great things.

It was a trying time for the world while "The Streak" was ongoing. The phenomenon kept the minds of Americans off of the happenings in Europe, as Hitler's military invaded Russia. "The Streak" offered a diversion from the global troubles.

The Yankees, who were leading the enthusiasm the country held for Joe and were on the road, paused on June 2 when learning of the devastating news -- their dear friend Lou Gehrig had died. Though the team lost two games, Joe continued to lead with "The Streak" while he was feeling equally downtrodden.

Lefty Gomez said, "From that moment on, there was no question who the leader of the team was."

Beginning on June 7, the Yankee spark returned with eight wins straight, and Joe taking home thirteen hits within those games.

Dorothy, halfway through her pregnancy commented how "The Streak" was impacting her, when questioned by reporters who stopped by to their midtown Manhattan penthouse.

"Joe is as calm as can be," Dorothy bragged to the press. "But it has me all on edge and tense. I can't say that I've been a baseball fan all my life, but I certainly am now."

There was one ballplayer who had an ax to grind with Joltin' Joe, and that was Philadelphia Athletics pitcher Johnny Babich, who lost to Joe when the two played in the Pacific Coast League. In those earlier days, Joe took a triple from Johnny's fastball and Joe's Seals took Johnny's Mission Reds, 1 to 0. Joe also achieved his twenty-ninth game that day in his streak that he reached with that team, which led to a total of sixty-one games.

Johnny undertook some plans to derail his old rival on June 28, with a plot to deliver Joe a fastball, which he successfully did, and the hit landed into shortstop Al Brancato's glove. Johnny had planned "junk" pitches to follow, however his plan was not clandestine and was broadcast to his detriment to local sportswriters, who emptied copious ink to alert their readers.

Joe had fair warning and hit everything in sight including the next ball, which he bashed back through Johnny's legs, nearly turning the pitcher's voice soprano. Joe took a double from his fellow San Franciscan.

When Joe broke George Sisler's record, George, enjoying his retirement, commented, "If the record has to go, I hope it goes to a player like DiMaggio. I liked DiMaggio the first time I saw him. He's a natural in everything he does. I'd hate to see my record beaten by some ordinary player who just hits a lucky streak. But if DiMaggio breaks it, fine! I don't know of any player I like more to do it."

A large hiccup occurred in the middle of "The Streak" at the Washington Senators game, where the Sisler record break occurred -- Joe's bat "Betsy Ann" was lifted. The handle of this particular D-29 had been shaved to conform to Joe's hand and the batboy was specifically ordered to guard it. It was the second of two thefts that day, with Lefty's mitt also swiped.

Tommy Henrich had borrowed another one of Joe's D-29's while Joe was in his slump. At first Joe jumped on Tommy that he may have taken his cherished "Betsy Ann" in error, and after it was resolved he had not, Joe borrowed it back. He hit a single to left field that left his teammates celebrating, as Joe conquered George Sisler's record.

Giuseppe, back in San Francisco, was proud yet as always, critical of his offspring.

He moaned to one of the local papers, which in turn published his commentary syllable by syllable of broken English and with his thick accent: "Joe, he wait-a too long. He waits until-a the seexth inning before he ties-a da record of Seesler. Then he waits until-a da seventh inning before he breaks-a Seesler's record in-a da second game. He makes his papa worry too long. Why cannot my son Joe do it in the first inning?"

Joe and his teammates celebrated on the train ride home from D.C., and the topic of "Betsy Ann" came up, with Joe's mood darkening. Joe had hoped to have that special lady for his trophy collection and mourned her disappearance over some vigorous puffs of his favorite Camels and rounds of beer that he bought for the boys.

"The Streak" albeit was a record achieving time for Joe, was a period as well that he felt his quality declined, because he swung at balls that were less than par, just to keep his momentum up for the record.

It was when Joe's "mistress" "Betsy Ann" was missing in action, that the DiMaggio Fever grew so great that the song "Joltin' Joe DiMaggio" was penned by bandleader Les Brown to commemorate "The Streak."

On July 1, Joe tied Willie Keeler's record and the following day, he garnered a home run in the fifth inning of a home game against the Boston Red Sox, helping his Yankees to keep the win in the Bronx in an 8 to 4 victory. Joe clocked the record-breaking ball into the lower stands beyond left field, adding an eighteenth homer onto his season stats.

"Betsy Ann" was tracked down in Newark, thanks to Joe's industrious friends in that city, who caught wind of her whereabouts after the thief bragged vigorously about his conquest. She was delivered back into Joe's hands on July 5.

With his "girl" and he joyfully reunited, Joe and "Betsy Ann" belted a 420-foot homer in game forty-six.

By game fifty, the excitement became further contagious, as Joe was the main attraction for ticket sales no matter where he traveled.

"It's all up to the pitchers to stop me now," Joe said by game fifty.

Joe headed for his fifty game record, with three singles in the game, and having achieved his twentieth homer over those nearly two months. The Yankees took home another win of 6 to 2, this time in St. Louis against the St. Louis Browns on July 11.

Joe's precious "Betsy Ann" would not outlive "The Streak." On July 14, his fifty-fourth game, the Yanks not only took a hit to the Chicago White Sox, succumbing to the team 7 to 1 and concluding their fourteen game winning streak, "Betsy Ann" splintered apart after Joe nailed a fly ball towards second base.

On July 17 "The Streak" then met its ending in Cleveland, on Indians' home turf, in front of more than 67,000 fans. It was two "ordinary" players who took Joe out. First, Southpaw Al Smith pitched to Joe three times within the first seven innings, and twice, third baseman Ken Keltner averted balls that headed in the direction of the third base line, knocking Joe out in both counts. Next, Jim Bagby was pulled from the bullpen in the eighth inning to pitch to Joe. Joe hit a ground ball to Lou Boudreau, who tossed it Ray Mack, and who threw to Oscar Grimes on first, who shut Joe out.

The inning it ended, Jim Bagby's first pitch was marked "ball one." The second was a fastball, which Joe fouled on. It was the fourth ball, a fastball that Joe nailed as a grounder, which in turn hit a pebble before it reached Lou Boudreau.

The audience was stunned into silence, as Lou tossed to Ray Mack, who threw it to Oscar Grimes.

Joe overran first base toward center field, then picked up his glove and momentarily headed back into position, emotionless.

The Yankees still took the game that night 4 to 3, though the Indians launched an attack against the Bronx Bombers in the ninth inning when the score was 4 to 1, with the Indians stealing an extra two runs, which almost brought the game into a tenth inning. The tenth inning could have permitted Joe another chance to continue his streak.

Out of all of them, Joe considered Ken Keltner the one who officially killed "The Streak."

"I can't say I'm glad that it's over," Joe told reporters, consenting to make goose egg shapes with his hands for the cameras. "Of course I wanted to go on as long as I could. But Smith and Bagby didn't break my string. The guy who turned the trick was that Keltner. He was a little rough on me."

That night, rather than being Cleveland's hero for ending "The Streak," police officers approached Ken Keltner and wife Evelyn, to escort the couple safely from the stadium. Though Joe was not a hometown hero, he had reached the status of American Folk Hero.

"There's a lot of angry people here, a lot of DiMaggio fans," the police told the Keltners.

Ken was in disbelief about it, until he hit the mound to pitch the next night and was greeted with a sea of "boos" from the Cleveland locals.

When "The Streak" ended, Joe did not pout or brood over it while in the limelight, and instead celebrated the accomplishment in the locker room with his team and their manager Joe McCarthy. Joe publicly took the ending in stride, graciously posing for pictures. On the way back to the hotel however with friend Phil Rizzuto, Joe confessed that he had been approached for an endorsement with Heinz 57, if he was able to meet and exceed fifty-seven games. He was silently downtrodden, though he had not let the world see. Joe headed for a local saloon, asking Phil if he could borrow money, since his wallet was left behind in the ballpark's safe.

Joe asked to be alone to reflect on the night's event in solitude, and in the company of strangers.

Phil was one teammate who would comment on "The Streak" many years later.

"Very seldom, if ever, would he hit a ball on the handle or on the end of the bat, like most of us 'normal' ballplayers. Every time he hit it," Phil explained, "it was almost always good wood. But now, he was outdoing himself. Everything he hit was a bullet."

"The 1941 streak was an unbelievable thing," Phil continued. "Day after day. I don't think he got a fluke hit the entire fifty-six games!"

Ted Williams, one of baseball's greatest batters, famed left-fielder with the Boston Red Sox, and friend of Joe's, once predicted of Joe's achievement, "I believe there isn't a record in the books that will be harder to break than Joe's fifty-six games. It may be the greatest batting achievement of all."

A milestone of a different kind would touch Joe's life on October 23, with the birth of his only child (Dorothy's as well), Joe DiMaggio, III, most commonly known as "Joe Jr." Although Joe would gush obvious pride over his son in the early part of his life, dedicating *Lucky to Be a Yankee* "To little JOE," father and son were estranged in later years.

In the book he wrote of the momentous occasion of his son's birth, which he celebrated at one of his favorite watering holes in Manhattan, a place he had frequented since his bachelor days, Toots Shor's.

Joe commented, "Even if Shor and I weren't such close friends, I'd always have a soft spot for him anyway because it was in his restaurant on the night of October 23, 1941, that I was able to pass around the cigars to celebrate the birth of Little Joe. Now there was another DiMaggio available to pick up the Yankees when I left off."

His only offspring was not at his father's deathbed on March 8, 1999, when Joe, an ardent smoker until 1969, succumbed to the ravages of lung cancer at age eighty-four. Joe Jr. would sadly lead a wayward life, working odd jobs and battling drugs and homelessness. The son of the golden boy of baseball often felt cast aside by both parents and struggled immensely. While at prep school in New Jersey, the young DiMaggio excelled in football and scholastics, although neither parent attended his games to support him, and rarely visited him at the school's campus.

In a tragic turn of events, Joe DiMaggio Jr., died shy of five months to the day of the anniversary of his father's death. Although the report of the younger DiMaggio's death indicated his death was of "natural causes," Joe Jr. was only fifty-seven years old when he was found without a heartbeat and not breathing. Attempts to resuscitate him failed after he was rushed to the hospital by ambulance. The media painted his death as a result of a drug overdose and so did biographer Richard Ben Cramer. In actuality, junior suffered from asthma and was often without an inhaler. The autopsy for the younger DiMaggio showed that he died from "hypoxia" aka "reduced oxygen," and "chronic pulmonary disease" -- "alcoholism" and "severe gastroesophageal reflux," were additional contributing causes.

Father and son, in happier times. An AP Wirephoto, from the author's memorabilia collection. The verso of the photo, is below.

HONOLULU—Joe DiMaggio grins broadly as Duchess Joy (left) and Carol Jean Hirota, both 9, kiss son, Joe Jr., 11, on his arrival for a vacation. "He likes sports—not girls," Joe said.

Joe Jr. who was often called "Joey" by those close to him, enrolled as a freshman at Yale in college, but disliked the winters on the East Coast and quit college there. His dad also told friend Morris Engelberg, that Joe Jr. was busy drinking and smoking marijuana already back in those days, confessing to his other friend Dr. Rock Positano in retrospect, that his son "got into the wrong crowd." Had he finished college, Joe Jr. would have graduated with Yale's Class of 1964. He moved to Los Angeles instead, where he was employed in random jobs before enlisting in the Marine Corps and heading to basic training at Camp Pendleton near San Diego.

After junior wrapped up basic training, Joe planned to snub his completion ceremony, as he was upset by his rebellious attitude. Marilyn chided Joe for his stubbornness and lack of support on Joey's achievement. Joltin' Joe still carried a chip on his shoulder that his boy did not complete his days at Yale.

"If you don't go, I will," Marilyn allegedly warned Joe. "You have let that boy down too many times. This time, either you go, or I will."

Joe followed Marilyn's orders this time around in their relationship and attended the ceremony.

Joe Jr. took a seventeen-year-old bride in 1963 after he completed his enlistment in the Marine Corps, her name now Dawn Novotny. She has since come out with her own memoirs entitled *Ragdoll Redeemed: Growing up in the Shadow of Marilyn Monroe*.

Dawn has described her interpretation of Joey's relationship with Marilyn as a combination of "friend, stepmother, idealized woman, and sexual fantasy."

While Dawn has countered that she has no regrets over their marital union, she has said she suffered emotionally during it. Joey, she described, still heavily mourned Marilyn's death, which happened only a year prior to their marriage. She said direct questions about Marilyn or the Yankee Clipper, were off limits. Joey also refused to talk about either parent and had not seen or spoken to Dorothy at that stage for two years.

Dawn described a meltdown Joey had in the supermarket, upon locating a magazine that boasted a headline about the Jolter receiving an endorsement from the Boys Club of America. She said Joey swiftly exited the store, leaving even their cart filled with groceries behind, and required hours of calming to normalize.

"Years later," Dawn wrote, "I thought how hurtful it must have been to see all that his father gave to other boys but never to him, his only son."

She said that Joey denied connections to the Yankee Clipper, when people viewed the name "Joseph DiMaggio" on their checks or his driver's license.

Though Joey would not admit to strangers about the affiliation to his famous dad, on the other hand after Dawn had been raped, Joey said the police should not be called due to the negative publicity the crime could generate. Both were distraught by the incident and instead retreated further in opposite directions.

She said Joey softened when remembering Marilyn.

"But with Marilyn he was different," Dawn wrote. "When speaking of her, his eyes became soft, almost misty. I could see his love for her."

Dawn said that Marilyn always made Joey feel special, and made time for him, rather than his parents, who he expressed to her would "only [take him] out of the closet for photo opportunities."

In her blog, Dawn articulated that she felt Joey wished to mold her in his own way, like Marilyn. He often asked Dawn to dress the way Marilyn did, for example, which was a style she was not comfortable with.

The marriage between Dawn and Joey fell apart a year later. Dawn has since recovered and moved on in the fields of counseling, teaching and mentoring. She has since become a mother and grandmother, and triumphed over breast cancer.

After his marriage with Dawn ended, Joe Jr. floated between odd jobs, until his uncle Dom in Boston became his employer. Dom owned a company that produced polyurethane foam.

During his employ with Dom he met Sue Adams, who is now employed as a realtor in the Walnut Creek California area and using the name "Sue DiMaggio Adams." Like Dawn Novotny, she appears in her photo as a confident and vibrant lady.

Sue and Joey married and he became the adoptive father to her two daughters, Kathie and Paula, from a previous marriage that left her widowed. Though Joltin' Joe was not fond of Sue (nor was he of Dawn), Kathie and Paula became the apples of the Yankee Clipper's eyes and he loved and treated his adoptive granddaughters as if they were his own flesh and blood.

Joe Jr. attempted to make a go of it himself in the polyurethane foam business and relocated back to California with Sue and the children, managing the business on the West Coast for Joe and his two business partners. This arrangement tickled Joe, since he was able to have his granddaughters nearby. Joe Jr. however had his usual difficulties relating to his father and turned to drinking and drugs for comfort. The company began to falter, as well as his marriage, with Joe Jr. doling abuse to his wife. During one incident, he broke three of her ribs and pounded on her face.

Sue told Joe's friend Morris Engelberg that Joey's drug of choice then was methamphetamines. The business tanked and junior took a job as a trucker in Oakland, often resorting to driving under the influence. He was ticketed when caught -- another moment in which he took out his anger on Sue at home. Sue and Joe Jr. separated in 1974 -- all the while it is said junior cavorted with other females while dangling Sue on the line.

In 1976 before they divorced, Joe Jr. asked Sue if he could use her station wagon one day. She reluctantly relented and he wrecked it. After being pulled from the twisted metal "Butchie," as he was nicknamed in childhood, survived the devastating car crash. He unfortunately developed a blood clot and it was necessary for doctors to extract a portion of his brain. The surgery further impacted his behavior and increased his temper. Junior began running with motorcyclists and landed in jail often after the accident.

Sue distanced herself and found her way into the real estate industry. Though she adored Joey as Dawn had, his self-destructive behavior and drug abuse took their toll on her feelings for him. The last time she saw him alive she was shocked by his appearance, which she described as "awful," as he carried his father's coffin the day the Yankee Clipper was laid to rest. However, the two were cordial to one another at Joe's funeral.

Joe the father apparently tried to help Joe the son with the purchase of a $75,000 Peterbilt truck, which Joe Jr. subsequently wrecked. The relationship became further strained and Joe Jr. spiraled additionally from his increased alcohol and drug use. At the end of the '80s, the roof over his head was a trailer nearby his father's birthplace of Martinez California.

Joe the father would try to seek out his son when he traveled back to California, though Joey purposely maintained a lifestyle without a phone and in meager accommodations to avoid his father. He shunned dental care and lost all of his teeth, while spending the bulk of any monies he received on the occasions that family and friends tried to help, on alcohol and drugs.

A cousin of the DiMaggios', Marie Amato Goodman, told the *Los Angeles Times* of the younger DiMaggio, "He had a brilliant mind. He lived in the shadow of his father, and could not rise above that."

Cousins Joe T. and Marina DiMaggio described him as a "con," though they said they have missed him terribly since his death.

Morris Engelberg, Joe's friend and lawyer, said he attempted to bridge the gap between father and son, which the Yankee Clipper refuted.

"You don't know my boy," he told Morris.

Morris was surprised that Joe used the term "my boy," rather than the more personal "my son."

It is likely had Marilyn survived beyond her thirty-six years, Joe Jr. would not have strayed down the path as he did. Marilyn adored him when he was a child, and he would often accompany his father and future stepmother on their dates. When Marilyn moved to San Francisco following her marriage to Joe, she would walk the city with Joe Jr. after retrieving him from school in the afternoons. Times with Marilyn were some of the happiest of his life.

Joe Jr. remained close to Marilyn following the couple's divorce. While Marilyn was married to third husband Arthur Miller, Joe Jr. stayed a part of her brood from a distance, and they would regularly speak on the phone. On August 4, 1962, he called his former stepmother (and future stepmother, as Joe and Marilyn were making plans to marry again on August 8, the day he would instead weep over her body as she lay in her coffin) to share the news that he had broken an engagement to a girl who Marilyn considered unsavory. It was the last confirmed phone call that she received -- Marilyn died a few hours later.

An envelope found in Marilyn's bedroom after her death contained photos of her stepchildren from her second and third marriages, as well as a young fan she had befriended named James Haspiel. Joe DiMaggio, III was included in this cherished category, and his call on that final day delivered a highlight of joy. Marilyn's housekeeper heard the star laughing and enjoying the conversation, in the moments before she retired to her bedroom to meet her untimely death.

Although the relationship between father and son remained tumultuous, Joltin' Joe however willed most of his fortune to his adoptive grandchildren.

As Joe was reaching major milestones, such as helping the team garner World Series wins from 1936 through 1939 and then again in 1941, achieving his famous hitting streak and simply becoming the legendary "Joltin' Joe," Marilyn had not yet become a bride for the first time. At this stage in the timeline, she was still a starry-eyed young teen named Norma Jeane, swooning over Jim Dougherty. While Norma Jeane batted her lashes at Jim, Joe was established and wealthy and on the surface, appeared to be enjoying life as a family man.

Little did the liquescent blue-eyed young woman know as she melted into her beau Jim's arms while they danced at a Christmas party in 1941, in slightly more than a decade she would not only be sought after by the great "Joltin' Joe Di Maggio," but would become the heart's desire for many men and screen goers worldwide.

There was a transformation that occurred in the young woman a year or so earlier and she now elicited attention everywhere she went. Initially taller and more awkward than the other girls, as she made her way into Emerson Junior High School, "Norma Jeane the String Bean," "Norma Jeane the Human Bean," or even "Norma Jeane the Jumping Bean," as fellow students named her, suddenly became shapely instead of skinny. The horns would beep, with offers to drive her to school. Male classmates, who previously passed her by, now tripped over each over and fought to carry her books. Though her grades were average, Norma Jeane participated in the school's glee club, was on the staff of the newspaper and was cast in stage productions.

Jim was the "boy next door," literally, who was tasked to drive his neighbors Bebe and Norma Jeane to school. He viewed the girls as "kids," and dated a local beauty queen. However, she dumped Jim, as she was seeking a man who could provide a lush lifestyle for her. Jim nobly worked the night shift as an aircraft worker at Lockheed.

The "kid" Norma Jeane blossomed in front of Jim's eyes at that dance, pushing herself closer to him, her eyes tightly shut as they swayed back and forth in time to the music. Jim swooned himself, and started to fall for her sweet personality. He recognized her maturity beyond her years. By springtime, Norma Jeane and Jim were steadies.

While things were heating up in the love department for Norma Jeane, things were fizzling for Dorothy and Joe. She considered Joe cold and inattentive, as he often spent nights out with the boys, especially at Toots Shor's. She also resented that she gave up her film career with the advent of their marriage -- marriage and motherhood bored her.

Joe was already not thrilled with the world of Hollywood. After marrying Dorothy, he quickly judged the Tinseltown facade as phony. He was long jaded about Hollywood before he met Marilyn. Joe was low-key following his games, preferring to sit in his team's clubhouse with Phil Rizzuto and Lefty Gomez to talk shop rather than attending glitzy Hollywood affairs. Toots Shor's was another stop where he would comfortably socialize and be guarded from the public and press by saloonkeeper and friend "Toots." He spent time there with the likes of other celebs, coincidentally from the institution he despised the most. Comedian Joe E. Lewis was a close friend, as was heartthrob Frank Sinatra, though that friendship would decline when Marilyn was at the center of it.

Dorothy felt excluded from this world and unlike Marilyn, crossed the threshold of the almighty Toots Shor's less frequently. The establishment was considered a sacred sanctuary of sorts for Joe. To her, it was the "boys' club." Here, Joe was the center of attention, not Dorothy, a point the attention hog resented.

After Little Joe was born, Joe was hardly around, which increased the tension in their home. He frequented his favorite place to escape the stress at their residence. Once when she did accompany him one evening at Toots Shor's, the gang there celebrated a new family addition for one of the patrons.

When Joe offered that he could teach the new papa how to hold a baby, Dorothy muttered under her breath, the question, "Whose baby are you going to use for teaching?"

In her eyes, Joe was not home enough, and her life as Joe DiMaggio's wife was growing duller by the minute.

In 1942, the year Norma Jeane and Jim married, Dorothy filed for divorce in Reno. Joe's performance on the field dipped and the club asked her to reconsider to help the Clipper get back on track, which she did. At the end of the season she filed again, this time with Joe pleading -- Dorothy dropped her case again.

After several back and forth scenarios, when Joe was stationed in Santa Ana during World War II, Dorothy used the opportunity to file the divorce papers in Los Angeles, and was granted an interlocutory divorce.

Dorothy showed to court attired in a mink coat, with a story similar to one Marilyn would later echo to a judge -- Joe could be cruel and distant, sometimes not speaking to her for days on end. Although the judge was a baseball fanatic, Joe was still obliged to pay out $14,000 to Dorothy, and then monthly support payments of $150 for Joe Jr. Joe apparently did not have the $14,000 handy and instead, reportedly sold his share of the DiMaggio's restaurant to Dominic, which ignited some bad blood between the brothers.

Since there was a year time-span in which the divorce was not fully finalized, Joe hoped it bought him additional time to reconcile with Dorothy.

He continued serving in the Army Air Force for the Special Services, teaching baseball to the troops to increase morale for the boys, beginning at the Santa Ana Army Air Base in Costa Mesa California. It was not all about baseball though, and the athletic DiMaggio endured the rigors of basic training like all the other recruits. He asserted he was ready to serve his country, in between the amusement. Joe was embraced by the ball team there, and was a valuable asset. He helped the team to garner a twenty game winning streak, in addition to his personal twenty-seven consecutive game-hitting streak.

Babe Ruth also recruited Joe onto his Armed Forces all-star team, which went head to head with the Boston Braves in early July.

In July of that year, Joe recalled in his memoirs that he was shipped to Hawaii, and now a Sergeant, served with the Seventh Air Force. While in Hawaii, he taught baseball to his new team, the 7th AAF, for a World Series in Honolulu with Army versus Navy players. Although Joe batted a 435-foot homer during their battle on the field with the Navy (playing against his own brother, Dom, as well as fellow pinstriper Phil Rizzuto), the team succumbed to the Navy, 6 to 2.

Perhaps the change of venue to Honolulu was a welcome relief for Joe following the angst surrounding his split from Dorothy. She retained custody of Little Joe, though Joe's mother Rosalie was then practically raising the boy.

Joe was susceptible to ulcers throughout his lifetime, with his bout in August 1943 most likely triggered by his stresses with his issues with Dorothy. There was another reason for his stomach woes, revealed later -- his dislike of Army life in general. Although Joe was more pampered than other enlisted men, rubbing elbows with generals and playing pinochle, Joe was bored. He missed his pals at Toots Shor's, and he missed Dorothy. His ulcers sidelined him. He required a break from military baseball and was hospitalized on the West Coast. His next transfer was with the special services to the Army Air Force Redistribution Station 1 in Atlantic City New Jersey, before he ended up with another round of ulcers and treatment in St. Petersburg Florida's Army Air Force's Don Ce Sar Convalescent Hospital.

This started the series of exams Joe was subjected to while in the military. A "Special Examination of Enlisted Man" on January 8, 1945, showed Joe's medical history included, in addition to issues with his ulcer and other gastric problems, the "usual childhood diseases," a tonsillectomy in 1938, and shockingly revealed gonorrhea in

1938, an illness he contracted the same year when he was already a Yankee (it was noted there had been "no recurrence" of the sexually transmitted disease).

A report from Atlantic City on July 19, 1945 shows that Joe was treated for "anxiety reaction, severe. He was hospitalized for observation, treatment and disposition."

Apparently, military doctors questioned Joe's history with duodenal ulcers, and indicated there was no ulcer found during a complete gastro-intestinal study. They described Joe as suffering from "hyperchlorhydria," which is a rise in stomach acid pH.

Joe in action, during a military game. From the collection of Pauline and Georgie Riggio.

"Although he denies nervous or mental disability," the report read, "he admits that he has always been moody, and it would appear that he has always been high strung, irritable, easily aroused and quick tempered."

One of Joe's complaints to the doctors was that military service was interrupting his ability to possibly reconcile with Dorothy, a task he grew obsessed with.

Their report noted Joe was already susceptible to depressive tendencies, for which, "the diagnosis was made of: anxiety reaction severe, manifested by depression, palpitation, restlessness, tension, epigastric distress and history of proven duodenal ulcer, non-combat stress moderately severe, predisposition moderate, functional capacity permanently and seriously impaired for all military service."

Joe underwent repeated psychiatric interviews, which all came to the same conclusion: he was pining for Dorothy -- and was additionally feeling guilty over their divorce, the shame he felt about it from church, and about the divorce's impact on Little Joe.

Another something that troubled Joe were the alterations to the family's restaurant management, which Joe did not agree with, and for which he was resentful. His stay in the military prevented him from taking action, and upset him because of some financial stake he still held in the restaurant.

Most of Joe's issues in the ten-page report focused around his angst triggering epigastric distress after his meals, which would keep him awake at night. He also said that he "felt he was exploited by being put on exhibition," while in Honolulu, and that if he wished to play baseball he "could have stayed in civilian life and made $50,000."

"He feels that in the Army on many occasions he was not treated as a soldier but was permitted to be lionized as a baseball hero by autograph seekers, that he was disturbed at times in his rest, and that he could not adequately adjust to military demands because of these factors," the account additionally read.

The testimony noted Joe's stormy relationship with Dorothy, and that it was subject to "frequent separations and reconciliations, which finally ended in divorce within the past few months."

Joe described himself as further feeling "reclusive, irritable, easily depressed, and resentful," since his stay in the Army.

Emile G. Stoloff, Major MC Chief of Neuropsychiatry, who penned the Psychiatric Certificate, suggested Joe be re-assigned as a physical instructor, that he no longer be exhibited in ballgames due to his aggravation about the topic, that accommodations be made to prevent badgering from autograph hounds and press releases, "or undue notoriety which single him out as a celebrity rather than a soldier." The remedy was to reassign him from Atlantic City to another post, where he would have a gastroenterologist supervising his diet of three healthy meals a day.

William G. Barret, Major in the Medical Corps, said, "He [Joe] has been a public character, in fact, an idol of the baseball masses for many years and he now no longer feels capable of living up to this position. In other words, a vicious cycle has been established, tending to undermine his self-esteem and perpetuate his anxiety. Each hospitalization has brought about temporary improvement in his condition, but it may well prove to be impossible, while he is in the service, to so alter the internal and external conditions of mental conflict, as to enable him to cope with his life situation, free from symptoms."

Joe was officially released from military duty on September 14, 1945.

While Joe mourned over the divorce from Dorothy and hoped for reconciliation (their divorce and marital struggles were not touched on in his book, in which he wrote, "Dorothy, of course, was the best catch I ever made in my life."), that would all change once he fell in love with Marilyn Monroe. With Marilyn, the Yankee Clipper was instantly smitten and forever in love with her, even as he lay in his own deathbed.

Norma Jeane and Jim's wedding on June 19, 1942, unlike Joe and Dorothy's at which about 30,000 fans crammed inside the cathedral, poured into the streets, and dangled in the trees in front of the Saints Peter and Paul Church in San Francisco, was a more intimate affair. About twenty-five guests gathered instead at the home of Grace's friend, Chester Howell, where Norma Jeane descended a swooping staircase. Most of the guests were family members of Jim Dougherty's, though the Bolenders were there and gushed over how pretty Norma Jeane looked. Gladys was one person noticeably absent from the day, as were Berniece (the two sisters had not met yet, but were corresponding) and the Goddards, who had already moved out to West Virginia. "Aunt Ana" Lower, Grace's aunt who had become a loving mentor to Norma Jeane, gave away the beautiful bride. A reception followed afterwards at the home, and then Norma Jeane, Jim and some of their guests, headed to the Florentine Gardens for an after-party celebration. Their honeymoon was a fishing trip, which Norma Jeane appeared to thoroughly enjoy from the photos.

In a somewhat parallel yet separate life, Jim Dougherty, then an everyday citizen (that would change once he became known as Marilyn Monroe's first husband), reported for the draft in summer of 1943 at Catalina Island. His base was only about forty miles from where Joe was stationed in Costa Mesa. Jim enlisted into the Merchant Marine where, much like Joe DiMaggio who was using his muscles for sport in the military, Jim became a physical instructor.

Jim was an athlete in his own right, having been a stellar football star at Van Nuys High School, and having turned down an athletic scholarship to the University of California at Santa Barbara to help support his impoverished family. Of course, many years earlier, Joe also experienced abject poverty and handed over meager wages to help put food on the table, yet at this time, his situation was much different. While Joe DiMaggio was fighting the Yankees for a difference of $25,000 versus $40,000 in his annual salary, in stark contrast, the Dougherty family was attempting to recover from the aftermath of the Depression. They were so deprived for a time the family camped in tents, picked fruit for a living and hunted small game for dinner to merely to subsist.

Norma Jeane unlike Dorothy Arnold would join Jim during his military stint, blissfully residing on Catalina Island with him through 1944. Norma Jeane tended to their home and walked the island with her dog Mugsy on the days Jim worked. However, Jim would soon be shipped overseas and Norma Jeane would return to the mainland, where she would live with his parents in the Los Angeles area and become employed at Radioplane.

Norma Jeane worked extraordinarily hard at Radioplane, a drone manufacturer, where she was recognized for her efforts. The job was exhausting and she was on her feet up to ten hours a day for a shift. Her pay was seventy cents an hour to start, or about $9.30 an hour by today's standards. The company was pleased with Norma Jeane and her efforts on the job. They commended her with awards to the chagrin of her co-workers, who were jealous of the favor she received, quickly earning raises in her pay as well. Norma Jeane had written to Grace that she was planning to save every cent possible to purchase a home with Jim following the war.

Photo of Marilyn, which had belonged to collector Frank Driggs, and is now part of the Jennifer Jean Miller Collection. Marilyn (far left), is featured in her first starring role.

Yet, unexpected guests to the Radioplane facility would influence a change in her path. One of those visitors to the factory was a photographer named David Conover, who first passed her by, suddenly stopped in his tracks for a double take, and then walked back to the beautiful girl who was busily toiling away.

Had the crew from the 1st Motion Picture Unit, which was then headed up by Ronald Reagan, not stopped by and located her, would there ever have been the phenomenon later known as Marilyn Monroe?

An even greater possibility that Marilyn Monroe may have never become a reality for the world was that Norma Jeane was busy seeking other employment. Norma Jeane reported to Grace in one letter that she had interviewed for an Army Civil Service position, yet there were too many men pursuing her at that potential job. Norma Jeane turned down the post, and the employer suggested she do the same, because she created such a distraction during her short visit to her prospective workplace.

"I was over there <u>one</u> day, There (sic) are just too many wolves to be working with, there are enough of those at Radioplane Co. with out (sic) a whole army full of them," she wrote to Grace on June 15, 1944.

Had Norma Jeane assimilated comfortably into that Civil Service job, perhaps she and Jimmie would have continued in their white picket fence life and Marilyn Monroe would have never existed.

Yet things would shift in a way, which would place Norma Jeane on a completely different route.

"The first thing I knew The (sic) leadlady (sic) and leadman (sic) had me out there having the Army taking Pictures of me," she wrote to Grace on June 4, 1945. "They all asked me where in the H_ _ _ I had been hidding (sic). I told them I had been back east on leave of absence to visit my folks."

Marilyn Monroe had a natural flair for quips, and her quick and innocent response to the inquirers from the Army proved how adept she was early on at holding her own in public relations situations. At the time, she had taken a leave to visit her half-sister Berniece for the first time, as well as the Goddards, in the latter part of 1944.

In the same letter, Norma Jeane reported to Grace that she had not worked at Radioplane since January. Jim had returned for a leave and she focused on her husband.

"I don't really want to do that kind of work anymore because it makes me so darn tired," she lamented.

By the time she had written Grace with her news, Norma Jeane had settled into modeling for area photographers, who were captivated by her enthusiasm in front of the camera, as well as her untrained command of it. David Conover was one for whom she worked as a paid model (a relationship she would describe to Grace as "strictly business," in spite of David's claims in his memoirs that there had been a romance), and his friend Potter Hueth was a second.

Husband Jim apparently approved initially of his wife's modeling endeavors, however as her career progressed, the moral support dwindled away. Norma Jeane rarely modeled when he was on leave, something that would change as their relationship declined. Jim believed modeling was something she would shed once they were ready to settle down and have a family. Joe DiMaggio would also consider Marilyn's career on the first leg of their relationship a passing phase.

Her career climbed to the next level during the late portion of the summer of 1945, when Potter Hueth's photos of Norma Jeane landed on the desk of Emmeline Snively, who headed up the Blue Book Modeling Agency. She enrolled with the agency using the name "Norma Jean Dougherty" and at times model under the professional name of "Jean Norman." "Mrs. Norman," was an alias she would later implement when leaving phone messages and sending telegrams to Joe in the early 1960s.

Soon, Norma Jeane became a sought-after model and cover girl, her beautiful nineteen-year-old face gracing the covers of magazines and pin-up photos, of which many would be held in the hands or tacked on the walls of servicemen worldwide.

As her career ascended, Jim asked her to make a choice. In turn, she headed to Las Vegas to temporarily reside while she filed for divorce. He received the "Dear John" letter, while stationed in the Orient, and ceased her allotment.

Although it was understood she was required to stay in Las Vegas until her divorce was finalized, which happened in September, Norma Jeane's interest in pursuing a film career led to a screen test in the summer of 1946. Thankfully, court officials did not learn that the Norma Jeane Dougherty, who had just attested that she had remained in Las Vegas the entire time since she filed for divorce, actually was reported in *Variety* on September 5 as having signed a contract at Twentieth Century-Fox Film Corporation.

After slipping back to Hollywood as an unattached woman, Norma Jeane underwent the studio's training program, with a work ethic unseen by the higher-ups at Fox of the contract players. She continually modeled and promoted herself with public appearances. Before the end of the year, she would undergo another change, as her professional name became Marilyn Monroe. Though Marilyn had hoped for the name "Jean Monroe," those guiding her in those early days told her this name combination was the best choice.

Over the course of her career, Marilyn acted in a total of thirty films, with that thirtieth one uncompleted. There are claims that exist that she was in some films as an extra, *the Green Grass of Wyoming* and *You Were Meant for Me* were a couple, though these roles have never been fully confirmed. Marilyn additionally has been cited as having had a part in *The Shocking Miss Pilgrim*, with her voice utilized as a telephone operator. Marilyn, in her lifetime, credited *Scudda Hoo! Scudda Hay!* as her first role, period and did not speak of participating in the others. *The Shocking Miss Pilgrim*, perhaps as a connection exists, because Marilyn asserted that film from the movie was utilized to film her initial screen text. However, outside of promoting the picture on a radio show as a starlet, that is where Marilyn's affiliation with that picture should cease.

In terms of production, early in her career Marilyn was an extraordinarily busy actress, especially in 1950 through 1952. During those years, her average output of films that she worked on totaled approximately five per annum. However, once the Freudians and Lee Strasberg took hold, even though Marilyn had achieved great heights of fame already on her own, the number of films she starred in declined. In 1955, the year she had arrived in New York, she did not star in any films. From 1956 through the end of her life, Marilyn worked on only six different films, with her final film, *Something's Got to Give*, never completed.

By early 1947, Marilyn landed a small role in the June Haver film, *Scudda Hoo! Scudda Hay!* which although most of her scenes hit the cutting room floor, her character "Betty," greeted June's "Rad" while descending the steps of the film's church, as June engaged in dialogue with the young actress Natalie Wood. The film was released in 1948.

There would be another opportunity that year in a vehicle called *Dangerous Years*. Marilyn was now emancipated at the age of twenty-one and could make her own career decisions. She played a waitress and donned a dress and cap costumed for that vocation.

Although she shone brightly in *Dangerous Years*, Fox dropped her, leaving the young actress scrambling for work. A married couple that took Marilyn under their wings as professional mentors, John Carroll and Lucille Ryman, helped to secure a spot for her in a local theater production. It would be the following year when Columbia Pictures would choose her for one of the lead roles in their B-musical vehicle, *Ladies of the Chorus*. The vehicle was a welcome relief in a difficult year, after Marilyn's beloved Aunt Ana passed away.

Marilyn was lovely in her role as a young showgirl named "Peggy," and had the opportunities to sing a few numbers as her first starring character.

"One of the bright spots is Miss Monroe's singing," Tibor Krekes, of the Motion Picture Herald crowed about Marilyn in her first review. "She is pretty, and with her pleasing voice and style, she shows promise."

Marilyn in a 1952 publicity photo from the author's collection.

Unfortunately, Columbia Pictures decided against renewing Marilyn's contract. Marilyn however was industrious, and plodded ahead during these early lean years.

While Marilyn's career was just commencing its ascension, Joe returned to the Yanks from his military hiatus, reporting for spring training in 1946. As it was a new horizon for her, it was a fresh start for Joe in his corner of the world.

"Three years away from baseball had increased my appetite for the game," he wrote. "Training was no arduous grind this time but a labor of love. Never before did I hit as well in spring training as I did in the spring of 1946, in the Canal Zone, in Florida, in Texas and all of the barnstorming stops on the way home. I felt certain I was going to have one of the best years of my life. I never had a sorrier one."

Injuries taxed the graceful athlete once again, as he dealt with another, this time a bone spur on his left heel that required surgery.

"I didn't know when I would be able to play and looked to the 1947 season with pessimistic foreboding," Joe would recall in his autobiography. "It turned out to be the most satisfactory season I ever had in my life."

Joe said he prepared for a great year in 1946, which did not come to pass.

Downtrodden and expecting a poor outcome in 1947, Joe was pleasantly surprised by the turn of events, including a first World Series win since his the same year as 1941 streak and having been chosen the Most Valuable Player for the American League.

"If I was unlucky in 1946, I was lucky in 1947," he wrote. "It all evens out."

In 1947, the Yankee fever rose higher as it marked the first World Series ever televised.

About being selected as Most Valuable Player, Joe wrote, "It was the third time I had gained this award but I don't think that even the first one, back in 1939, gave me as big a thrill."

Dorothy also began showing her face again around the Yankee games, fueling the rumors that the couple reconciled, though they told the press, as he and Marilyn would often say of themselves they were "just friends."

Joe began experiencing problems with his throwing arm, which although it pained him, it did not stop him from contributing to his team's win against the Brooklyn Dodgers. The victory however, was not a sweeping one, as after the Yankees took the first two games, the Dodgers beat them in the third 9 to 8. Then the score evened out, with the Dodgers ahead by only another point in their win for the fourth game at 3 to 2. The Yanks edged the Dodgers in the fifth game by 2 to 1. Joe expected the Yankees would take the victory in the sixth game, however the Dodgers shut them out this time. The Yankees wrapped it up in the ninth game, taking the World Series win back to the Bronx.

Ralph Branca was a pitcher for the Brooklyn Dodgers, Detroit Tigers, and later for the Yankees in 1954, the year that Joe and Marilyn married. Ralph knew Eddie Lopat, who started with the Yankees in '47, after being traded from the White Sox. Eddie told him a story about a game he played with Joe.

Eddie Lopat was amazed one day to discover how synchronized Joe was with his teammates. It was Eddie's first game with the Yankees. It was a home game with the bases loaded, there was three and then two on the hitter. He looked back and saw Joe centered in center field. Eddie pitched and the hitter, as Ralph recalled from Eddie's story, "hits a screamer to left center."

Eddie was expecting doom, until Joe caught the ball.

"'I couldn't wait for him to get to the dugout,'" Eddie recalled to Ralph.

Eddie was itching to know how Joe made his way to the left side.

"'I knew you had to come in with the pitch,'" Joe said, "'so I just moved over twenty feet.'"

"Joe D. was so graceful," Ralph reminisced overall.

Ralph played with the Dodgers then, while Joe was with the Yankees.

"I mean," he continued, "you didn't realize how fast he was because he looked graceful. I watch video clips of him now and you realize he was really running hard, but when you saw him play, it looked like it was easy. But he played the hitters very, very well. He knew how to play the hitters. And he made everything look easy because he was so graceful."

The Dodgers played an exhibition game in Louisville in 1947, with Ralph pitching inside fastballs Joe's way. An umpire, who traveled back with the team on the train named Larry Goetz, reported back compliments he heard from Joe about Ralph.

"'Joe D,'" Larry shared with him, "'said you have the best stuff he'd seen in all spring.'"

Joe continued to play ball over the next few years, though his body grew tired from the wear and tear of the game. In 1948, he achieved his 300th career home run. His team, however, fretted this year.

"We had aging stars like Joe DiMaggio and Tommy Henrich, and a bunch of platoon players," wrote Yogi Berra.

The season itself, Yogi described as "disappointing," with the Yankees in angst that Joe might have to miss the season because of an injury to his foot.

Left fielder, Charlie "King Kong" (nicknamed for his ability to grab fly balls) Keller, before his back troubled him too from a ruptured disc, read the group the riot act in the form of a locker room lecture. Charlie told teammates to become more serious and unified. Many teams, he expressed, treated the Yankees as if they were a one-man team, meaning that Joe carried the group, and hinted Joe's absence should not be an excuse for slacking.

In 1949, now the only player to receive $100,000 a year (by today's standards close to $981,500), a bone spur on the right foot next troubled Joe.

Yankee pitcher Whitey Ford recalled in his first year (1950), he received a $5,000 salary. The next year, after some haggling and a suggestion to be paid at $9,000 was denied, Whitey settled for $7,000.

In his third year, when proposing a raise, he was rebuffed since payroll was estimated at $600,000 that year.

"And then later on they said," Whitey recalled, "'Nobody's ever going to make more than Joe DiMaggio.' You know, Mickey [Mantle] played for $100,000 his last five or six years. They would never let him go above $100,000 because they said nobody is going to make more than DiMaggio did."

Joe's heel bone spur, which caused him pain through the 1948 season, left him unable walk, run or stand up comfortably. Doctors assured him that surgery would correct the issues, yet play was still rough on his body, and the surgery performed was later considered a botched one. During 1949 training, blood flowed from his foot, and he bit his lips from the pain, yet he still endured.

Joe DiMaggio teaches batting techniques in Japan at top in 1950. The image and text on the photo's verso, shown at the bottom of this photo collage, is part of the wire photo documenting this event. Author's Collection.

Carl Erskine was another Dodger who pitched to Joe in his first World Series game in 1949 when the Dodgers played the Bronx Bombers. He was called in as a reliever and found Joe waiting for him at the plate. After pitching a fastball to Joe, Joe hit a towering fly in the direction of shortstop. Carl could not recall if it was Harold "Pee Wee" Reese the shortstop who actually grabbed the ball, or Jackie Robinson from second base, all he remembered is it took some time for the ball to make its way back down from the atmosphere into his teammate's glove.

"That's the only time I actually faced DiMaggio," he said. "But he was near the end of his career."

The two would become friends later on in life well after baseball, when Joe gave his endorsement to the Bowery Savings Bank and Carl worked in the banking industry himself.

Boston and New York fans have faced one another on a lifelong battlefield of bitter rivalry, yet even Boston fans were amazed by the grace of Joe DiMaggio, while he persisted through his injury. Sox fans were awed to their feet.

The 1949 World Series was a poignant one for Joe, who hobbled on the field from the bone spur, and was weak from a viral infection. Yet Fenway Park in Boston was electrified by his very presence as he hit a single, then a home run. The next day Joe whacked two more homers, and the day after one more.

On the return to Yankee Stadium for the final two days when the team took the pennant from Boston, Joe whammed a single and double before exiting from center field, the effects of his illness and bone spur taking their toll. The day for the 69,551 fans was magical as they celebrated Joe DiMaggio Day and he further cemented his place into sports infamy.

"Joe was extremely gracious, thanking everybody, and even acknowledging the Red Sox, our opponent," wrote Yogi Berra, one of his Yankee teammates, about the day Joe uttered his now famous quote, "'I want to thank the good Lord for making me a Yankee.'"

Marilyn gained more traction in her career during this year, enjoying some successes in films including a small and memorable role in *Love Happy*, a Marx Brothers vehicle. Johnny Hyde, a powerful head as the vice-president of the West Coast office of the William Morris Agency, took her under his wing and a love affair blossomed. Johnny pleaded with Marilyn to marry him, stating that when he would die (he struggled with heart troubles), she would become very wealthy. However, money was never important to Marilyn, who told Johnny although she loved him, she clarified she was not *in love* with him.

While money was no object for the rising starlet, it was still necessary for survival. She had never planned to pose nude, but was in need of money, even as Johnny Hyde looked after her. She contracted with photographer Tom Kelley under the name of "Mona Monroe" on May 27, 1949, to be paid fifty dollars for her appearance against a backdrop of red velvet. Nudity, in her first agent Emmeline Snively's eyes, was always the kiss of death for a model. However, once the word was leaked that Marilyn Monroe was the girl who posed for the "Golden Dreams" calendar because she struggled for cash, it worked to her advantage.

She bounced between MGM and Fox with three more films in 1950, *A Ticket to Tomahawk*, *Right Cross* and *The Fireball*, which brought some attention, yet did not push Marilyn over the popularity precipice. Her next spots during the same year in *The Asphalt Jungle*, garnered Marilyn some credentials as a heavyweight. She returned to Fox for *All About Eve*, in which she played a secondary character named Miss Caswell, a vapid vixen who was unknowingly quick-witted at the same time. It was a role she so brilliantly approached, that one of Johnny Hyde's last acts before his death in December 1950, was to negotiate a seven-year contract for Marilyn with Twentieth Century-Fox.

More roles would come in 1951 with *Home Town Story*, *As Young as You Feel*, *Love Nest,* and *Let's Make It Legal,* turning her into one of Hollywood's busiest working actresses. In this same year and with her quest for knowledge strong, Marilyn quietly enrolled herself at UCLA for literature and art appreciation courses, but because she was becoming noticeable and was pursued for autographs on campus, she dropped her studies.

While Marilyn's star was rising, Joe set his feet on the path that would lead to Marilyn and soon, the two would form their own constellation.

Though Joe played in the 1950 World Series, the Yankees did not win this time. Joe's mother also died this year, with his father Giuseppe having predeceased her the year prior.

Lefty O'Doul, who had seen success in his early career as a member of the New York Yankees, Boston Red Sox, New York Giants (for two separate occasions), Philadelphia Phillies and Brooklyn Robins/Dodgers, had become the leader who brought professional baseball to Japan prior to World War II. He invited Joe on one of his trips in 1950, while Joe still donned his Yankee pinstripes. In Japan, Joe joined his mentor for his goodwill tour as ambassadors for the sport and to visit soldiers recovering in hospitals. Joe repeated the same trip in 1951, as he pondered his future with the Yankees.

That season, Yankees Manager Casey Stengel sometimes pulled Joe out of the lineup to help him rest. Joe was not thrilled with this idea, as he was there to play, but Casey recognized his pain and did so out of concern. The stoic Joe finally consented to sitting out an inning or two.

Even as his performance declined, he still took 122 runs for his team that season and earned thirty-two homers, his average at .300. As the sun began to set for Joe's days as a Yankee, it rose for a young dynamo, his teammate Mickey Mantle.

Joe and the other ballplayers he travelled with in Japan had an unforgettable time there, which helped to soothe Joe's spirit as he finalized his decision about his career. Two of them recollected their adventures with Joe and Lefty.

Chuck Stevens, former first baseman for the St. Louis Browns, was also on the trip. The troupe of baseball heroes that joined Lefty, were honored in a parade upon their arrival. Chuck said that Lefty and Joe cancelled the parade, because the crowd was so deep, they were fearful of the cars being turned over by the crushing masses.

Joe DiMaggio (below), the day he announced his retirement in 1951. This wire photo had been in Yankee Shortstop Phil Rizzuto's wire photo collection, which was sold at auction following his death, and is now part of the Jennifer Jean Miller collection. Author's Collection.

Another attendee on the baseball trip in '51 was Mel Parnell, starting pitcher for the Boston Red Sox, who also shared some commentary about the Japanese experience.

"We were riding in cars that didn't have automatic transmissions," Mel mused, "and they were burning up clutches, because of the crowds, and they couldn't hardly move."

"It was like he [Joe] was a national hero," Chuck remembered. "There was no contest, Joe was the man."

The hero worship was evident one day when Chuck and Joe headed for the Ginza district, to purchase custom-tailored and inexpensive silk shirts. As they left and continued chatting while walking down the street, the pair suddenly turned around and realized they were followed by three thousand Japanese citizens, who chanted, "DiMaggio...DiMaggio."

Chuck busted Joe's chops, when he joked about Joe's followers, "I get so sick of this, I can't go anyplace."

Joe punched his friend in the arm, which caused Chuck to step into the street, and he was almost struck by a car.

"Jesus, Big D," Chuck laughed. "You almost got me killed."

The incident left Joe in stitches.

"Joe was like a king over there," Mel also remembered. "Baseball was really big at that time in Japan."

"Lefty, I think he could have run for Emperor over there," he added. "The Japanese were treating us royally, mainly because of these guys."

Mel and Joe were on a white water rafting trip together in Japan, with Joe saturated from sitting up front.

"Joe said he didn't care to go on one of those again," Mel recalled.

In 1951, Joe's performance on the field slipped, due to his injuries and even after the 1951 World Series win and enticement from the Yankees to be signed in 1952 again for $100,000, on December 11, he shocked sports fans by announcing his retirement.

This statement was published in *Sporting News* on December 19: "I feel like I have reached the stage where I can no longer produce for my club, my manager and my teammates. I had a poor year, but even if I had hit .350, this would have been my last year. I was full of aches and pains and it had become a chore for me to play. When baseball is no longer fun, it's no longer a game, and so, I've played my last game."

"He quit because he wasn't Joe DiMaggio anymore," brother Tom told reporters.

By the end of his career, Joe had played 1,736 games, averaged .325 over his career, hit 361 homers, and struck out 367 times. Comparatively speaking, Mickey Mantle struck out 1,710 times while garnering 536 home runs. Reggie Jackson may have achieved 563 homers, yet he struck out 2,597 times.

Number Five was retired in 1952, the same year in which a life-changing, whirlwind chapter would commence and Joe DiMaggio met the love of his life and woman to whom he would remain devoted beyond her natural life: Marilyn Monroe.

Chapter Two - Love and Marriage

As Marilyn made her way through the Hollywood publicity machine, there were several more films she stuck under her belt as one of Hollywood's busiest actresses, adding *Clash by Night, We're Not Married, Don't Bother to Knock, O. Henry's Full House* and *Monkey Business* to her roster by 1952.

Her days were filled not just with the task of creating movie magic, but also photo shoots, interviews and personal appearances to augment her star.

One of these staged occasions was a photo shoot with Gus Zernial. Gus was shy a decade the Yankee Clipper's junior, and played for three teams during his career, bursting his way onto the field as Joe's professional playing career was dwindling down.

Gus Zernial (left) and Joe Dobson (right) in a publicity photo with Marilyn. From the author's collection.

Gus, who was nicknamed "Ozark Ike" after an athletic comic-strip character, was not the powerhouse like Joltin' Joe, yet he could hold his own. With a batting average of .265 he was still no slacker and trailed slightly behind Yankee players Yogi Berra (with an average of .265) and the team's latest prodigy Mickey Mantle, who averaged .298.

Joe holding an average of .325, still left them all in the dust, though his average never touched that of predecessor Babe Ruth at .342 or contemporary Lou Gehrig (who also played with Babe, aka "The Sultan of Swat") at .340.

Known as "The Iron Horse," the versatile Lou Gehrig was lauded for his endurance and hitting ability, both which would sadly be lost when his performance began to dim in 1938. The following year, his game further declined. Amyotrophic lateral sclerosis or ALS, a disease that degenerates the body's nerve impulses and today is still a death sentence for those who are diagnosed with the devastating illness, took the great Lou Gehrig in 1941. The disease not only stole his life but his name as well, as it is now commonly coined "Lou Gehrig's Disease."

Gus Zernial played for the Chicago White Sox beginning in 1949 and was on the team's roster until he was traded to the A's in 1951 (which at that time the team's home base was Philadelphia and then midstream in Gus's career, moved to Kansas City -- the team headquartered to Oakland California in 1968). He finished his career with the Detroit Tigers.

It was in that small window of time within his trade to the A's when Gus was at the March 1951 spring training for the White Sox in Pasadena California. It was where he would be posed with Marilyn Monroe.

There was another player there that day that made a stir, though his name did not have the notoriety with the event as Gus did. That player was Gus's teammate, pitcher Joe Dobson.

Joe Dobson began his career a few years after Joe DiMaggio with the Cleveland Indians in 1939 and then held a few separate tenures with the Boston Red Sox. He played with the Chicago White Sox from 1951 through 1953.

"Ozark Ike," is often credited as the lucky man to have placed his arm around Marilyn's waist that day in one of the most famous photos from the session where Marilyn was adorably attired in a tight top, white short-shorts and peek-a-boo heels, topped off with a beret tipped on her head. The man with that honor however, was Joe Dobson.

Hank Majeski, the team's third baseman, was another who posed for photos. He played through 1951 for the White Sox and held an admirable batting average himself of .279. He played with a range of teams over his sixteen-year career. Beginning with the Boston Bees in 1939, like Joltin' Joe, he ended up in the military playing for the Coast Guard for two years, before joining the Yankee Clipper on the Yankee roster for 1946. His career with the Bronx Bombers was short-lived -- after eight games, he was traded to the A's, then to the White Sox, then back to the A's, where he played with Gus Zernial during the 1951 season. The Cleveland Indians bought his contract in 1952, where he stayed until a trade with the Baltimore Orioles in 1955. He finished his career with the Orioles at the end of that season and retired.

Out of the three, both Hank Majeski and Joe Dobson had the most physical contact with Marilyn Monroe that day. In two less famous photos, Marilyn is pictured parading around the camp with those two players in separate snapshots, her arm linked within theirs', a bat each swung over their opposite shoulders. Hank Majeski was beaming in his picture, while Joe Dobson appeared more serious.

In one more known photo, the three players were photographed while Marilyn was seated above them, her legs draping down a rock wall. All three players grinned, especially "Ozark Ike" who seemed the most photogenic of the three.

In 1976, Joe Dobson was interviewed about the photo session, which he said took place following a charity game in Hollywood. Joe Dobson reported on the rivalry between the autographed photos they each received from Marilyn afterward.

"A month or so later, we both received autographed pictures from her," he told the *Lakeland Ledger*. "On Zernial's picture she wrote, 'Hope to do it again sometime.' Old Gus was tickled pink until he saw what Marilyn wrote on mine, 'Can't wait to do it again.'"

It was Gus Zernial who would gain the most fame from the photo op, and show off the most about the session.

"She was the most beautiful girl I had ever seen," he reportedly said, as quoted in the book *Marilyn & Joe DiMaggio*. "She was wearing shorts and a halter. It was a fantastic outfit. She was incredible! She was lovely. She was intelligent. I should have paid them to let me pose with her."

The dashing "Ozark Ike" said he considered asking Marilyn to dinner, except wife Gladys, who he wedded in 1946, was in the stands. Obviously, this was not a strong union, as Gus thought about inviting the blonde bombshell on a date, and he and Gladys divorced after twelve years of marriage. His second marriage to wife Marla lasted for fifty years until his death in 2011.

It was Gus who would be one of the connections between Joe DiMaggio and Marilyn. However, some accounts noted Joltin' Joe grew annoyed over the years with Ozark Ike's reports that he set Joe and Marilyn up on a blind date.

Some have said that the two players discussed the beautiful blonde at an exhibition game and other accounts said it happened when Joe visited the White Sox training camp.

In either case, Joe asked Gus, "How come I never get to pose with pretty girls like that?"

Gus pointed Joe in David March's direction.

David March was a business manager who knew both Joe and Marilyn. In January 1952, David March connected Marilyn to a small West Hollywood apartment on Hilldale Avenue. He was acquainted with Joe from his New York romps at Toots Shor's. According to writer Maurice Zolotow, David's ulterior motive was to snap up Marilyn's account for his firm Leslie and Tyson.

Marilyn's train of life was careening at high speed early that year. She was awarded the Henrietta Award as "Best Young Box Office Personality" that winter at Santa Monica's Del Mar Club. She was also filming *Monkey Business* at Fox with Cary Grant, Ginger Rogers and Charles Coburn.

Some have attributed her lack of interest in meeting Joe DiMaggio to her aversion that he was a potentially obnoxious sports player. She believed those in the industry were brash and tacky. For that reason, it has been said she feigned fatigue from her schedule as an excuse.

Marilyn was leading a hectic life and on top of that, was battling a health setback. On March 1, about a week prior to her blind date with Joe, she suffered from stomach pains so severe she was forced into bed rest at Cedars of Lebanon Hospital for a week, and diagnosed with an appendicitis attack. Her appendix surgery was postponed until April 28, with concerns her operation might damper her studio commitment.

Marilyn was not kidding David when she advised him how exhausted she was, the night he phoned her to ask if he could introduce her to a friend of his who wanted to meet her. That friend was Joe. David eased Marilyn, who was also shy by nature, into the double date. He would bring his girlfriend, Peggy Rabe and then Marilyn could meet Joe DiMaggio, an arrangement he thought seemed comfortable for all.

David confirmed with Marilyn that the foursome would meet at the Villa Nova Restaurant at seven o'clock on the evening of March 8. David, Peggy and Joe headed for the far left corner booth. The trio arrived early and Joe nervously sipped his glass of sweet vermouth on the rocks, as he fidgeted by folding his menu into quarters, then eighths.

Then, David, Peggy and Joe waited for Marilyn.
And waited.

A matchbook, from the author's memorabilia collection from Villa Nova in Hollywood, where Marilyn and Joe shared their first date in 1952. Photo courtesy of the author.

Notoriously known for tardiness, David placed a call to Marilyn about an hour later. She was at home resting after an arduous day on the set, telling him that she honestly forgot and was exhausted.

Marilyn pleaded with David for another time to meet, and he stood his ground.

"No," was David's staunch response.

She relented.

Several months later, when Marilyn was apparently insecure after an incident in her relationship with Joe, she blasted David. The outburst was triggered as Marilyn was waiting for Joe's call and after not hearing from him, phoned David in a rage.

"What did you tell him?" Marilyn demanded.

"Tell him about what?" David asked puzzled.

"Well, I don't know, you must have told him something," Marilyn asserted.

Joe phoned later that day, apologetically, and said, "I didn't have time to make the call before boarding my train."

Marilyn reportedly still broke off the friendship with their matchmaker -- this night though, all of the stars were aligning, even if Marilyn was behind schedule.

Marilyn arrived an hour later, donning a white silk blouse and blue suit. Joe rose for the beauty and they greeted one another.

The conversation was quiet between Marilyn and Joe during most of the meal, except for some minor dialogue in which she complimented how a polka dot was arranged squarely within the knot of his tie. Like Marilyn, Joltin' Joe had timid tendencies. Most of the chatter took place between David and Marilyn as they discussed *Monkey Business* over the meal of anchovies on pimento, Veal Scallopini and spaghetti laced with garlic.

Joe was a man of few words and a nervous conversationalist himself, yet he was a keen observer. Joe was impressed with what he saw in front of him in Tinseltown's latest and greatest screen goddess. Eventually, the conversation started to gain momentum between the two guests of honor, and David was pleased -- until an unexpected interruption occurred.

"Joe DiMaggio!" Mickey exclaimed excitedly as he approached.

There was another star struck player in this scene who did not sit at the table and who was not drooling over Marilyn. That was actor Mickey Rooney, who had been a co-star of Marilyn's in *The Fireball*, one of her earlier vehicles. The gregarious Mickey, who was also a diner at Villa Nova that night and a devoted DiMaggio fan, crashed the table -- and did so by posing an endless stream of questions to Joe to wiggle his way in. David attempted to shoo Mickey away without luck.

"After Rooney joined the party, Joe and Marilyn couldn't get a word in edgewise," David told Maurice Zolotow during an interview.

The interruption piqued Marilyn's interest, as she saw someone with Mickey Rooney's fame falling all over her date.

Yet, her bed was calling, as Marilyn had an early arrival at the studio the following morning. She excused herself from the table at eleven.

Joe was not ready for the evening to end. He offered to hail her a cab and ride with her. She thanked him, and said she had driven herself to the Villa Nova.

However, Joe's expression shifted from disappointment to hopeful when Marilyn offered him a lift to his hotel.

From there the accounts again vary.

Some have said the couple remained silent in their drive until they reached the stylish Knickerbocker Hotel, when Joe suggested they continue to drive for a while. Others have said she parked the car and then snuck through the kitchen to join Joe for a nightcap at the establishment's bar. Another account -- a kind of dull one -- had Marilyn drop off Joe and simply drive home. More lore has placed the two in bed at the end of their first night, or for a lovemaking soirée in the back of her car -- neither a likely scenario since Joe was the archetypal gentleman and Marilyn was not promiscuous as has often been rumored plus was battling appendicitis.

And yet, another story about that night emerged from famed director Elia Kazan. Marilyn and Elia Kazan had been involved in a relationship of some depth following the passing of Johnny Hyde. In 1951, Elia introduced Marilyn to his friend Arthur Miller when he was in town from New York. Arthur escorted Marilyn to a party at producer Charles Feldman's home. Charles would eventually negotiate Marilyn's contract after Johnny Hyde's death.

Elia Kazan held a philandering reputation, having bedded a number of young actresses while promising them roles in his films. Elia was married to wife Molly until her death in 1963, yet became involved with many beautiful starlets. Molly was said to have turned a blind eye to her husband's behaviors -- Marilyn was said to have been one of those starlets.

The cunning Kazan was admired by some and hated by others. His testimony in front of the House Committee on Un-American Activities (HUAC) in 1952 brought down eight of his former colleagues from the Group Theater, including Marilyn's later acting coach Paula Strasberg (née Miller), for their participation with the American Communist Party. Elia Kazan avoided the blacklist by naming names and stating that he relinquished his membership in 1936, which brought about traitor status in the eyes of some. His friendship with Arthur would also eventually topple over for a period of time because of what Arthur viewed as a betrayal.

Arthur Miller was married to his wife Mary at the time he met Marilyn, and although the pair appeared wildly attracted to each other, nothing intimately happened officially between the two until 1955.

Elia Kazan claimed that at three o'clock in the morning after Marilyn's date with Joe she snuck into his bed. He alleged to have told her earlier that evening that he would leave the door open and to crawl into bed with him. He maintained that Marilyn spoke excitedly about a date with a man she planned to marry. Elia thought at first she referred to her crush who he was already aware of, Arthur Miller. He said after Marilyn relayed her news, their night concluded with a romp in the hay, which he asserted was the final secret meeting between the two.

Although the validity of this story only relies on Elia Kazan's account, an undated "Dear John" letter on Fox stationary from Marilyn confirms that a relationship had taken place between the director and actress, with an ending not favorable for Elia. If Marilyn had been a plaything, he could no longer count her as one. Instead, Marilyn turned the tables on him.

In her note, Marilyn thanked "Gadge," (his nickname) for everything.

"...Nothing that you <u>gave</u> was wasted," she wrote, "but was received and I want to thank you for it..."

Yet, Marilyn's postscript at the top of her correspondence above the studio logo was stern: "I know you will respect my <u>wish</u> do not write to me or call."

Not only did Marilyn put the brakes on with Elia Kazan, she supposedly did so as well with Joe DiMaggio initially.

With the rated-G version of the story, the phone rang as Marilyn settled into bed, with an eager Joe inviting her to dinner the following evening -- Marilyn declined. Joe aimed for the night after that, and Marilyn once again turned him down.

Always aggressively pursuing what he sought, a determined Joe persisted with up to three calls daily over the next several days, with Marilyn rejecting the other invitations. The calls soon ceased.

This was something that had to make Marilyn even more desirable to Joe if this scenario of cat and mouse is true. Although she was devoted to those that she loved, Marilyn was a person who would steer clear of those at times, if she sensed them too aggressive. While Joe subdued Dorothy, Marilyn was more free-spirited in some ways, and to him appeared as if she was playing hard to get. He enjoyed the chase.

And she was Marilyn Monroe, who had now become the world's most photographed and desirable woman -- she could choose to evade those who pursued her, including Joe. She held that power in her hand. And when she cut someone loose, she cut him or her loose entirely. She would take people back if it was to her choosing, not the other way around. Though she did not use this tactic in a calculating or bitchy way, she was beguiling in her own innocent manner. Letting someone go was not an easy task for her, as she was empathetic, kind, sweet, forgiving, and carried guilt easily, as well as held a fear of hurting the other party. She was loving and eager to please, yet could easily retreat into her own sphere and shut people out. Handling relationships this way brought later trouble in her life. Her compass in gauging those she could trust from those she could not was not always the most precise -- manipulators easily roped Marilyn in.

Marilyn possessed a unique way of compartmentalizing the various people that she knew from her different walks of life. Some of her friends did not get along with one another and she had an exceptional approach in those days of playing pacifist while maintaining all of the friendships. Later in her life, she handed this ability over to those who controlled her. These parties, including her gurus the Strasbergs, her psychiatrists, the Greenes and Arthur Miller, acted on her behalf alternately to slice those out from her life for her. All of them competed with one another for the top spot in her life. The main issue was Marilyn opened her emotional doors to the wrong people, who led her to her downward spiral.

Perhaps at this point with Joe Marilyn was playing a game of "catch me if you can," though that is unlikely. She was impressed with the Yankee Clipper. She was sincerely busy between filming, the usual round of publicity activities and sessions with acting coach Natasha Lytess. Natasha was one of the first who Marilyn permitted to monopolize and control her.

To top it off, Marilyn was still recovering from the precarious situation with her appendix (which might negate the sexual rendezvous possibilities with Gadge or Joe, with her health in peril due to the enflamed appendix).

There was something else unexpected that cropped up, however, in terms of a ghost from Marilyn's past.

An industrious journalist by the name of Aline Mosby dug up the "Golden Dreams" calendar, creating a potential nightmare for the emerging star.

Some at the studio advised Marilyn to deny she was the calendar's model, while a few trusted advisors like makeup man Whitey Snyder, columnist and confidante Sidney Skolsky, and Fox President Spyros Skouras (it was this power player who also gave Elia Kazan the ultimatum to name names for the HUAC, or never work in Hollywood again), told Marilyn it was best to fess up.

The United Press Association Reporter met with her at Fox's publicity office. Aline asked Marilyn if she was the woman on the calendar.

"Yes," Marilyn replied softly.

"I had to have the money," Marilyn confessed to Aline, in the story that broke on March 13, 1952.

She was a week behind in her rent. In 1948 after a minor car collision on the way to an audition, the photographer Tom Kelley was one who aided the damsel in distress. He fronted her cab money since she was penniless, and handed her a business card. Marilyn ended up meeting him for a few modeling assignments, and turned down the ones he offered requiring nudity. Marilyn in fact told Tom Kelley she would never pose nude.

"This time I called him," she recounted in her interview, "and said I would as soon as possible, to get it over with."

Tom Kelley, his brother Bill, and wife Natalie commenced the two-hour shoot, as "Begin the Beguine" played softly in the background. Afterward, Marilyn, Tom and Natalie enjoyed some chili and coffee together at Barney's Beanery.

"I was told I should deny I'd posed," Marilyn shared with the inquisitive newswoman, "but I'd rather be honest about it."

Marilyn's candor, instead of having repulsed fans, drew them closer.

She and Joe soon grew nearer to each other too. Marilyn decided to figuratively reopen the door, this time calling Joltin' Joe to suggest he take her to dinner. The astonished Yankee Clipper proceeded with caution as he headed to her front door at seven o'clock on the evening of their second date, and was pleasantly surprised when she literally opened it for him, beaming her magnetic smile that he adored from the moment they met.

Joe and Marilyn found a secluded Italian restaurant that night with no Mickey Rooney nearby to interrupt them this time, and then enjoyed a drive together along the Pacific Coast Highway. They passed through Malibu and Escondido Beach, still driving three hours later. Eventually they found a diner, where they stopped for more conversation, burgers and coffee. They relished in the evening, with its further treat of a beautiful moon and purple sky.

It was the next date when he confessed his initial attraction to her from the photo with Gus Zernial.

"You must have posed with celebrities for lots of publicity pictures when you were in baseball," Marilyn mused.

"The best I ever got was Ethel Barrymore and General MacArthur," Joe laughed. "You're much prettier."

"That [the compliment about Marilyn's looks] had an odd effect on me," Marilyn would later say. "I had read reams and reams of writing about my good looks, and scores of men had told me I was beautiful. But this was the first time my heart had jumped to hear it."

On March 17, a lucky day for both of them, Marilyn watched her slugger play in the only game she would ever see him grace the field in, a Kiwanis Charity Game, with major leaguers versus Hollywood heavy-hitters.

Marilyn was also given a warm-up opportunity of sorts for her four-day stint in entertaining the troops in Korea in 1954. On April 4, she made an appearance for the

The press, in the spin doctor role, purposely cropped Cary Grant from photos, to hone in on the blossoming romance between Marilyn and Joe. The couple, however, still told the news hounds, they were, "just friends." AP Wirephoto, from the author's memorabilia collection.

Marines stationed at Camp Pendleton near San Diego. Bob Hope commenced the weekly morale-boosting event for the military there in 1941, and Marilyn was one of his guests in 1952.

It is said she crooned a sultry version of the Gershwin song "Do It Again," which drove the Marines wild. She recalled to journalists that she wore the controversial red gown she sported at the Henrietta Awards (also at a UCLA dance), a sleek number with large tassels draping down her shoulder and a basket weave front. She was spotted in this dress several times over 1952. Several of her female contemporaries slammed her for wearing something they considered so risqué. The Marines, however, begged to differ on that opinion.

Though she was reported to have performed in front of 10,000 Marines, in a clip from 2003 aired on Larry King Live that paid tribute to Bob Hope, Bob said in the audio, "Had her [Marilyn] on my show from Camp Pendleton and there were 800 kids that came down from Roosevelt's Raiders out of the mountains after the training. And she walked out, and she said, 'hello.' That's all. They went right to the ceiling, and I was with them."

During an interview with Pete Martin of *The Saturday Evening Post*, Marilyn remembered the stir she created at Camp Pendleton when asked about the rumored whistles she received after she took the stage.

"They wanted me to say a few words," Marilyn recalled, "so I said, 'you fellows down there are always whistling at sweater girls. Well, take away their sweaters and what have you got?' For some reason, it seemed to kill them. They screamed and yelled."

On April 7 the Monroe train continued along its route at lightning speed as Marilyn appeared in a sultry pose by photographer Philippe Halsman on the cover of *LIFE,* her first for the famous magazine.

The front of the magazine proclaimed, "Marilyn Monroe: The Talk of Hollywood." And that she was.

She was also the focal point in Joe DiMaggio's life, as he visited her on the last day of filming on the set of *Monkey Business*. Originally her co-star Cary Grant was in the photo, but the spin-doctors in the press world cropped him out.

"Just Friends" reported the photo cut line, but the press rubbed in how Joe stopped by on the set prior to a return to his assignment in New York as commentator for the Yankees.

The gossip columnists began asking her questions about marriage in light of her new affiliation with the slugger, and if she would leave her career in the event that she ever tied the knot.

"A career is wonderful, but you can't curl up with it on a cold night," she nudged back to one inquirer with one of her usual quips.

Marilyn had the inborn gift to leave interviewers amused and hanging at the same time, especially after they would attempt to trap her with a question. They would be the ones left swinging from their rope from her witticisms.

Marilyn rode some other roller coasters during that month. Her acting coach Natasha Lytess for one exhibited her immediate disdain for Joe. Natasha had an enveloping possessiveness over Marilyn. Whitey Snyder was less gullible than Marilyn and he heavily disliked Natasha's grip on her. Marilyn attempted diplomacy as an intermediary who tried to placate the weighty egos surrounding her. Jealous Natasha pouted over her fixation's new love.

During this time, Marilyn also received a raise to $750 a week, which kept her trapped as one of Hollywood's lowest paid and one of its hardest working famous stars.

Another event with great impact in this time period was the revelation about Gladys being alive. Publicity yarns had previously placed Gladys as deceased. Marilyn had been painted for years as Hollywood's Cinderella, with tales of having grown up in multiple abusive foster homes in slummy neighborhoods, as well as the orphanage. This was an exaggerated fabrication that partially originated from Marilyn and Grace, and was maintained by studio campaigns to boost her popularity. Grace, who was back in California, was then Marilyn's business manager as well as her dear family friend.

Grace and Marilyn were correct in their assumptions -- the public further sympathized with Marilyn, laden with the impression that she had been a waif.

Unfortunately, parasitic people who would later cling to Marilyn thought they were entitled to do so and knew the truth about her background, yet maintained she had no family in order to influence her.

It is a myth that perpetuates through today.

In a 1952 *Screenland* magazine article, Marilyn said the studio told her to "forget the past, everybody thinks you're an orphan, so let it stay that way. It's good copy."

What could have been disastrous to her career like the calendar, Marilyn's justification was a white lie that readers embraced as she further told them: "My close friends know that my mother is alive. Unknown to me as a child, my mother spent many years as an invalid in a state hospital. I haven't known my mother intimately, but since I have become grown and able to help her, I have contacted her. I am helping her and will continue to help her when she needs me."

At the end of the month on April 28, nurses at Cedars of Lebanon Hospital prepared to wheel Marilyn into surgery to remove her appendix. Once under anesthesia, Drs. Marcus Rabwin (who had been Jean Harlow's physician) and Leon Krohn pulled back her gown and found a note taped to her belly.

"Dear Dr. Rabwin, cut <u>as</u> <u>little</u> <u>as</u> <u>possible</u>," she began.

Marilyn's plea, she expressed, was not for vanity's sake.

"You have children and you <u>must</u> know <u>what</u> it means," she continued.

She begged especially that her ovaries remain intact and secondarily, that the doctor prevent large scars.

Perhaps with Joe in her life children became a priority. Babies were not on the radar with Jim Dougherty, though she once impulsively begged Jim to impregnate her when he entered the military. She was concerned that he could to die in service and maintained that a baby could carry on his legacy.

The inability to sustain a pregnancy (she suffered three miscarriages during her marriage to Arthur Miller) plagued Marilyn until her last days. She considered adopting a child. Over the years, there have been false rumors of secret births and multiple abortions. Dr. Krohn especially would go on record to refute the abortion falsities.

And those who have claimed to be love children of Marilyn's always do so without taking into account the actual timeline of her life, declaring they were born at times when photos show her evidently without a baby bump. As one of the world's most photographed women of all time it would have been impossible for the public to have missed one of these reputed conceptions. When she announced her pregnancies, the world rejoiced with Marilyn, as she miscarried her children, her followers grieved.

Sustaining a child for Marilyn was a challenge since she suffered from endometriosis and ectopic pregnancies. At Cedars of Lebanon Hospital, she later underwent three gynecological surgeries in 1953, 1954 and 1962 respectively, with the hopes of improving her situation.

Marilyn pulled through her appendectomy with flying colors. Though Joe was out of town working on his television show, he sent his love in the form of a dozen roses and a card. Whitey Snyder stopped by to make up his famous client. Marilyn posed demurely for the cameras in her hospital bed, photographed smiling as she read her cards from well-wishers and a book with a smiling cartoon banana on the front entitled *No More Appendix*.

Fans clambered over their star, which inhibited her recovery. Marilyn, who had been nomadic during these years and moved from residence to residence around the Los Angeles area (including living in hotels), next headquartered herself at the Hotel Bel-Air to regain a slice of privacy. Joe and Marilyn kept each other company and took regular excursions to dine at the home of his friend Vic Masi in Ensenada in the Baja area. There they would savor home cooking and television. Otherwise, there were hotel meals in her suite, where Joe the television addict parked himself while eating.

Joe Jr. was attending school nearby at the Black-Foxe Military Institute and started to tag along with his father for visits with Marilyn for swims. Joey held fond memories of swimming in the Hotel Bel-Air pool.

When Little Joe spent time with Marilyn and his father, it was the first time he truly felt comfortable around his dad. For once, Joey sensed Joe was not putting on a show -- he usually talked about sports or grilled junior about school. The man he now witnessed instead was down-to-earth and relaxed.

Joe Jr. really liked Marilyn instantly and in his opinion, she had an easy nature. He was amazed that she did not speak in the whispery voice as she did onscreen and told his friends so.

Butch warmed up even greater to Marilyn when she told him, "I can never be your mother, because you already have one, but I want to be your friend."

In contrast, Dorothy was beginning to irritate him in all ways. She grew more loud and obnoxious in front of her boyfriend of the week when he would visit her at home, showing off to her revolving door of new suitors. Dorothy sought so desperately for attention. Joey recalled her behavior became erratic and inappropriate. Once she did a handstand in front of his friends, her skirt touching the ground, revealing she wore no underwear. Joe Jr. was mortified.

Once Dorothy caught wind from Joe Jr. of the time spent with Marilyn, not only was she displeased, she involved the court system to jealously strong-arm the blossoming relationship between Marilyn and Joe, dragging poor Joey into the middle of the mess.

The Jolter questioned the confusion he perceived must have existed in Butch's head, because of Dorothy's many boyfriends, leaving him scratching in speculation that the boy might "wonder how many fathers he has."

Dorothy sought full custody of Joe Jr. in retaliation, in place of the partial custody each shared.

"I sure don't understand it," Joe said of Dorothy's outburst.

Dorothy vouched she had no issue with Marilyn, though privately she confessed to her sister of her paranoia that Marilyn and Joe left Little Joe to fend for himself, in search of a bedroom. Perhaps Dorothy falsely envisioned this because of the days that she lived in the Waldorf-Astoria and sent junior out to cruise up and down in the elevator for entertainment, while she was holed up with the beau du jour.

"Miss Arnold made her announcement after DiMaggio took his son swimming last week with Marilyn Monroe, blonde actress," one newspaper report leaked on May 29. "She said she didn't think the swimming party was proper for the boy."

The press reported Joe's countering statement: "I never have and I never will take my son into places that would not be proper for a boy of his age to enter."

Though Marilyn did not comment on the swim date, she described her relationship with Joe as "good friends."

While Dorothy accused Joe of exposing their son to amoral behavior, Joe retorted that Dorothy's accusations were "ridiculous." He condemned her with a retaliatory legal response, alleging that she spent child support on indulgences for herself. His cross-motion was a request for full custody.

On June 3, another publication reported that Dorothy lifted her squeeze on Joe slightly and wrote: "She will not object to DiMaggio continuing to have reasonable rights to visit the boy."

Joe's counterattack on Dorothy disassembled some of her frivolous assertions.

Yet, her caveat was her plan to battle it in court, and to prohibit Joe from taking Joe Jr. to "places where there is drinking and where there are no other children."

"He's a little young for the smart set," Dorothy commented, obviously still bristled about Joe's affiliation with Marilyn.

The fact was there were other individuals around the pool and children to play with. There was also no drinking -- Joe's indulgence that day around his son was coffee. Joe was comfortable enough to leave Marilyn and Joey alone for a few minutes as well to grab a cup. He and Marilyn strolled around the pool too as junior splashed around with the other kids. It was an overall peaceful time and for once, the boy was having fun and allowed to be a kid.

Dorothy was obviously looking for an ax to grind with Joe. She had no steady at this stage and had already remarried (in 1946) and divorced stockbroker George Schuster by 1949. In spite of Dorothy's adamancy and accusations about drinking alcohol, she drank freely in front of Joey and later married a man by the name of Ralph Peck, with whom she opened up a Palm Springs nightclub, Charcoal Charley's. Dorothy was allegedly partial to Gin Gibsons and took to the stage there in an early and unofficial version of karaoke. Broadway music was her favorite genre to sing and she supposedly worked in the nightclub industry until her death from pancreatic cancer in 1984.

Marilyn's recovery time wound down and she headed back to work. The film *We're Not Married* was next on her slate, along with costume tests and musical rehearsals with vocal coach Phil Moore for her next film *Niagara*.

On her twenty-sixth birthday, Marilyn received a very special gift -- she was notified that she had been selected for the role of Lorelei Lee in *Gentlemen Prefer Blondes* -- one of the roles that would cement her into cinema history both figuratively and literally (it was on the occasion of the film's release that Marilyn and co-star Jane Russell would have their hands and feet immortalized at Grauman's Chinese Theatre). Marilyn celebrated her birthday and the news alone in her room that night over some steak and champagne. Joe was back in New York, and was one of the few genuine people in her life who showered her with congratulatory flowers and telegrams.

Marilyn headed to New York for a stay at the Sherry-Netherland Hotel for her publicity tour of *Monkey Business*. She and Joe connected in the city. While there, Marilyn had hoped to take in some cultural excursions, though Joe was uninterested. She instead tagged along enthusiastically to Toots Shor's and other places he liked to frequent.

Joe's friends were surprised by the change in their pal, who they viewed as a new man. He confessed to them he would rather be wherever Marilyn was. *The Joe DiMaggio Show* meant little to him anymore and it drove him nuts to be apart from her. Joe grew to love and adore her in a way he never had with another human being. His insides quivered and his exterior melted when he set his eyes on her. Her heart jumped as well at the sight of him. When she complimented him in return on how great he looked, her sentiments liquefied the regal DiMaggio into a human puddle.

She provided Joe with a view of New York through fresh eyes. He enjoyed escorting her to the fine restaurants and nightclubs he frequented. She visited Yankee Stadium where she mingled with those sitting in the box seats, and was engulfed for autographs.

Marilyn, Joe, and Joe Jr. also shared some unforgettable moments together in the city. According to Joe's friend Morris Engelberg, the three strolled through Central Park one day. After their walk, Little Joe asked to stop for an ice cream soda at Rumplemeyer's, the upscale ice cream parlor in the Hotel St. Moritz. Since Joe could be frugal, he told junior he would make him a soda at home. However, when Joe had his back turned, Marilyn passed a twenty to the young man. She urged him to pick up his drink while she browsed in the hotel's boutique. This incited a fit from the Jolter, who grabbed Marilyn's arm and chewed her for it as they walked along Central Park South, while Joey trailed behind slurping his drink. For the remainder of the day Joe stewed and remained silent towards his girl and son. This "conspiracy" strengthened the glue, on the other hand, between Marilyn and Butchie.

After Joe cooled his heels over the ice cream soda incident, he reaffirmed his first instinct was to protect Marilyn from the world. Eventually that impulse rose to the point of overzealousness, with his jealousy and then taciturn nature kicking in often.

Joe was growing impatient with Marilyn in the nuptials department. She asked for Joe's patience and to postpone the process to tend to her further blossoming career.

"For at least a year," one publication would eventually report, "Joe DiMaggio has been and still is the only man in her life. What the outcome will be, she won't say -- not because she is reticent about it, but because she honestly doesn't know."

Marilyn during her stay at the Sherry-Netherland Hotel in 1952. Original photo courtesy of the author's collection.

Yet Marilyn hinted she sought a family for her future. During an interview with one magazine, she showed the reporter her three pet goldfish, Marmaduke, Mike and Mo. She swore to the news hound she could not explain how she named them.

"My favorite name is Antonio," she said, "but you can't really name a goldfish that. But I hope to name my son Antonio, someday."

While in New York, Marilyn embarked on a special excursion to New Jersey's seaside resort of Atlantic City. There, she was the Grand Marshal for the Miss America Parade, appeared at the Stanley Theater on August 29 for the *Monkey Business* premiere and visited the Betty Bacharach Home for Afflicted Children in the nearby Borough of Longport. At the hospital, Marilyn was filmed signing autographs and handing out candies to the kids. She missed a game in New York that Joe appeared in while spending time with these children.

Following her trip to New York, Marilyn headed for Niagara Falls to begin filming the thriller, *Niagara*.

In the film, the beauty and wonder of Niagara Falls paled in comparison to Marilyn, who was cast as the gorgeous and cunningly unfaithful wife, Rose Loomis. It was this film that would memorialize Marilyn's hip sashaying famous walk into cinematic history.

While in Niagara, Joe was never far from Marilyn's heart, in spite of salacious and fabricated reports that a con named Robert Slatzer would come out with years later, of romps in her hotel room.

Jock Carroll was a photographer who vouched for Marilyn's devotion to Joe. In his book *Falling For Marilyn: The Lost Niagara Collection*, Jock wrote of Marilyn's excitement to potentially return for the weekend to Manhattan to visit Joe. She was met with disappointment when required to stay for filming.

Afterward, she reluctantly picked up the phone to call Joe and break the news. Jock and Whitey, who had been applying her makeup, exited to allow her privacy. They could hear her through the door pleading with Joe for his understanding. It was then apparent that an enraged Joe hung up on Marilyn. Marilyn reopened the door ten minutes later, with trails of mascara traced down her cheeks.

In spite of his insolence, Marilyn made consistent efforts to please Joe. One day, she recruited Jock as a model to size a sweater for Joe from a shop in the General Brock Hotel lobby. She perceived Jock as the same height and body type as Joe and for an hour, the photojournalist tried on cashmere sweaters for her. Insistent that it would take days to clear customs, the pair crossed the border with the sweater to have it shipped from the American side. In the meantime, Jock forgot about a case of beer in his car trunk, an oversight that customs officers quickly forgave him for since Marilyn was his passenger.

To make her temporary home in the hotel more familiar, Marilyn traveled with her mobile library of favorite books, and on her nightstand sat a photo of Joe.

Jock moreover witnessed Marilyn's fidelity to Joe in other ways, an allegiance Joe would reciprocate as he protected her in life and death.

Hy Gardner requested that Marilyn call in to his radio show and conversely the host wanted more on the scoop about the romance between Marilyn and Joe than she was willing to discuss. Hy was advised in advance that Joe, as a topic of conversation, was off-limits.

"I know Joe wouldn't like it," she stated.

Hy attempted another route -- could she speak about baseball? Marilyn affirmed she would and he tried that route to force her to into the Joe subject again. She refused a second time. Sly interviewers often did this to Joe following Marilyn's death, gently guiding the interview, and then...slam! They would interject with a question about Marilyn. Those episodes left Joe storming from conference rooms, with interviewers, though prepped the topic of Marilyn was disallowed, stunned.

Could she talk about Butchie?

Marilyn slapped her forehead at the suggestion.

"No!" she exclaimed. "Why does he want to drag the child into this? Doesn't he understand? Joe's [ex] wife has already named me in a legal action. It's completely unfair to everybody. My personal relationships are important to me. I don't care if it is a coast-to-coast show!"

Marilyn would later be upset to learn when Joe Jr. was teased at school after she became his stepmother, and when stepson from her third marriage Bobby Miller, hid one magazine because it contained slanderous copy about Marilyn.

Marilyn remained true to those she cared deeply for especially the children in her life, frustrating the radio show host, and losing the spot.

Frank Neill, the publicist attempting to negotiate the appearance, chided Marilyn and said, "It wouldn't have hurt [to discuss her private life] -- it's a big show."

"It's my personal life!" Marilyn retorted angrily.

Marilyn dropped the name of Fox President Spyros Skouras in retaliation. Frank backed down though only temporarily.

"Honey, it's perfectly alright, we're only trying to look after you," though in the same breath, he threateningly and sarcastically reminded her, "remember, you're ours now."

The studio may have perceived Marilyn was their property but she was making strides on her own. In August of that year she received a tribute much like Joe did in the height of his career, with a song penned in her honor. She arrived at a star-studded event in Sherman Oaks at the home of bandleader Ray Anthony where "Marilyn" was unveiled. Mickey Rooney was there as a guest and jamming on the drums. Marilyn wore the sexy red dress from *Niagara* with the cutout in the middle above her waistline. She posed for photos by a military helicopter that landed on the lawn and with a collie that jumped to greet her. Footage taken that day shows a beaming Marilyn who recognized the day belonged to her in more ways than just having the song written about her.

It was a blessing that Marilyn was so considerate of the feelings of others otherwise Dorothy may have further initiated attacks against her. In November, Dorothy tried another tactic to punish Joe for replacing her with his new love. This time her angle was usurping more financial support from him. She demanded to have child support increased from $300 to $1,000 a month.

A 1953 AP Wirephoto, from the author's collection, taken during the period when Dorothy Arnold, attempted to arm wrestle Joe in court, started by her jealousy over his relationship with Marilyn. At this stage, Joe and Dorothy, were already divorced nearly a decade, and she already held a second marriage and divorce under her belt. Dorothy's attack against Joe, failed in the legal system. Courtesy of the author's collection.

The year prior Dorothy had contended she was so financially strapped that it was necessary to sell her mink coat Joe had presented her with during their marriage. Joe believed the lie and forked over another $2,000 to the woman he then hoped to win back.

Dorothy's fight was a lost cause. The judge ruled that Joe was a fine father who paid for summer camp and Little Joe's tuition. One example of Dorothy's financial foolery that the judge lectured her for was when Joe bought Joey a piano, which Dorothy turned around and hocked for cash.

His Honor Judge Elmer Doyle scolded Dorothy in court, as he was a Joe sympathizer. He ignored Dorothy's groundless charges of Joe carting their child to inappropriate venues, denied her child support increase and rebuked her for misguidedly terminating her marriage to Joe almost a decade prior.

Joe Jr. spent a couple of minutes in His Honor's chambers and the judge reached a verdict -- no more cash for Dorothy -- and visitation for Joe was permitted on alternating weekends.

At this point, the press was reporting that Marilyn and Joe were on the verge of breakup, which was likely above all, the envious Dorothy's goal. Dorothy's mantra at this point was probably that if she could not have Joe, no one could. She seemed to do all she could to wreck his relationship since she was no longer his main focus. She considered Marilyn a threat. The breakup report was most possibly a ruse to keep the media and Dorothy at bay. Joe and Marilyn craved privacy -- well, Joe more than Marilyn. There was no way Dorothy could edge her way back into Joe's life now. He was entirely committed to Marilyn and Dorothy was a distant memory.

If Marilyn and Joe were really on the fritz, Marilyn had platoons and platoons full of suitors clambering for her. Only a few days following Dorothy's most recent move, Marilyn still outdid her in the press in a positive way.

The papers reported that on a visit to Korea, Anna Rosenberg the United States Secretary of Defense learned soldiers there asked for a visit from Marilyn above anything.

"All GIs Want In Korea Is Marilyn Monroe," the headlines yelled, though not as loudly as the GI's did.

"Send us Marilyn Monroe," one GI shouted as the Secretary of Defense visited GI's and Marines on the front lines fighting against the Chinese Communists.

Marilyn was prominently on their minds. One paper reported about a road soldiers named after their dream girl. Earmarked the "Marilyn Monroe Stretch" on the supply route's signage, following twenty-three curves and two-miles the second sign quipped to drivers inquisitively, "See why?"

Little did they know in only slightly a year more, their wishes would come true when their poster girl Marilyn would appear in the flesh.

Marilyn spent Christmas Eve of that year at a studio party and reluctantly returned alone to her room at the Beverly Hills Hotel. She missed Joe, who was up in San Francisco with his family.

After opening her door and switching on her light, she was astonished to find a Christmas tree in the corner, adorned with tinsel and lights and topped with an angel. A large card was in front of the tree, which read, "Merry Christmas."

Suddenly, Joe emerged from the closet, echoing the words on the card's face.

Marilyn began to cry, "You didn't forget me Joe. That's the sweetest thing anybody has done for me in my whole life."

Not to say drama was absent between Marilyn and Joe -- it always existed in these early years.

At the start of the New Year in 1953, Marilyn's star further rose, as she officially became "the blonde" in *Gentlemen Prefer Blondes*. She also became the world's preferred blonde for that matter.

During this time, Marilyn garnered seventy interview requests daily, 20,000 fan letters weekly (separated in stacks of 200) and eighty marriage proposals each seven day increment.

Many likened her to Jean Harlow in terms of her star power.

"Dozens of reporters have compared her to Jean Harlow," director Howard Hawks told *Family Circle*. "Isn't that ridiculous? Jean was bright and sharp -- she exuded authority and self-confidence. She led a life of her own, made her own rules, and everybody loved her. No, Marilyn is nothing like Jean. She's the perfect paradox -- the shy sorceress, sexy and self-conscious. The reluctant tease. Cold facts, these."

Once when Joe visited the set a photographer requested to photograph the couple, which Joe agreed to at the end of Marilyn's workday. While she rehearsed, he signed baseballs and then played the waiting game while she changed from the red sequined outfit that she wore from the song she had been rehearsing that day, "A Little Girl From Little Rock," into her street clothes. Joe entered her dressing room in protest and a yelling match ensued. The two exited the dressing room, Joe expressionless and Marilyn pale and emotionally exhausted.

A member of the press hanging around the soundstage asked where they two were headed for dinner.

When Marilyn replied that she would ask Joe, the stringer turned to the Jolter for a response.

"None of your damn business," Joe barked storming away, with Marilyn apologizing to the reporter.

While the press corps received unsolicited morsels about skirmishes between Marilyn and Joe, they prayed to no avail for ferocious catfights between Marilyn and her equally beautiful and buxom brunette co-star, Jane Russell. They were sorely disappointed. Jane and "Blondl" or "Blondel," as she so lovingly nicknamed Marilyn, mutually and greatly admired one another instead. They were equals, with Jane known as "The World's Most Talked-About Brunette," and ended up compatible friends during this period of Marilyn's life.

Marilyn sought Jane's advice, especially in the love department, as one would consult an older sister.

Marilyn was always a bundle of nerves on the set, working after hours with the demanding Natasha Lytess. Jane was shocked when Natasha attempted to overstep Howard Hawks. The annoyed director eventually booted Natasha from the set.

Harry Evans from *Family Circle* witnessed Natasha in action too.

"During the third take, I was conscious of a woman near me who seemed to be quietly having a stroke," he reported in his story. "At the conclusion of the scene, she muttered, 'No! No! No!' Her dark eyes flashed disapproval."

He was told that members of the crew referred to Natasha as "Marilyn's Svengali," for she made it a requirement that she remain on the set with Marilyn at all times.

"Some refer to her as 'Monroe's Svengali,'" he wrote, "but don't use 'Svengali' in front of Natasha, unless you're ready to duck."

Natasha's take on Marilyn's talent also surprised the writer: "Marilyn has been called a 'natural.' The word sickens me! There is nothing natural about make-believe."

While Marilyn was known for lateness, Whitey Snyder told Jane that Marilyn was often only puttering around in her dressing room. Marilyn was on the set long before the rest of the cast, nervously fearful of emerging.

Jane gently urged her friend out of her shell with subtle camaraderie.

"So from then on," Jane expressed in her autobiography, "I'd stand in her doorway and say, 'Come on Blondl, let's go,' and she'd say, 'oh, okay,' in her whispery voice, and we'd go on together. She was never late again."

Since Jane was married to an athlete, Marilyn would ask for her perspective.

"They're birds of a feather, and you'll get to know lots of other athletes -- otherwise, it's great," Jane counseled her.

Although Marilyn still flashed the "good friends" card to strangers and press people in terms of defining her relationship with Joe, commentary from Jane Russell helped the media to connect the dots. In one interview she referred to "Joe and Robert" [her own husband, Bob Waterfield] collectively, when confessing to interviewer Gene Handsacker that the two sports figures [Bob was a retired football star] complemented she and Marilyn respectively as mates, since they worked in other fields (both literally and figuratively).

Jane pointed out as well that both "Joe and Robert" were "sensible money wise. Marilyn isn't and I've never been. That's another opposite quality, which is great. Then you have a whole."

Marilyn's whole was sometimes a "half" when it came to Joe, who despised Hollywood affairs. *Photoplay* awarded Marilyn their "New Star Award" recognition in 1953. Joe refused to accompany her and friend Sidney Skolsky was Marilyn's token escort. Marilyn arrived to the gala two hours late, sewn into a gold lamé gown designed by William Travilla. Marilyn wore this dress in *Gentlemen Prefer Blondes*, though it was only visible from the back in one scene due to the plunging neckline, which lost out to the scrutinizing censors. She created a stir, irritating fellow industry actresses, who watched as the men of Tinseltown became silly over her, including emcee Jerry Lewis, who jumped on a table whinnying like a stallion. Joan Crawford was especially critical, which hurt Marilyn's feelings tremendously.

Sidney was always thrilled, on the other hand, to be on Marilyn's arm.

"Mickey Mantle can take DiMaggio's place with the Yankees -- I much prefer to take his place with 'The Monroe,'" he wrote.

In spite of the criticism some naysayers flung her way, Marilyn enjoyed a sincere balance of friendship with Jane and companionship with Joe. She reached a special pinnacle on her twenty-seventh birthday when she and Jane clasped their hands together in solidarity, as each cemented their hands and feet into cement at Grauman's Chinese Theatre in Hollywood.

Marilyn and Jane Russell place their names in cement at Grauman's Chinese Theatre in 1953 in Hollywood, in a rare color image from the original slide from the author's collection.

For Marilyn and Jane it was a rite of passage, as both young women were locals and spent time pushing their hands and feet into the prints of their Hollywood favorites during their youth. It was a tradition for Marilyn, who often visited Grauman's with Gladys and Grace. For Jane and Marilyn as well, they were the last in a line of stars to be immortalized in cement on cement sculptor Jean Klossner's watch. He was instrumental in making possible the first prints for Mary Pickford, Douglas Fairbanks and Norma Talmadge -- then many other notables to follow. After Marilyn and Jane's ceremony Jean Klossner retired.

Marilyn and Jane celebrated with their special men "Joe and Robert," for dinner at Chasen's in Hollywood following the festivities.

John Gilmore author of the book *Inside Marilyn Monroe* had interviewed Jane, who recalled Marilyn's delight in putting her hands in the cement.

"I'll never forget her saying, 'This is for all time, isn't it?'" Jane remembered. "Yes, I told her, it's for all time or as long as the cement lasts."

"She was so thrilled she was beside herself," Jane continued, "and she told me how she'd come to Grauman's when she was a kid and looked at the prints of everyone, and how she dreamed about being a movie star more than anything. It was something precious to me, her saying that."

Marilyn's next role was in a film that was the first in history to be shot using the CinemaScope widescreen techniques, plus partnered her with two major Hollywood powerhouses, Betty Grable and Lauren Bacall, in *How to Marry a Millionaire*. It was an excellent experience for her, as not only was she brilliant once again in her natural comedic timing, this time as the bumbling and myopic "Pola," but she gained the admiration of two established stars. However, it was known that Marilyn was ascending as Betty Grable was climbing down from her star. The press prayed again for flying fur between the ladies, as they had previously done with Marilyn and Jane, and were disappointed yet another time. Instead, Betty told Marilyn to "go get yours," in terms of reaching for the golden ring and apparently tore up her own Fox contract with five years remaining on it.

In spite of the confidence boost from her female co-stars, Natasha Lytess continually undermined Marilyn's self-esteem. Betty and Lauren were friendly to her, though frustrated with the constant retakes as Marilyn sought Natasha's approval on the sidelines and would instead be met with snippy criticism.

"Well, I suppose that wasn't bad dear, but I thought you could do better," Natasha lectured, chipping away at Marilyn's fragility.

As a people pleaser, it was hard for Marilyn not to take Natasha's advice as if it were gospel. After Marilyn eventually fired Natasha, she breathed in the vapors of the Lee Strasberg teachings. Natasha was easygoing in comparison to Lee, in terms of her levels of dominance and control.

As Marilyn's future began to form, a part of her past was fading away including a person whom she could truly count on and who genuinely loved her. Even though her star was rising and she now held the adoration of one of sport's greatest figures, her devoted Grace Goddard, who had been her guardian and mother's best friend, passed away suddenly in September of '53. Grace had cancer, though it was learned her cause of death was actually a result of an overdose of Phenobarbital. Grace was a rock in Marilyn's life since she was a baby and someone who had supported her in her dreams of stardom. Grace's death was another difficult blow she endured. It created a void that Marilyn refilled with the negative parties who would in the next few years overtake her life without Grace there to shield her from them. Unlike Grace, they were insincere in their intentions with Marilyn.

Marilyn was radiant at the premiere of *How to Marry a Millionaire*, as she clung onto the arm of director Nunnally Johnson. She wore a white gown that she borrowed from the studio, along with a fox fur stole and muff that were her own. She excitedly squeezed into photos with co-star Lauren Bacall and her husband Humphrey Bogart. Joe was noticeably absent again from this occasion, having ripped into Marilyn with accusations of double talk -- he criticized her about her aspirations to become a serious actress, while attending campy events such as film premieres.

Becoming more of a household name by the minute, Marilyn wore the same white gown when she appeared on *The Jack Benny Show*, which was her television debut. Marilyn was gifted with a new car for her appearance.

Her next picture was *River of No Return* co-starring Robert Mitchum and with Otto Preminger directing. Robert was familiar with Marilyn before she was famous because he worked with Jim Dougherty. Marilyn and her director mixed like oil and water. First, he despised Natasha and barred her from the set on location, which distressed Marilyn. Overall, he was a tyrant.

There was however another incident. Marilyn's friend Shelley Winters, who was also in Canada filming her movie, *Saskatchewan*, said she was there on the day that Marilyn was filming a scene on a raft. Marilyn shivered and struggled through the day. Otto Preminger behaved like a dictator to start, with his attitude beginning to escalate take after take. He grew vulgar with his vocabulary, even with the presence of child star Tommy Rettig on the set.

When Marilyn made her way back to the pier, Shelley took her arm and escorted Marilyn back to her limousine. Shelley said she noted to Marilyn after she slipped on the pier that she ought to "watch her step or she could break a leg."

After the ladies arrived to the hotel, Shelley said she exited the limo but Marilyn stayed behind.

"I can't get out," she told Shelley, "I've broken my ankle."

Everyone scrambled around Marilyn and rushed her to bed. After time on the phone with the Fox bigwigs, she insisted she needed a walking cast and said she could hide it under her long skirts during filming.

Although doctors x-rayed Marilyn the following day and concluded she may have had only a sprain, she demanded a walking cast and crutches. Both were provided and she showed back for her raft scene. Otto Preminger was now forced to treat his star with a softer attitude.

The director was mandated to grit his moods further behind his teeth when Joe showed on the scene to rescue her during the last two weeks of location filming. Joe and friend George Solotaire were there to hunt and fish while Marilyn worked. The friends rejoined her later after her workdays though it was later revealed fishing and hunting were covers (and hunting was a stretch for two city slickers, who both were spooked out by a bear that they encountered). Joe was there only to assure that Otto Preminger watched his p's and q's around Marilyn after hearing her tales of woe about the abusive director. Pictures show many smiling times in Canada together, in spite of the drama behind the scenes. Marilyn and Joe, who also taught her how to golf during their stay, formed pleasant memories.

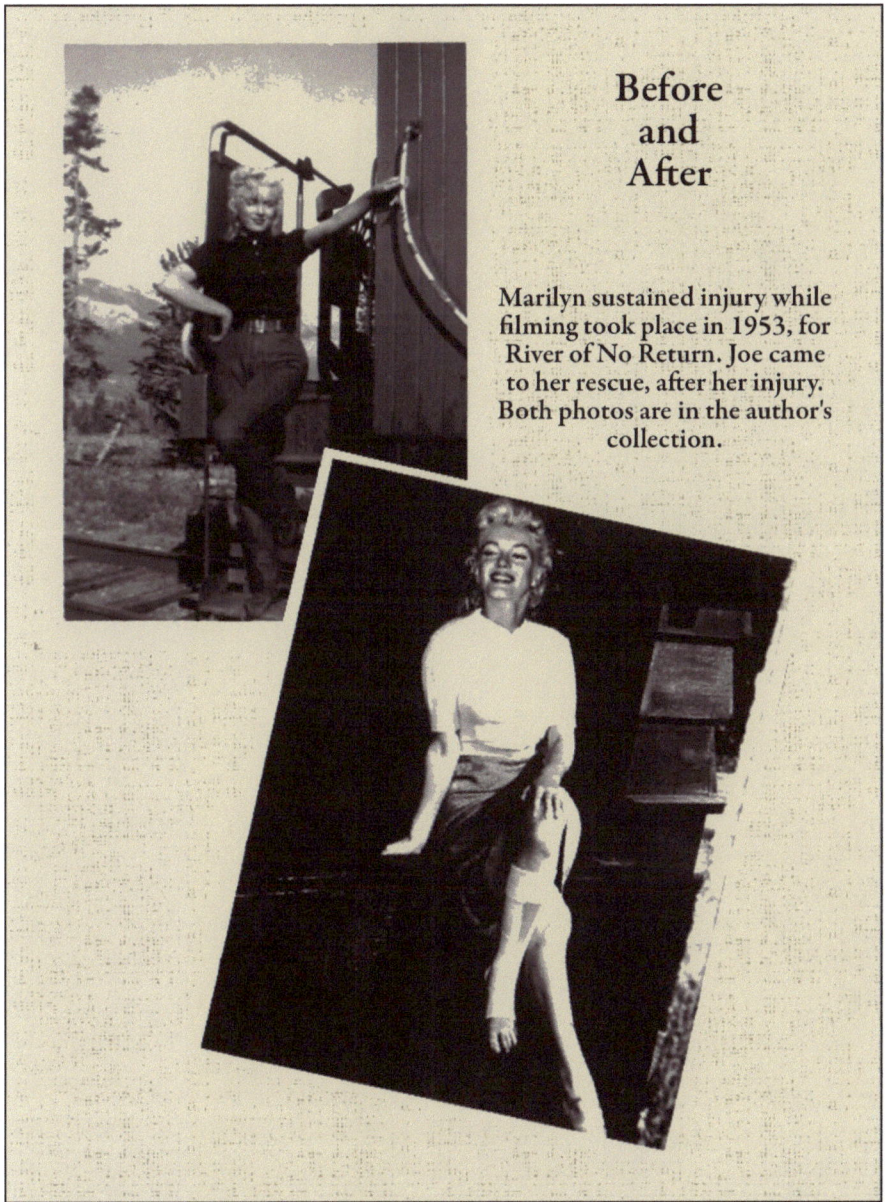

Before and After

Marilyn sustained injury while filming took place in 1953, for River of No Return. Joe came to her rescue, after her injury. Both photos are in the author's collection.

Marilyn and Joe also lavished in weekend excursions together in San Francisco after her return to Los Angeles. Marilyn would conceal her identity with a scarf around her head and Joe took her to the beach where he taught her to surf-cast. The two would savor romantic moments along the shoreline and appetizers often doled out on the house from his friends' local eateries.

Dario Lodigiani told author Richard Ben Cramer how he spent a day fishing and boating with Marilyn and Joe on his boat the Yankee Clipper, and was impressed when she nailed a striper. The fish was a persistent and weighty sea creature that wriggled a lot on Marilyn. Dario suggested Joe help her.

"She hooked it," Joe said. "Let her bring it in."

Marilyn unwillingly entertained Joe, as she pushed the pole into her bosom, still holding onto the bass.

"She's gonna pop one of them things!" Dario exclaimed, referring to Marilyn's chest, which sent the Yankee Clipper aboard the Yankee Clipper with Marilyn and his friend, into stitches.

Marilyn finally reeled the bass in on her own and Joe and Dario grabbed it with a net. Marilyn subsequently dropped the pole and was finished with fishing for the rest of the day after that.

Having Marilyn in San Francisco was a treat for Joe, who was so enamored by her that he would watch her as she slept. As her eyes were breaking open for the day, she would catch Joe standing nearby in the doorway of their room with his cup of coffee and a shy smile on his face. On those peaceful days in the fall of '53, Joe was in awe of how much their relationship had blossomed over that year.

Marilyn and Joe really began to bond earlier that year in the spring of 1953 after they were delivered the devastating news that Joe's brother Michael died from drowning in a fishing accident (it was suggested he had a heart attack and fell overboard). The couple rushed to San Francisco for days of mourning. The enormous DiMaggio clan embraced Marilyn with hugs and tears, weeping as they drank wine, spoke Sicilian and broken English and consumed large quantities of Italian fare leaving the DiMaggio kitchen in an endless stream. His sister, Marie was elated to meet a woman as supportive to Joe as Marilyn had become and watched as Marilyn tenderly comforted him within the depths of that tragedy. To the DiMaggios, it was family that was the core and Marilyn was now a part of their lives. The DiMaggios fussed over her and reveled about her beauty, bragging to her about Joe buying the family home for his mother. She saw Joe in a light, which drew her deeper in love with him. It was then during this time that the two agreed they would find a time to marry after the completion of *River of No Return*.

A photo taken in 1953 of Joe, when he visited Marilyn on location in Canada during the filming of River of No Return.

The photo was taken at the same time as when Joe was signing the autograph.
Both the autograph, photo and negatives from this day are part of the author's collection.

After Canada then Michael's death, Marilyn admitted to Sidney Skolsky. "It's the nearest I've been to marrying him."

Sidney questioned the rumors if the couple was already secretly wed.

"Where could Joe and I marry secretly?" Marilyn asked. "No, we're not married. I wouldn't want to keep my marriage a secret. There wouldn't be any reason for keeping it secret. I'll let you know when I do."

"Hold a good thought for me," she asked of her friend.

"I saw Marilyn Monroe once more," Sidney recalled. "The time after that she was Marilyn Monroe DiMaggio."

The rumors started flying about Marilyn and Joe immediately around the holidays. Were they heading to Vegas to tie the knot? Why was Marilyn not answering her home phone? The media frenzy commenced and those who wanted to know began the search, assuming Marilyn was still in San Francisco with Joe.

Only a day earlier, Marilyn had failed to show up for *The Girl in Pink Tights*, a musical production that Fox had scheduled her for and Marilyn was dissatisfied with. She refused to participate in it and from there the studio suspended her.

Joe became fed up with the Hollywood machine and how it exploited Marilyn. When he did on a rare occasion show up on the set, he drank coffee, dealt with numerous requests for autographs from the crew and overall grew annoyed at what he considered the phoniness. He despised the parties and banquets, with Marilyn accompanied at times by friends instead like Sidney.

Joe was most definitely the one who instilled in her the itch to break free of the system. He felt they demeaned her with substandard roles that only focused on her sexuality, while Fox worked her like a dog.

"Occasionally listening to her plots for the future, Joe would offer some sage advice from his own history," a journalist reported. "'Never mind all the publicity, baby,' he'd say. 'Go for the money.'"

Marilyn's boycott of the vehicle incited the nuptial rumors, yet the studio denied them.

Behind the scenes though, Joe was telling her the role would demean her and marrying him she could avoid the further embarrassing picture and abuse from the studio.

It was earlier that year that Joe helped Marilyn to purchase the rights to a novel called *Horns For The Devil*, after her agent Charles Feldman sent the couple novels to review. The agent considered it another way to usurp some extra cash from the greedy studio. Charles suggested that the novel rights become part of Marilyn's contract and that the studio, in order to sign Marilyn again, would have to purchase the rights to the screenplay from this novel. Marilyn paid screenwriter Alfred Hayes from *Clash by Night* to complete it for her. In the end, Charles would split the commission once the deal was finalized and his agency took over Marilyn's contract. The contract was still with William Morris, Johnny Hyde's agency, instead of Charles's agency Famous Artists. Eventually, the agency and Joe helped Marilyn to grab $150,000, with the studio purchasing the rights of *Horns For The Devil*.

The studio acknowledged that Marilyn was a no-show to her latest picture because she sought a raise. Considering Joe's track record of standing up the Yankees when he was dissatisfied with his compensation and as an overall dollar smart man, he was the one that told Marilyn to further hold her ground. Joe already knew that his friend Frank Sinatra, who would be Marilyn's co-star, was earning $5,000 weekly -- she was making a quarter of that.

Natasha covered for Marilyn by telling the press that she did not have the opportunity to review the script, which is why she failed to report to work. However at the same time, Natasha made attempts to lure Marilyn back to the studio -- if Marilyn was suspended, then Natasha was technically too. Natasha demanded $5,000 from Marilyn, who sold her mink coat from Johnny Hyde to raise $1,000 towards Natasha's financial request. Natasha continued to push that she must have $5,000 and attempted to extort the entire sum of monies from Marilyn.

The studio reminded Marilyn ad nauseam that she had a contract.

She felt cornered and unsure of what to do. Typically, Marilyn would concede to bullies until she was pushed against a wall. From there, Marilyn would sometimes shove back, then subsequently run and hide. Instead, Marilyn ran for safety in San Francisco for Thanksgiving with the DiMaggio family, with Marie cooking for the entire crew. Marilyn returned to Hollywood with a plan and Joe in tow to go to bat for her.

Marilyn was scared by the pushback and Joe helped to keep her strong. First, was to resist the threats that the studio, specifically its president Darryl Zanuck, was doling out via her agent because of Marilyn's attempts to stand up to the script. Joe advised Marilyn to ignore them no matter how tempting it was to give in. Charles, who was in Switzerland while his ex-wife had surgery, attempted to secure Marilyn the role of Nefer in *The Egyptian*. Darryl denied the request. In the meantime, Charles did not care that Marilyn was unhappy with the situation with *The Girl in Pink Tights*, a commission was still a commission to a money hungry agent and he made attempts as well through his office while in Switzerland to order Marilyn, who he condescendingly referred to as "the girl," to return to work.

Then Darryl tried lure number two, which was for Marilyn to report to the studio to redub a song from *River of No Return*. Once again, Joe urged Marilyn to not show and that request faded away.

The next bully in line was Natasha, with a mission to order that "selfish" Marilyn come to the studio at once, since she would lose her pay without Marilyn at work. Joe intercepted the phone call at Marilyn's Doheny Drive apartment and notified Natasha that Marilyn was unavailable.

After Darryl's attempt to reach Marilyn through Natasha was thwarted, he sent Roy Craft from the Fox Publicity Department to her residence and was sure Marilyn would take that bait. Instead, the full six feet and two inches and nearly 200 pounds of Joe DiMaggio answered the door. He instructed Roy to take a hike.

In between her standoff with the studio, Marilyn attended events including a party for General William Dean at Bob Hope's home, which Joe acted as Marilyn's escort and most definitely squired her around town as her bodyguard to intimidate the potentially long line of tormenters and harassers that had formed. Marilyn and Joe enjoyed their time at Bob's home -- she had spent some time with Bob and Jack Benny earlier that month at a charity event and now the suggestion came up at the party for Marilyn to join Bob on a future USO tour.

Marilyn photographed in the airport in Canada during the filming of *River of No Return*. The man to her left is potentially Joe's friend, George Solotaire, who also visited Marilyn with Joe on the set.

The author owns the negative and original photo above, plus the autograph below, obtained on the same day as the photo in 1953, and written by Marilyn in pencil.

The threats continued, with Darryl Zanuck attempting to blackmail Marilyn that he would destroy her through the press. Joe, now back in San Francisco, urged Marilyn to ignore the bluster and stay strong. She hopped a plane to San Francisco under the name of Norma Jeane Dougherty and decorated the Christmas tree at Joe's Beach Street home with Marie. Joe surprised Marilyn with a beautiful black mink coat, which far surpassed the quality of the one from Johnny Hyde that Marilyn felt compelled to sell after Natasha's threats. Marilyn was pictured wearing that coat frequently in upcoming months.

The closeness of Joe's family warmed her the most through this trying time. With the loss of Grace, her mother in the mental health system, Berniece far away and not someone she saw frequently and the war with studio bosses, she appreciated the DiMaggios' open arms.

"Whenever possible, Marilyn would take a trip to San Francisco, for she became almost like a member of the family," Sidney Skolsky wrote. "She and Joe's sister Marie became very friendly. 'She's just about the closest to a real girl friend I've ever had,' Marilyn told me."

Marie took Marilyn under her wing like a younger sibling. That was Marie's role anyway with Joe, who was seven years her junior. Marie nurtured most of the DiMaggio siblings and remained the matriarch of the Beach Street home until she was elderly. Even in those later years, she still managed Joe's business affairs. Marilyn was an additional twelve years younger than Joe and could have been comparable to a daughter for Marie with the age difference. Marie and Marilyn frequently enjoyed shopping trips in town with Marilyn making attempts to appear incognito with her hair tucked underneath a scarf. It was then impossible to conceal Marilyn and San Francisco was already under Marilyn watch anyway.

Joe loved to observe Marie and Marilyn communing together over the stove as Marilyn learned Marie's tomato gravy making techniques. He gazed at her in those moments, a love struck expression forming across his face.

Writer Dale Corvino's grandparents Helen and Tony Rizzo were neighbors of the DiMaggios. He shared a charming story fifty years following Marilyn's death, which detailed relationships Marilyn formed in San Francisco with his grandmother, mother and cousin. Helen became especially sociable with Marie too. The Rizzos had a daughter also named Marie, who is Dale's mother.

In late 1953, Joe first introduced Marilyn to the Rizzos. Dale's great aunt Rose learned of Marilyn's arrival to her family's home and flew in specifically from New York. In photos, Rose fawned all over Marilyn. Marilyn posed for pictures, her face free of makeup, and only agreed to photographs in black and white that day since she had a rash on her face.

Marilyn took a liking to little Marie and her cousin Laraine. She offered to take the girls for a day of fun at a nearby amusement park, Playland. Marilyn, now with her recognizable face painted on and a scarf on her head, stopped to a photo booth with the two young ladies and they snapped a souvenir picture together. Marilyn's joy was evident as her smile bubbled from behind the children. She was far removed from the Fox drama, in a moment now forever frozen in time in a tattered photo within a frame on Dale's desk.

The scarf blew from Marilyn's head after the photo and revealed her famous curly mane. A soldier spotted her and asked for a picture with the star. Marilyn and the children were soon mobbed. San Francisco Police Officers helped the trio out of the park, with their afternoon of fun ceasing early.

Dale Corvino treasures the relic of his mother and cousin with Marilyn, and the preparation of his article generated warm recollections of that day for his mother and Laraine.

"Whatever she is to you," Dale expressed about Marilyn in a Salon.com article, "she's the smiling blonde lady who beams at me from behind my mom's curls, and binds me to the women of my family, across divides of generations, loss and modern displacement."

Thankfully, Marilyn had the moral support around her, and enveloped herself with diversions like the trip to Playland. It was necessary because more haranguing from Darryl Zanuck took place. Joe told her to remain grounded. However, she was soon notified of her suspension and crumbled.

Afterward, the press began to write scathing editorials about Marilyn. At first Marilyn was upset, and sure Joe did not understand. She accused him of supported her strike to keep her out of movies. Marilyn was spot on in her assumption that Joe wished her to leave the industry, however he could not and would not stop her. Unlike Dorothy, he recognized Marilyn was unstoppable. He smoothed over her feelings by reiterating how he did understand. He told her that after his own fights with the Yankees he was down at first, and at the end of the day though the Yankees begged him to stay. Joe explained to her that his tenacity and game of hardball finally forced their hand to approve the pay increase.

"Yet she had a hard choice to make -- between security in marriage and security as an artist," one publication printed. "Much of her trouble with her studio can be traced directly to this conflict. She shunned cocktail parties, publicity stunts, and the empty business of being seen at the right places. Joe came first."

This was when plans began to further solidify for the couple's future together.

"Marilyn promised to notify us if she decided to get married," the studio commented to the press as their star remained quiet and the rumors grew.

Even Fox however was secretly worried.

One news source reported that a wedding was scheduled at Hotel El Rancho the Monday Marilyn was set to report to work, and was suddenly cancelled.

So the press waited with bated breath on their wedding watch.

Not all of the banter about it was positive.

'With the right attitude, and the proper approach, there is no reason why Miss Monroe can't make a happy Mrs. DiMaggio," one writer cackled.

There were naysayers out there who doubted the relationship would work.

"The biggest gamblers in the world, would never place a bet on this relationship...to them; it is a one hundred to one shot," wrote Joe Franklin and Laurie Palmer, who penned the first Marilyn biography.

"Rumors spread that the couple had eloped everywhere from Reno to Istanbul," one magazine wrote.

"Will Mr. America marry Mrs. America?" the baffled press pressed. "And if they split, who gets custody of the Wheaties?"

"In matters of the heart, Marilyn Monroe is also a faker," one magazine wrote. "But in an odd sort of way."

The publication mused that Marilyn realized a romantic component was an integral part of her publicity plan.

"So she has one," Jim Heneghan the author continued. "You've read about it. He's Joe DiMaggio."

"Joe fills the bill as the publicity lover," he added. "The only gimmick is that Joe and Marilyn are very much in love. The fact of this love is a secret that she shares with few people. When she has been pressed for details, her stock answer is that she likes him very much -- and doesn't know if they will marry."

A day later, after both Marilyn and DiMag were missing, Joe resurfaced, this time with a hint -- he told reporters, "If and when we are married, it will be announced in a blanket statement to everyone. No scoops."

Representatives for Marilyn denied the union between the Hollywood beauty and the Yankee Clipper, indicating, "There is absolutely no foundation to those marriage rumors."

The following Thursday January 14, the studio learned otherwise -- they received a last minute call from their star, which Harry Brand in the Fox Publicity Department, desperate for news on their commodity, picked up on.

"I'm getting married, Harry," Marilyn gushed.

"When?" he asked astonished.

"Today," she dropped.

"But, who? How? Where?" he stammered.

"I'm marrying Joe in a few minutes, Harry, wish me luck," Marilyn revealed in a giddy manner before rapidly hanging up the phone.

Fox summoned a small group of reporters to San Francisco City Hall, after receiving the tip, unbeknownst to Joe. After 30,000 fans strong waited outside after his first wedding, he sought absolute peace.

Joe asked best friend Reno Barsocchini, who helped to coordinate some of the nuptials, to keep it private. He was already aware from his past experience with Dorothy the kiss of death there was on that marriage with the press intrusiveness. He was more familiar that with Marilyn, the appetite of the press was even greater.

"I don't want any of those news reporters, I don't want any photographers," he instructed Reno. "I don't want any mobs outside the judge's chamber. "Keep it quiet."

It was, however, too late, and Joe could only smile for the cameras.

Presiding Municipal Judge Charles S. Peery joined the beaming Marilyn and Joe in wedded bliss during a single ring ceremony at 1:45 p.m. The judge was so flustered by the whole event and star power before him he later confessed he forgot to gift the bride with a congratulatory kiss, something he said he regretted.

Judge Peery commented after being bombarded by reporters, "Sometimes I'm glad I'm not Joe."

Joe, however, did not forget his role in the love scene as newsreels show the repeated kisses while the newsmen urged encores. Joe in a blue suit and polka dot tie embraced Marilyn. She donned a brown broadcloth suit, accented with a fluffy ermine collar. She toted a trio of orchids as her bouquet.

One group that was apparently annoyed with Joe for taking the vows with Marilyn was the San Francisco Archdiocese. According to Morris Engelberg's biography about Joe, the bishop Fulton Sheen allegedly reprimanded Joe for divorcing Dorothy, and then marrying Marilyn in a civil ceremony. Joe supposedly stormed out of a meeting with the bishop following his wedding. He continued to go to mass though he was reportedly excommunicated. Obviously the situation was rectified since the Catholic Church led Joe's funeral mass in San Francisco and later permitted a memorial service in New York's St. Patrick's Cathedral.

The wedding party included a small group of guests, among them: Reno and his wife, George Solotaire, Lefty O'Doul and wife Jean and Joe's brother Tom (whose wife Lee also attended) who witnessed the certificate.

Marilyn glowed and said she "couldn't be happier" and "I'm terribly excited."

Marilyn told reporters that she planned to continue her acting career and added, "I'm looking forward to being a housewife, too."

Joe confessed that he and Marilyn had planned the wedding for a while, yet only recently finalized their details.

"We decided to go through with it about two days ago," he said. "It's snap judgment, you know. It's been talked about for some time."

The question arose about children.

"Sure there's going to be a family," Joe blushed.

When asked how many babies Marilyn replied, "I'd like to have six."

"One," Joe quickly contributed in a corrective manner.

Marilyn and Joe, overjoyed on their wedding day, January 14, 1954. This original photo had been in Yankee Phil Rizzuto's wire photo collection, which was auctioned off following his death. Phil's photo, is now part of the Jennifer Jean Miller collection. Photo courtesy of the author.

As the couple emerged from the building, running to his car, the question collectively posed was where they were headed for next. Joe said they would take ten days for a honeymoon before he voyaged to New York on a business trip.

Joe told reporters, "We are going to climb into the car and take off. The car's all packed, jammed full of stuff. We are just driving. We have a lot of miles to put behind us."

The couple sped out of town in his midnight blue Cadillac, dodging paparazzi. Joe and Marilyn stopped in Monterey for lunch, creating a stir at the Hot Springs Hotel where they ate. Next they registered to stay at the Mission Inn Hotel, with the crowd convinced Marilyn and Joe were spending their first night as husband and wife there.

Instead, Marilyn and Joe strolled into the office of the Clifton Motel about 175 miles south of San Francisco in Paso Robles. They stunned sleepy proprietor Ernest Sharpe at around 8 p.m. He had to rub his eyes at the vision of the couple to verify he was not dreaming, after having dozed just previously as he watched TV.

Joe asked for a room with a television.

"I don't suppose you want twin beds?" Ernest asked Joe.

"Oh boy, I'll say not," was Joe's reply.

After helping the couple to their room, Ernest eagerly informed his wife about their guests.

"You won't believe this," he gasped excitedly, "we've got Joe DiMaggio and Marilyn Monroe staying right here with us, and they're married."

He was right -- his spouse did not buy the story.

"Marilyn who?" his wife echoed.

"Marilyn Monroe," he repeated.

"Sure, and I'm Gloria Swanson," she snickered.

Marilyn and Joe spent their wedding night in a room that ran a $4 tab for the stay, hanging a "Do Not Disturb" sign on the door. They emerged fifteen hours later at 1 p.m. the following day.

Ernest tipped no one off about their presence respecting their privacy. After paying their bill, the DiMaggios turned down Ernest's offer for cups of coffee and said they planned on breakfast down the road.

Ernest Sharpe would commemorate the couple's stay with a brass plaque outside their room that read, "Marilyn and Joe Slept Here."

From there, Joe and Marilyn disappeared off the radar, with many speculating they were headed for Mexico or Hollywood since Marilyn was required to report back to work. Instead, they evaded attention again and quietly headed into the mountains beyond Palm Springs where they stayed in the secluded home of their friend and attorney Loyd Wright near Idyllwild. Looking back later on this portion of their honeymoon, Marilyn viewed it as a time in which they bonded for two weeks, luxuriating in walks in the snow for hours. There were none of the usual interruptions from the phone, television, press or studio. The two simply appreciated one another's company.

"Joe and I talked a lot," she said. "We really got to know each other. And we played billiards. There was a billiard table there, and Joe taught me how to play."

A week following their honeymoon, reporters were sniffing around for news on the couple again. They reached out to the studio for tips, which only produced a dead end. All the media knew is that Marilyn and Joe were "believed to be honeymooning somewhere in Southern California."

Marilyn obviously had one up on the studio, which bit its tongue when asked if Marilyn was still under suspension.

Evidently keeping the sour grapes under wraps, yet still attempting to maintain their tough guy front, the studio offered a smooth reply when questioned if they planned to take action against Marilyn for her failure to show. They said she had five more days until she was mandated to report back for duty.

Yet, was Marilyn aware of this deadline?

"No we haven't heard from her," the studio answered.

It was clear Fox was seething at their hot property standing her ground, and reiterated that Marilyn did not have final script approval over her films.

Little did the studio realize, Marilyn was nearby as she remained in disguise in Westwood. She stayed in a motel under the name "Norma Baker" while Joe tended to some business in New York. Joe rejoined her then they flew back to San Francisco.

Only five days later Lefty O'Doul tossed a bone to the nutritionally deprived press -- he was heading to Japan to open the country's baseball league for its 1954 season before he officially took his own post as the Pacific Coast League's Manager for the San Diego Club.

This could have been an innocuous news ditty, minus one small and important leak: "O'Doul said he expected Joe DiMaggio, former New York Yankee star now in New York, to join him in Tokyo -- if DiMaggio's new wife, actress Marilyn Monroe, will let him go."

Chapter Three - Love in Japan and Korea

The Marilyn-hungry press swarmed upon Joe and his bride on Friday, January 29, having previously been on an unwilling diet and starved of Marilyn and Joe news. Now, the local and overseas press media rolled again, as the couple headed for their trip to Tokyo. The photographers' lenses awakened when she re-emerged publicly in San Francisco, beaming while she carried a large hatbox and her mink coat from Joe. She sported a diagonally buttoned black wool dress with a leopard-print scarf demurely tied around her neck. Joe appeared dapper as usual, attired in an elegant suit.

The honeymoon to the Eastern part of the world was planned to continue for about another four weeks and Marilyn remained under a loose suspension with the studio.

The pair headed from San Francisco with Lefty, the three waving goodbye to local supporters. The trio boarded a Pan American Clipper and prepared for their first stop in Honolulu, where 2,000 Hawaiians strong waited at the airport.

"It's what you might call an extension of their honeymoon," Lefty, then manager of the San Diego Padres, told reporters.

For Lefty, the trip to Japan was a regular occurrence. Joe traveled to the Orient several times in his life. For Marilyn, it was her only trip and the Japanese still continue to talk about her visit as if it was yesterday.

Sportswriters in San Francisco crowned Lefty "The Father of Baseball in Japan." Though baseball was introduced in the country long before Lefty's birth, Lefty's inauguration to the game in Japan commenced with a trip in 1931 with American all-stars, who challenged Japanese university students. There were seventeen games, which drew more than 450,000 fans in total.

Lefty fell for the nation and then developed friendships with industrialist and newspaper publisher Matsutaro Shokori, and his assistant, Sotaro Suzuki. The pair asked Lefty to act as a liaison to bring Babe Ruth to Japan. "The Sultan of Swat" rejected the opportunity at first, but once his numbers slipped and the Yankees released Babe in 1934, he acquiesced.

The crowds in Japan went wild, with a welcoming parade packed so tightly with Japanese citizens that the cars were at a complete standstill. The mob at that parade was estimated at one million strong.

Joe, Marilyn, and Lefty, as they prepared to depart for their trip to Japan. United Press Telephoto, with description on verso, from the author's collection.

When he played, Babe Ruth was so moved by the enthusiasm of 100,000 fans in attendance at one game, a downpour did not deter him from participating in the event. One fan politely delivered an umbrella to the field for Babe, and after the two bowed thanks to one another, Babe played the entire game with the umbrella in hand to show his gratitude. It was only when he was batting that a bat replaced it.

The American team took all seventeen games, yet were almost shut out by an eighteen-year-old high school pitcher, Eiji Sawamura. This baseball prodigy later played for the Yomiuri Giants and sadly died in 1944 when he served in the military and his ship was torpedoed during World War II.

Marilyn and Joe, on one leg of their journey, during their trip to the Far East.
An original photograph, from the author's collection.

The Japanese were extremely awed by the height of the American players, with most over six feet tall.

One of Lefty's major contributions was to help establish professional teams for the country, with the Yomiuri Giants the first. In 1935, Lefty rounded up an American team to play against the Giants, since there were no other teams. The Giants also headed to the United States for training in San Francisco with the San Francisco Seals, of which Lefty was now the team's manager.

World War II postponed Lefty's next visits to Japan and he returned swiftly in 1946. His trips ended in the 1950s.

His own San Francisco Seals toured to Japan in 1949, a time when Lefty observed the Japanese were greatly depressed.

"You know, when I was there three years ago," Lefty remarked, "their cry was always, 'banzai, banzai' ('bravo, bravo'). But in '49 they were so depressed that when I hollered 'banzai' at them, they didn't even respond."

That changed by the end of the six weeks, as the emotional sunshine returned to the people of Japan. Over a course of eleven games, in excess of $100,000 was raised for Japanese charities.

The visit from Lefty's team was an icebreaker and morale-booster, which greatly restored Japanese and American relations.

"All the diplomats together would not have been able to do that," General Douglas MacArthur marveled. "This is the greatest piece of diplomacy ever."

Japan's Emperor Hirohito was so grateful, he invited Lefty and the Seals brass to his Imperial Palace for personal words of thanks.

In 1950, Joe made his first trip to Japan, returning in 1951 with the "O'Doul's All-Stars." Dom DiMaggio was on the team roster too. Dom had been included on the 1937 tour, which cancelled because of the war, and asked Lefty to remember him when the chance arose again.

The impact that Lefty has left on the Japanese baseball culture, is evident in the Yomiuri Giants uniform -- it is almost identical to the one Lefty wore when he played with the New York Giants in 1933 and 1934. Other teams have since caught on to the pinstripe tradition, which was the Seals' uniform style.

The pinstripe spirit was on its way back to Japan in 1954, though a layover was required along the way in Honolulu first. That diversion was less than tranquil.

Marilyn in Japan - two similar photos from the author's collection.

The Hawaiian frenzy was too much for Marilyn. The papers sugarcoated their coverage of the power couple's arrival at the airport. Or perhaps they were even unaware of the true mayhem. Fans reportedly cheered, though it was not noted that the people of Hawaii who waited for her excitedly grabbed at Marilyn's white-blonde locks as she passed by. They yanked pieces out because these fans were so enamored with its shade, not accustomed to such fairness. It was something that truly frightened Marilyn. Police had difficulty holding back the throng.

"They keep grabbing at my hair," a stunned Marilyn informed Joe, as the violation was in process.

They attempted to navigate through the crowd.

A photo from the author's collection, of Marilyn and Joe traveling together in Japan. Her finger is visibly bandaged in this picture.

"Do you see what they're doing, Joe?" she asked. "They keep grabbing at my hair."

Are you all right?" Joe asked Marilyn after they located a safe corner of the airport.

"I'm alright," she responded in between the trembles and dusting herself off.

"I tried to keep them off of you," Joe contributed. "I've never seen anything like it."

"Neither have I," a stunned Marilyn interjected, close to tears, "it was mad, just mad. I never thought there'd be such a crowd here."

She lovingly took his protective arm, leaning against him. Her breathing relaxing slightly as she straightened her hair, and the smile he so loved began to curl on the sides of her lips again.

"You didn't expect it, did you, Joe?" she inquired.

"No," Joe snapped, irritated by how the rabid fans converged on his wife, and he was not able to guard her from the intrusion.

Marilyn, Joe, and Lefty were adorned with leis, greeted by hula dancers and ukuleles and consented to a brief interview at the airport. Marilyn attempted to de-stress after feeling as if she had been partially scalped, while she sipped on a glass of freshly squeezed pineapple juice. At this point, she felt ready to return home.

When asked if she would be in another picture soon, Marilyn replied she did not know, and then confirmed her suspension.

"We're not concerned about that now, we're on our honeymoon," Joe chimed in.

Joe informed reporters that San Francisco would become their permanent home upon their return.

Marilyn also publicly made it clear she was unabashed by Fox's stance.

"Marriage is my main career from now on," Marilyn cooed to the press, though in other breaths she indicated she would not leave the industry, and simply on leave because she did not like *The Girl in Pink Tights* script.

The trip to Tokyo had some other hitches in addition to pulled hair. The couple had scrambled previous to it to acquire a passport photo of the world's most photographed woman. That Friday Marilyn was without a passport for her first trip abroad. Joe rushed out to a Market Street arcade, and a half hour later emerged with a photo of Marilyn.

There was something else amiss with Marilyn that night as they departed. She hid something under her mink coat. When the newlyweds first emerged from hiding, it ended up visible and remained so throughout most of the trip in photos. It was her right thumb, bandaged in a splint, something that her doctor ordered she must wear for three weeks.

When asked, Marilyn explained her thumb was broken.

"I just bumped it," she told reporters. "I have a witness. Joe was there. He heard it crack."

Some have accused Joe of having been the reason that Marilyn's thumb was injured -- an unconfirmed rumor was that he threw a glass at her while the two quarreled.

Their marital relationship was known to have been stormy, yet there was a mutual love and admiration that stretched beyond its legal bounds as husband and wife, as well as beyond life. Joe was her shining knight who ran to her rescue many times after their divorce and following her death.

Having already been prepped by the throng in Honolulu, Marilyn, Joe and Lefty took additional precautions as they planned to head for Tokyo's Imperial Hotel when they arrived on Monday February 1.

Before they exited the plane, a General who introduced himself with the last name of Christenberry, proposed to Marilyn that perhaps she might consider entertaining the soldiers in Korea. Marilyn turned to Joe for guidance.

"It's you're honeymoon," Joe said, "Go ahead if you want."

As Marilyn, Lefty and Joe debarked from their aircraft in Haneda Airport, the first 4,000 that greeted them at the airport rushed them. This was not because of Joe and Lefty, who had intended to be the main stars of the trip and had been in the past, but Marilyn was the reason. Hopefuls vied for a glimpse of the bombshell. Joe instinctively pulled her back into the plane from the ramp as fans charged them.

Police attempted to urge the masses to return to their homes, yet to no avail.

The excited crowd knocked over photographers on their stepladders, as well as reporters, American Airlines Executives and Japanese stars, who also waited for the beauty.

As other passengers who acted as decoys left the plane, Joe and Marilyn instead made their escape through the luggage hatch.

Police and jeeps held back the crowd with difficulty, and a Japanese police official swore to the press that the throng was so unruly in their excitement he feared Marilyn's clothes would have been ripped off if she had attempted to greet them. A few broke through the barricade and landed atop the vehicle that transported Marilyn and Joe, nearly crushing the roof.

Marilyn in Japan - Feb 1954 - From the Author's Collection

Although hundreds of thousands of fans waited in the Ginza district of Tokyo praying for a peek of the DiMaggios as they headed to the famous Frank Lloyd Wright Imperial Hotel, Joe instructed the driver to take an alternate route. Safety was paramount for the concerned husband.

Fans along the way adoringly chanted "mon-chan," which translates to "sweet little girl."

"Malyn, Malyn, Malyn Monloe!" some additionally were heard repeating in Japanese pronunciation, which often substitutes an "r" with an "l."

There were two hundred police officers guarding the hotel, where the clambering continued. Those who missed Marilyn, Joe and Lefty at the Ginza now assembled. There were ten entrances at which the fans all stationed themselves. People were so energized they pushed into one another, knocking each other into the hotel Koi ponds, and jamming and breaking both the revolving door in the lobby and the hotel lobby windows adjacent to the main entrance. The riot birthed injuries, screams, bloodshed and more pandemonium.

When the riotous crowd learned they could not summon Marilyn with mayhem, the fans held a vigil outside the venue. They shouted her name until it was impossible to concentrate.

Officers and the crowd catch a glimpse of a smiling Marilyn, after she has arrived in Japan. Photo from the author's collection.

Joking about feeling like Eva Perón, "Like I was a dictator or something," a jetlagged Marilyn consented to a step outside onto a balcony where she waved and blew kisses. Her appearance simmered down the crowd.

The following day, the press began reporting that a trip was planned for Marilyn to head to Korea to entertain the troops.

"I have wanted to go to Korea to see the boys for a long time," she said. "Now, even though I am on my honeymoon, I have the chance to go -- and I'm going for at least four days."

"She will be most welcome," Army officials replied.

When asked if Marilyn would wear an ermine bikini to perform as actress Terry Moore had for a previous show, Walter A. Bouillet a special services officer replied, "She'll wear dresses, plenty of clothes."

He added that Marilyn would "sing a few numbers but mostly she'll just stand there."

Twenty-one-year-old Corporal Al Guastafeste of Unionville Long Island had the assigned honor to be her accompanist. He played with the troupe of musicians called "Anything Goes," which was scheduled to perform two shows daily with Marilyn.

Joe would be unable to join his wife, tied down to his previously planned coaching schedule with Lefty.

This was the same day as well that Marilyn and Joe held a news conference at the hotel. In addition to the newsmen, a Japanese fan and loyal *Modern Screen* reader named Yoko Hazama finagled his way into the room. It was clear to those in attendance Marilyn was the focal point, and lapped up the interest. Some noted that Joe who had previously been the attention monger, stewed as the press honed in on his gorgeous bride.

Marilyn, above in an original photo from the author's collection during the press conference in Tokyo. She is wearing the Mikimoto pearl necklace that Lefty picked up for Joe.

She wore a more conservative outfit, as well as a string of pearls around her neck. The Mikimoto pearls were picked up by Lefty on Joe's behalf, and would become a source of contention years following her death and about two months before Joe's. The pearls were then long out of both of their hands. Marilyn would later be photographed wearing them when she signed the divorce papers to end her legal union with Joe.

"Do you know where the pearls are?" Anna Strasberg demanded in 1999.

Anna Mizrahi Strasberg is the widow of Lee Strasberg, Marilyn's guru acting theorist who eventually controlled her spirit and wallet. Lee became the major beneficiary of Marilyn's estate, which Anna further dominated following his death as a primary beneficiary. Anna never met Marilyn, which is a strange irony that she would inherit the bulk of what Lee received from Marilyn in her will.

Susan Strasberg, Lee's daughter, recognized this herself in her unpublished memoirs discovered following her death: "A good part of [my father's] estate was seventy-five percent of Marilyn's estate."

Susan also wrote that Marilyn thought Lee would "care for her, protect her in death, as he tried to do if unsuccessfully in life. Now she would be in the hands of people who had never known or loved or respected her as she so desperately wanted. Marilyn Monroe, who was not so unreasonably paranoid about strangers now belonged to them."

While the author of this book does not fully agree with Susan's statement, believing instead that Lee Strasberg was a stranger and leech who weaseled his way too into Marilyn's life when he barely knew her, the author does agree that it is even less appropriate for Anna Strasberg and her children to have "control" over Marilyn Monroe.

Anna has remained a mysterious figure in some ways since she entered into the Marilyn Monroe picture. She typically refuses to comment when articles have been written which cite something about her and her part in the Marilyn Monroe legacy. What is commonly known is that Anna has exerted a territorial demeanor over all aspects of Marilyn's likeness, something she rarely challenges when reporters quote others who make statements about her influence. She typically replies "no comment."

Marilyn's right of publicity has been one of those components, although courts have judicially estopped Anna several times for her control, wagging their fingers at her. Courts have exerted that Marilyn's right of publicity died with her in 1962. Anna has however earned millions in licensing fees on Marilyn's image when she was never legally entitled to. Lee received Marilyn's personal effects and was a residuary beneficiary of the estate.

He never inherited her right of publicity. That right also did not exist in 1962 and Anna has attempted to challenge it posthumously, even seeking legislative assistance when the courts did not rule in her favor.

Marilyn showered with flowers during her stay in Japan. Photo from the author's collection.

Secondly, Marilyn died with only a few thousand dollars in her bank account and her beneficiaries received her royalties for her work following her death. How then have parties like Anna, who never knew Marilyn, been able to make millions each year from her image and lay claim to it? It has stretched to the point Anna has sued others who she alleged had infringed on the "rights," demanding exorbitant licensing fees from the defendants.

Shortly following Marilyn's death, her business manager Inez Melson reached out to Joe, already suspicious that the puzzle pieces of Marilyn's demise did not fit. Inez was the only one who challenged Marilyn's Last Will, accusing Lee and Marilyn's therapist in New York Dr. Marianne Kris of undue influence. These main beneficiaries had been cut from Marilyn's life towards the end. Inez said they coerced Marilyn to sign the will in 1961, before Dr. Kris tossed Marilyn into the Payne Whitney Psychiatric Clinic in New York. Berniece confirmed this in her book too about her half-sister -- she said Marilyn was not pleased with the will and wished to change it. Sadly Inez's claim was dismissed -- she did have a valid point -- these parties victimized Marilyn.

The true colors of the recipients of Marilyn's estate eventually crept to the surface. Lee demanded from Inez certain items that he said belonged to "the estate" and was angry when the furniture in Marilyn's Brentwood home, not considered personal effects, sold with the house. Dr. Kris also brazenly raised a stink before her death in 1980 that the value of her portion of Marilyn's estate significantly declined due to the overwhelming taxes it was subject to. It was no longer about Marilyn, only about money.

Dr. Kris was actually the beard for Anna Freud's share, a topic the author will explore later in the book. The Anna Freud Centre is where Dr. Kris willed her portion. Anna Freud unlike the other Anna at least met Marilyn once in her life -- that is where the contrasts stop.

Lee and his wife Paula lived in the same building as Dr. Kris. They had been already acquainted with her when Marilyn started therapy. The Strasbergs also referred Marilyn to her East Coast attorney Aaron Frosch, who mishandled her estate while maintaining an inappropriate relationship with the Strasbergs. He breached his attorney-client privileges with Marilyn through this relationship.

While Marilyn magically wowed the press with her mere presence and Mikimoto strand in Japan in 1954, she would never learn of the later battle behind her cherished piece of jewelry after having it delivered in a brown paper bag on Christmas Eve in 1957 to the front door of the Strasberg apartment. She knew Paula always admired the pearls and Marilyn's gift provided some closure from her marriage to Joe. Paula was delighted with the gesture. Paula was actually enthralled with every morsel of cash and other valuables she sucked up from Marilyn.

The pearls ended up in Susan's hands after Paula died from cancer. Susan would also adore this necklace, although one clumsy night she caught it on her car door, snapping the string and scattering the pearls on her garage floor. After the mishap they were restrung, once she and a friend located every bead.

A rare color image of Marilyn and Joe exiting from their plane at Itami Air Force Base in Japan, February 1954.

Gentlemanly Joe holds an umbrella for his new bride as she descends from the aircraft on a rainy winter day. This image is from the original slide, which is now in the author's collection.

However, Susan befell the same health fate as her mother, and succumbed to financial challenges too. Susan wished to provide for her daughter Jenny. Lee had verbally offered to establish a trust fund for his granddaughter. Unbeknownst to Susan and her brother Johnny, Lee financially snubbed and disinherited the two children from his first marriage in lieu of Anna and their two sons David-Lee and Adam-Lee. Susan neither received a dime at his death, nor any items back that she had given her father. Susan was the financial rock for her parents before Marilyn's estate, handing over her proceeds from her first thirteen years of her own successful acting career.

Susan, in desperation, consigned the necklace to Gotta Have It! The business is a pop-culture and memorabilia store in New York. The dealer located the perfect buyer -- Mikimoto in New York.

The day in 1999 that Robert Schagrin from Gotta Have It! was prepared to hand-deliver the check for $100,000 to Susan, he entered her bedroom and found her limp body stretched across her bed. Susan took her last breath in his arms.

Anna Strasberg strode in after being informed of Susan's death to orchestrate her funeral. Though it fell on deaf ears, Susan's friends told Anna her final wishes were to have her ashes scattered.

Anna ignored the directives and advised Jenny as soon as she stepped off the plane, "Don't sell those pearls."

Anna indicated that the necklace belonged to "the estate," meaning they belonged to her.

Jenny told *Vanity Fair* in an interview, an article that Anna declined to comment on, "I knew that [the pearls belonging to the estate] wasn't true! But I was in a state of shock. My mother had just died, and Anna was telling me not to sell the pearls. I knew they'd already been sold, but I didn't say anything. I just listened. All I could think of was Mom didn't want a funeral, and she certainly didn't want Anna to pay for it."

Anna manipulated Jenny into signing a Power of Attorney after she learned the pearls were sold and Robert Schagrin delivered the check to Anna's attorney. The check was written for "Jennifer Jones Strasberg, c/o Susan Strasberg estate."

Jenny snapped out of her shock after her return to Los Angeles and regained her Power of Attorney via a court of law. Anna's grip on her check was removed.

A metal slide from the author's collection of an image taken by an unknown soldier.

Jenny disclosed to *Vanity Fair* she had signed her mother's cremation order the day before the memorial without Anna's knowledge -- Jenny described Anna as having a "ballistic" reaction.

"She is all about control," Jenny said of her step-grandmother.

Anna claimed she had suggested she oversee the Power of Attorney to "protect Jenny," and wanted to "get her more money for the pearls."

In 1988, six years following Lee's death, Anna had asked to meet with Susan. The two discussed Jenny's future. Anna offered a receptionist job to Jenny at the Strasberg Institute in Los Angeles, the acting school on the West Coast, though she insisted Jenny could not use the name "Strasberg" while working. She could only refer to herself as "Jenny Jones." Susan had reminded Anna of the trust fund Lee had considered for Jenny, which Anna said she would speak to her attorneys about. Although Susan never heard back from Anna on the fund, she did not pursue the matter, fearful Jenny might lose her employment.

When Susan suggested one percent of Marilyn's estate for Jenny as a trust, Anna replied, "Oh, darling, the Marilyn Monroe estate isn't going to be worth very much!"

By 1994, Anna ended up pocketing $7 million from the sale of Marilyn's likeness and right of publicity.

Four months following Susan's death, *Vanity Fair* reported that Jenny received the $100,000 check from the sale of the pearls, quit her job at the institute and worked at a bookstore.

According to the current LinkedIn Profile for Jenny Strasberg (who has most recently listed herself as "Jennifer Strasberg") she was employed at Dutton's Brentwood Bookstore until 2006. It does not specify when she commenced her job as an office assistant for her current employer, which at present is again The Lee Strasberg Theatre and Film Institute.

A rare color image taken by a member of America's military stationed in Japan, from the collection of the author's negatives, of Marilyn and Joe, as they arrived at Itami Air Force Base. The couple was showered with flowers at this stop, as they were on the others, on the evidently rainy day, in February 1954.

Anna directed both the Roger Richman Agency, then CMG Worldwide to manage the licensing of Marilyn Monroe's image. She sold what was left of the "estate" after massive legal bills racked up from multiple court battles, to Authentic Brands Group (ABG) for an approximate $20 to $30 million. Anna is still a minority partner in the venture with ABG.

If only Marilyn on February 2, 1954 had warning over the battles that have since ensued over her legacy, she would have likely been sickened. The living Marilyn in Tokyo never saw that type of cash during her lifetime, and though she was wealthy, she was a simple woman by nature. At the same time, she was constantly broke because of being consistently financially milked by those around her, excluding Joe. In her final days, Marilyn finally caught on to the shenanigans.

Yet that day in Japan the press obviously did not foresee her tragic future and was instead swooning over the blonde sex goddess. There was a two-hour wait for her arrival -- she greeted them in a red clingy wool dress, accented by her pearls and fur coat -- it was a vision worth their wait. They pitched questions to her that she batted responses back with home run precision out of the park.

"How long have you been walking like that?" a Japanese reporter inquired.

"I started when I was six months old, and haven't stopped yet," she quipped.

"We are told you do not wear anything under your dress," another from the Japanese press corps stated before asking, "Is that true?"

"I'm planning to buy a kimono tomorrow," Marilyn replied coyly.

"What kind of fur is that?" a reporter questioned pointing to her coat.

"Fox -- and not the 20th Century kind," she retorted with an obvious swing at the studio.

"What is your first impression of Japan?"

"I just arrived here only yesterday, but I heard about Japan from my husband," Marilyn explained turning to Joe. "I really never expected so many cameramen waiting here."

Marilyn also noted that she had never seen Joe play ball, not referring back to the charity game that she attended in 1952.

"I met my husband after he retired from active baseball," she said.

"Is it true you want six children?"

"You should ask *me* that question," Joe interjected though the press mainly disregarded him.

Two days following the press conference papers reported about an upset of the Japanese underwear industry, with women there allegedly shedding their skivvies with the knowledge that Marilyn was potentially commando under her dresses.

The whirlwind in Japan began to take its toll on Marilyn. Between her vaccines for Korea and then suffering from a nervous stomach from the barrage of fans following the DiMaggios and the O'Douls the entire trip, her health was delicate. She first took to her bed in Tokyo, dealing with what the press coined as "autograph hound fatigue."

While Marilyn noted that in her travels she rarely had opportunities to enjoy the sites, she managed to take in some shopping in the Ginza district and a Kabuki theatre performance. She and Joe were photographed with locals as they enjoyed some moments of solitude in the fishing village of Kawana. In the mornings though, Joe was her focus while she watched him coach at the stadium.

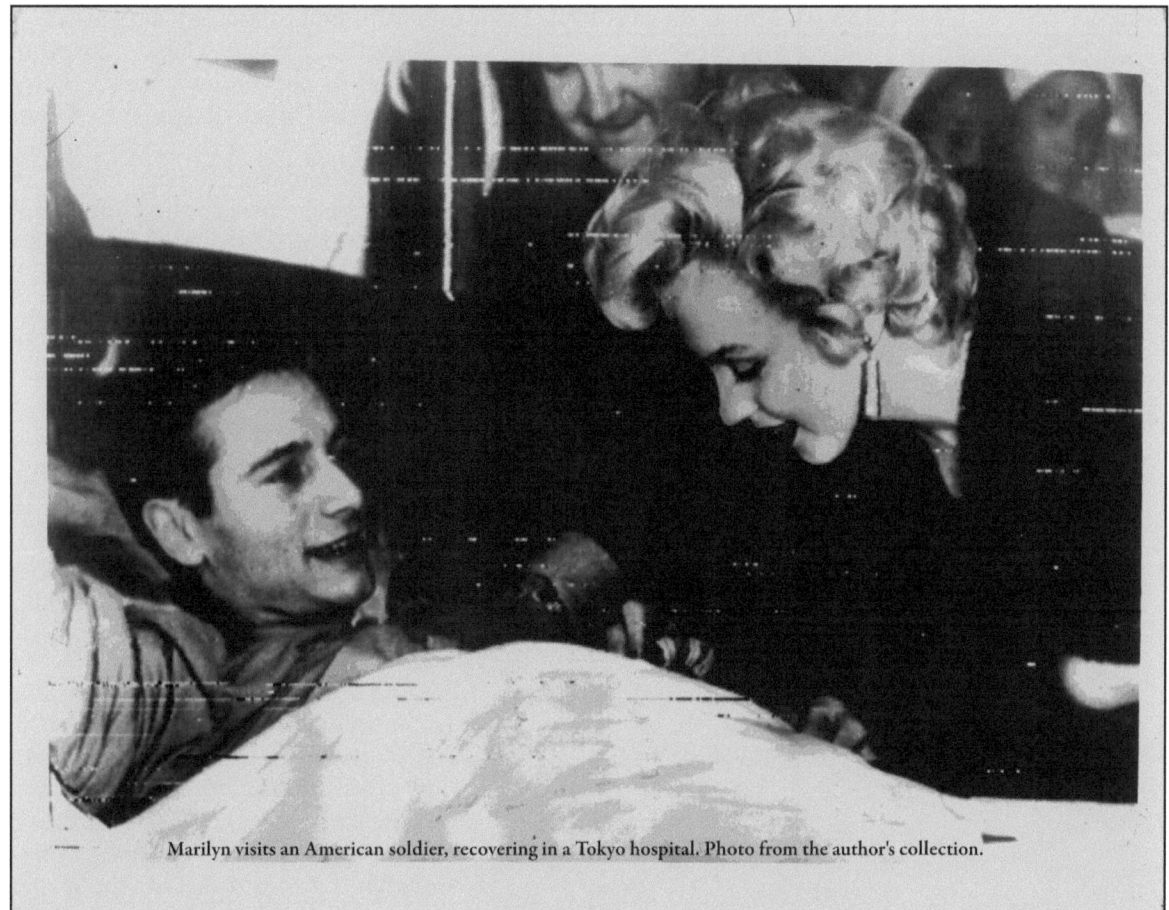
Marilyn visits an American soldier, recovering in a Tokyo hospital. Photo from the author's collection.

On Friday February 5 Lefty and Joe enjoyed some camaraderie and golf in the seaside town of Kawana before training Japanese ball players in the fine art of the game. While they did so, Marilyn rested and luckily received some female friendship from Lefty's spouse Jean the next day. Jean flew in from the States, and was the one who accompanied Marilyn to Korea.

The following day, the press reported that Marilyn received her vaccines to prepare her body for her travels to Korea. It was Joe's friend and Yankee infielder Dr. Bobby Brown who administered the shots. While Bobby played ball, he simultaneously earned his medical degree and served in the Army as a doctor in Japan.

"He [Joe] was a little skeptical of the army, having served in the army in World War II," Bobby would later say. "Marilyn was going to Korea to entertain the troops. She was going to need some injections for cholera and yellow fever and typhoid and so forth."

Bobby said that Joe announced he would only permit one army doctor to treat Marilyn -- that was First Lieutenant Brown.

"So of course," Bobby continued, "from all over the Far East came the calls, 'Who the hell is First Lieutenant Brown?' He just didn't want anybody who he didn't know dealing with her."

Marilyn ended up dining in her room for the remainder of the stay in Tokyo (she told the press she "wasn't stuck up," and did so because "I just couldn't use my hands to eat in public."). She was up that Friday night for steak and orange juice with Lefty and Joe in Kawana. Joe kept his worried hawk's eye on the fan activity and tenderly over his bride while they dined. Following dinner, she cheered her husband on with many an enthusiastic "Good shot, Joe," while he and Lefty played snooker. The game is Japan's equivalent of pool. As Marilyn watched the game fans ogled over her.

Earlier that morning Marilyn did put aside her fatigue to do one of the things that she did best, connecting with people. She made a stop at the Army Hospital in Tokyo where she visited with several soldiers. One of them was Corporal Donald L. Wakehouse of Iowa City Iowa who was headed back to the States after having been a prisoner of war. He would return home with a souvenir -- a cast autographed by Marilyn. The other, Private Albert Evans of Canton Ohio was suspended upside down in his bed after a jeep accident broke his back and had the unique experience of Marilyn speaking to him as she lay on the floor under his bed to look up at him.

On one of the makeshift stages in Korea, where Marilyn elatedly performed for soldiers. Photo from the author's collection.

Meeting with these hospitalized members of the military was a warm-up of sorts for Marilyn for the upcoming days.

On Monday February 8, a week following their arrival, the couple made a stop at Itami Air Force base on their way to Fukuoka. The DiMaggios and O'Douls were approached for picture and autographs by a small crowd on their rainy stop and were greeted with flowers and a small press conference.

After their arrival, the group headed to the Kokusai Hotel, and by morning the hotel was packed with fans. One local journalist, Shoji Kawamura of the Fukunichi newspaper, was assigned to track down the news on Marilyn. He headed to the hotel, armed with three photographers.

The trip had become slightly discouraging for Joe, who had been the king in the eyes of the press in his past trips. Nothing prepared him for the rush he was experiencing as a result of Marilyn's fame and interest in the public eye. The fascination far surpassed the Japanese natives' adoration of him.

Joe's guard was immediately up when Shoji rapped on the door of their room, number 313.

"Nobody talks to my wife until I get back," Joe ordered.

Joe headed to the Kashii ballpark to coach the Shochiku Robins, while Shoji and his photographers waited nervously. On the Yankee Clipper's return, Shoji anxiously knocked and had an unexpected treat -- a beaming Marilyn herself answered the door. She glowed in a black beret and white turtleneck.

The tongue-tied Shoji asked if she would consent to an interview and some photos. Normally speaking fluent English, he sputtered out his request in Japanese through Marilyn's interpreter.

"Of course, I would like to pay my respects to the local media and my fans," Marilyn consented in reply.

The two paced in the hotel hallway, with Marilyn blowing kisses out the window to fans. One of the photographers with Shoji took photos from a ledge outside the window, thankfully not plunging from the side of the building as he did so. The other two busily burned through flashbulbs as Shoji interviewed Marilyn.

He noticed her bandaged and splinted finger and asked about it.

"It's a blister from signing too many autographs," Marilyn fibbed.

Shoji would return after Marilyn granted permission for one photo. He would have that developed for her autograph, an item he proudly displayed in his living room as a treasured souvenir. Before then, he cranked out a feature story with photos of the star entitled "Marilyn hits Hakata like an H-Bomb!"

He followed Marilyn the day after their interview to another location, an American base at Uminonakamichi Koen, then known as Gannosu. After a drive around Higashi Koen for some sightseeing, Marilyn and Joe joined the O'Douls at the American Center to watch the baseball newsreels. Marilyn was apparently bored, according to the projector operator Akira Ogata, who sat next to her. She spent time watching everything but the newsreels.

Marilyn gladly signed Akira's bus pass, the only thing he had on hand. She met other fans outside of the center and posed for photos. A photo from the visit is apparently still hanging in the American Center. That night, Marilyn and Joe ate at the Royal Bakery in Nakasu and had to exit on the sly through the back to avoid the crowd.

After their departure on February 11, Shoji learned after questioning the hotel bellboy, Marilyn and Joe had been considered the tidiest visitors that ever patronized the hotel. When Joe was gone at training, Marilyn washed her own underwear in the sink. After the couple checked out, hotel staff combed the room for remnants of her hair, which sold for high prices on the black market.

Although the trip was intended to promote baseball, Marilyn instead stole the show and enraptured the Japanese.

On February 14, Marilyn was in Hiroshima with Joe and Bobby Brown. They toured the Atomic Bomb Memorial Hall to view a replica of the damage to Hiroshima. Afterward, they took a walk around the city. While there, Marilyn also took in a game. When a local announcer mentioned she was in the park, 5,000 fans mobbed the location, which caused difficulty when Marilyn sought her seat by Jean O'Doul.

A scan of the original negative, in the author's collection, taken by U.S. Army Staff Sergeant, Anthony M. Aprile, who was stationed near the Yalu River. The soldiers greeted Marilyn with this sign, which she beamed joyfully over, and leaned over in gratitude, for photos.

The paper reported an insight about something that occurred repeatedly while the group visited Japan and that rubbed Joe the wrong way the entire trip, after having previously been the reigning attention grabber: "On the field, the blonde's husband Joe DiMaggio, Lefty O'Doul, and former Yankee third baseman Capt. Bobby Brown were forgotten by the fans."

She was a real nice gal," Bobby said later as he remembered Marilyn.

Marilyn suited up for baseball with the 25th Division. Description of the photo-op below. Wire photo from the author's collection.

WIDE WORLD PHOTOS   PLEASE WATCH CREDIT

MARILYN MONROE CONTINUES THE WHIRLWIND TOUR OF THE FRONT LINE DIVISIONS IN KOREA FOR THE THIRD DAY STILL PLAYING TO A MOST ENTHUSIASTIC AUDIENCE. MARILYN EMULATES HER HUSBAND JOE DIMAGGIO AND GETS A FEW BASEBALL POINTERS FROM TWIN BROTHERS ERNEST (LEFT) AND MONROE MANUEL ABRIL, OF COLTON, CALIF. THE BROTHERS ARE WITH THE 25TH DIVISION BASEBALL TEAM.
2-19-54

Bobby and his wife joined the DiMaggios and O'Douls for some of their tour.

"We had a great time together," he said.

"The Japanese just went wild," said Bobby about the DiMaggios' stay there. "At that time, the two biggest things in Japanese lives were baseball players and movie stars, and you had the two biggest, right there."

Though Marilyn entranced the people of Japan, Joe attempted to refocus on baseball and to continue coaching with Lefty, while Marilyn headed off on her own with Jean to Korea.

Before Marilyn's arrival in Korea, she had spent about a week's time rehearsing in Osaka with Al Guastafeste and "Anything Goes." "Diamonds Are a Girl's Best Friend," "Bye Bye Baby," "Somebody Loves Me" and "Do It Again," were among the numbers.

Bandleader Don Obermeyer was surprised by Marilyn's humility. He was amazed at her sensitivity overall -- she even questioned if singing "Diamonds Are a Girl's Best Friend," would be appropriate to croon to the troops. She recognized that they subsisted on meager wages. She then decided to weave in a small dance number at the end of the song, which she thought could counter the possibility of any offense.

"She was easy to get along with," Don recalled to biographer Jenna Glatzer. "Just charming."

Don also met Joe, and described them both as "friendly."

He was amazed that Marilyn had never used an upright microphone before, with all of the sound equipment in Hollywood overhead booms.

"She walked up to it like she was afraid of it," he commented, "but she soon learned to use it. We got her trained in on the PA system. She did just about everything we asked her to do. She was so willing to be cooperative and nice. I don't think she had a mean bone in her body."

Don said that Marilyn constantly sought feedback from the band on how to improve her performance and politely asked them what they required from her.

On a flight to Busan he said that Marilyn was seated in the front of the plane with colonels and generals, and later excused herself during the trip to make her way towards the rear of the aircraft. There Don said, she took a seat and spoke with every member of the band. She asked where each of them was from, where they had attended school, about their families and hometowns and their ambitions.

"She wanted to know more about us," Don told Jenna. "She didn't want to be with the brass, she wanted to be with 'the guys.'"

"We all appreciated her interest in us," he continued.

This was typical of Marilyn, who on her movie sets often socialized with members of the crew.

Marilyn arrived in Seoul on Tuesday February 16, where 600 servicemen greeted her before she headed for the Western Front. She was about to meet the men who had been asking the government to specifically send her for close to two years.

Marilyn showed up in her C-54 transport plane attired in military garb and heavy boots. As Marilyn flew in, she asked the pilot to circle the crowd while she lay down on her belly. She waved and blew kisses as two soldiers in the aircraft held her feet. Although not outfitted in her typical feminine way, her beauty and effervescent spirit still radiated. The men were smitten and affectionately showered her with wolf whistles and howling.

"Gosh!" she exclaimed. "I've never seen so many men in my life."

"I am just sorry Joe couldn't come along," she added.

The last visitor who garnered as much news coverage and enthusiastic attention (without the wolf whistles of course) was President Dwight Eisenhower in 1952. The President still did not top the Monroe phenomenon.

Marilyn planned on ten shows in four days for an estimated 100,000 members of the military strong that cheered for her. She switched her outfits in makeshift changing areas, discarding her Army surplus apparel for something very sexy.

She performed on improvised stages, many accented with burlap curtains suspended on four poles, where it was so frigid, snow flurries were visibly blowing in some shows in the newsreels and icy pellets could be seen on the stage floor in photos from others. Braving the gray skies and damp air as she started to develop sniffles from the chill, she performed in a skintight purple beaded cocktail dress with a flower pinned near the décolleté area of her dress, gold heels, hooped earrings and wearing a pearl bracelet. Bundling up she considered a disservice -- she sought to deliver to the soldiers the woman of their dreams as she warmed their spirits.

"I thought I might wear it to a cocktail party," she told a reporter of her dress. "I really didn't know I was coming to Korea."

Marilyn was able to fight off the chill of the winter Korean air bundled in her military surplus jacket. She is hanging onto a sign, which soldiers painted in honor of her visit to Korea. This is an original negative in the author's collection taken by US Army Staff Sergeant Anthony M. Aprile, who was stationed with a group by the Yalu River.

"You're on next, Miss Monroe," she was signaled as the tap dance number before her wrapped up.

A cue was only a formality -- her cue was the ability to hear the thousands of voices calling for her.

"We want Marilyn!" they chanted while rhythmically clapping their hands in unison.

She never once looked miserable in the plunging neckline and chilly temperatures. She smiled, danced, pranced and sang her way across the stages and around the bases. She never once lost the sparkle in her eyes or the enthusiasm in her carriage.

Marilyn on tour in Korea -- the stage is covered with frozen precipitation. Photo from the author's collection.

Her joy was evident in the photos and newsreels. It was Marilyn in command over those bases. The soldiers excitedly photographed her during her visits whether they were up close or watching from a distance.

In a later interview she said: "The highlight of my life was singing for the soldiers there. I stood out on an open stage and it was cold, but I swear I didn't feel a thing except good."

Her first show, the number of soldiers reported there varied. By some reports, it was 13,000 and from other sources the numbers ranged between 19,000 and 23,000. The group included men from the First U.S. Marine Division and M.P.'s, who dropped their tough personas to whip out their cameras and take pictures of Marilyn.

"Anything Goes" accompanied Marilyn as she sang the numbers, "Diamonds Are a Girl's Best Friend," "Do It Again" and "Bye, Bye Baby." Her performances elicited monstrous cheers and calls for encores. One of the generals was upset with "Do It Again" and its suggestive lyrics. Marilyn reminded him it was a classy George Gershwin tune, a bit of trivia that did not lessen the blow of the general's dissatisfaction with the song.

"I sing it as a straight, wistful love song," Marilyn countered.

Though Marilyn's time onstage was brief, lasting only about five minutes per show, it was well worth it for the soldiers. Some of them trekked more than five miles of muddy terrain for a glimpse of the star. The members of the military watching that day, and at the other shows, shimmied up telephone poles and stood on jeeps and tanks for better views and pictures of the star.

Ed Barrus, another soldier cited in the Jenna Glatzer biography *The Marilyn Monroe Treasures*, hoofed it to watch Marilyn perform.

"When we arrived at our destination," he said, "we tried to spruce up in case she called out to one of us to come up on stage with her...we were a bunch of dreamers. They had some other entertainers perform -- they did a good job, but we wanted to see Marilyn."

Ed said that she arrived on a tank and when she exited, she backed down and the soldiers ended up with a rear view. They showered her with whistles and cheers in approval.

"We just stood there and stared at her," he said. "She was very beautiful. I felt my three-year enlistment was worth it, even though I was about forty rows back."

Don Loraine was one GI in a group that Marilyn socialized with for a few moments during her stay.

"I was a young Marine in Korea," he described to biographer Michelle Morgan. "Marilyn came out dressed in a heavy parka. She started to sing, suddenly stopped and said, 'That's not what you came to see,' and took off the parka. She was dressed in a low-cut purple cocktail dress. She was so beautiful, we all went wild, and I might add, it was colder than hell that day. She brought a lot of joy to a group of combat weary marines, and I for one will never forget her."

Marilyn waves as she is driven by soldiers. US Army Staff Sergeant Anthony M. Aprile, was fortunate enough to catch Marilyn's wave through his lens. His negatives are now part of the author's collection.

R.J. Vannucci, another Marine who Michelle Morgan interviewed, set out on foot for his show. He first walked, and then hitched a ride for the fifteen-mile distance.

"I remember it was a very cold day," he said, "typical for Korea in the winter."

Another soldier had similar memories.

Marilyn, as she is transported by jeep, is thrilled as she is greeted by soldiers. There was literally a documented film shortage following her trip to Korea. Anthony M. Aprile, US Army Staff Sergeant took this photo. His negatives are now part of the author's collection.

"Marilyn knocked herself out for the troops," John T. Jones shared in his recollections, when interviewed by Jenna Glatzer. "While planes were strafing just north of us, she sang, joked, and gave the troops a good show. They were appreciative and gave her much applause. After the show, some of my guys went up by the stage and got her autograph and photos. I knew Marilyn because she was on the radio at night on the Armed Forces Radio Network. Yes, we loved that gal -- hated to see her get kicked around in life."

Her next stop, the 7th Infantry Division, drew the same reaction.

One paper reported, "The Reds probably thought the 7th Infantry Division was on night maneuvers. The sky kept lighting up from the constant flashing of bulbs as cameras clicked."

Marilyn reached over to one of the soldiers, who she realized was so enthralled to have her in front of his eyes he forgot to remove his lens cap.

"Honey, you forgot to take it off," she remarked as she removed the cover.

He blushed and swooned, his fellow soldiers hooting and hollering behind him.

One soldier in that group was quoted as sighing, "I sure hope she outlives Joe," as one of the many millions of men who she would dazzle with her presence who would have gladly waited on a line for a chance to be with her.

The sad irony in that soldier's statement, was in slightly more than eight years, Joe would commence his lonesome journey in outliving Marilyn.

As Marilyn traveled along dusty road to dusty road, she received a warm welcome at every destination. While navigating her way to particular bases, she spotted signs of her presence.

"Drive carefully -- the life you save may be Marilyn Monroe's," one road sign read.

Although she enjoyed her time in Korea, it was obvious Marilyn's heart was back in Japan with Joe. The Army arranged a phone call for the newlyweds from one of the mess halls.

"Do you still love me, Joe?" Marilyn asked, following up with, "Do you miss me?"

Annoyed by the grilling in front of a live audience, Joe replied, "I do. Yeah."

From the privacy of her tent, it has been reported that Marilyn asked Joe if he could join her. He apparently replied that there were too many commitments in Japan for him to do so.

During her stop at an officer's mess for two cheese omelets at the 7th Infantry Division, there was a blank wall. It previously held Marilyn's "Golden Dreams" calendar.

"We thought it might embarrass Miss Monroe if she came here," a mess hall attendant told a reporter who inquired.

The same picture was hung throughout the bases, and did disappearing acts during her stay.

Except, Marilyn located one of the calendars in a mess hall and her reaction was opposite from what members of the military who made the great efforts to spare her feelings anticipated.

"I'm very pleased to have my picture hanging in a place of honor," she smiled.

Culinary ventures were aplenty when Marilyn visited Korea. In addition to downing her omelets, she was photographed serving up cake, eating cake and being fed cake. Marilyn sported a chef's cap at one stop and dished out food on the chow line next to Jean O'Doul,

"The fellows don't eat those rolls Marilyn hands out with her little fingers," one sergeant grinned in his confession to a reporter.

She was also photographed as a recipient on the chow line, her meal scooped onto her tray.

*Marilyn greets soldiers in Korea from a Jeep
Negative from the author's collection.*

Many of the infantrymen felt slighted with Marilyn often pulled into the officers' clubs. Later in her tour, ten enlisted men per stop were invited into the officers' messes, after their complaints that Marilyn was only accessible to those at the top were heard.

One officer was inadvertently snubbed. Major General R.M. Pate of the First Marine Division expected to dine with Marilyn until her helicopter crew overshot its mark and ended up a few miles away. Marilyn munched on the omelets while her steak grew cold with the Major General.

Marilyn also made certain that members of her band were never excluded from entering the officers' clubs.

"I'm not going to that officers' club without my guys," Marilyn stated firmly. "Where I go, they go."

"She insisted that the band be with her," Don Obermeyer recalled, "so we were in some nice officers' clubs!"

The enthusiasm augmented as the number of Marilyn's shows increased. At the U.S. 40th Infantry Division, an M.P. was nearly trampled by the crowd of 10,000 who sought a closer glimpse of the beauty queen.

At one of her stops on the U.S. 45th Division show on Thursday February 18, soldiers grew impatient over the forty-five minute show prior to Marilyn's act, demanding for Marilyn to come onstage and the other show to exit.

The soldiers began flinging rocks and chanting, "Bring on Marilyn, bring on Marilyn!"

Army officials including Colonel John Kelly stopped the pre-show. The Colonel threatened to obstruct their view of Marilyn, who he was now guarding, until "every last man moves back." That quieted the group temporarily, though some of the 6,000 soldiers rushed the stage prior to the finish of her three songs. In the melee, one soldier was injured and taken away by ambulance. Following the show, Marilyn was heavily shielded while the noise level of the crowd escalated to the point that Marilyn's voice was drowned out. She was sequestered offstage with an Army parka flung over her shoulders, before a military sedan rushed her away.

Marilyn later blamed herself for part of the riot. On that stop located in the Korean Eastern Front she yelled, "Eleewah!" ("Come!"), after she meant to shout "Sayonara!" (the Japanese phrase meaning "Goodbye!"). This occurred as she was being driven around the base in an open jeep and waved to some soldiers in the trenches -- her jeep was swarmed in moments.

"I've never seen so many men in my life, we were besieged, overwhelmed by them," Marilyn would recount in 1956.

Once the crowd was calmed, an M.P. asked what happened. He explained to Marilyn why they were bombarded.

She surmised innocently, "Thinking back on the incident, I don't consider it as much of a faux pas as it may have seemed -- because subconsciously, I'm sure it was the way I really felt."

Marilyn performing in Korea at the Bulldozer Bowl.
Photo from the author's collection.

On her final day, Marilyn performed for 8,000 in Taegu followed by a more intimate performance of 200 Airmen at an airbase near Chunchon. Afterward, she grabbed some lunch at the officers' mess.

"What a fuselage!" an Airman shouted out, complimenting the star in her final show.

"I love you," she yelled to the crowd in Taegu when she concluded.

For the soldiers who were there, Marilyn's visit left them with a lifetime of photographs and memories they handed down. Those who are still living continue to tell their stories too. The papers said that Marilyn's appearance fully depleted the film supply in Korea.

Marilyn's departure day did not have the fanfare as her arrival did, with a few members of the Air Force and press on hand.

She described her visit in Korea as "the climax to everything in my career," and "the high point of everything."

"I never felt like a movie star before -- really in my heart -- before I came to Korea," Marilyn told reporters.

The experience of performing onstage implanted some desires in Marilyn's being about live performing -- a validation that film did not offer her.

"It was so wonderful to look down and see a fellow smiling at me," she said. "Gosh, you should see the effect, it was really wonderful. After this I hope to go on the stage."

She credited her success in Hollywood to those who served in Korea, which is one of the reasons she desired to give back through her performances. Marilyn explained how letters from Korea catapulted her from bit parts and as calendar girl to superstardom.

In a later interview, Marilyn would attribute those in Korea to skyrocketing her popularity with a jump from fifty to 5,000 fan letters weekly.

An original color negative from the author's collection of an elated Marilyn beaming a magnetic smile to the troops who greeted her when she visited Korea. This photo was taken by US Army Staff Sergeant, Anthony M. Aprile, who was stationed by the Yalu River.

"I sort of feel the guys over here were responsible for a lot of what happened to me," she credited. "They are very close to my heart."

Even closer to her heart was Joe who greeted her that Friday night in Japan with embraces and gentle kisses as she descended her plane.

In other ways, Joe was a cold welcoming committee.

"Joe, you never heard such cheering," Marilyn told him excitedly.

"Yes I have," Joe replied blandly, bursting her bubble. "Don't let it get to your head. Just miss the ball once. You'll see they can boo as loud as they can cheer."

The rigors of the side trip to Korea combined with the glacial temperatures (Marilyn admitted to reporters that her normal sleep in the nude, was now replaced with white woolen long underwear), caused Marilyn to become ill. She began running a fever prior to her departure from Korea.

Joe was irritated at first after Marilyn's return from Korea, deep down annoyed that she had left. He missed his bride and underneath his façade was jealous of the attention she was receiving -- it was Joe who was normally the star in Japan.

He suggested they go to a pizzeria for dinner that he was familiar with in the city.

Miffed by Joe's lack of interest in her anecdotes about Korea she rebuffed him, snapping back that she was not hungry. There was more though.

Marilyn poses for Korean Troops
negative from the author's collection.

"I don't feel well," she muttered to him curtly, her feelings hurt, while at the same time experiencing physical symptoms.

"You're tired," he remarked, slightly concerned yet still matter-of-factly. "Let's get something into your stomach."

"I think I've got a fever," Marilyn persisted.

He laid his hand on her forehead, and Joe's eyes suddenly widened.

"You're hot!" he exclaimed.

Joe grabbed her hand and rushed Marilyn to the hotel. From there, he contacted the Army Post in Tokyo for a physician, who clocked her fever in at 104. She was diagnosed with a mild case of pneumonia.

For the next few days she rested, and Joe fussed over her. Some reports have erroneously alleged that the couple fought on those final days in Japan, which was incorrect. Once she had recuperated slightly, they quietly took in some more tourist destinations.

Marilyn smiles as she takes to the stage in Korea.
Her thumb is still visibly bandaged in this photo, from an injury she sustained before the trip.
Photo from the author's collection.

The DiMaggios and O'Douls headed back stateside on Tuesday February 23 for the thirty-hour flight. During their stop in Hawaii, the worried Joe insisted Marilyn be checked at the hospital where doctors observed her for a second opinion -- they diagnosed her with a case of bronchial pneumonia.

On the return flight from Hawaii to San Francisco, Connie Jorgensen was a flight attendant who looked after Marilyn.

"She's the greatest sport I ever saw," the Pan American employee remarked about Marilyn's positive attitude as she flew at high altitudes with a severe respiratory ailment.

"I'm ill and I just want to go to bed," a hoarse-sounding Marilyn told the fifty members from the press corps and about one hundred fans, who waited to greet them in San Francisco after they landed. "My doctor ordered me to bed, and that's where I'm going."

The next day, it was reported that she was "feeling better," and Joe's concerns of Marilyn potentially requiring hospitalization were lifted.

As Marilyn recovered and planted her roots in San Francisco for her next chapter with Joe, some press swirled around negatively about Marilyn's show in Korea. The negativity smoked out a few soldiers who flurried to her defense. The *Pittsburgh Post-Gazette* published a bash, stealing a quote from *The New York Times* "distinguished military observer" Hanson Baldwin.

The editorial that appeared on February 25 entitled "Soldiers, Not 'Cowboys,'" incited members of the military who were alerted to it. The editorial attributed Marilyn's visit as one factor that added to lowered morale and lack of discipline in the military.

"On two occasions during the visit of the motion picture actress, troops rioted...and behaved like bobby soxers in Times Square, not like soldiers proud of their uniform," was the quote that the editor published and repeated Baldwin's complaint. "Sweater girls and young ladies scantily clad in ermine-trimmed bathing suits, have nothing to do with military morale: tours by such as these are not the stuff of discipline and pride and toughness."

With the 1950s Puritanism, the *Post-Gazette* agreed with a "Bravo," and "It was time that someone reminded the Army Special Services, that it is not the burlesque business. Military morale grows out of a feeling of personal dignity, of pride, of confidence in leadership. It is not something that comes from high-class, 'kootch shows,' into forward areas or military camps. In short, you don't make a good soldier by treating him like a drugstore cowboy."

Three of those "drugstore cowboys" with an A.P.O. address from Marilyn's new hometown of San Francisco lashed back.

"We think it rather difficult to observe the military and especially the conduct of the individual soldier from a distance of approximately 9,000 miles," the trio retorted. "Perhaps Mr. Baldwin has not 'observed' carefully enough to discover how often top talent is available for such shows. Has he taken into consideration just what we are doing in Korea and what few diversions we have?"

The soldiers resented the snobbery in the editor's commentary and ardently defended Marilyn.

"Mrs. DiMaggio, while in the public light, is unfortunately only too open to snide criticisms, based on biased views of past performance," they wrote. "In her defense we would like to say that in the Second Division at least, her show was beyond reproach. She is an entertainer and she did her entertaining decently. It was far from a 'kootch show.'"

Chapter Four - True Love Never Dies

Marilyn settled into married life in San Francisco, tending to Joe's needs and taking on some tasks as a housewife as she felt interested and able. Joe's sister Marie, a widow, handled most of the domestic duties in the family home like cleaning, and especially cooking. At Joe's advice, he would ask Marie to step aside for Marilyn to take the helm when the mood swayed her.

"Marilyn Monroe, the voluptuous blonde bombshell who has become the unrivaled glamour queen of Hollywood, made news by telling a columnist that her principal concern in life (at least for the moment) was learning how to cook spaghetti the way her husband likes it," one publication chimed.

Marilyn did take an interest in cooking items beyond pots of spaghetti. Though in her previous marriage to Jim Dougherty she would become known for cooking peas and carrots as an ensemble because she liked the color combination, and he initially offered words of displeasure about her cooking, Jim noted later how Norma Jeane learned to skillfully prepare game dishes with acquisitions he brought home for dinner after hunting.

Frequently slammed as not having been a stellar housewife, Marilyn enjoyed cooking as was evident by her *Fannie Farmer Cook Book* -- the lucky bidder paid $13,800 for it at Christie's in 1999. A treasure within the treasure was a shopping list inside handwritten by Marilyn. Marilyn's copy of *Joy of Cooking* was another book of hers that the final hammer dropped for $29,900 at the end of the auction.

It is possible that Marie may have sparked Marilyn's interest in a couple of special recipes, which most definitely came from San Francisco. For one, the recipes were written on paper from the City Title Insurance Company, a San Francisco based business. Secondly, one of the dishes was a special stuffing, which among ingredients included Sourdough Bread. San Francisco remains the most famous location in the country where that variety of bread is an integral part of the city's culture. Some of the other ingredients -- pine nuts, raisins and Parmesan cheese -- would give a nod to the DiMaggio Sicilian background. Joe additionally was normally was light on the garlic. Some friends have said so and the stuffing recipe in particular called for "no garlic." Marilyn emphasized those words specifically at the top of the page. Morris Engelberg, Joe's friend and attorney would claim in his biography that Marilyn disliked the odor of garlic on Joe's breath, though she would enjoy eating foods with garlic herself. If correct, that could be another potential reason why she excluded garlic from the recipe. Whatever the reason, Marilyn obviously liked this recipe, as well one for a roasted chicken, which appeared on the stuffing recipe's flip side.

Joe expected Marilyn to ditch her career and become a San Francisco housewife, yet the world would not let her forget she was Marilyn Monroe. During the afternoons, Marilyn would retrieve Joe Jr. from school and walk with him around the city. Marilyn and Joey often visited the zoo too, to the chagrin of the Yankee Clipper -- he was a privacy seeker who preferred she maintain some anonymity and quiet. That was impossible as Marilyn's very presence raised the popularity of the city as a tourist destination even greater while she lived there. He forbade her from walking after visitors in town pursued her, and insisted she drive from then on.

San Francisco afforded her more solitude than Los Angeles, where she learned to fish (though often became seasick in the process), would sit in the back of the family restaurant (which closed in 1986) while Joe played host, enjoyed time with the DiMaggio family, would embark on picnics with Joe, and in the evenings wound down the day with him and a little television.

Trouble in paradise was evident on the docks of San Francisco after Marilyn and Joe passed one morning with some fishing off of the Yankee Clipper. Fishermen witnessed Marilyn running from the pier onto the road -- she was crying hysterically with Joe in pursuit. The fisherman pretended they did not witness the incident, attempting to respect the boundaries of their local hero and his famous bride.

Marilyn enjoyed an evening walk one of those nights while Joe was out of the house on business, ignoring his orders to take the car from now on. Marie tried to reinforce Joe's directives, to no avail.

Marilyn reveled in the foggy conditions and the eerie glow from Coit Tower.

"I felt like I was walking in a strange and different world," she recalled in amazement. "It was like I was moving away from the earth into some beautiful and mysterious lands that have never been discovered."

She quietly looked down on the city after ascending to the tower. Marilyn's silence was soon broken by footsteps. She said she saw the shadow of a man, yet could not scream. For a moment, the person was there and then disappeared into the fog, perhaps as frightened to discover an unexpected person nearby.

"Maybe he thought he was seeing things," Marilyn joked when she retold the story years later, "or thought I was a femme fatale."

To Joe's dismay, the call from Hollywood soon became too strong. They began splitting their time between San Francisco and an English Tudor rental in Beverly Hills that April. At the end of May, Fox began drawing her back from her Hollywood exile and onto the lot for *There's No Business Like Show Business.*

At home, Marilyn would attempt to fuss over Joe, placing his favorite chair in front of the television while delivering his dinner to a folding table. Dinner was frequently steaks or burgers. She also took pride in ironing his shirts.

"He won't have to move a muscle," she would say. "I'll treat him like a king."

She vowed in addition to shining his shoes, laundering and pressing his shirts, overseeing the household budget and meal planning and hiring a capable maid (at the advice of Jane Russell), that she would cull and arrange flowers from their lush garden in the back.

Marilyn envisioned a room for Joe Jr. in their new dwelling with masculine furnishings and pennants on the walls, and a nursery for the baby she hoped to conceive with Joe -- she prayed for a little girl.

From the exterior, it appeared that the couple was surrounded by many amenities and aspirations for their future. Pleasures surrounded them, including their swimming pool, dinners by candlelight and vintage wines to savor.

"Since going with Joe she'd learned how to make spaghetti expertly and had acquired a taste for Italian wines with meals," was another news tidbit in Marilyn's progress towards her housewife transition.

As Marilyn's workload increased at the studio, her household duties and dreams of domestic divaship took a back seat. Joe absorbed the budget task after Marilyn confounded it and within a week, his shirts took a regular journey to the dry cleaners instead. With her late work nights, candlelight dinners were a mere fantasy, often sidelined for meals out at restaurants.

Leon Shamroy, cinematographer for *There's No Business Like Show Business,* spotted the couple one evening at the upscale Chinese Restaurant Bruce Wong's. He witnessed over a two-hour period how neither Marilyn nor Joe uttered a word to each other and instead sat stone-faced.

Unlike many of her Hollywood counterparts, Marilyn downed the idea of separate bedrooms. She preferred enormous double beds, with girth ample enough for husband and wife to enjoy what she referred to as "their own sleeping independence."

"Separate bedrooms are lonely," she told interviewer Pete Martin in 1956. "For a man and woman to live intimately together is no easy thing at best. If it's not right in every way it's practically impossible."

Marilyn also commented that she believed televisions did not belong in the bedroom. One publication reported a year earlier that Marilyn had a television in her bedroom, which was a gift from Joe.

"Did you and Joe have one in your bedroom?" Pete pressed.

"No comment," Marilyn replied demurely. "But everything I say to you I speak from experience. You can make what you want of that."

"I don't believe in that," she confessed to friend and confidante Sidney Skolsky, about the idea of separate bedrooms. "Often in bed you think of something you want to say, or something you've forgotten. You're not going to get out of bed and chase down the hall to another room. I don't buy it. This separate bedroom deal is not in the American tradition. In the pioneer days, did you ever hear of a man and his wife sleeping in separate covered wagons?"

Trouble however, was already lurking on the horizon, shrouded within a confession she also made to Sidney shortly following her honeymoon and after raving about her wonderful new life.

"Do you know who I'm going to marry?" she asked Sidney.

"Marry? What are you talking about?" he fired back, stunned.

"I'm going to marry Arthur Miller," Marilyn volunteered.

"Arthur Miller!" Sidney exclaimed. "You just got home from a honeymoon. You told me how wonderful Joe was, how happy he made you, and what a great time you had! Now you tell me you're going to marry Arthur Miller. I don't understand."

"You wait, you'll see," the starry-eyed Marilyn offered.

The rumor mill was already astir with gossip about the deteriorating relationship between Marilyn and Joe.

At a party one night, Marilyn whispered to tattletale queen Louella Parsons, "Joe is going to pick me up after the party. There are too many people here. You know he doesn't like all this publicity, and he won't get dressed up even for me."

Marilyn reviewed her new contract, which no longer included *The Girl in Pink Tights.* It permitted more money, but did not authorize the creative control that she sought. Joe and Charles Feldman advocated that she sign it anyway because the cash was better.

On the surface, Joe acted supportive.

"When you win the pennant, your Oscar," he said, "then I'll put on the soup-and-fish and sit out there in public, mighty proud of you."

Privately, Joe was beside himself with *There's No Business Like Show Business*. He was dismayed to watch Marilyn sashay her hips seductively in her sensual numbers like "Heat Wave" in scantily clad costumes. He remained annoyed with Natasha who parked herself night after night in their home, dictating to Marilyn as they reviewed the script. Overall, Natasha was a thorn in Joe's side -- she relished in that role.

Joe's fire engulfed the best of him and there were horrendous fights between he and Marilyn. He would scream at her, then she would lock herself into a bedroom where she would cry her eyes out. Following the fights, she would down some sleeping pills to attempt to sleep. The mornings were set aside for walks around the set and in her dressing room to sweat the pills out and help emerge from her haze. This ugly cycle in turn, ticked off the production because of the schedule delays it created on the set.

A distraught Marilyn, the day she announced her divorce from Joe, on the arm of her attorney.
Photo from the author's collection.

Joe's evident anger upset Marilyn to the point that she was visibly intimidated. She fumbled through scenes when he showed up with George Solotaire on the set. Rather than watch Marilyn rehearse, Joe relayed to another person he was there to see Ethel Merman, a regular patron at Toots Shor's. Joe coined "The Merm," as his favorite performer, not Marilyn. Those words cut Marilyn to the core and incited a scrap between the two at home, accusing each other of the side interests in their marriage.

Joe vocally made a stink about the way Marilyn was dressed in the film. Marilyn was so nervous by his presence that she fell in her Carmen Miranda style costume and headdress. Assistants helped her up and dusted Marilyn off. The publicity machine at Fox suggested a photo with Marilyn and Joe, an idea that he declined because he was displeased with the way Marilyn was dressed. In his opinion she had no clothes on. Instead, he posed with Irving Berlin.

Watching from the sidelines was Susan Strasberg, who was in Hollywood at the time with her mother to watch Marlon Brando on another soundstage as Napoleon Bonaparte in *Desiree*. Susan and Paula joined Sidney and his daughter Steffi (Susan's friend) on Marilyn's set. They saw Marilyn's eyes fearfully dart in Joe's direction before her fall.

"That's DiMaggio," Steffi told Susan in hushed tones.

"He doesn't like anyone to look at him," she added while Susan already had.

Susan gasped as Marilyn tripped and fell. She watched as the limping Marilyn headed towards Joe. Susan described Joe's appearance as emulating the look of an "Italian marble sphinx."

Joe retreated as Marilyn attempted to near him for a warm embrace, crumbling up his body at her approach. Susan saw a look of rejection cross her face.

"I almost got makeup on you," Marilyn noted quietly in a subservient tone to the still silent DiMaggio.

She pecked his cheek before trotting off to her dressing room for a retouch. It was here where Marilyn made the acquaintance of Susan Strasberg for the first time.

"I really admire your father, I've heard such wonderful things about him," she told Susan. "I'm going to come to New York and study acting with him. It's what I want to do more than anything."

At the time, Susan did not believe the larger-than-life blonde goddess, who topped almost six feet (her actual height was shy of five feet six inches) when outfitted in the gigantic platform heels and headdress.

Marilyn's hopes and dreams were thwarted the second she stepped into her home with Joe, now an emotionally dark place. When Marilyn would return to the set in the mornings, she reportedly did with bruises. The explanations included, "I bite myself in my sleep" or "I walked into a door."

Joe criticized her for her habits of leaving clothing draped throughout their home on pieces of furniture, toothpaste tubes uncovered by the bathroom sink, faucets left dripping, her lateness and her time commitment with the studio.

Marilyn was known especially for disorganization, although in her first marriage she prided herself in keeping house well. As she progressed in her career and relied on others and slipped into the haze of pills that her doctors and acting gurus attached her to, she became less organized.

Billy Wilder, one of her directors, was stunned when he hitched a ride with Marilyn once.

"I didn't realize what a disorganized person she was," he commented about the experience, "this is until I see in the back of the car. It is like she throws everything in helter skelter because there's a foreign invasion and the enemy armies are already in Pasadena. There's blouses laying there, and slacks, dresses, girdles, old shoes, old plane tickets, old lovers for all I knew, you never saw such a filthy mess in your life. On top of the mess is a whole bunch of traffic tickets. I ask her about this. Tickets for parking. Tickets for speeding. Tickets for passing lights, who knows what. Is she worried about this? Am I worried about the sun rising tomorrow?"

"I could just have well have stayed a bachelor," Joe shouted in one heated confrontation. "You're married to that goddamned movie studio. You complain about my watching television. What the hell else have I got to do, Marilyn? It's worse than being a bachelor. I'm rattling around this big house with nothing to do, no one to talk to."

Joe was honestly bored in his retirement.

My life is dull," Joe told a reporter, "I never interfere with Marilyn's work. I don't go to the studios to see her act. It's the same stuff all the time. You only see a little of it. Shoot a scene -- then hang around for the last ones. I'd rather wait and see the whole picture."

Joe volunteered that he would rise early to play golf, scoring an eighty-three in those days, and that he had purchased a set of clubs for Marilyn.

"She takes a hell of a cut," he commented about his wife's swing. "She hits a long ball when she hits it."

Even as he chided her behind the scenes, Joe openly acknowledged Marilyn's drive.

"She was working hard long before she met me," Joe added before asking, "And for what? Don't think it's easy work acting in the movies. It's hard work. When she's working she's up at five or six in the morning and doesn't get through until around seven. Then we eat dinner, watch a little television, and go to sleep."

"We're people who don't go out much," Joe confessed. "We don't go to parties. We don't get mixed up in many crowds."

Far from sociable, the Yankee Clipper was needy and sought attention above all from his love, despite the confident exterior.

A slide from the author's collection of Marilyn in New York with fan and friend, who became one of her "children," James Haspiel. His photo was included in an envelope with pictures she kept of her stepchildren and was found in her bedroom after her death.

"He was too proud to beg for it," biographer Maurice Zolotow penned.

Always the one to acquiesce, Marilyn scribbled a note to Joe on the back of a dry cleaning receipt, something which was found still folded in his wallet after his death.

"Dear Joe, I was wrong! I acted the way I did and said the things I did because I was hurt -- not because I meant them -- and it was stupid of me to be hurt because actually there wasn't enough reason -- in fact no reason at all. Please accept my apology and don't, don't, don't, don't be angry with your baby -- she loves you. Lovingly, your wife (for life), Mrs. J.P. DiMaggio."

It was during this time period that Morris Engelberg, Joe's friend and attorney in his later life, indicated that Marilyn miscarried a child with Joe. This was a tidbit he said that the secretive couple did not share publicly. Naturally this seems strange for a longtime Marilyn fan to digest since she was normally open about her life happenings. She had already disclosed to the press about baby plans with Joe (perhaps that was her hint of a pregnancy). Marilyn was regularly open with reporters -- her candor was evident during her pregnancies with Arthur. Some have downed this idea of a pregnancy with Joe, though to this biographer, it could have been a pregnancy that terminated early. There is nothing wrong with this possibility -- they were husband and wife. Joe was just private period, with a wife who was more of an open book, so it could have been natural he wanted to keep the baby news under wraps. Morris also said that Joe and Marilyn talked about adopting a blue-eyed blonde baby from Northern Italy.

"She probably would have quit Hollywood [if we had a baby]," Morris quoted Joe.

Joe did not permit that friends visit with Marilyn at home and she began to drink alone upstairs in the bedroom upon her nightly return from the studio. She glugged from a hidden bottle inside of her vanity drawer while Joe remained glued to the television. As the couple drifted from one another Marilyn sought comfort in psychotherapy, something she had dabbled in years earlier when living with Shelley Winters. The two friends invested in counseling sessions with celebrity psychiatrist Dr. Judd Marmor.

Marilyn's friendship with her vocal coach Hal Schaefer further ignited rumors of marital issues between the DiMaggios. Hal's presence enflamed Joe's temper and spiked a rise in his jealousy meter. Marilyn enjoyed Hal's company and often joined him in disguise for Jewish fare at Canter's, a popular deli restaurant in Los Angeles. Marilyn never admitted to anything deeper than friendship, though Hal claimed she planned to divorce Joe, marry him and convert to Judaism. Marilyn's devotion to Hal was evident in either case, as she was one person that kept vigil by Hal's hospital bed that July after his botched suicide attempt, when he had downed acetone and sleeping pills to end his life.

Marilyn made plans for her next film *The Seven Year Itch*, which required a stay in New York. New York was where she plotted an upcoming escape and planned to collaborate with Milton Greene. Milton was a photographer who she had met and took a liking to at first. He offered to help Marilyn start her own production company. The lure of the Actor's Studio in New York with Svengali Lee Strasberg was another draw.

Marilyn headed to New York for filming and Joe pursued her. He attempted to smooth the situation over with Marilyn, and even volunteered to seek counseling, aware of her interests in Freudian psychotherapy.

The press was already teeming with rumors that the DiMaggio marriage was on the rocks. The reports were about to become worse. Though on the surface, the picture appeared sunny between husband and wife.

Devoted Marilyn fan James Haspiel actually showed to the St. Regis Hotel where Marilyn was staying and found her room. He rang the bell and a man answered the door, rejecting James and another boy's try to visit their favorite blonde goddess. After the rebuff, the boys bumped into Joe in the elevator and asked him for assistance. He retrieved Marilyn and delivered her to the boys. Marilyn gratefully posed for photos before returning to her room.

James described the scene outside of the hotel with a dense crowd so thick that Joe and Marilyn could not even figure out an exit route. They attempted to circumvent the group for a night on the town. One girl stood atop a taxi for a view of the Golden Girl, eventually crushing the roof and falling into James Haspiel's arms.

No one knew the firestorm about to hit, as Marilyn and Joe were photographed while enjoying an evening at the Stork Club.

In fact, the press was only reporting joyous occasions for the couple.

"But come the fall, they plan to make up for lost time with a long vacation together," was the news about Marilyn and Joe after the hubbub of Hollywood moviemaking died down. "They haven't made up their minds yet if it will be Europe or South America."

Three nights later, Joe would not be so amenable.

Columnist Walter Winchell suggested he and Joe head to Lexington Avenue and the Trans-Lux Theatre where Marilyn was filming a scene. It would become one of cinema history's most iconic with Marilyn standing over a subway grate while a large fan blew her white halter dress above her head as if it was a subway passing underneath.

Joe was not keen on the idea, knowing already how nervous he made Marilyn. He did not wish to tread on already thin ice. However, Walter Winchell had in mind the copy it would create, not just Marilyn's performance but the fireworks he anticipated would fly from Joltin' Joe because of Marilyn's visible panties. Joe and George Solotaire, who had been having a few drinks in the bar of the St. Regis Hotel, were convinced and headed to the location, with Joe obviously clueless what Marilyn's scene was comprised of.

George, according to the biography written by Morris Engelberg, was the friend who Marilyn vented to about Joe.

George would say to Marilyn: "He's not the easiest guy to get along with, but he loves you, he always tells me that, so you have to try to make allowances for his moods."

George apparently attempted to diffuse the situation that night and whisk Joe from the scene, yet was unsuccessful because the horde was too deep.

James Haspiel said that the shooting had begun around midnight and continued until five in the morning.

What Joe arrived to, was the horror of watching his wife's skirt fly up as the crowd of 2,000 yelled, "Higher!" and "More!" Photographers were intrusive with their lenses, pointing them in the direction of Marilyn's private parts.

"What the hell is going on here?" Joe demanded, his fury returning.

Billy Wilder described the expression on Joe's face as "the look of death."

When the press asked Joe for his response to Marilyn's scene, Joe dryly replied, "No comment."

Joe stormed away from the scene while a meddlesome Walter Winchell smirked as he tailed Joe.

James Haspiel would recall: "I must confess, I had no trouble seeing through Marilyn's sheer panties. Actually, she had two pairs of panties on [Marilyn typically it is known, did not wear underwear], but still I had no trouble seeing through them. Most of the published photographs from that night do not illustrate this intimacy. I think they shot the scene over fifteen times, so it was a very exciting, intimate situation being played out over and over again before my eyes! Nonetheless, I could fully appreciate DiMaggio's anger. Indeed, Joe stood there sour-faced. In defense of Monroe, I am reasonably convinced that in her dressing room she did not see what the powerful Kleig lights then put on display for what the press later called, 'five thousand onlookers.' And there were people everywhere I recall for a time watching the action while sitting on the roof of a four-story building across the way."

Obviously at that time, James Haspiel was unaware of the consequences Marilyn faced behind closed doors, although a closed door does not signify confidentiality.

That night there was a major scuffle in the couple's suite at the St. Regis, disrupting the sleep of all of the guests on the eleventh floor. Allegedly Marilyn headed to the set the next day, with makeup magic required by her team to cover bruises on her shoulders.

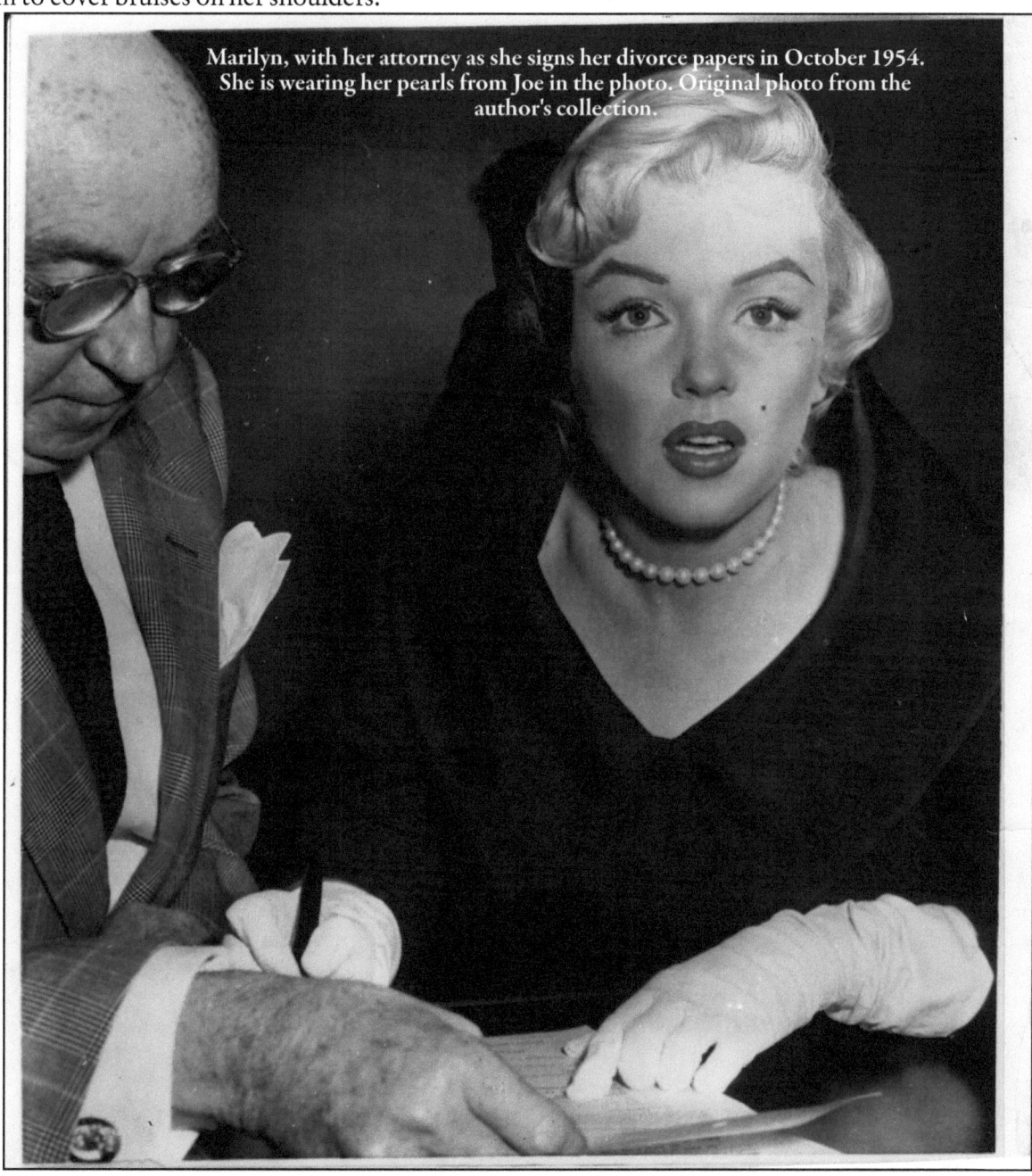

Marilyn, with her attorney as she signs her divorce papers in October 1954. She is wearing her pearls from Joe in the photo. Original photo from the author's collection.

Morris Engelberg's biography about Joe denies his hitting Marilyn out of anger ever. After years of listening to reports that he had, Joe blew up in Morris's office about the topic one day. He said the only time that he touched Marilyn was to revive her when he found her tanked once on drugs or alcohol, he was not sure which one. He tapped on her face to arouse her and swore that was the only time it ever happened.

There were never any complaints from the Dorothy Arnold camp of physical abuse. If Joe were hitting Marilyn he would have likely done the same in his relationship with Dorothy. And there were no reports of hitting Joe Jr. The major gripe for both ex-wives and son was his emotional distance and not speaking with them for days. Marilyn also never mentioned physical abuse in front of the judge during divorce proceedings, only the emotional wounds. Her testimony and Dorothy's were mirrored.

When later asked by editor Pete Martin to clarify the differing rumors that he had heard about Joe's reaction to the scene, if he was annoyed or calm, Marilyn replied, "One of these two is correct. If you'll give it a little thought, maybe you can figure it out for yourself."

It was the last straw for Marilyn, who advised Joe that their marriage was over. Joe had mutual sentiments, though he was not the one who initiated the divorce. He was sick of the headlines where he was referred to as "Mr. Monroe." *The Seven Year Itch* fiasco was also his last straw.

"The battling lovebirds were cooped up in the same little cage," the papers snorted as word escaped that Joe's sleeping quarters were now the sunroom.

It was where he snuggled with the television, instead of his spouse, to keep warm at night.

On October 5, 1954, the *Daily News* leaked that Marilyn planned to file for divorce the next day following talks with Joe and her attorney Jerry Geisler as the mediator.

The day after, the press was camped on the couple's lawn waiting for them both. Marilyn emerged weeping after having been primped by her hair stylist, makeup man and dress designer William Travilla. She was attired fully in black, wearing a high collared top that she had been photographed wearing in Japan only nine happy months earlier. She was visibly and terribly upset with real emotion, although the lawyer coached Marilyn to hang onto his arm and not speak at all to the press. He addressed them instead.

"Miss Monroe will have nothing to say this morning," Jerry told the paparazzi. "All I can say as her attorney is, that this is what we would say is a conflict of careers."

Marilyn swayed as she held onto his arm, appearing faint. She was escorted to his car, her head swinging limply in her distress, while he backed the car from the driveway.

Marilyn's studio stand-in Irene Crosby said no one at Fox knew there was major trouble and they were blindsided by the news.

"I came to the studio the morning it happened," she said, "expecting to go right to work. When Marilyn didn't come in, and we heard the announcement, we were all amazed. I tried to call, but she wouldn't talk to anyone."

Joe headed out at 10:30 that morning after Marilyn. Reno Barsocchini carried out two suitcases and a bag of golf clubs to Joe's Cadillac. Joe sullenly appeared and fielded the reporter questions for a few moments.

"Where are you going?" one newsman asked.

"I'm driving to San Francisco right now," Joe responded.

"Is that going to be your home?" the press pressed.

"That is my home and always has been," Joe snapped.

"Are you coming back?" was the next inquiry.

"I'll never be back," Joe fired in reply.

Joe took his place behind the wheel of his car, glancing over at Marilyn's car before departing.

Later on that day after the paperwork was filed, Jerry Geisler reported further about the action. He said the couple would part company without any financial dispute or settlement.

At court Marilyn summarized, "We are still friends. You can say that I still don't know a thing about baseball."

Two days later, Marilyn arrived for duty at Fox to continue her work on *The Seven Year Itch*.

"I feel alive for the first time in days," Marilyn stated. "It's good to be back at the studio."

Although Marilyn's life was in horrendous personal turmoil during both *There's No Business Like Show Business* and *The Seven Year Itch*, she still radiated the inner Monroe Magic and light onscreen.

Up in San Francisco, Joe kept mum with "no comment," while attempting to stay busy with games of golf.

While Joe would remain silent about his marriages and especially their endings, his friends, fearful of being cut out from his life, fed some stories to the press in whispers and anonymity.

"He married someone who talked about having six kids," a friend shrouded in mystery leaked. "Then, when they were married, it turned out she didn't mean six kids. She wanted to have six goddamn Oscars."

Gossip gal Sheilah Graham wrote, "Item: Joe, a quiet, publicity shy husband, objected heatedly to the fanfare of sexy photos attending Marilyn's public appearances."

Instigator Walter Winchell flapped his trap and threw his two cents in with, "Marilyn and Joe have both found outside love interests."

"If there were someone I was really interested in, I'd go with him all I could," Marilyn retorted, when a snappy comment like this came up. "But why go out on dates just to be going out?"

On October 9, columnist Harold Heffernan ran his editorial "Marilyn May Find Joe Has Last Laugh," noting that Joe, as he had with Dorothy, might launch a counterattack. The writer predicted like Joe did unsuccessfully when he sought permanent custody of junior, he might attempt to invoke the "share your wealth" law for equal share of the earnings.

"Although independently wealthy through his well-invested $750,000 in baseball, Joe hasn't had a steady job since his marriage to Marilyn last January 14," the column sneered. "He made a couple of television appearances, and more recently by-lined an 'expert' account of the World Series for a news service. A liberal estimate of his earnings since marrying Marilyn, however, would only be $5,000."

Harold Heffernan estimated Marilyn's earnings at about $175,000 for 1954.

"It isn't entirely inconceivable that Joe's attorneys might have a plan," he stated. "They might want to toss all the community earnings into the pool -- her $175,000 and his $5,000."

The columnist hinted as well about neighbors around the DiMaggios' Beverly Hills home, who overheard the loud discourses between Joe and Marilyn. Originally reporting them as "heated," they were later describing the couple as "screaming at the top of their voices."

Harold Heffernan touched on the relationship between Marilyn and Hal Schaefer, yet alleged, "Marilyn's movements both at the studio, and in her personal life, were governed by a 'Svengali' type of chap, who always remains in the background."

The world was yet to know about several Svengalis in Marilyn's life lurking around the bend, including Milton Greene, Lee Strasberg, her therapists and Arthur Miller, though Marilyn denied talk of any Svengalis.

Marilyn had a journalist sympathizer in her corner, Nanette Kutner, who had interviewed Dorothy when she and Joe were married. An open letter that she wrote to Marilyn entitled "Don't Blame Yourself, Marilyn," was published in a 1955 edition of *Photoplay*.

"Well Marilyn, it was not your fault and it had nothing to do with your career," Nanette wrote. "I think the separation would have occurred anyway. You see I saw how your Joe acted during his previous marriage to Dorothy Arnold. I am an observing reporter, Marilyn. Of course, a person can change, but only a great one. Joe was a superb ballplayer. Still, is he a great person? I doubt if he will change. It is impossible for me to believe you or any other bright, alive, cooperative well-meaning woman -- career bent or no -- could have liked a marriage, like the one Dorothy had, for long."

The newswoman revealed that when visiting Dorothy for an interview, Dorothy recounted her uneventful life as Mrs. Joe DiMaggio. She pointed to their library.

"Some days I take down these books, every one," Dorothy said. "They're hard to dust. But it helps pass the time."

She also showed Nanette her mink coat, stating she had the garment, but rarely was out on the town to wear it.

Dorothy expressed her devotion to Joe during the interview.

"I go to the game every day," she said. "When I don't go Joe likes me to listen [on the radio]."

Dorothy also added about Joey, then ten months old, "Joe wants him to grow up a ballplayer. So the whole time I was pregnant I never missed a game."

Nanette said that Dorothy contacted her after the meeting, asking her to kill the story since she was leaving for Nevada to divorce Joe.

"I know what I'm doing," Dorothy reportedly said. "I can't rot away."

Nanette left Marilyn with a final nugget of wisdom: "You had a nasty jolt, Marilyn. Grieving is no disgrace. But know you are not alone in your grief. There are some who understand."

Natasha for one gloated that Marilyn was now "free." She had described Joe as a "brutish bore," and a man who viewed "his" women as "broads." Joe had called Natasha out as a phony early on, which was still not yet evident to Marilyn.

The press swooped down on the Santa Monica Courthouse on October 27 for Marilyn's testimony. The divorce was to be granted by default since Joe did not respond. Like the divorce with Dorothy it was interlocutory, expected to take another year to become fully official during a "cooling off" period.

The following day, Florabel Muir of the *Daily News* reported that the divorce remained uncontested and Marilyn described Joe during her testimony as "cold."

"My husband would get into moods where he wouldn't talk to me for seven or eight -- one time it was ten days," Marilyn said again dressed in black.

There were patches of white in her ensemble like her Mikimoto pearls and gloved hands.

"When I tried to find out what was the matter with him he would say, 'Leave me alone' and 'Stop nagging me,'" she added.

Marilyn said the estrangement impacted her health and she had been under the care of her doctor.

Business manager Inez Melson testified the same, indicating she witnessed Joe push Marilyn away and state, "Don't bother me," when Marilyn would attempt to cuddle.

Inez additionally said that the two slept in separate rooms for a week in September -- Marilyn upstairs and Joe downstairs.

Inez recalled how Joe stated, "'I know I am wrong in my approach of coldness and indifference. I regret it but I cannot help it.'"

Marilyn would later lament about those days with Joe, "He didn't talk to me. He was cold. He was indifferent to me as a human being and an artist. He didn't want me to have friends of my own. He didn't want me to do my work. He really watched television instead of talking to me. So what I said in my testimony was really so."

Although Marilyn and Joe divorced they still attempted to remain cordial.

Their friendliness prompted reporters for the *Oakland Tribune* to seek out Tom DiMaggio for his opinion on the situation. They questioned if reconciliation was already brewing. Perhaps as one of the older siblings, Tom did not fear the repercussion from his younger brother for venting his opinion. Or perhaps there was a family feud already in process, over the restaurant or another matter, typical activity for Joe and his siblings.

"That's a lot of baloney," Tom retorted. "Their marriage is a dead fish."

Joe still maintained his possessiveness over Marilyn. Feeling a great sense of entitlement and jealousy over the possibility that Marilyn could be with another man, combined with the upset that there was a court judgment already against him for his cold indifference, Joe whined to Frank Sinatra. Joe strategized a way to counter the allegations with an adultery charge against Marilyn. Frank, then one of his Toot Shor's pals, hired a detective for Joe to begin tailing her. Joe enlisted his own detective too. Joe's detective located Marilyn at Hal Schaefer's address, also the residence of Marilyn's friend Sheila Stuart.

On the evening of Friday November 5, Marilyn enjoyed dinner with Sheila, unaware of the brooding anger outside the building. Joe was ready to knock down what he thought was Hal's door, hoping to discover Marilyn in an uncomfortable encounter with Hal.

"Well, I'm not fooling around here," Joe said. "Let's kick in the door and find out."

Joe's detective, Phillip Irwin, encouraged him to hold off until Frank's arrival. Once Frank arrived with his detective Barney Ruditsky, they knocked in the door. The group flicked on the lights, cameras in hand and then their eyes opened widely in horror.

After they all tore in like caped crusaders, an older woman named Florence Kotz Ross shot up in bed, awakened from a sound slumber. She began screaming once her door was kicked in around 11 p.m.

Marilyn and Sheila fled from the scene after hearing the commotion.

"We're in the wrong place!" the men all exclaimed, tearing into the other direction.

Hal Schaefer commented that he had other pupils including Jane Russell visit him at his home.

"It's ridiculous that Mr. DiMaggio could be any more jealous of me than he is of other people working with Marilyn," Hal said. "She's a wonderful girl. And kind to us all."

The press had a field day, especially with Frank Sinatra. They accused him of past activities in Hoboken New Jersey as a bushwhacker. He was said to have hired detectives too to trail wife Ava Gardner. According to one article Frank found Ava hot and heavy with Lana Turner after one of his tips. He was said to have torn through the house searching for male companions and only found the ladies together.

In 1957, both Barney Ruditsky and Phillip Irwin were hauled in to testify in front of a committee with the California State Senate. The committee formed to investigate the incident, coined "The Wrong Door Raid," after a story was released in *Confidential* magazine about the blunder. Frank Sinatra was subpoenaed and offered differing testimony -- he denied helping to knock down the door. Joe avoided questioning since he was out of the area and out of the country traveling for work. Phillip Irwin alleged to have been attacked by six men who accused him of selling details of the story to *Confidential* magazine and ratting out Frank when he was questioned by the State's Bureau of Private Investigators and Adjusters.

The court awarded the victim Florence Kotz Ross $7,500 (in excess of $53,000 by today's standards) for her troubles after she filed a suit against all parties including Joe for their intrusion. The initial request was for $200,000. Frank's attorney Milton Rudin (who would eventually represent Marilyn) was able to whittle it down. Frank denied his involvement and claimed he innocently sat in the car outside.

"Frankie, by his own thinking," a publication wrote, "was the only batboy who helped DiMaggio hit a foul ball."

This was the beginning of the end for the Frank Sinatra and Joe DiMaggio friendship. It began to decay when Ava Gardner, knowing how to tap into Frank's jealous side, would reportedly pen flirtatious love letters to Joe. Joe never responded to the advances, having respect for another man's woman. Yet tables turned following Joe and Marilyn's divorce when Frank offered to set Marilyn up on dates and Joe caught wind of it. This was circa 1960 and '61 after Marilyn and Arthur had split.

Frank and Joe were still pals in 1958 based on a photo released from Morris Engelberg's collection. Frank and Joe posed during a party held at the Italian embassy. Once on the Joe grudge list, a person typically remained on the list and Frank Sinatra was no exception. He was the recipient of the Joe "evil eye" at events and Joe banned Frank from Marilyn's funeral.

In 1995, the resentment still present on Joe's end, Frank learned that Joe would be in Los Angeles for an award ceremony. He had plans to dine at Matteo's and Frank arranged to be seated at Joe's table. Frank hoped to offer him an olive branch. One of Joe's friends, Dr. Rock Positano, jockeyed the schedule at the last moment after learning of Frank's plan to force himself on Joe. Rock opted instead for The Palm restaurant.

Always sharp, Joe asked what prompted the change.

After Joe was alerted to the situation, he paused and told his friend, "Rock, you did the right thing."

Less than a month later and even following Joe's role as a conspirator in "The Wrong Door Raid," Marilyn recovered from gynecological surgery for her chronic endometriosis and Joe rushed to her side. The two were spotted enjoying dinner at the Villa Capri Italian Restaurant with Dom DiMaggio for Joe's birthday. Joe was extremely doting on her and she questioned privately if she may have made a mistake in leaving him. The press did too and both denied reconciliation.

However, on November 22, the papers reported that Joe's ulcer had flared again and he was hospitalized in San Francisco. Marilyn did not return the favor of a bedside visit.

"In Hollywood, DiMaggio's divorced wife, Marilyn Monroe, said she does not intend to visit him in the hospital," one paper blared. "Joe visited her every day at the hospital where she was recovering from an operation earlier this month."

In the midst of her recovery from surgery and inner turmoil over her departure from Joe, Milton Greene flew back to Los Angeles at the advice of his legal team, fearful that Marilyn was backing away from the idea of making their potential company Marilyn Monroe Productions a possibility. He reignited the fire with pep talks and expected profits.

Shortly before the holidays, Marilyn would gift herself a Christmas present that she believed would change her life and offer her a fresh start. Under the assumed name of "Zelda Zonk," Marilyn, as she did a year earlier when she flew to San Francisco to spend Christmas with the DiMaggios, headed to New York City.

It was in January when she would formally announce her connection to a new man in her life, business partner Milton Greene, and their new company, Marilyn Monroe Productions.

"I formed my own corporation," Marilyn informed the press, "so I can play the better kind of roles I want to play. I didn't like a lot of my pictures. I'm tired of sex roles. I don't want to play sex roles anymore."

A reporter asked her what made her think she was capable of more serious roles.

"Some people have more scope than other people think they have," she replied.

"Do you want to play *The Brothers Karamazov*?" a member of the press corps inquired mockingly.

"I don't want to play the brothers," Marilyn stated gearing up for one of her home run replies. "I want to play Grushenka. She's a girl."

The press creamed Marilyn left and right with insults.

"Minus the acting talent of a Brando who can afford to be independent, without the seniority of a Grable, who can walk out and be wooed back, sans the public to keep her shoulders in ermine and her smile in public view -- Marilyn is on the spot," one publication *Tempo & Quick* reported. "August 1958, the date when 20th Century must release her, is a long way off. When it comes, forgetful fans may greet her name with a puzzled, 'Who?' instead of a dazzled 'Wow!'"

About columnists of that genre, Marilyn was upset by their comments and at the same time surmised, "You know, most people really don't know me."

Marilyn shook the dust of Hollywood off of her feet, yet she still had misgivings. Milton had checked with his attorneys to pacify her that she was not breaking a contract with Fox. Marilyn did not check in with any of her business advisors if this transaction was sound and strictly listened to the advice of those representing Milton. He also reassured Marilyn, who was concerned how she could financially defend herself, that he would agree to fiscally support her for three years. He offered to pay for her clothes, hotels, beauty bills and even psychoanalysis.

Marilyn informed Milton she no longer attended her sessions.

"Well, you should start," Milton suggested. "We'll get you the best analyst in New York. You can't separate yourself as an artist from yourself as a human being. The happier you are as a person, the finer you will be as an artist."

Milton was a regular on the analyst's couch himself.

Marilyn did hesitate before taking the final leap of faith. She spent nights on the town and suddenly, the papers were connecting her with every eligible bachelor from Marlon Brando to Mel Torme to Sammy Davis, Jr.

The nationwide release of *There's No Business Like Show Business* was what pushed her over the edge and forced her to sprout wings to head to New York, following miserable reviews.

What an odyssey it had been for Marilyn since her previous Christmas -- first, spending the holiday with her future family the DiMaggios, next marrying Joe, afterward her trip to Japan and Korea, next her return from her voyage to become a wife, then back to work, lastly the soap opera with Joe and finally the traumatic finish to their marriage.

Would Marilyn have envisioned on Christmas of 1953 that on Christmas Day 1954, she would be celebrating her holiday at Milton's sprawling Connecticut home with his family?

Truth can be stranger than fiction sometimes.

In Maurice Zolotow's book, Milton's wife Amy was quoted as stating that Milton had "saved Marilyn's life," and the couple and son and Joshua were the "only real family Marilyn had ever known." The author claimed this was not a new line and the same was said of the DiMaggios. The DiMaggios of course were different because Marilyn was legitimately their family member.

Whether this is correct or not, Marilyn already had family and her newest East Coast "friends" especially urged her to steer clear of her past.

This myth of the Greenes as the "only family she has ever known," has been ingrained so deeply into Marilyn Monroe history that the line was even written into the quasi-fictional film *My Week With Marilyn*. The Milton Greene character shouted out the line.

Joe was not far behind from Marilyn in a co-dependent type of relationship, which still had yet to mature. He helped Marilyn to move into her temporary new home, the Gladstone Hotel on East 52nd Street.

Marilyn and Joe would continue with this push-pull relationship for a while, leaving those around them baffled by their actions. One example happened on the occasion of a meeting in Boston that Marilyn attended with Milton about Marilyn Monroe Productions. With this new company, Marilyn held fifty-one percent of the shares and Milton the vice-president carried forty-nine percent of the ownership (Arthur Miller noted in his book *Timebends*, that it was initially the opposite). The company was Marilyn's attempt to gain the creative freedom that she sought though she was still under contract to Fox.

While in Boston however, Joe made a showing and Marilyn ditched Milton for Joe. The couple spent time in Boston with Joe's brother Dom and his family. The divorce did not dim their need for one another and only reinforced the interest of the press.

Eddie Corsetti was a newsman for the *Boston American* during the time period when Joe and Marilyn were in the city. He was assigned to hunt them down. He and photographer Carroll Myett staked out in front of Dom's house along with the other news outlets. After waiting approximately two hours, Joe and Marilyn emerged and drove away in a Cadillac convertible. Marilyn was "incognito" in a floppy hat and sunglasses.

After the news team quietly pursued the couple for five minutes, Joe realized he was being tailed and laid on the gas.

"He had to be going eighty miles per hour," Eddie remembered.

Attempting to pull next to Joe for a photo, Joe pulled his car towards the left, which forced Eddie to brake and back down as well.

Joe next gunned the car into overdrive and accelerated to about one hundred miles an hour.

"We let him go," said Eddie. "I'll give him credit, he was a helluva driver."

About Joe and Marilyn he remarked, "They were as big as anything in the country at that time."

Marilyn and Joe puzzled the masses by keeping each other company after their vicious breakup.

One comment was: "Since their divorce, she and Joe have been seen together more often than might be expected from two people who are through with each other. On one occasion, they disappeared together for three days. Everyone decided that they would return with all differences patched up. As one friend worded it, 'If this isn't a reconciliation, what is it? It's a heck of a lot of time to play Scrabble.'"

Joe learned of his induction into the Baseball Hall of Fame this year, yet the honor did not fill the cavern in his heart. He missed Marilyn terribly.

Marilyn announced that *The Seven Year Itch* would be her final film for Fox.

Studio executive Darryl Zanuck retorted, "This will be her last picture for anyone but Twentieth Century-Fox for three years and four months. She's under contract to this studio and she'll fulfill it."

Marilyn made a special public appearance at the end of March at Madison Square Garden to benefit the Arthritis and Rheumatism Foundation. Amy commissioned designer Norman Norell to fashion a black silk dress for Marilyn's arrival to the circus gala. It was Marilyn's first major public event since her departure from Los Angeles. Marilyn was outfitted in a special corseted showgirl costume complete with beads and a feathered train in the back of the outfit.

Marilyn radiated, as she emerged into the packed auditorium for the Ringling Brothers spectacular atop a cooperative pink elephant. Milton Berle was the ringmaster for the event. The crowd went wild for Marilyn and any other star there that night was quickly forgotten about.

Ed Feingersh was one of the main photographers who captured this glorious moment as well as Marilyn lapping up those early days in New York before life became too complex there. She posed at Grand Central Station, in a subway car, at the Ambassador Hotel (including some famous rooftop photos), at Costello's Restaurant, for her costume fitting, at Elizabeth Arden's Salon and primping herself (her favorite Chanel No. 5 and powder included) for the premiere of Tennessee Williams' *Cat on a Hot Tin Roof*. Photos show her at the after-party at El Morocco.

Marilyn was interviewed on Edward R. Murrow's live show *Person to Person* from the Greenes' sixteen-room home in April. In this television appearance many sympathized with Marilyn. She seemed shy and nervous in front of the cameras. It was noticeable Amy trumped Marilyn by answering her questions for her.

Edward R. Murrow noted that Milton's photos have been seen for years on covers including *LOOK*, *LIFE* and *Vogue*, though he aptly remarked "few people outside magazine and advertising offices ever heard of Milton Greene until he became Vice-President of Marilyn Monroe Productions incorporated."

The program started in Milton's studio with a tour of his cover photos and then a trip into the kitchen where Amy and Marilyn were sitting. Amy told the host that Marilyn was an "ideal" houseguest who picked up after herself and helped frequently as a babysitter. Amy revealed the family employed a cook, who was off on the night of the broadcast.

Amy suggested the crew move into the den closer to the fire, since it was a chilly night.

"I sort of take care of Milton, which is very important -- and Josh and Marilyn," she replied when asked what her role was in the company.

Author Bob LaBrasca in the book *Marilyn: March 1955* summarized the relationship between the three as follows: "Throughout these spring months she was treated as a welcome member of the Greene family, with Milton guiding her business affairs and future plans and Amy, then a fashion model, coordinating her wardrobe and playing the role of a more settled and sensible older sister -- though she was in fact half a decade younger than Marilyn."

In time, Marilyn grew resentful of them both, with the same author stating her "relationship with Greene soured in suspicion and dissolved."

Amy jumped in for Marilyn when she was asked about her smallest roles, chiming in about Marilyn's appearance in *Scudda Hoo! Scudda Hay!*

Marilyn referenced *The Asphalt Jungle* and *The Seven Year Itch* as some of her more prominent roles during her interview and mentioned John Huston and Billy Wilder as directors she considered influential. She especially recognized Natasha and the classes she attended with Michael Chekhov as beneficial -- she never mentioned a word about the Strasbergs, whose classes she had already begun attending.

Marilyn expressed her love of New York and Connecticut to Edward R. Murrow. She said in Connecticut it was the first time where she had seen the woods and enjoyed walks with the Greenes' dogs on the approximate eleven acres their home was on (though obviously not correct since she had been in the woods up in Canada for *River of No Return* and had been in forested areas with both Jim and Joe before).

Towards the end of the interview one of the dogs stopped by for some petting. Marilyn seemed to anxiously pet and grab the canine's coat as she spoke, to the point the animal slightly snapped at her in warning. The whole session overall appeared uncomfortable for her.

Amy reminded Marilyn to tell the interviewer about the excitement among spectators in the balcony who watched her ride the pink pachyderm.

After watching the interview some suggested to Darryl Zanuck that instead of Marilyn, Fox needed to sign a contract with Amy Greene, who they considered very poised and beautiful.

The relationship was starting to strain quickly between the two women according to an unidentified female visitor to the Greenes'. This witness attended an event at their home and disliked how Amy treated Marilyn. She recounted the evening to author Maurice Zolotow.

"I got the feeling that Amy looked down on Marilyn as a stupid little bitch," the woman insinuated. "Amy was better dressed, more chic, more sophisticated, and much cleverer than Marilyn. She even looked better. In fact, you couldn't believe that this queer little duck you saw sitting around the Greenes' was really Marilyn Monroe."

This individual said that during a game of charades, Amy poked fun at Marilyn when the topic of poetry quotations came up and pressed, "Come on, Marilyn, give us a book title, will you? You're always reading all those books."

"I got the feeling," she said about Amy, "that Amy was implying that Marilyn was a phony about being intellectual, and didn't read any of the books she pretended to read, and that Marilyn knew Amy had this low opinion of her mind."

The press had also hinted of an affair between Marilyn and Milton, which was far from the truth. What this person attested to, she said was a result of those rumors and was the catalyst of Amy's mistreatment of Marilyn.

"She wanted to show us," the party guest said of Amy, "that she was in command of the situation."

At about half past midnight during a break in the festivities the group decided they were hungry. The guest reported that Amy directed Marilyn to make sandwiches for them all, ten people in total.

"She didn't ask her," the woman recalled, "she ordered her, the way you would a servant -- 'Marilyn,' she said, 'Marilyn, go in the kitchen and make sandwiches.' And Marilyn obeyed her. She went into the kitchen and made sandwiches and coffee and served them to us."

Marilyn was slowly breaking the apron strings to Joe, though little did she realize she was tying herself to people who would eventually wrap the ropes around the stake and light the fire at the bottom. Amy, based on the testimony of her anonymous guest, was apparently included in that group of naysayers.

One such person who also fit into this category was Lee Strasberg the acting theorist at the Actors Studio in New York. Marilyn began attending classes there in early February 1955 led by this manipulative mind-twisting man. She hoped to transform herself into a "serious actress," as if she had no previous talents. Little did she realize Lee was one of the many who was convincing her that she had something which required fixing and never told her that she already held her innate gifts. Often showing to the Actors Studio in casual clothing and no makeup, Marilyn would become entranced and fixated with the classes -- and him.

The Actors Studio was a "members only" institution. Students were admitted solely by audition. Many stars like Marilyn audited classes, though she was never officially made a member. In addition to what she paid the Strasbergs for their tutelage, the Actors Studio solicited Marilyn for her contributions and she willingly donated. In turn, the Actors Studio used the names of these actors who attended their classes, to bolster their own publicity and reputation.

In an article published in 1956 about the Actors Studio, *Collier's* magazine noted that, "Director Lee Strasberg oversees all studio classes, prods his students into intensely realistic performances with sharp, severe, illuminating criticism.

He summed to his students that, "Acting is no mere imitation of life. It is *living*."

This is the same man who once asked actor Paul Newman why he redid a scene, with Paul replying he did so to improve it and Lee countered harshly and condescendingly, "Darling, you improved it into a failure."

In pictures that Ed Feingersh photographed to accompany the *Collier's* article, Lee appeared determined and forceful, his hand in a tight fist in one, his eyes widened in an irritated stare. In another photo, he loomed over actors onstage with an accusatory finger pointed at them.

"The studio's mainspring director Lee Strasberg," the story continued, "fires the youngsters' talents by cajolery, rough criticism and seemingly daffy exercises designed to shatter even the hardest-shelled inhibitions."

Behind the scenes Marilyn was receiving extra "lessons" from Lee. One evening Paula shushed teenage Susan Strasberg at home, informing their daughter that Lee was working with a student in his study. She had known of only one other student that had broken this personal barrier, the actress Jennifer Jones, who was a woman that Lee was obsessed with. Susan pondered who else could elicit such a pull.

Out stepped Marilyn, who stunned Susan. Unbeknownst to Marilyn, she was slowly becoming an obsession of Lee's too. She was evolving similarly as the trusting and vulnerable character Christine Daaé was to the "Angel of Music" in *The Phantom of the Opera*.

Lee could have represented that "Angel of Music." She mistakenly thought without him, she was nothing. He convinced her of that too. However it was the other way around. It was Marilyn who brought fame his way by attachment to her name. Marilyn Monroe was the reason that Lee Strasberg became "something."

"She seemed very fragile -- not fragile breakable, but fragile, 'handle with care,'" Susan remarked.

Her previous vision of Marilyn had been the woman undulating under the harsh lights at Fox with heavy pancake makeup and a garish costume. The woman she saw now appeared more like a girl, fresh-faced and shy, with her translucent skin, blue eyes and blonde hair creating the appearance that a halo of light encapsulated her.

"My father took Marilyn's arm, and she glommed on to it," Susan said. "This surprised me. He never took anyone's arm, they took his."

Marilyn sat to have dinner with the family, with Lee serving her the very best cut of meat from the table. There would be many more nights like this where Susan would hear laughter emanating from behind the study door, alternating with crying and complaints about those who had affronted Marilyn in her past.

Susan observed this, yet she did not truly realize the sick obsession her father possessed.

Susan had experienced a disconnect from her father over many years and took a back seat to the actors who he "mentored." In her later life, Susan plunged into dangerous relationships with older men like Richard Burton. Her marriage to Christopher Jones was additionally extremely dysfunctional. Overall, she had been cast aside and exploited by her parents.

"In his acting classes," she wrote in her memoirs entitled *Bittersweet*, "my father spent hours cajoling actors to contact their innermost feelings and express themselves without fear. 'Are you a human being?' he would demand. 'Then just get up and act like a human being, don't complicate things.'"

Lee often compared himself to a doctor in front of students. He considered himself a doctor of the theater and implemented Freudian and Pavlovian behavioral modification techniques within his teachings. He viewed actors as habitual by nature and believed they required circumcision from their previously patterned rituals to optimize their performances.

Marilyn felt so strongly about the level of Lee's skill in transforming her in a way that he saw fit for her. In her blind adoration, she elevated Lee to the level of "best finest surgeon," in an account she had written when she was a resident at the Waldorf-Astoria.

"In addition to being aware of Freud's work with the unconscious, Lee drew from scientific results and analytical work of Nobel-Prize winning Russian physician and groundbreaking behaviorist, Ivan Pavlov," wrote Lola Cohen, who edited *The Lee Strasberg Notes*.

Ivan Pavlov was most famous for his experimentations on dogs and the "conditioned reflex," with canines adopting a subconscious reaction (salivating) from a sequence of events (food presented after a buzzer has sounded). Pavlov experimented with removal of one of the components (food) though one of the presenters in a lab coat was still present. The activity triggered salivation anyway because the dogs anticipated food.

Pavlovian mind-control experiments have been considered brutal. Ivan Pavlov surgically implanted a saliva catch container in each of his canine subjects to monitor their physical reactions to the stimuli. Later, he supervised conditioning experiments on children and these children were also subject to the same surgically implanted catch containers.

"Pavlov's theories on conditioned responses in animals and humans contributed to the recognition of the damaging and self-limiting role habitual behavior can have on expressiveness in acting," Lola Cohen continued. "Lee's development of procedures and exercises for actors to free themselves from the problem of habitual responses is based in part on Pavlov's studies. By siding with modern psychologists, he was reacting to Denis Diderot, author of *The Paradox of Acting*, who postulated that great acting is the ability to laugh or cry at will, but if an actor can't do that, he or she must use an external technique."

In Marilyn's account that she had chronicled during her stay at the Waldorf-Astoria, which her cousin Jason Kennedy who has reviewed what she had written and refers to as "The Surgeon Story," Marilyn described a "mental operation" that she endured with Lee and the psychiatrist he recommended she see. In an unethical twist and large conflict of interest, Milton Greene's therapist Dr. Margaret Hohenberg began treating Marilyn with Lee's blessing. Lee and Dr. Hohenberg essentially succeeded at reconditioning Marilyn's behaviors for their own purposes and beyond the need for a better stage performance. Those who had known her before she left for New York noticed a negative change in Marilyn after she endured the barrage of emotional violations that Lee and Dr. Hohenberg subjected her to, though they never knew what exactly triggered her decline.

Lee Strasberg devotees and followers suggested, "'Lee, you should have been a therapist,'" Susan recounted.

"'Why darling?'" Susan said Lee quizzed one disciple. "'I have more freedom in my work.'"

"Relaxation and sense memory exercises deal with the areas of the acting process and of the acting instrument which previously had evaded observation or had been treated purely externally," Lee stated in lectures at his classes. "We try to eliminate the habits of non-expression and inhibitions created by conditioning so that when the impulse starts, it will lead to behavior different from the one to which you're accustomed. Related to Pavlov's work on the process of conditioning and the basic connection between the physical and the mental, we seek a conscious control of the faculties. A twenty-year habit may take as long as a year to break, but we believe everything that was conditioned can be reconditioned."

With Marilyn it was a matter of wiping the slate clean for a fresh start, to reprogram her and mold her into the person that Lee and the Freudians needed her to be -- the person who could be the platinum cash cow for their endeavors.

"He said that often the depth of the emotional problem was correspondent to the degree of talent," Susan added. "Because of this, he was accused of doing therapy."

The accusations were correct, though something Susan was oblivious to. Marilyn was navigating herself into a comfortable trap without realizing it, like a lobster enjoying warmer and warmer water, until it is cooked alive. If only Joe knew, he certainly would have intervened and ceased Lee's reprogramming activities on his girl.

The private sessions were actually attempts for Lee to gain control. Marilyn's account on Waldorf-Astoria stationary might appear cryptic, and in fact many have written off what Marilyn wrote as free verse or her account of a dream. Yet, what she documented was actually the start of her living nightmare commencing. What Marilyn chronicled could be best termed as her victim's impact statement.

In her narrative, Marilyn described how Dr. Hohenberg prepared her with an anesthetic drug while Lee "waits to cut me open." Cutting open was not physically slicing with a knife it was the words Lee used instead to cut her. He was already famous for being sharp with his tongue. With her doctor of psychiatry and her doctor of theater, she wrote that both "doctors" agreed that her "operation" was required to help her.

"An operation to bring myself back to life," Marilyn penned, "and to cure me of this terrible dis-ease (sic), whatever the hell it is..."

The next step was the surgery to "cure" Marilyn's "dis-ease."

"A surgeon," Lee often told his classes, "when he's going to do a great operation, he doesn't work at it for three hours before he starts, he'd be dead by the time the operation came along."

The "surgeons" went to work as quickly as possible on their "patient" aka Marilyn. There was no time to waste. What Marilyn recounted in her testimony would have been something she knew little of, unless she experienced it firsthand.

They gave her a dose of what they referred to as "anesthetic." Dr. Hohenberg had a background in neurology as a medical doctor and she had more than adequate training to administer intravenous drugs.

The "doctors" then wheeled Marilyn into a monochromatic room.

"...Everything in the room is white, in fact, I can't even see anyone, just white objects," she wrote.

Next the procedure began, with its purpose to strip away her previous experiences and habits through a coercive technique.

The dissociative anesthetic drugs they pumped into Marilyn's system helped to begin the disconnection process.

The team skillfully implemented sensory deprivation techniques. Psychiatric research was important to both Lee and Dr. Hohenberg. Marilyn also advocated Freudian endeavors and of course, Lee's acting techniques employed the use of Freudian and Pavlovian elements. Dr. Hohenberg's mentor was believed to be Anna Freud herself.

As Marilyn expected to relax under the influence of the mind-numbing substances, she had anticipated an opportunity to emerge fresher than before. However, the drugs they fed her during the procedure were harsh in their own right and created a frightening and trippy experience. She was subjected to undue influence and when she thought something beneficial would happen to her it did not. While under the influence of the drugs, instead her acting coach and doctor placed emotional pressure on her. Pressure that elicited feelings she did not anticipate. She had hoped to feel good following this procedure and they told her she would. In its place she felt worse. Guilt, emptiness and void were some of the emotions elicited from the experience.

Marilyn buckled under their coercion and in less than a year later in 1956, these two individuals who she barely knew, would be on her first Last Will and Testament. Lee hammered in about the need for his theater and Dr. Hohenberg continued to push over and over about the Freudian needs for a psychiatric cure.

The pair continued to emotionally dissect her until Marilyn was psychologically gaping at the climax of the "operation."

"...And there is absolutely nothing there," she wrote. "Strasberg is deeply disappointed but more even -- academically amazed that he had made such a mistake. He thought there was going to be so much -- more than he had ever dreamed possible in almost anyone but instead there was absolutely nothing -- devoid of every human living feeling thing -- the only thing that came out was so finely cut sawdust -- like out of a Raggedy Ann doll -- and the sawdust spills all over the floor &[and] table..."

"...Dr. H is puzzled," she continued, "because suddenly she realizes that this a new type case of puple [Marilyn also crossed these two words "of puple" out in her original manuscript]. The patient (pupil -- or student -- I started to write) existing of complete emptiness..."

Only a mile from where Marilyn stayed at the Waldorf-Astoria was a hotbed in the 1950s for psychic driving techniques combined with the use of dissociative anesthetic drugs in sensory deprivation chambers (white rooms) at Cornell University Medical School. Here was where the MKUltra program, a CIA front, was in full effect during Marilyn's stay in New York. Years later, many victims (most schizophrenic) who were subjected to mind-control experiments under MKUltra were compensated for the crimes committed against them. Based on what Marilyn has written in the account, she was likely taken by her doctor and acting theorist to a hospital facility nearby with a white sensory deprivation chamber.

In 1961 while the MKUltra program was still in effect, Marilyn's psychotherapist incarcerated her in the high security Payne Whitney Psychiatric Clinic, a facility affiliated with Cornell University Medical School.

It was then a strange time in America with the fear of the communist Red Scare and operatives working against other operatives, attempting to snuff out communism. Though Lee and Dr. Hohenberg mingled with communist types and had their own motives, there was a bigger picture.

There were some other players named in the scenario. Marilyn wrote about Arthur Miller and Hedda and Norman Rosten in her account. Arthur, Norman and Hedda were eventually named in her 1956 will, with only less than a year under their belts as acquaintances of Marilyn's. While Arthur was named as a beneficiary, his divorce from his first wife was not yet finalized.

Milton was another name she had written. Milton was not on the will but his address was named as her residence on it.

Above this the CIA, which was overseeing the MKUltra experiments, was busy watching some of Marilyn's friends and in turn, developed an interest in her. She was also under watch because of these connections, with suspicions that her Marilyn Monroe Productions monies were funneled into the communist party and commies surrounded her in her company. In fact, Arthur was identified by an anonymous source right after their wedding that tipped off the press, as a "cultural front man" for the party.

While the author of this book does not believe a government organization executed Marilyn and instead those on her will were responsible for orchestrating her death, this author does believe Marilyn was under watch because of these affiliations. Although Lee for example, was dabbling in techniques that organizations like the CIA then used to extort information from citizens, a bigger brother watched him because he was a suspected communist sympathizer.

This scenario sounds far out and in many ways it is, yet it is realistic because Marilyn was an innocent victim in a bigger picture (Lee, the therapists and crew), which was under the microscope of yet another group.

One of the biggest Achilles heels of Marilyn's whole being was the trust she gave over to those who were taking advantage of her. They suggested she forget her past and move on, as cult-like movements often do. They insinuated they were her "family" and the "only family she has ever known." This technique isolated her from those who were truly her family members, or those like family who had been genuinely close to her.

During this time, she naturally drifted farther away from Joe, did not see sister Berniece again in person until 1961 and separated more from Inez Melson who visited Gladys in the hospital on her behalf (Marilyn financially provided for Gladys). There were other relatives too who knew her in her earlier years that were shut out. Jason Kennedy's grandmother was one of them. Rebecca, William Marion Hogan's daughter and Gladys's first cousin, was a year younger than Marilyn. When the two were small, Rebecca and Marilyn spent time running under sprinklers together on sweltering days and met up for roller skating excursions. Marilyn lost touch with the Hogans as well.

Anne Karger was one person mentioned in "The Surgeon Story." Anne was a longtime friend and mother figure that adored Marilyn. Marilyn was also close to Anne's daughter Mary, visiting her often at her home in New Jersey. The two met Marilyn at the beginning of her career when Anne's son (and Mary's brother) Fred dated her. He had been her vocal coach at Columbia. Though the relationship between the two fizzled (Marilyn was head over heels for him), the friendship with the Karger women was always there. Yet, Marilyn ended up seeing the ladies less frequently as time marched on and those who were preying on her told her, as she wrote in "The Surgeon Story," to forget these early ties in her life.

"Make no more promises" and "make no commitments, or tie myself down to engagements in future -- to save not being able to keep them and mostly to avoid feeling guilty, which is now the case," was something she had written in a side note at the top of the page by Anne's name.

"Disappointment" was another theme of this horrific session. If Marilyn did not fulfill their wishes they would be disappointed. If Marilyn underwent true psychic driving techniques in a sensory deprivation chamber, persuasive messages were likely fed through a speaker instructing her of the need to grow both a Strasberg theater and further Freudianism, actually an interchangeable request if one looks at it.

"Disappointment" was a theme slightly over a year later. Marilyn found Arthur's diary with that word screaming out at her, reflecting his feelings about her. Arthur's psychological game only a couple months into their marriage, sent her into a tailspin, something from which she never recovered.

Marilyn Monroe for all of them became their conquest. She was someone they manipulated so deeply and into whom they dug their fingernails, grabbing her emotional psyche to retain a grip. The ultimate goal was to gain control over Marilyn, her career and finances. Her newfound "family," like a cult, offered her their phony embrace, and brought her into their lair like a lamb to slaughter. There was a powerful hold that these individuals influenced over Marilyn, as exemplified in Susan Strasberg's book, which she deliberately entitled *Marilyn and Me: Sisters, Rivals, Friends*.

In notes that Marilyn scrolled during her visits with Lee, the snake oil he sold her about Method Acting was obvious, and he manipulatively sacrificed his own daughter for Marilyn as leverage to bolster Marilyn's confidence in his bill of goods.

"Like Susie," Marilyn dictated as Lee told her, "where you are wherever you walk there is a kind of light about you -- no acting can give you this quality. The sensitivity is so strong -- much deeper and stronger than that of Susie's."

Marilyn had family. Susan Strasberg surely was not her sister, though the substitute family encouraged Marilyn to believe so. Marilyn had Berniece. These individuals blurred the lines for Marilyn, crossing over from professionalism to "family." They sucked up a place in her life, which should have belonged to her blood, not bloodsuckers.

"I'd like to think of my life as having started right now," she told interviewer Pete Martin, in the midst of her transition into the hands of the Strasbergs and Freudians. "Somebody asked me when I was born and I said, 'Just recently, in New York.'"

This statement reads chillingly, when one places into perspective Marilyn's emotional timeline and the manipulation she endured especially in 1955.

On the other end of the spectrum, there was Joe, banging at her door night after night at the Waldorf-Astoria hoping to maintain that thread.

Marilyn was already in deep with her love interest Arthur, who in 1955 was still married to wife Mary, though he had allegedly been miserable for years, even when he met Marilyn for the first time in 1951. Their trysts were secret and sometimes happened unbeknownst to Joe as he moped in front of the door of her suite at the Waldorf-Astoria. Marilyn was then holed up with Arthur, who had his own role in infiltrating her mind.

While many believed Joe and Marilyn to be opposites, and in many ways they were, in others there were mammoth similarities between the two. Marilyn wanted to believe that she and Arthur were compatible. He wooed her with his intellectual talk and demeanor, yet they had little in common. This was not yet apparent to her in the early stages of attraction. Arthur simply looked to mooch off of her financially. There was another reason too.

Most looked at them as the "Egghead and the Hourglass," with Marilyn attracted to his academia and ideals. She liked that he appeared to be for the underdog. In her naïveté, she did not realize how he was a champion for communism. Arthur's relationship with her was one way for him to restore his image from the communist black eye. The relationship of course yielded many consequences in a time when there was a mission to out communists. She outwardly defended Arthur when he refused to name names to the House Un-American Activities Committee in 1956 and when he was charged with Contempt of Congress in 1957. Some feared her popularity would dim from it.

Marilyn and Arthur became the topic of conversation for a satirist who wrote, "Arthur sought his passport from his Uncle Sam, and when he couldn't get it, he was sure in a jam -- but he knew what to do, and so he hauled off and married Marilyn Monroe."

The writer continued his rant with the ditty, "I'm just crazy over Mrs. Arthur Miller! Mrs. Arthur Miller's my number one thriller. With her new-style dumb-intellectual blend, she can show you how Timon is a girl's best friend...if her countrymen forget her real talent when she's dead, you can wager they'll remember her for something else instead, for she's made a public hero of a one-time Red -- Mrs. Miller, the queen of them all."

While the miserable team of the Strasbergs, Greenes, Arthur Miller and the therapists worked together with the collective goal to gain control of Marilyn, the internal mechanisms of the group soon fell apart. They began to attack and down each other, like bigger fish gobbling up smaller ones. In the end, each of these parties ended up resenting the other, with each one eliminating the other at a time from Marilyn's life, In the end, the Strasbergs remained of the biggest shareholders in her life though by that stage she was near to ridding of them too.

An even bigger player later in the scenario was her therapist Dr. Ralph Greenson, who was an advocate for Freudianism. He attempted to eliminate the Strasbergs entirely from her life. The doctor surmised her estate would have been sweeter for those with a Freud allegiance if more money was allocated towards Freudian causes, instead of a pesky theater run by a man who had difficulty attaining success on his own without piggybacking on others. And on August 6, 1962 there were plans for Marilyn to draw up a new will with her attorney, who also happened to be Dr. Greenson's brother-in-law. While Marilyn planned to make Joe a major benefactor, this incited the jealous therapist who wanted Joe and anyone else she had loyalty to out of the way. He wanted the estate for himself and even his daughter Joanie would later leak that that it was planned for her family to be placed on Marilyn's 1962 will. Marilyn was dead, however on August 4, her body found only a day before this appointment.

In the midst of this, Marilyn would briefly allow Joe back into her life, while she was already involved with Arthur Miller. Amazingly as much as he despised the Hollywood system, Joe made a showing on Marilyn's arm at the premiere of *The Seven Year Itch*, which less than a year prior he had fumed so angrily about the skirt raising above her head. Of course, he had also chewed her for the hypocrisies of attending premieres yet there he was. It was the first and only film premiere of Marilyn's he ever attended with her, even with a fifty-two foot high replica of Marilyn with the dress blowing over her head at the Loew's State Theatre, a reminder of that tormented evening. Joe confidently smiled as Marilyn gently cradled his thumb within her hand while the two walked together.

It was her twenty-ninth birthday when the premiere took place on June 1, 1955. She looked radiant and a vision completely in white with platinum hair, white dress, white gloves, white shoes, and all accented with a white fox fur stole.

Marilyn and Joe, at the premiere of The Seven Year Itch in 1955, following their divorce. Photo from the author's collection.

Joe threw Marilyn a small surprise birthday party at Toots Shor's afterward.

He also threw out their usual line to the press about their relationship: "We're just good friends. We do not plan to remarry. That's all I care to say."

Joe and Marilyn remained loosely connected through Joey, who would speak with his former stepmother on the phone frequently while he was in prep school in Lawrenceville New Jersey.

"JD has tried to be charming in his miserable sort of way," the young Joe penned to Dorothy in a letter about the Yankee Clipper.

Both parents were very distant to the boy, while Marilyn held an empathy, love and understanding for Joey.

Joey grew more into a rebel, to Joe's dismay. Thankfully the boy had Marilyn, who appeared to keep him somewhat grounded. Joe Jr. started heading into deviance by hanging out with the wrong crowd. While he was at the Lawrenceville Academy, the school reported to Joe about his truancy. Joe showed up on the campus on this rare occasion to speak to him about it in his dorm room and Little Joe never showed.

Marilyn still carried a small torch for Joe in her heart, even with her adulation for Arthur. His photo was still visible in her closet. Her jewelry box was a constant reminder too, with the combination "5-5-5."

Yet, she sunk further into the Arthur Miller abyss. Arthur gloated about being the victor for her heart. His feelings though were not properly reciprocated, he simply responded to her overtures for his own selfish gain. Arthur even commented later in a negative manner about Marilyn's relationship with Joe to a reporter. He pointed out that Marilyn's marriage to Joe failed from a lack of joint interests and intellectual connection. He also stated that Joe had a propensity towards physical violence in those days. Obviously, Arthur was looking to divert the press from suspecting his own poor behaviors.

Though not yet married to Arthur (and he was still not divorced -- that finalized in June) she drew up her first Last Will and Testament in February 1956. In the will, most of the members of the wayward band written about in "The Surgeon Story," were beneficiaries. Their ploy was working, they had snaked their way onto Marilyn's will.

Marilyn listed her residence in 1956 on the will as Milton Greene's and asked that monies be distributed as follows: $100,000 for Arthur, $25,000 to Lee and Paula, $20,000 to Dr. Hohenberg, $10,000 to Xenia Chekhov (the widow of her former acting instructor in Los Angeles), $10,000 to the Actors' Studio, $10,000 for Patricia Rosten (Norman's and Hedda's daughter) for her education and $25,000 for the care of Gladys.

Strange how a man she barely knew who was technically still married, was the primary beneficiary. Odd too how monies for the perpetual care of her mother equaled that of acting gurus she had only become acquainted with a year prior (and technically exceeded that with their acting school also allotted an additional $10,000). Curious how a psychiatrist was earmarked the third major recipient of monies. Xenia Chekhov on the will was potentially acceptable, as Marilyn had grown close to her when she took lessons with Michael. Yet Marilyn provided for Patricia Rosten, a child she had just met, when there were other children dear to her including niece Mona.

Mona was not far from her mind, since she sought to ensure provisions for the girl as a receiver for Gladys's social security benefits. Why was her niece not on this will, or her sister?

Actress Maureen Stapleton befriended Marilyn when they were at the Actors Studio together. She recalled the fierceness of the control that the group had over her. Maureen had full confidence in Marilyn's abilities as an actress when the two worked on the scene from *Anna Christie* together. While they did, Maureen and Marilyn became better acquainted, discussing such topics as Marilyn's therapy sessions with Dr. Hohenberg. Maureen was quickly suspicious of the obvious undue influence the doctor was placing on Marilyn.

"She described one hour when she and the analyst were looking at photographs of Marilyn and Joe DiMaggio," Maureen said.

"'Look at this picture,'" Maureen recalled Dr. Hohenberg would tell Marilyn of the wedding day photos. "'You and Joe DiMaggio are kissing. Look at your hands, though; they're flat against his shoulders. You see, you really didn't want to marry Joe, because you're kissing him and at the same time you're pushing him away with your hands.'"

Marilyn then turned to Maureen and said, "'See Maureen, deep down I didn't want to marry Joe DiMaggio."

Maureen did not buy into the Freudian techniques that the therapist was using to extort Marilyn. She told Marilyn it was obvious she wanted to marry Joe, whether or not her hands were flat against him, because she married him.

"Poor Marilyn," Maureen recounted, "as if she didn't have enough problems, she had to deal with the doctors. With everyone telling her this and that and the other thing, it's amazing she survived as long as she did and that she was as pleasant as she was."

Her insight into Lee Strasberg and his grasp over people was similar.

"I was fond of Lee and his family, but I never knew what the hell he was talking about," Maureen said. "For my taste things got too guru-ish and cultish at the Actors Studio. I wanted a teacher, not a god."

Shelley Winters told author John Gilmore how Lee extended his exertion of control over Marilyn, through other students and friends like her.

Lee held a private meeting with Shelley. Behind closed doors he informed Shelley of Marilyn's importance as a star and his belief in her potential. Shelley recollected that Marilyn's affiliation with the Actors Studio was not just any ordinary feather, but a proud plume in Lee's cap. He asked Shelley for her assistance.

"He asked me to help her feel secure and to put her trust in Lee," Shelley expressed to John Gilmore. "He said, 'We're her family now, Shelley, and you can be a true blue sister to Marilyn.' This was all right with me, except it was peculiar for Lee to be saying, and the manner in which he said it, like he was involving me in some underhanded activity. But what he meant was that Marilyn was not in control of her own ambitions or kind of like he was saying her stability..."

Another observer was Marlon Brando. He was Marilyn's friend, fellow actor and someone she briefly dated. As Joe had been her escort, she diverted from Arthur too at the end of 1955 to be Marlon's date at the premiere of *The Rose Tattoo*.

"Marilyn was a sensitive, misunderstood person, much more perceptive than was generally assumed," Marlon said of her. "She had been beaten down, but had a strong emotional intelligence -- a keen intuition for the feelings of others, the most refined type of intelligence."

Marlon, who was often associated as a pupil of the Actors Studio, admitted in his book that Lee only used his name to help propel the school. Marlon was actually a follower of Lee's adversary and competitor, Stella Adler. Stella had been a part of The Group Theatre that Lee helped to found. Stella parted ways with him and left the group, because of her major disagreements with Lee over his interpretation of Stanislavsky's Method Acting techniques. She disliked how he used "sense memory" and "affective memory" techniques to draw out actor emotions. She told *People Magazine* so during an interview.

This acting technique was how he manipulated Marilyn. The system encourages the actor or actress to dig into the recesses of their psyche to bring up past memories. Even if repressed memories are painful, Lee believed them necessary to enhance actor performances. For a fragile person like Marilyn this technique was the kiss of death. Lee and Dr. Hohenberg took their "therapy" further by implanting false memories and guilty feelings into her during their "surgeon" sessions. The purpose to do so was to extort from her, not ameliorate her performance.

Stella was so angry about how Lee taught Method Acting she confronted Stanislavsky himself, the master who conceptualized it. From him, she learned that Lee bastardized the "Method" with his own interpretation and it differed from the authentic Stanislavsky technique.

"He [Stanislavsky] understood that asking the actor recall his personal life could produce hysteria, so he abandoned that. He believed now that the actor must rely on his own imagination," Stella told *People*.

She described Lee's attempts at psychoanalysis and vented how he elevated himself to the level of a medical practitioner as "sick."

After Lee died in 1982, Stella asked from her students a moment of silence upon hearing the news.

She broke the silence by adding, "It will take fifty years for the American actor to recover from the damage that man did."

Marilyn photographed during the filming of Bus Stop, in a slide from the author's collection.

Marilyn's sister Berniece, was closing in on the theory of the games being played with Marilyn's mind, after Marilyn was hospitalized for her emotional breakdown. For a fleeting moment, Berniece pondered the connection between Method Acting and Marilyn's hospitalization. She asked Mona about the case of actor Lee J. Cobb, who coincidentally starred in Arthur's play *Death of a Salesman*. The actor, she had heard, was so indoctrinated with Lee's version of Method Acting that he had suffered a nervous breakdown. Mona explained that the actor had been instead, so wrapped into his character, that he was still immersed in his role when he came offstage. Mother and daughter wrote the idea off that the acting techniques were a catalyst in Marilyn's breakdown, though in her book Berniece toyed with the possibilities that Marilyn's personality was too fragile for Method Acting. Berniece considered how Method Acting removed Marilyn's coping mechanisms and forced her to dig into deep and painful recesses of her mind. Berniece believed some of Marilyn's memories were better left behind.

Those that could have helped Marilyn, truly did not realize what peril she was in.

"After I had some success, Lee Strasberg tried to take credit for teaching me how to act," Marlon Brando said. "He never taught me anything. He would have claimed credit for the sun and the moon if he believed he could get away with it. He was an ambitious, selfish man who exploited the people who attended the Actors Studio, and he tried to project himself as an acting oracle and guru. Some people worshipped him, but I never knew why. To me he was a tasteless and untalented person who I didn't like very much. I sometimes went to the Actors Studio on Saturday mornings because Elia Kazan was teaching, and there were usually a lot of good-looking girls. But Strasberg never taught me acting. Stella Adler did -- and later Kazan."

The gall the Strasbergs held in Marilyn's career and their control over her, also shocked Elia Kazan.

"He'd [Lee] influenced her [Marilyn] to demand that his wife, Paula, be on every film set (at $2,500 per week) to help Marilyn with her performance," Elia wrote. "Paula would station herself directly behind the director, and after each take, when Marilyn looked in her direction, Paula would either nod or shake her head. If she shook her head, Marilyn would demand that the scene be shot again."

Elia further elaborated that the Strasbergs held conferences with Marilyn the evening prior to a scene's shooting, and excluded the director from the private meetings.

"Didn't Lee realize how insulting this was to the director?" Elia asked.

Elia contemplated what a power trip Lee was on to have Marilyn rely so greatly on him. He also reminisced about Lee's days as a "director" at Fox in the '40s, when he was never promoted higher than one who filmed screen tests. They kept Lee busy with tests before firing him. It gave Lee great satisfaction to pull rank, as he was vengeful after they had held him back all those years ago. Marilyn was innocently used as his pawn.

"What kudos to have the great public's greatest movie star depend on you for advice that would supersede that of the filmmaker for whom she was working," he wrote. "Now Lee had power over producers like those who, twenty years before, had hired him to make tests of actors, then fired him. A failure as a director himself, he was now directing directors of the first rank."

Even Arthur took pot shots at Lee and Paula in his autobiography *Timebends*. He considered Paula comical, especially how she bragged that actors from their school were found worldwide. To the contrary, some who she named Arthur also knew. He said they barely schooled with the Strasbergs. Paula, he said, even attempted to convince others that dress designer Jean Louis was "one of our best designers." Arthur alleged Paula misled the public, alluding that the designer learned his trade from the Strasbergs.

"Strasberg is a hard taskmaster. There is no 'right' and 'wrong' in his method of instruction, but only individual honesty," wrote journalist William Barbour in 1955. "Under relentless prodding, the actor must project his deepest feelings to the audience. All else is phoniness."

"Although Strasberg pales at the thought," the reporter continued, "his technique resembles psychiatric therapy. He strips his students emotionally bare and then forces them to parade in public. Several of his protégés, less high strung than Marilyn, have recoiled against self-exposure and fallen by the wayside."

Marilyn could not see the walls closing in around her, nor could she recognize the infighting between the members of the group clambering for her, each competing for their piece of the Marilyn angel cake.

Early in 1956, Marilyn made her way back to Hollywood to begin filming *Bus Stop*. She was now jumping between all of her Svengalis. Sometimes she fell figuratively and literally into Lee's arms, before alternating between Milton and Arthur for emotional support.

Dr. Hohenberg continued with the steady stream of barbiturates and mind-altering medications to keep Marilyn "controlled." She also kept her patient roped in with her costly therapy sessions. After five sessions of "therapy" each week, Marilyn would head to Lee's apartment for more "therapy," aka "private sessions." With Lee, there were more regressive acting techniques to tap into her "affective memory."

All Marilyn sought was betterment and she did not realize the dangerous slippery slope she was travelling on.

One control freak was cut loose, as Natasha was let go as Marilyn's acting coach. The Strasbergs replaced Natasha, who did not go away quietly. After Natasha knocked on Marilyn's door at her home in Westwood that she rented with the Greenes as she filmed *Bus Stop*, Marilyn's agent Lew Wasserman threatened Natasha. He told her that her job at Fox would be in jeopardy if she did not back off. Natasha saw Marilyn watching over the confrontation from the safety of the home.

Paula who presided over the set and Marilyn, and called the shots like her predecessor, was more hated than Natasha ever was. Later, Marilyn affectionately nicknamed her "Black Bart," because of her attire. Marilyn nicknamed most everyone she knew. Film crews on *The Misfits*, especially capitalized on it as a negative moniker.

Paula and Lee milked Marilyn greater than Natasha ever had. By 1960, Paula had billed Marilyn $10,000 for her four weeks on *The Misfits*, monies that Marilyn willingly doled out. Marilyn also shelled out $11,000 for one hundred shares of AT&T stock for Paula. She additionally funded a trip for drama study that Lee took to Japan. Paula made calls to Marilyn from Paris once, reversing the charges to Marilyn, then requesting money for a plane ticket back as well -- that tab ran Marilyn another $411. If Marilyn had appeared in the television version of *Rain* as discussed in 1961, she pledged to donate her full compensation of $100,000 to the Actors Studio.

Marilyn followed a similar path with Arthur, who she married in June of 1956. Arthur was not working, spending many of their years together writing *The Misfits*, while Marilyn carried the financial burdens of their New York apartment at 444 East 57th Street by Sutton Place and their home in Connecticut.

It was also in 1956 that Marilyn officially and legally changed her name to "Marilyn Monroe," a name that she had been using professionally, yet was still known as "Norma Jeane" privately. It seemed as if she was attempting to rid of any link to her past.

On the outside, all appeared rosy for Marilyn with Arthur. Unlike Joe and Marilyn, they were an odd looking couple. Joe and Marilyn certainly gave off an "appearance" of compatibility and she looked awkward with Arthur.

Many times in these early days at press conferences, Marilyn would snuggle herself into Arthur's shoulder like a shy child. This increased the false cuteness factor, though Marilyn's feelings for Arthur were totally loving and genuine.

Marilyn announcing her wedding to Arthur, in this wire photo from the author's collection.

(NY9-June 22) MARILYN IN HALLWAY CONFERENCE--Screen star Marilyn Monroe is all smiles as she talks to newsmen in hallway conference outside her apartment yesterday at which she confirmed her wedding announcement to dramatist Arthur Miller. The scheduled wedding, the date a secret between the couple, will be Marilyn's third and Miller's second. (AP Wirephoto)(See Wire Story)(m61025mz) 1956

Of course, looks are not everything and many have chastised Joe for his treatment of Marilyn. At the same time, they were co-dependents because their emotional grasp on one another was so strong. Once this cycle was broken and the romantic relationship was reinstated after Marilyn's ended with Arthur, the connection between Marilyn and Joe became closer to "normal" and "healthy."

Arthur Miller simply married Marilyn to benefit from her, and like the others exploiting her, he sought to gain emotional dominance over her. Marilyn truly did fall in love with Arthur. While some, like author Jerome Charyn, have incorrectly referred to Joe DiMaggio as the beard for Arthur when he escorted Marilyn to the premier in 1955, it was more that Arthur was the beard in the transaction for the Strasbergs and others. Arthur was just as guilty for attempting to grab Marilyn's fortune.

As part of the transformation in submitting herself to Arthur, Marilyn converted to Judaism.

She was close to Arthur's parents, Isidore and Augusta. Marilyn asked Mrs. Miller to teach her to cook.

"You can cook," she said. "You make a very good steak and a nice salad."

What Marilyn meant was Jewish cuisine. She wanted to learn to make "what Arthur likes."

Marilyn's first request was Gefilte Fish, which her future mother-in-law advised her was too difficult as a beginning. Instead, the ladies started with stuffed cabbage. Marilyn would pride herself in later making other Jewish specialties and Matzah Ball Soup was one of her culinary creations.

It should have been considered an omen of misfortune the day the couple announced their impending marriage, when a few members of the press tailed Marilyn and Arthur in hot pursuit on the winding country roads near the couple's Connecticut farmhouse. Arthur's cousin Mort was behind the wheel as Arthur and Marilyn's chauffeur. The press vehicle careened into a tree, fatally wounding Mara Sherbatoff from *Paris-Match*. Marilyn was totally shaken with splotches of blood covering her sweater, as she ran quickly from the car past reporters after speeding into the driveway. Marilyn changed her soiled clothes and attempted to compose herself for the press conference. That evening June 29, Marilyn and Arthur were secretly married in a civil ceremony and two days later on Sunday July 1 Lee gave the bride away in the religious ceremony.

The danger signs came early on, in the same summer as their marriage while the two stayed in England during the filming of *The Prince and the Showgirl*, for what would also mix in as a honeymoon. The film, which was the first and only one Marilyn Monroe Productions' released, was riddled with difficulties behind the scenes. Laurence Olivier, her co-star and director, clashed especially with Paula and Hedda Rosten. He deemed both intrusive to Marilyn's success.

Laurence considered Milton Greene a voice of reason and urged him to rid of both Hedda and Paula. Milton was able to accomplish those tasks in September and October. Marilyn suffered an emotional collapse following their departures (as well as one when Arthur returned briefly to the States). Some considered Marilyn's disintegration an act (likely orchestrated with some coercion by Lee and Paula behind the scenes and over the phone) and the ban on the set against Paula was lifted. The commotion was enough for Dr. Hohenberg to fly to England and set up a private session with Anna Freud for her star patient. Milton's involvement in ridding of Hedda and Paula caused Marilyn to begin viewing him further as a traitor. She was angry that he sided with Laurence, who Marilyn now sarcastically referred to as "Mister Sir."

Another relationship began to fall apart when Marilyn stumbled onto Arthur's notebook. He purposely left his thoughts out in the open on the dining room table. The first few words slapped her in the face and were additionally repeats of what she had written in "The Surgeon Story." She saw a self-fulfilling prophecy coming to fruition.

Marilyn and Arthur at the press conference in Connecticut, to discuss their upcoming marriage. An original photo from the author's collection.

The word "disappointed" was the first to fly out at her, a word she had previously penned with grave sadness on the Waldorf-Astoria stationary. She read that Arthur initially viewed her as an angel, but now he agreed with Laurence Olivier that she was really "a troublesome bitch."

Arthur's confession in the diary became the ultimate betrayal for Marilyn, one that she would talk about years later with her sister following her divorce from Arthur. Arthur would include the effect of a diary entry on a character he created in his play *After the Fall*. Though Arthur piddled around on his work projects and usurped her funds during the marriage to Marilyn, he quickly cranked out this play after she died, with an underlying theme about her. In his script, life imitated art. And it is likely Arthur created this drama between he and Marilyn simply for the character development of *After the Fall*. The author of this book views his marriage to Marilyn as an intelligence-gathering mission for that play, since Arthur understood Freudian psychology. Maggie, the Marilyn protagonist of the play, discovered a diary entry disparaging her, which crushed her spirit.

Marilyn knew right away something was twisted with Arthur's action. Susan Strasberg, who described her family as embracing a "cross section of modern psychology," because of Lee's interest in Pavlov and Susan and Paula's interests in Carl Jung and Wilhelm Reich, said Marilyn attempted to interpret the incident with Freudian psychology.

"Even Freud said sometimes a cigar is just a cigar," Paula told her.

"This cigar was on purpose," Marilyn surmised. "It wasn't an accident."

Arthur quickly learned that the "test" worked. The short-term litmus was the notebook and the word "disappointment" drove Marilyn into a more dependent and despondent direction. She never wished to disappoint anyone that she loved. The diary was a tool to further implant guilt into Marilyn and set her on her emotional roller coaster to break her spirit.

The first to go from the group was Milton Greene. That break was initiated with a lot of urging from Arthur, though it was not a bad riddance. Milton like all of them had his own agenda. Yet Milton, although he was one who wanted to benefit off of Marilyn, was not in the inner circle with the Strasbergs and Arthur. His Hohenberg affiliation did not make him immune from the ax.

Arthur starting laying the tracks for offing Milton from the group before he was divorced and even married Marilyn. A letter he sent to Marilyn addressing her as "Dearest Poo" on May 25, 1956 exhibited this.

Arthur prefaced the letter by indicating he did not know really know Milton, however Arthur viewed Milton as having "some kind of proprietary function over you in his mind. It seems to me sometimes that he conceives of you as something he almost created himself. And now that you have grown into a human being, as opposed to a commodity ("something that is traded for money") [Arthur defined the word for Marilyn as if she was too stupid to know the definition without his assistance at almost thirty years old], his security is threatened."

It is obvious Arthur demeaned Marilyn's intelligence as well as her place in the human race. To even allude that she had "grown into a human being," showed he viewed her as something less before he had graced her presence. Had she not been a human being all along?

Arthur was projecting sole blame onto Milton for opinions that he and Lee also shared. Marilyn was a commodity to the "theater doctor" and the dramatist fiancé. Arthur was attempting to fool Marilyn that he viewed her as something greater than a good to be traded.

Arthur also referred in this letter to fights the couple was having about Paula and arguments they already were having about money. Why would they be arguing about finances when not yet married? Why would he have argued with Marilyn, the true breadwinner who held the larger stake in their finances? It was never his place to do so even after their marriage.

After a long-winded bashing of and diatribe about the photographer in his two-page letter of what he perceived as his Milton's philosophies, Arthur added, "I have absolutely nothing against Milton."

Obviously with such a lengthy rant about Milton, Arthur lied.

Arthur also pointed out that Milton was "tuned-in very sharply to his own advantage and to money-making," and "he is marshalling all his allies in the hope of forcing you back into the cage he found you in."

Again, this was another diversionary tactic because Arthur was doing the same. It was not long after Arthur's poison pen letter to Marilyn about Milton that things began to come further undone between the business partners. While the relationship was naturally falling apart, Arthur planted another seed.

Marilyn began to turn on Milton and received validation from the Strasbergs to oust him as well. While she visited them in their apartment on the "family" evenings, Marilyn vented to Paula and Lee about Milton and Amy. She had become distrustful of both. She confided to Paula and Lee that Milton excluded her from her own business decisions and he had also allowed Dr. Hohenberg to be a part of the decision-making process, which she was unhappy with. Marilyn also often felt inferior to Amy she said, who especially chided Marilyn about her wardrobe.

Dr. Hohenberg was a whole other topic. Marilyn believed there was competition between she and her partner in terms of their care. Dr. Hohenberg used Milton as the messenger to alert Marilyn when she disapproved of their business decisions. Why would a doctor be involved in a patient's business decisions? The doctor later told biographer Donald Spoto she disapproved of the partnership altogether and warned Milton not to become involved.

While Arthur and the Strasbergs grew resentful of Milton, Milton also harbored bitterness in return. During the filming of *Bus Stop*, the partners argued over the cost of flying out Lee to the location. Right after the heated discussion, Marilyn took a tumble and fell from a six-foot ramp. As she writhed in pain from the fall, bystanders watched Milton continue to photograph her.

His excuse for not assisting her as she lay on the ground, a witness to her fall said was that "I was a photographer before I was a producer."

When filming *The Prince and the Showgirl*, Jay Kanter, Milton's friend and MCA Agent, recognized the influence he waved over Marilyn.

"It was important for Milton to control her, just as it was for Strasberg and for Miller to control her," Jay said.

It was not the first time that anyone noted Milton's emotional hold over Marilyn.

Jean Negulesco, Marilyn's director from *How to Marry a Millionaire* also pointed out Milton's control. He discussed the topic with biographer Maurice Zolotow.

"Well this Greene," he explained after Marilyn showed photos to the director that Milton had taken, "he had some kind of hypnotic power over her, because he did get her to pose in certain ways she had never posed before. Greene saw something virginal in her, something sweet, pure, and he caught it with the camera. This was how she wanted to see herself, so maybe that's why she thought he was a movie genius. There was no other reason for her to come under his influence."

Hal Schaefer also feared that Milton was subduing Marilyn and expressed so in his final call to her after she headed to New York. He accused Milton of brainwashing Marilyn to abandon him. Marilyn never talked to Hal again after this discussion.

"Don't blame him," Marilyn sided in her conversation with Hal. "Milton is a friend of mine. It's just that I'm here [New York], and we [Milton and I] need time...if it's supposed to be, it will be."

Milton exerted his chemical control over Marilyn too. He acted as Marilyn's personal kingpin in obtaining prescriptions for her. He kept her medicated with the help of Marilyn and Amy's doctor Mortimer Weinstein, requesting two-month supplies of Dexamyl (an amphetamine and barbiturate mix) shipped in small envelopes while they were filming in England.

"He [Milton] was a great manipulator and there were gallon bottles of pills being flown in for her," said Whitey Snyder, Marilyn's makeup artist.

While in England, Marilyn learned she was pregnant. Those around her continued to enable her -- Hedda was supposedly an alcoholic who passed the time drinking with Marilyn while Milton continued doling out pills. Marilyn soon lost her child.

Marilyn also accused Milton of using company proceeds to purchase lavish antiques while in England.

In the meantime, reporter and biographer Maurice Zolotow had heard rumored that Arthur would replace Milton as one of the heads of the company. Arthur denied the rumor in a reply telegram to Maurice on October 24, 1956, his response obviously peppered with lies.

"I have no more than the normal family interest in my wife's business affairs, and am happy to state this works out fine," Arthur responded. "Rumors of conflict between myself and Milton Greene are space fillers for unimaginative columnists."

This was another misleading statement from Arthur, who continued to stick his nose into Marilyn Monroe Productions. By 1957, the partnership completely disintegrated. The game of conflict of interest continued, with Arthur's attorney stepping in to accuse Milton of mismanaging Marilyn Monroe Productions. Soon, a new legal and accounting team was on board, with Milton and his attorney Irving Stein and accountant Joseph Carr dismissed in lieu of Arthur's counsel Robert Montgomery, his brother-in-law George Kupchik and friend George Levine.

"It seems Marilyn doesn't want to go ahead with the programs we planned," Milton told the press. "I'm getting lawyers to represent me...I don't want to do anything to hurt her career...but I did devote about a year and a half exclusively to her. I practically gave up photography."

"He knows perfectly well that we have been at odds for a year and a half and he knows why," Marilyn replied in one April 1957 article. "My company has been completely mismanaged by Mr. Greene. He has made secret commitments for the company without informing me. He has misinformed me of what certain contracts contained. As president of the corporation and its only source of income, I was never informed that he had elected himself to the position of executive producer of *The Prince and the Showgirl* and secretly signed contracts to that effect."

"The company was not set up to merely parcel out 49.6 percent of all of my earnings to Mr. Greene for seven years," Marilyn continued. "My company was formed because I wanted to make better pictures, improve my work, secure my income and help others to make good pictures. Instead, I have had to defend my aims, my interests and conditions of work against the demands of Mr. Greene himself."

Naturally, the company was named Marilyn Monroe Productions, not Milton Greene Productions. Milton, in her eyes, sold Marilyn a bill of goods in order to edge his way in.

Milton and Marilyn never saw one another again, though he and his family have contended otherwise, even claiming they spoke to her just prior to her death. The Greenes though were not in Marilyn's 1962 address book, which contained the names of those she had regular contact with. The process for Marilyn to buy back his $100,000 worth of stock dragged out for more than a year.

Milton would have the last word in his own way, literally. Milton later indicated that Marilyn handed off the manuscript to him of her life story. It was supposedly the one that Ben Hecht was penning in a project she contracted him for in March of 1954, before Marilyn and Milton became partners. The contract explicitly stated that Ben would write Marilyn's story for magazine publication only and he would receive proceeds for the sale as compensation. The agreement also specifically stated the manuscript was not intended for book format.

However Ben Hecht's agent Jacques Chambrun stole and doctored the manuscript for publication in the London *Empire News* without Ben's consent and the journalist subsequently fired his agent.

Though some have argued over Marilyn Monroe biographer Donald Spoto's stance on this point, he has indicated that the book *My Story*, allegedly written by Marilyn and copyrighted by Milton Greene as the publication of her "memoirs" in 1974, does not match the first sixty-six pages of the Ben Hecht draft. The original draft planned for the article is within Ben Hecht's papers at the Newberry Library, which Donald Spoto said he reviewed.

Some have also said that Milton collaborated with Ben Hecht on the 1974 book publication, however Ben Hecht died a decade earlier and two years after Marilyn. Ben Hecht has been credited as the ghostwriter for the work copyrighted by Milton Greene. How could this be possible? Or could Milton have waited until both Marilyn and Ben Hecht were deceased, so he could not be challenged about the authenticity of these memoirs?

If this was Ben Hecht's manuscript, Milton Greene not only published something in book format that was originally stated in the contract with Ben Hecht to not be published in a book, he is often accused of reworking the draft for the final product. Meanwhile, Milton profited off of the book almost two decades after Marilyn terminated their relationship, with materials for which he claimed in the byline were the words of Marilyn herself.

And of course, Milton and now his estate have generated additional income from the photos he took of Marilyn during the years they knew one another.

Biographer Maurice Zolotow expressed concern for Marilyn in his 1960 biography because of those surrounding her. The biography contained interviews with Marilyn as well as with others who knew her.

Many in Hollywood, he wrote, believed that Lee and Milton were taking her for a ride and those individuals described her as a "pawn."

Maurice conducted an interview with director Billy Wilder in 1955, who concurred she was also being exploited by these characters.

"Here you have this poor girl and all of a sudden she becomes a famous star," Billy said. "So now these people tell her she has to be a great actress."

The director likened her to the person who wrote the campy jingle, "Doggie in the Window." The tune became successful and Billy posed what could happen if that songwriter was then forced into writing symphonies. To Billy, the hypothesis was not a formula for Marilyn's success as a gifted comedienne. In his own snarky manner, he also felt Marilyn would have had better success if she headed to Switzerland for training at Patek Philippe to learn timing, since tardiness had become such an issue for her.

"They're trying to elevate Marilyn to a level where she can't exist," he added. "She will lose her audience. She is a calendar girl with warmth, charm, great charm -- and she's being compared to Duse. Duse! They tell her she's a deep emotional actress. I don't know who's to blame. Kazan? Strasberg? Milton Greene? Who is Milton Greene anyway?"

In his eyes, Billy felt that people like Milton and Lee were only small fish in the pond swimming in the waters of Marilyn's success. He described those now mentoring her as "the kind of people who don't believe in under-arm deodorants. They believe in sitting on the floor even if there are six comfortable chairs in the room."

He predicted that by Marilyn handing her life over to this crew, she would lose "everything of her own, make herself ugly," and the "crowd in the bleachers will hate her."

Eventually the bloodsuckers took what was most important from Marilyn -- her life.

Already her newfound artistic freedom was off to a shaky start. Though Marilyn experienced some interesting highlights including meeting Queen Elizabeth II and Princess Margaret while in England, when *The Prince and the Showgirl* was released in 1957 the reviewers panned the picture, including the performances of both Marilyn and Sir Laurence Olivier.

A few commented otherwise and referred to it as the "season's sparkling comedy surprise." They said that Marilyn had "never seemed more in command of herself as person and as comedienne."

Chapter Five – True Love Comes to the Rescue

Following Marilyn's breakup with Milton Greene, Dr. Margaret Hohenberg was also excised from her life. Her departure was not at Marilyn's consent. Marilyn became attached to the doctor who was her emotional captor. She had a tendency to feel anxious in their times of separation.

In one letter during the filming of *Bus Stop*, this uncertainty was evident when Marilyn wrote: "I've been feeling I was taken away from you (with your consent) or that you sent me away from you."

The relationship was obviously doomed from the start with the doctor's willingness to treat two patients who were business partners and with her true loyalty to Milton Greene.

Dr. Hohenberg was most likely removed for a greater and more sinister cause and willingly backed down, because she was not as elevated on the Freudian food chain.

Although Dr. Hohenberg referred Marilyn to Anna Freud during the filming of *The Prince and the Showgirl* in London, she was not one of Anna Freud's "pets." The next two therapists who "treated" Marilyn were. Although she fought for the Freudian cause, Dr. Hohenberg was not as close to it as others and certainly was not in the Anna Freud inner circle.

For Anna Freud, the magic word was "funding." Funding could only help further their programs and studies for their cause. Marilyn subscribed greatly to Freud and Freudianism already, with even Jane Russell noting that while she tried to bring Marilyn closer to God (Jane was a born-again Christian and held services in her home with other stars and Marilyn attended once), Marilyn tried to introduce Jane further to Freud, which did not stick either.

Marilyn was their perfect victim. She was already a fan of the Freudian methodologies. She lapped up their theologies and naturally, wished to help them forward their agendas. Little did she realize as a sweet and trusting person, their eyes and prying hands were reaching for her wallet, with minimal concern for her well-being. They simply wished for Marilyn to remain in the cloudiness while they dug into her deeper and deeper. Their plan was to walk away with the pot of gold in the end and discard her once they conquered her financially.

Though Dr. Hohenberg was gone, she would appear briefly back into the picture following Marilyn's passing with a bill for "telephone services." The doctor alleged that these consultations took place with Marilyn during the months of May through July of 1962 and she sought $840 for her purported consultations. It is highly possible that Marilyn did reach out to the doctor when she was unable to get a hold of Dr. Ralph Greenson while he vacationed in Europe during those final months of Marilyn's life. Perhaps Marilyn reached out to Dr. Hohenberg as the relationship between she and Dr. Greenson disintegrated.

In Dr. Hohenberg's place, Dr. Marianne Kris would assume responsibility for Marilyn's care. Dr. Kris, who resided in the same building as the Strasbergs, was the wife of Dr. Ernst Kris. Ernst Kris was a famous Austrian psychoanalyst versed in studying and writing about the recovery of childhood memories. Lee implemented this technique to bubble characters to the surface through Method Acting's "Affective Memory." Dr. Marianne Kris's father had been a personal friend of and family physician for Dr. Sigmund Freud and she had personally lived with Anna Freud. Anna Freud was the key player who assigned her minions like Drs. Kris and Greenson to seek out wealthy and influential financiers like Marilyn to fund the Anna Freud Centre.

The section they dedicated to Marilyn's memory in the Anna Freud Centre is called the Monroe Family Assessment Service. This is part of the Tavistock Clinic, which was initially created to treat shell-shocked soldiers. Naturally, there is a connection to this as well since Dr. Greenson later worked with soldiers dealing with traumas following their service.

The Tavistock Clinic sweeps its history of acting as a breeding ground for mind-control experiments including MKUltra, under the rug. Lee's hero, Ivan Pavlov, was one of the inspirations for the early work at the Tavistock Clinic since splitting personalities became a fascination for the doctor, as it would be to Lee when he worked with his actors. The soldiers who walked through the doors of the Tavistock Clinic came for assistance yet became reluctant subjects, when inhumane tests were administered to them against their will.

With Tavistock having been connected to MKUltra, there were other underlying sinister connections. In the MKUltra program worldwide, pregnant mothers were exposed to radiation, children suffered through electroshock therapy and LSD trips, and developmentally disabled tots had plutonium mixed in with their cereals at breakfast.

Those affiliated with these programs eventually worked with Marilyn and subjected her to some of their techniques. Marilyn's money was handed over by her benefactors to support an institution that supported experimentation on human beings. It likely would have broken Marilyn's heart, as a woman who spent considerable time supporting children's charities, to know one was fronted with her name that had a place in history in committing such barbaric acts against humanity.

While those who spent time jockeying for control over Marilyn's life fought bitterly amongst each other to climb to the top of her list, life for Joe without Marilyn had turned into a merry-go-round of boredom. He snagged a job in 1958 with the V.H. Monette Company, a military post supplier, and as he did in his days in the military, Joe would golf and dine with generals and colonels. Joe was simply passing time and wished to be with Marilyn. It is a shame he was not able to either as without his protection, she plunged further into darkness between the Strasbergs, the therapists and Arthur now leading her by the hand.

Press Photo from the author's collection.

Joe was not a guy who dated frequently. He was shy and had two long-term female relationships, the first with Dorothy and the second Marilyn. After Dorothy and before Marilyn, he was spotted once on a date with Marlene Dietrich and then with a woman named Bettie Pearson. Joe was certainly no prude and appreciated beautiful women -- he often attended beauty pageants and even judged one in Miami Beach in '49.

Since Joe could not have Marilyn anymore, he was known to date Marilyn look-alikes. The gossip columns linked Joe with actress Liz Renay and burlesque star Dixie Evans. Miss Americas current and past were also said to be in Joe's little black book. Lee Ann Meriwether Miss America of 1955 was one he was allegedly dating and photographed with and the marital rumors circulated. Walter Winchell chased and staged that scoop, as he had with the mess he created on the set of *The Seven Year Itch*. Yet the relationship, with the buzz beginning of remarriage a month after Marilyn's, did not stick.

Miss America 1957 Marian McKnight was another who the rumor mill paired with Joe. During the pageant's talent portion she performed "Diamond's Are a Girl's Best Friend," in Marilyn style. Joltin' Joe was apparently in the audience as she did her number. Marian worked as well for V.H. Monette Company too, though she denied a romantic relationship with Joe. She currently owns Carmody McKnight Estate Wines and Vineyards.

Another girl was aspiring actress Lola Mason, a Joe admirer who was only nineteen when they reportedly began dating. It was said to be a relationship that was on and off for five years. A platonic male friend who she was out on the town with allegedly asked her why she was single. She expressed that the only man she would ever like to date was Joe DiMaggio, a man who she had never even met. As the story goes, by chance Joe was at El Morocco with Lee Meriwether where Lola and her friend were when this dialogue took place, and she had her opportunity afterward to date the man of her dreams.

Miss America 1951 Yolanda Betbeze was another one, though the two had little in common.

The window for Joe to find his way back into Marilyn's life was reopening. After the continued decline with Marilyn and Arthur's relationship, three miscarried pregnancies, a suspected affair with actor Yves Montand, and the many difficulties she experienced while working on the films *Some Like It Hot, Let's Make Love* and *The Misfits*, she and Arthur called it quits.

She depended further on the Strasbergs to approve every move she made, which drove Arthur, her directors and film crews mad.

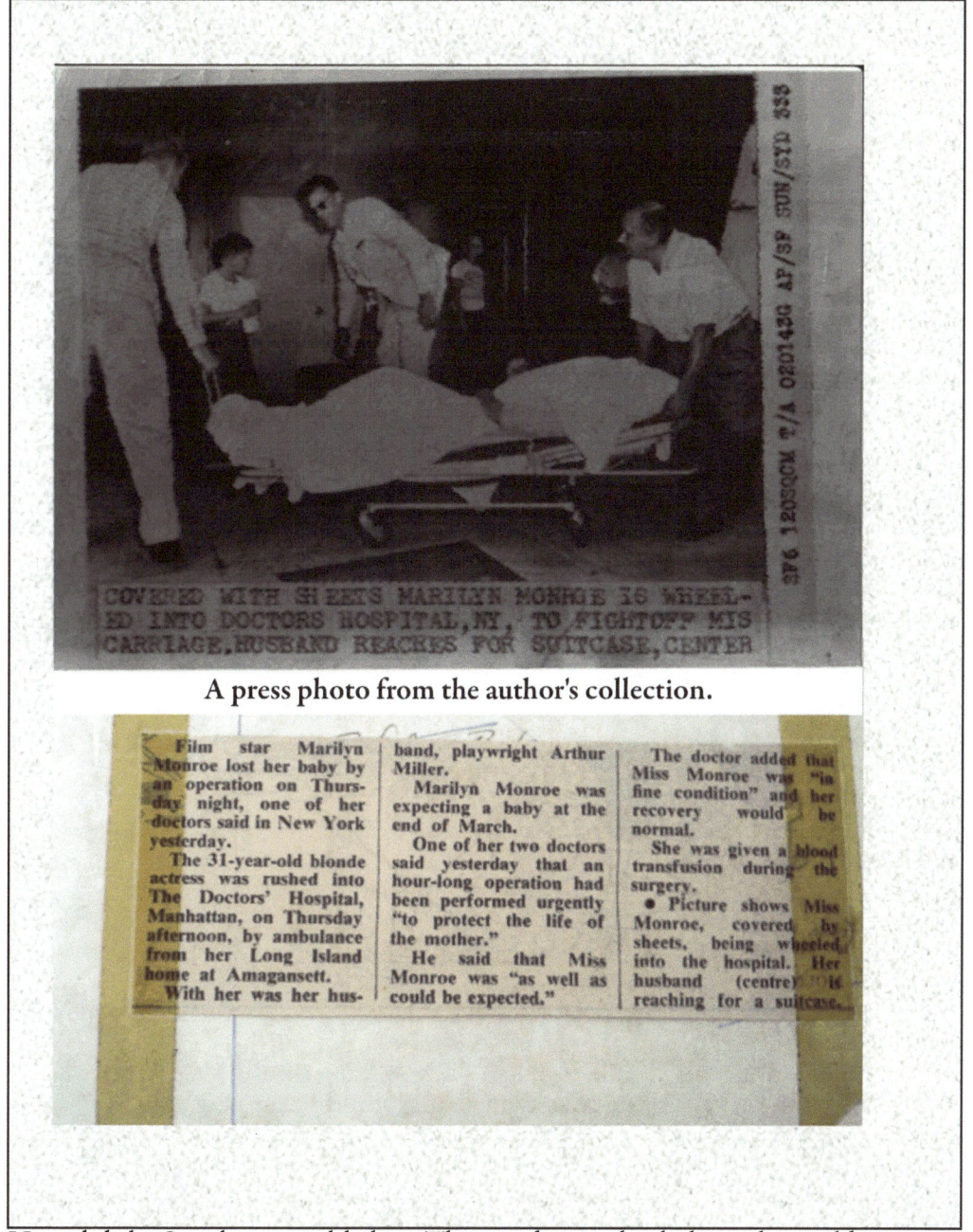

A press photo from the author's collection.

How did the Strasbergs enable her? They made Marilyn believe she could not survive without their approval on any step she took. Natasha Lytess had done the same. All of them convinced Marilyn to pay them exorbitant compensations for their services. She was still making peanuts per picture versus her contemporaries who had lesser star power, plus was cashing out generously to her Svengalis.

Yet, unlike Natasha, the Strasbergs took the game a step further -- they encouraged Marilyn into therapy, something Natasha did not. Of course they implemented elements of "therapy" into their acting techniques.

Natasha was never on any will for Marilyn (the relationship ceased around the time the first will was drafted). The Strasbergs additionally enabled Marilyn in her prescription drug abuse, with Paula administering the supply as Milton had previously.

Marilyn's life overall had become enveloped with greater sadness towards the end of her marriage. Notes in 1958 from her days at their farmhouse in Roxbury Connecticut where Arthur would remain after their divorce (she would take the New York apartment when they physically parted ways in 1960) expressed her angst.

"I think I hate it here because there is no love here anymore," she poured onto paper. "I regret the effort I desperately made here."

Arthur moved out from their apartment by the end of 1960, leaving Marilyn period, as well as alone to fend for herself over the death of Clark Gable. Marilyn has often been blamed for his death, because of her lateness and illnesses when they filmed *The Misfits*. He died from a heart attack two weeks after the grueling conditions during the filming ended.

Clark's passing was a huge blow in many ways. Marilyn told half-sister Berniece that strangers on the streets of New York would refer to her as a "murderer," when they passed her by. Clark was a person who she cared for deeply, and as a girl when she did not know the true identity of her biological father, she substituted him with an image of Clark Gable in her mind. This is because she had seen a photo of Charles Stanley Gifford, suspected to be her dad, and he held some resemblance to the famous actor. Marilyn held an even greater affinity for the fatherly performer for this reason. In 1954 she proudly danced with him at a special party in her honor. His death and the accusations that she held a role in it further obliterated her spirit.

All of these factors caused Marilyn to unravel more. She felt there was no one genuine in her isolated circle to turn to -- and then Joe stepped back into her life.

He could never escape the memory of Marilyn. There was always a reminder, whether it was a news clipping, word from Joey, or some acquaintance or stranger who made the mistake of asking about her.

Joe sent what Marilyn described in a letter as a "forest-full of poinsettias" that Christmas. He signed the card with "Best, Joe."

When her publicist Pat Newcomb opened the card, she told Marilyn that she did not know who the sender could be.

Marilyn replied, "Well, there's just one Joe."

Marilyn called Joe and asked why he sent the flowers.

"First of all," he replied, "because I thought you would call to thank me. Besides, who in the hell else do you have in the world?"

Joe asked if they could have a drink sometime and what she was doing that Christmas night. She told him she was there "with a friend" [Pat] and otherwise was unoccupied.

"Then he asked me to come over and I was glad he was coming, though I must say I was bleary and depressed, but somehow still glad he was coming over," Marilyn explained in the retrospective letter that she wrote on Thursday March 2, 1961 to Dr. Ralph Greenson, while she was hospitalized at Columbia Presbyterian.

As 1960 turned into 1961, Marilyn did not realize the further horror only months ahead.

She did her best to keep her chin up. On January 6, the press reported that Marilyn and Lee had commenced negotiations with NBC for a television production of the film *Rain*, W. Somerset Maugham's story of Sadie Thompson. Other great actresses prior to Marilyn had portrayed the beloved fictional American prostitute. Originally there was a silent film entitled *Sadie Thompson* with Gloria Swanson, then reprised in *Rain* with Joan Crawford, and finally *Miss Sadie Thompson* with Rita Hayworth. Jeanne Eagels starred in the stage version of *Rain*.

Marilyn anticipated the role as Sadie, who escaped to the South Seas for a new future, to encounter a religious zealot pursuing her instead. He ended up falling for her.

"I am so glad to hear that you are going to play Sadie in the T.V. production of 'Rain,'" W. Somerset Maugham wrote to Marilyn on January 31. "I am sure you will be splendid. I wish you the best of luck."

The project never came to life. Lee was appointed "production supervisor" and when he demanded the role of director, NBC denied the request. The network expressed that Lee did not have adequate experience. Lee's ego was bruised and he insisted the plug be pulled entirely on the project.

"And the Strasberg stranglehold on Marilyn Monroe continued," penned author Ernest Cunningham.

"The tragedy of the Strasbergs' influence," exclaimed columnist Radie Harris, "they motivated her [Marilyn] into a lot of pretentious rot!"

"I want to change that will they showed me!" Marilyn exclaimed to half-sister Berniece who helped to care for Marilyn following the removal of her gall bladder over the summer of 1961.

"I want to work on a will to get it the way I want it!" Marilyn continued with her emphasis on the word "I."

Marilyn was most upset about having the will shoved in her face in the winter of 1961, indicating to her sister that her secretary May Reis and attorney Aaron Frosch were the ones who coerced her to sign it. The will was already drafted for her and she never had a previous chance to review it. It was neither in her words, nor under her terms.

"I was furious, I told them I was not going to sign it," Marilyn added. "I stood and argued."

However, Marilyn still caved in and placed her signature onto the document. Only weeks later she was tossed into the Payne Whitney Psychiatric Clinic.

The date Marilyn's will was allegedly signed was January 14, 1961. By coincidence if Marilyn and Joe had stayed married, it would have been their seventh wedding anniversary. An appointment was noted for Aaron Frosch in her datebook (now in the hands of a collector, and which the author of this book has reviewed) the day prior on Friday January 13 at 5:30 p.m. There was no notation on the calendar on January 14, the date when it was purportedly signed.

Why would an attorney and his secretary who witnessed it, have a client sign a will on a Saturday outside of normal business hours? The date does not make sense, nor does it that no appointment was registered in the appointment book the day that it was allegedly signed.

A check that Marilyn wrote to May Reis, her secretary -- who also benefitted from Marilyn's Estate, on her Last Will and Testament. This check is now in the author's collection.

Inez Melson, her business manager, also felt strangely about the transaction after Marilyn's death. She mailed a letter to Joe about it only a month following Marilyn's death. Inez noted car rental charges that day totaling seven hours. She asked Joe if he knew how to "obtain the information quietly." She was afraid to ruffle feathers by inquiring.

"I know it sounds like a '*Perry Mason*' television script but I am (between thee and me) very suspicious about that will and my only interest lies in the protection of future care of Mrs. Eley," Inez confessed to Joe about Gladys. "I have pretty well constructed what happened on that day and I find it impossible to see why Mr. Frosch had to be a witness along with his secretary. I know that you will understand how very discreet I must be about this."

According to a letter written to Inez to memorialize a conversation with Aaron Frosch on December 3, 1963 about a year and four months following Marilyn's death, his end claimed further details regarding the process of how the will came to be.

The will was completed ten days prior to her divorce's finalization from Arthur Miller. Apparently, there was a second will completed during their marriage with Arthur as sole beneficiary for it. Though a copy of this document has been written and spoken of, it has not surfaced publicly to date.

"Will was drawn in eighteen minutes and it was just a fluke that it was done when it was," Eileen Atkinson who typed the memorandum indicated. "Otherwise everything would have gone to Miller and no provision was made for Mother [Gladys]. Who knows whether he would have taken care of Mother or not."

The above was definitely true about Arthur because in addition to his act of fleecing Marilyn, he despised Gladys.

The will from 1961 was extraordinarily fishy for many reasons. One of the smelly components was Aaron Frosch acting in many roles, as Marilyn's attorney, plus executor, plus trustee, plus witnesses to her signature and finally as friends with the Strasbergs.

Marilyn's 1961 will consisted of many nuances, which were carefully plotted out not by Marilyn herself, but by many of the intended recipients of her earnings. Outside of her sister and mother, every other beneficiary on the will is suspect.

Although Norman and Hedda Rosten were said to be longtime friends of Marilyn's (at that point she had known them six years) previously they were friends of Arthur and his first wife. Like Arthur, they appeared in Marilyn's first will drawn up in 1956 when they were only becoming acquainted and Arthur was still technically wed to Mary. The Rostens were again in the 1961 will, though their award had been downsized from the first from $10,000 to $5,000.

"If they should predecease me," the will read, "then to their daughter, Patricia Rosten."

The sum of $5,000 was claimed to be a wish of Marilyn's for Patricia's education. However, the funds were not released until 1977 when Patricia was thirty-one years old and past college age.

What happened to the funds then?

And why were other children who Marilyn equally adored including niece Mona, and her three stepchildren not mentioned? Following both of those divorces she remained in touch with the children. Marilyn again, cared enough about Mona to suggest to Grace in a 1953 letter (now in the hands of a collector) about appointing Mona as Gladys's beneficiary of her Social Security funds. It seems unlikely she would snub all of the other closer children altogether.

Removed from the will shortly before he was officially and legally circumcised from her life, Arthur Miller still had an "in." May Reis, Marilyn's secretary, was a beneficiary of $10,000 plus an additional $40,000 (or twenty-five percent of Marilyn's estate, whichever was less). May had never been on Marilyn's first will. Arthur, part as the "inner circle," who helped to raise emotional torment in Marilyn's life, was the one who referred May to Marilyn. She had previously been Arthur's secretary before working for Marilyn, and then worked for Elia Kazan. Her brother, Irving Reis was a director who collaborated with Arthur Miller on the film version of his play, *All My Sons*.

Why would a secretary receive such a cut when Marilyn had other devoted employees that she looked to, including Inez, who was also Gladys's guardian? There was nothing apportioned on the will for Inez in light of this delicate task and she faithfully visited Gladys regularly in Marilyn's stead, even following her death. Could it have been that the $10,000 and the $40,000 or residuary was not meant for May Reis but was veiled for Arthur Miller in his role in assisting the Strasbergs and Freudians? What kind of a conflict of interest was it for May to join Aaron in cornering Marilyn to sign the document?

Lee (Paula was eliminated from the 1961 will and would never garner monies from Marilyn's estate through Lee, as she died from cancer in 1966) ended up the residuary beneficiary of the estate and was also gifted Marilyn's clothing and personal effects. The document specified those items were to be distributed to her friends -- that never happened. Anna Strasberg sold all of Marilyn's personal effects including her furniture (which technically should not have counted as personal effects) at Christie's in New York in 1999. In fact in the 1963 letter to Inez, it indicated that Lee was "miffed," about the selling of Marilyn's furniture, most likely during the sale of her California home, even though he "realizes this isn't personal effects" and complained to Aaron Frosch about it.

The trust was something missing from Marilyn's first will, with only flat payments to all the beneficiaries. The 1961 will was designed for perpetual payouts. In it a trust was set annually for $100,000, there was $5,000 per year for Gladys and $2,500 for Xenia Chekhov. Xenia died in 1970 and Marilyn's will did not leave probate until 1977. It was also created so if Dr. Marianne Kris survived both of them (she predeceased Gladys by four years -- Gladys passed away in 1984) the funds could be used "for furtherance of the work of such psychiatric institutions or groups as she shall elect."

Dr. Kris craftily made provisions for her cause, transferring the trust to the Anna Freud Centre in her will. The institution acted as the beneficiary after the deaths of all three ladies.

Dr. Kris replaced Dr. Hohenberg on Marilyn's 1961 will. The goal for both of these women was to secure monies not for personal gain but for their "higher power." That power player was Anna Freud. Even though Dr. Kris was excised from Marilyn's life after the Payne Whitney mistake, she was still the twenty-five percent residuary beneficiary.

Unbelievably, Dr. Kris still griped after she said that her portion dwindled from $1.6 million to $101,229.

The Freudians cause reached out its tentacles through their local connections -- Drs. Hohenberg, Kris and also Ralph "Romi" Greenson. Dr. Greenson was on the scene at her death and one who was actively involved in seeking millionaires for Anna Freud to finance their work. The Freudian psychotherapists would use underhanded psychological techniques to extort these funds. Marilyn was one of their victims.

Dr. Greenson was the most suave of the "recruiters," nailing his prospects by roping in Hollywood stars, who subscribed to Sigmund Freud. He made Freud appear glamorous as he worked the town hand-in-hand with his brother-in-law Milton Rudin, who was a famous entertainment attorney. The family members swapped clients, often with those in therapy using the services of the brother-in-law attorney and vice-versa.

Between them, there were no secrets and no attorney-client privilege or patient confidentiality existed. Romi Greenson not only invited Marilyn to stay for dinner and to sleep at his home so he could "monitor" her, he also would invite famous guests simultaneously to his home for Sunday afternoon shindigs comprised of chamber music and cold cuts. Co-mingling his notorious party attendees at a single event was obviously another breach of their secrecy.

Although Dr. Greenson would shy away from the idea that he promoted Marilyn's drug use, he made claims that he was attempting to wean her from her medications -- a downright lie -- pharmacology was in his genes. His father Joel Greenschpoon owned a pharmacy in Brooklyn and advertised to hire an enterprising pharmacist. A woman named Katherine answered the call and eventually became Mrs. Greenschpoon too. Later, she gave birth to twins comically named Romeo ("Romi") and Juliet in 1911.

Romi's father headed to medical school and earned his degree in 1914. Romi himself followed in his father's footsteps and entered medical school at the University of Berne in Switzerland. He began using the name "Ralph Greenson" when he joined the profession. It was in Switzerland where he met the woman who would become his bride, Hildi, and also delved into Freud. He evolved as one of the leaders in the movement, and became Anna Freud's personal friend.

In the mid-1930s, Romi became reputed as a therapist in Hollywood and then headed during World War II to serve in the military as a psychiatrist in a convalescent hospital. In another violation of ethics, Dr. Greenson allowed his friend Leo Rosten (no relation to Arthur's friend, Norman) to write a book loosely based on Dr. Greenson's experiences as a military shrink, *Captain Newman, M.D.* The book was later adapted into a film version in 1963, which starred Gregory Peck. Of course, Romi earned royalties off of the picture.

It was a bizarre game that he played with his clients, who all seemed to know what Marilyn's business was. Actress Celeste Holm, who was one of the principal players in *All About Eve,* a film that Marilyn starred in as a secondary character, was beside herself one day after she drove to Romi's home. He was her analyst too and she was confronted with the sight of Marilyn at his dinner table. Another unethical twist was that Celeste often spent time at the Greenson home as well. She openly expressed her jealousy to the doctor that Marilyn was invited to dine there and she had never been.

The icing on the medical code cake was that Celeste and Dr. Greenson engaged in conversations about Marilyn following that encounter. Celeste approached him in her fit of envy.

"Celeste, this woman [Marilyn] has no concept of family life," he replied.

Another client Janice Rule learned of Marilyn's attendance at the chamber music events and was upset because she had not been invited either.

"How come you never invited me?" she asked.

"Because, you were never that ill," he replied.

Leo Rosten was another one who knew when Marilyn was present at the Greenson resident. Once while they were both there Leo was upstairs speaking to Ralph's son, and Romi attempted to encourage the author to come downstairs to say hello. Leo refused, feeling uncomfortable with it all.

The Greenson household all interacted with Marilyn, something not permitted in therapy today and likely not condoned in those days. It was an extreme abuse of patient rights and privacy. His daughter Joan and Marilyn apparently would spend time together like girlfriends, with Joanie gossiping with Marilyn about boys. Marilyn once attended one of Joanie's birthday parties as well. His son Danny, who was studying at UCLA, would talk politics with Marilyn and she also supposedly helped him hunt for an apartment.

In a strange twist of fate Danny Greenson would follow in the footsteps of his father to also breach ethics, though he would be punished for his improprieties. Danny ironically died on Marilyn's birthday June 1, 2011 at age 74.

Danny was slapped with ethics charges in 2002 and remanded to surrender his license to practice medicine. He signed off on this action on December 5, 2002, more than forty years after Marilyn died. The author of this book has reviewed the report from the Medical Board of California documenting the charges against him.

While Danny was a psychiatrist in Berkeley California, he began engaging in a sexual relationship with one of his clients in 1995, a relationship which continued for two years. He was slapped another charge of gross negligence for gossiping with the patient since 1992 about his other clients. He had permitted her to listen to phone messages of these patients. He also spoke with her about his sexual relationship with his wife. Those acts carried into a third charge for their inappropriateness. And Danny was issued with another charge for failure to provide adequate medical records, prescribing the patient victim with sleeping pills and drugs such as Valium and marijuana for chronic gastrointestinal pain, without documenting any of the drugs on her record.

It is obvious that the apple did not fall far from the tree in the Greenson family, with son receiving his "ethics" education (or lack thereof) from his father.

It is a shame there is no way to posthumously slap Dr. Greenson for ethics violations charges. Hopefully this biographical account will further reiterate the quandary Marilyn soon found herself in. It was a place where she did not belong, in an abyss of users, where she has always ended up since her death carrying the blame. People like Romi Greenson accused her of committing suicide while he was the one who initiated her killing.

For Dr. Greenson, celebrities and artists were horses of a different color and his muses. He was a researcher who studied, tested and analyzed them. The painter Tony Berlant was one of Romi's patients, who was at that time struggling financially and unable to afford sessions. Romeo was able to extend a professional courtesy and gratis sessions to the artist, because he received a grant that was applicable to the study of artistic types.

Marilyn was truly above her head without realizing it and was a test case herself.

It took years to sort through Marilyn's estate, not only because of the many dishonest hands in the pot all looking to benefit, but also because of the complexities in the way it was set up.

Marilyn died a non-California resident, which required documentation to prove and was requested by the Inheritance Tax Appraiser in Los Angeles.

In 1967, the Inheritance Tax Appraiser advised that while Marilyn was a New York resident at the time of her death, her estate was still required to pay $777.63 in California Inheritance taxes.

Marilyn's earnings were still subject to income taxes in her former home state and in 1975 the California Franchise Tax Board determined that Marilyn's work generated monies. Aaron Frosch was forced to dole out $51,243 and $12,810 in penalties to the California State Board of Equalization.

"No millionaires materialized," wrote Anna Freud's biographer, "but ironically enough, the Clinic did get a sizeable portion of the tardily settled estate of Marilyn Monroe."

Anna Strasberg was appointed executrix over Marilyn's estate in 1989 following the death of Aaron Frosch. It was the same year that the Anna Freud Centre duked it out in court with the other Anna, accusing Lee's widow of not increasing residuals on a couple of Marilyn's films and dragging her feet on licensing opportunities that were depriving them all of revenue.

The Anna Freud Centre attempted to replace Aaron Frosch with counsel that they recommended, Joseph D. Garon a New York patent and copyright attorney. Anna Strasberg's attorney Irving Seidman insisted that Anna was the more legally entitled party for the role as well as the more deserving and the judge sided with him.

"All of this meant diminished revenues for the Center -- revenues, it claimed, that were earmarked for the very psychiatric services she [Marilyn] sought to finance," David Margolis reported in *The New York Times*.

Marilyn specified no particular request of any psychiatric service and it is shocking to read how her will eventually became so grossly misinterpreted, turning her into a commodity.

The book *American Monroe: The Making of a Body Politic*, reminds readers how in 1992 these parties were garnering between $20 and $30 million annually on the sale of many novelty items, from clocks to key chains, on which her image had been emblazoned.

Roger Richman, who represented Anna Strasberg prior to CMG, described her viewpoint to *The Wall Street Journal* as to "keep making money."

Her attorney William Wegner then divulged to the publication, "Anna thinks about and handles [Marilyn's image] from the moment she wakes up."

Anna has developed a reputation around those who know her as a "shrewd businesswoman," and immediately went to work licensing Marilyn's image beginning in 1982, only a few months after Lee died. She was also the one who handled the business matters for the Lee Strasberg Theatre and Film Institute while Lee focused on teaching. Elia Kazan remembered in those later years, Lee was chauffeured around in a Mercedes limousine, living off of the monies from Marilyn and the marketing of his institution. His school now on both coasts, there was and remains a Marilyn Monroe Theatre at each location.

Marilyn had become immortal, and sadly fiscally more valuable to the heirs who profited from her death than she had been to them while she was living.

The author of this book, a devoted Marilyn admirer since childhood, purchased and was gifted many of the plates and dolls sold by her "estate." If it was known the purpose and whose pockets were lined, the author has vouched she would have saved her monies, and suggested others purchasing presents for her of this type to do the same.

There have been too many suits and countersuits initiated from the "estate" camp. One of the more recent skirmishes emerged between Anna and the children of photographers who took photos of Marilyn, Sam Shaw, Milton Greene and Tom Kelley.

Anna attempted to assert that she held rights over the works of these photographers, now in the hands of their heirs. They faced her in return court volleys and won.

Anna wrestled with Marilyn's domiciliary and has wavered between the ideas of Marilyn having been a New York then a California resident. She did so to strengthen her own position and govern Marilyn's right of publicity. Anna asserted that she controlled all aspects, including those held by the photographers. She argued it to the point that she attempted to change legislation in both California and New York to garner her post-mortem residuary rights. It was determined Marilyn's rights died with her (post-mortem celebrity publicity laws were not in effect in 1962, nor did Marilyn assign rights to her image to anyone). Anna successfully pushed legislation through in California though not in New York. Courts overturned Anna's ownership of Marilyn's image and use of her name though they have applied for a registered trademark. There has been a gross misrepresentation of her "owning Marilyn," which she has masked for many years, sucking millions up in licensing deals when she was never entitled to. It is not known if those licensees ever pursued her in court for restitution.

Marilyn exiting her New York apartment, following her split with Arthur, with Pat Newcomb in tow. Photo from the author's collection.

The Shaw Family Archives was forced into bankruptcy by the legal wrangling and licensed their photos to Anna Strasberg and ABG, as did the Milton Greene Archives.

Eventually, her company Marilyn Monroe LLC declared bankruptcy and Anna started anew with The Estate of Marilyn Monroe LLC, selling her "rights" (though none technically existed per above about Marilyn's rights having died with her) from the previous company to ABG.

The response to many of the questions regarding Marilyn's controversial Last Will could be answered swiftly following the activities in the weeks after it was signed. Marilyn headed to Mexico the next week on Friday January 20 to divorce Arthur. The divorce was officially finalized on Tuesday January 24, 1961.

It was Sunday February 5 that was the true kicker. Marilyn's calendar the Friday prior was packed with appointments and the next date in her appointment book, Wednesday February 8 eerily listed an appointment with Lester Markel *The New York Times* Sunday Editor and name "Henry R.," meaning Henry Rosenfeld the investor that Milton had wanted Marilyn to meet with when they were in Boston (he and Marilyn continued with a friendship). Then all activity dropped from Marilyn's appointment book until Sunday March 5 with an appointment listed with "Dr. K," meaning Dr. Kris. That was on Monday March 5 at 5 p.m. On Tuesday March 7 was the notation "Left Neurol PysD," which was most likely affiliated with her stay ("Neurol" short for "Neurology" and "PysD" "Psychologist."). Then some of the appointments returned to her roster with the usual suspects, the Strasbergs, Aaron Frosch and "Dr. K."

As an afterthought in her book, Berniece reflected about Marilyn's emotional breakdown in 1961 by stating: "I know that the eight years of therapy that she'd had at the point she died hadn't created a strong, healthy, self-confident person. In fact to me, Marilyn had been stronger, healthier and more self-confident before she went to New York."

Marilyn had an amazingly forgiving heart and ability to easily forget wrongs committed against her.

For it was on Sunday February 5, when she endured the ultimate betrayal.

With Marilyn thinking that she was about to enter into New York Hospital for other reasons, which Dr. Kris suggested to her due to the various stresses she had been under, Marilyn followed Dr. Kris's advice like a lamb to the slaughter even down to admitting herself and signing in under the name "Faye Miller." However Dr. Kris had other plans for Marilyn, who soon found locked doors closing behind her at the Payne Whitney Psychiatric Clinic. To her own shocking surprise, she was placed in a padded cell in the area for the most disturbed patients.

There were no windows in the white room. Perhaps one could have considered it a sensory deprivation chamber of sorts. Marilyn was held captive there for further reprogramming from her keepers.

Marilyn banged on the doors until her fists bled and sobbed hysterically to the extent that the following day an intern classified her as "extremely disturbed."

Well of course she was "extremely disturbed," she was locked up there against her will under false pretenses…who else would not turn "disturbed" under those conditions?

Marilyn was able to pen a note to the Strasbergs asking for help -- they never responded to her letter.

"Dear Lee and Paula," she pleaded. "Dr. Kris has put me into the New York Hospital – psychiatric division under the care of two idiot doctors -- they both should not be my doctors. You haven't heard from me because I'm locked up with these poor nutty people. I'm sure to end up a nut too if I stay in this nightmare -- please help me Lee, this is the last place I should be -- maybe if you called Dr. Kris and assured her of my sensitivity and that I must get back to class so I'll be better prepared for "rain" (sic). Lee, I try to remember what you said once in class "that art goes far beyond science." Please help me -- if Dr. Kris assures you I am all right -- you can assure her I am not. I do not belong here! I love you both. Marilyn."

She followed up with her postscript: "P.S. forgive the spelling -- and there's nothing to write on here. I'm on the dangerous floor it's like a cell. Can you imagine -- cement blocks. They put me in here because they lied to me about calling my doctor and Joe and they had my bathroom door locked so I broke the glass and outside of that I haven't done anything that is uncooperative."

In her book, Susan Strasberg neither mentioned the letter nor indicated that her parents visited Marilyn. She glossed over the topic of Marilyn's hospitalization classifying it as "detoxification," which she said that her parents also advocated.

However in his book *Timebends*, Arthur Miller recalled an episode during the filming of *The Misfits* as Marilyn was becoming more dependent on sleeping pills. Paula and Lee staged a tantrum when director John Huston, like many directors Marilyn worked with, refused to deal with her acting advisors. Following the incident, Paula led Arthur into her apartment and then bedroom where Marilyn lay, a doctor seeking a vein in her hand and dosing her up with Amytal (a barbiturate with hypnotic properties, also called "truth serum." It was used to care for shell-shocked soldiers after World War II. This was another drug used during MKUltra experiments). Marilyn screamed at Arthur to leave. Their relationship by now was severely disintegrated. In his memoirs he claimed his stomach turned at this sight and he visualized himself breaking between the doctor and himself, though he took no such action.

"She [Paula] wanted help and she wanted credit for her mothering love even as something in her could not care less because it was all hopelessly disconnected," Arthur said.

Such were the dysfunctional relationships surrounding Marilyn, which her co-dependents latched onto her in unhealthy ways as well.

Yet fully aware of her incarceration in Payne Whitney, Arthur also never came to Marilyn's rescue or stopped the control exerted over her. He also benefitted from it and turned his back.

Essentially, the whole lousy bunch of them were relieved she was locked up. In fact, the author believes they hoped Marilyn would be able to continue her stay there. The author of this book also asserts their eventual plan was to rule Marilyn incompetent in order to gain further leverage of her assets.

While some may find it uncharacteristic for Arthur to permit Marilyn to be tossed to the wolves, he was in reality, cold and calculating. He has been outwardly and falsely perceived as a sensitive humanitarian. Why would

Arthur not help his ex-wife, knowing full well that she was controlled? How could someone who had claimed love easily wipe his hands clean? It is because he was a participant.

There were other reasons too. This was characteristic of Arthur, who thought it acceptable to toss his own son Daniel, born in 1966 with developmental disabilities, into an institution. Plus, he was now occupied with his new love Inge Morath, a photographer he met on *The Misfits*. Marilyn was a memory in the short distance.

Marilyn was heartsick to learn before her death that Inge was pregnant since she struggled so fiercely to maintain her pregnancies. Arthur and Inge's daughter Rebecca was born in September 1962, a month after Marilyn died.

Inge who predeceased Arthur in 2002 (he died in 2005) visited Daniel weekly. Arthur never mentioned their son to friends or visited him. He also omitted his child from his memoirs *Timebends*.

The New York Times analyzed this subject following Arthur's death. While some made no judgment of Arthur, others were shocked and saddened, expressing that their image of him was tarnished. They recognized a deeper, darker picture and character of a flawed man.

"There's more to Tennessee Williams than being a dope addict," commented Martin Gottfried, the only biographer that revealed Daniel's existence before Arthur's death, "and there's more to Arthur Miller than this."

If placing Arthur's own flesh and blood into an institution and ignoring him was so simple, so was abandoning a newly discarded ex-wife into a mental ward.

Marilyn on the set with Arthur Miller and John Huston during filming of The Misfits. Slide from the author's collection.

On February 9, several papers were reporting that Marilyn was hospitalized at Payne Whitney, though they said she was allowed out on day passes during her stay at the hospital.

"For two months, while most of Broadway and Hollywood thought she was studying acting and readying herself for a super TV role, a badly shaken Marilyn Monroe has been quietly undergoing treatment at Payne Whitney Psychiatric Clinic of New York Hospital – Cornell Medical Center," the *Daily News* reported. "Marilyn has been able to carry off the deception because she is registered under the name of 'Miss Faye Miller,' and has the privilege of periodically leaving the hospital on a pass and being seen around town."

One publication reported that Marilyn had been under treatment for two months, since December 5, while she had been allowed out to leave for Mexico to divorce Arthur, attend the premiere of *The Misfits* with co-star Montgomery Clift on January 31 (which reporters described her demeanor as "cheerful," in spite of the fact that Arthur was there separately with children, Bobby and Jane) and had been spotted on dates with Joe. The medical facility would not disclose her condition, though it was described as "satisfactory" and a spokesperson said that Marilyn had been battling a sore throat and cold the week prior.

Reporters like George Carpozi were baffled and frustrated as they received little information. He said Chiari Pisani from *Gente*, an Italian Magazine, was able to achieve a breakthrough when she asked a doctor friend on staff to phone Payne Whitney while she eavesdropped on the call.

When asked if Marilyn inherited schizophrenia, the Payne Whitney physician replied that Marilyn was not schizophrenic but, "psychiatrically disconnected in an acute way," due to the stress of her last two films and divorce.

Marilyn sought desperately for a phone during her first few days at Payne Whitney, after enduring physical examinations and lies that she would have phone privileges. Angrily, she slammed a chair several times against the small glass window at her door, through which the medical professionals peered in on her as if she was a caged zoo animal or sideshow freak. After breaking the glass, she kept a sliver of it concealed in her hand and told them, "If you are going to treat me like a nut, I'll act like a nut."

She bluffed and told the doctors she would harm herself, looking back to her experience in the film *Don't Bother to Knock*, when her character held a standoff to inflict self-harm with a razor blade. Soon she said she found herself lifted by four stocky orderlies, two male and two female, who carried her by her arms and legs face down from the sixth to the seventh floor. Marilyn wept until her arrival into another cell. One of the women orderlies, who she described as "an ox of a woman," forced her to bathe.

"As soon as you change floors, you have to take another bath," the orderly ordered.

It was here a doctor, who Dr. Kris told Marilyn was the "administrator," began questioning Marilyn and told her she was a "very, very sick girl and had been a very, very sick girl for many years."

"Don't you think that perhaps Greta Garbo and Charlie Chaplin and perhaps Ingrid Bergman they had been depressed when *they* worked sometimes?" Marilyn snapped back to the "administrator."

The enterprising newswoman Chiari Pisani wooed one of the hospital's Spanish-speaking orderlies with a cup of coffee and five dollars, informing him that she spoke Spanish and asked for further information. In turn as they sipped coffee together on February 9, he confirmed that staff feared Marilyn might harm herself and she was carted to the security ward, where she was further guarded. She was administered IV sedation, as well as IV feedings during that lockdown.

This type of a confinement and kidnapping, including intravenous drugs and nutrition, is typical of one in which patients have been subject to emotional torture by their captors.

Soon a suitor would be on the way to thwart the further attempts that the Freudians and Strasbergs exerted over Marilyn to break her spirit. On February 9, when the press began their major swirling about Marilyn's hospitalization, a sympathetic and unidentified employee permitted Marilyn one phone call. After attempts to reach several so-called friends, she contacted one she knew she could always count on. It was the loyal Joe who she was able to track down in Florida. Joe was busy coaching the Yankees during their training and immediately headed up to New York, arriving that evening.

The following day, Joe took charge of the situation, his Sicilian temper letting loose. He began barking orders to the Payne Whitney staff.

"I want my wife," boomed an enraged Joe, as he shook the facility's reception desk, neck bulging.

No one dared to correct the Jolter that on paper, his marriage to Marilyn had terminated in 1954.

The Freudian effort to emotionally subjugate Marilyn soon began to disengage, as Joe demanded Marilyn be discharged into his care. It was not what her handlers anticipated, a rescuer in the form of a persistent and intimidating DiMaggio to gallop in from the horizon.

The Payne Whitney employees, who had been initially cocky towards Joe, quickly became timid under the force of the Yankee Clipper. They still dryly informed him he must speak to Dr. Kris.

Joe cautioned Dr. Kris he would "take the hospital apart brick by brick," if Marilyn was not released to him by the end of that day. Everyone knew Joe meant that sincerely and there would be hell for all of them to pay. Dr. Kris began discharge proceedings and then accompanied Marilyn back to her apartment, where Joe was waiting. Ralph Roberts, another referral from the Strasbergs and Marilyn's masseur and confidant, drove the car while Marilyn delivered a tongue lashing to the doctor.

Ralph Roberts was another shadowy character in Marilyn's life. Though considered Marilyn's friend and confidant, he was referred to her by the Strasbergs and reported conversations back to them. Joe was additionally suspicious of Ralph Roberts. However, Marilyn cared deeply for him and divulged many of her secrets while she relaxed on his massage table.

Joe was disconcerted when he was united with Marilyn, who was trembling, disoriented and gaunt. He delivered her to the Neurological Institute of the Columbia University-Presbyterian Medical Center, where he believed she could have peace, medical care and recuperation. While she rested, Joe often stayed with her and visited her daily.

A bill from a portion of her stay there, now in the hands of a collector, reflected free use of the telephone, television, a guest dinner and around-the-clock nursing care. The bill from Payne Whitney, on the other hand, was more cryptic. Charges were broken down differently and included lab services. The invoice was sent to "Miller M. Miss" at 135 Central Park West -- that was Dr. Kris's office address. Her doctor listed on the statement was Dr. Mastrovito.

Joe averted the press and safely sequestered Marilyn at the Neurological Institute. It was not without trauma and drama though. Chiari Pisani attempted to obtain information without success, pretending to be a friend of actress Simone Signoret. The crafty reporter also reached out to Henry Fonda's wife Afdera, a personal friend of her's. Chiari asked her to call Lee who was a mutual friend. Lee told Afdera he did not have a clue where Marilyn would be hospitalized.

Marilyn, in a wire photo, following her release from the hospital. "I had a nice rest," she told reporters. From the author's collection.

Joe had his own brush with the press that day when *Journal-American* photographer John Dolan and reporter James Clarity staked out Joe at Payne Whitney and spotted Joe as he carried a suitcase. Joe recognized John Dolan and jumped into a cab, which led the reporting staff's unsuccessful pursuit. Joe warned Marilyn's escorts and the group headed through the hospital passageways into the basement where the car met Marilyn at an exit.

The press sought their nuggets with difficulty until February 11, when it was announced that Marilyn was checked into the Harkness Pavilion room 719.

While Marilyn recovered, the press discovered what they could about Marilyn's health.

"She went to the hospital for what amounted to exhaustion and nothing more," Joe told reporters, who spotted him carrying in a bouquet of flowers.

Naturally, the visit initiated the chatter about their relationship again. The talk led to reconciliation questions about the two and out came the usual reply from Joltin' Joe.

"As to a reconciliation, I can only say we are friends -- good friends -- and nothing else," Joe countered.

Then, the airwaves remained silent.

George Carpozi described how the press backed away and explained, "There seemed to be a common knowledge that, 'this is for real, boys, let's take it easy. This is no press agent's gimmick. Let's give her a chance.'"

Joe returned to Florida and insisted Marilyn join him for further relaxation.

On Sunday, March 5, the wheels of the press corps began to turn as the announcement was made that Marilyn would be discharged from Columbia Presbyterian.

About four hundred fans crunched into Marilyn as she was escorted out and it was Marilyn mayhem as usual. Fans yelled and reporters shouted out questions while Marilyn's voice was drowned out. Six security guards pushed back the crowd to form a small path for Marilyn to squeeze through.

She was pale and thinner, wearing a tight sweater and skirt.

"You're beautiful," members of the crowd yelled.

"I feel fine," she told reporters. "I feel wonderful. I had a nice rest."

Only two days later, Marilyn was thrust back into a stressful mode when Arthur Miller's mother passed away. The following day in Jewish tradition, the funeral took place. Marilyn attended to provide comfort especially to her father-in-law, with whom she continued to remain close. Marilyn was cordial to Arthur and presented her condolences.

It was two weeks later that there was a large note in her datebook written by May Reis for Tuesday March 21. It was a reminder in immense letters to call Joe Jr. and emphasized that with an underline. That day as well Marilyn headed for Florida to reconnect with Joe.

Although Marilyn and Joe attempted to remain incognito, they were spotted quickly and unsuccessfully made attempts to avoid the press at the airport.

Marilyn and Joe attempt to avert the paparazzi as they spent time together in 1961. Photo from the author's collection.

"Marilyn in Florida," one news blurb shouted.

On Thursday, March 23, Marilyn and Joe were grilled again, as they baked in the sunshine under a cabana on Redington Beach while the Yankees played in nearby Bradenton against Milwaukee. At first, it was just Joe on the beach, and then Marilyn emerged from the hotel, wearing a blue strapless sun bra, white capri pants and a white jacket.

"We're just friends, that's as far as it is," Joe replied. "We're here to visit and rest. We want to be left alone."

Only ten minutes later, they retreated to their rooms in the Tides hotel to escape the swarm that had congregated on the beach.

Although Marilyn touted to reporters she was there for "sun, rest and to visit with Joe," she ended up requiring a rain check on the sunshine, as press and fans descended on her at times during the trip.

Dining offered the same amount of privacy invasion. One night, the couple headed into the hotel's Bath Club dining room, only to be greeted by a Bavarian dance scene. An irritated Joe asked the manager Phil Dross for suggestions where the couple could catch some quiet. They headed to the Wine House in North Redington Beach where manager Bob Purvis set up the glassed-front dining area for Joe and Marilyn. The two dined on filet mignon, holding hands and speaking quietly, as they enjoyed dinner until about 11 p.m. Marilyn smiled gently at the waiters and otherwise showed little expression.

Marilyn was seen attired in a black fur coat, in spite of the Floridian weather, her eyes with their typical Marilyn lush lashes and scarlet painted onto her lips.

"Gad, she is really beautiful," murmured a parking attendant.

The curiosity-seekers peeked in for a view by peering into the restaurant's windows.

"She's not so hot," one female passerby sneered.

"She's a doll, I hope they get back together," another woman chimed in.

Attempts for Marilyn and sister Berniece to visit one another while she was in Florida with Joe were interrupted by stalking reporters and then Joe's wish to have Marilyn accompany him on a fishing expedition. Marilyn was crushed, as she had hoped to visit with her sister.

The visit overall to Florida for Joe and Marilyn was not necessarily about time with loved ones, dining, beaching, fishing and relaxing. Baseball was another component, with Joe's initial mission as the Yankees' batting coach. His goal shifted though unlike their time in Japan with his new primary focus now Marilyn. If necessary and able, he would drop his work as well as his time with the Yankees, to dote on her.

Yet like in Japan, overall public attention transferred from baseball to Marilyn. This was in a time and place where Joe Torre, years later a Yankee manager, was a rookie catcher for the Milwaukee Braves playing against the Yankees. Even Mickey Mantle, who was the crowd pleaser, recognized Marilyn's presence, though it is said he was too intimidated to greet her.

"The most momentous announcement of the spring was made in the press box in the third inning -- Marilyn Monroe is joining the Yankees at St. Petersburg Thursday," reported *The Milwaukee Sentinel*. "One of her former husbands, Joe DiMaggio, is batting tutor for the Yanks and a second romance between the two is rumored."

Marilyn and Joe joyfully walk together in Florida, in March, 1961. This original negative comes from the author's collection.

Instead of departing Florida when his time was up, Joe bailed on a business trip to Guantanamo Bay for his company to extend his stay with Marilyn.

Once again, Marilyn drew a crowd and this time Joe did not seem to mind. He seemed to have finally come to a place of peace and acceptance regarding the popularity of the beloved woman in his life. While Joe worked with the players at the Yankee training grounds at Huggins and Al Lang Field, Marilyn visited daily. She typically waited in a car. She was often also spotted casually dressed in slacks and sweater, sometimes wearing a scarf on her head and sunglasses. Occasionally, she was seen donning a Yankee ball cap.

When a press person witnessed Marilyn lifting a bat, Joe laughed when he read that one paper reported that Marilyn was batting "fungoes" (for laypeople, "fly balls"), which Joe smiled and dismissed as "a pipedream."

However, a columnist with the *Daily Mirror* Arthur Richman, was greeted with a surprise one day, He spotted two people on the practice field. One was Joe and the other was Marilyn, who Joe was teaching more about the fine art of batting.

Following her return from Florida to New York, Marilyn attempted to resume her regular activities. Yet she battled extreme pain on her right side and issues with digestion. On June 28, Ralph Roberts chauffeured Marilyn to the Manhattan Polyclinic, where she was diagnosed with acute inflammation in her gallbladder as well as a massive influx of gallstones. Her gallbladder was removed the following day in a two-hour procedure.

Publicist and friend Pat Newcomb visited during her recovery, delivering to Marilyn a special gift on behalf of Frank Sinatra, a fluffy white poodle puppy. Natalie Wood's mother, a known poodle breeder, bred the pup. Pat acted as the beard for the transaction on Frank's behalf and Marilyn named the dog "Maf Honey" or "Maf," in playful recognition of Frank's suspected mob connections. Marilyn's friendship with Frank was a sensitive and upsetting subject for Joe.

Marilyn insisted Berniece come to stay with her, which it had been years since the sisters met in person. Berniece made her way to help her recovering sister. Berniece's husband Paris had visited with some business associates while he was in New York and Marilyn was still married to Arthur.

It was obvious to Berniece that Marilyn and Joe cared deeply for one another, though Marilyn still distanced Joe from particular segments of her life. His gripping jealousy had not fully disappeared in spite of gains in his emotional maturity. One example of Marilyn's holding out on Joe was about Frank Sinatra again. Marilyn told Berniece she had planned to continue some of her recuperation at Frank's home while the crooner was out of town.

"You mustn't tell anyone," Marilyn clued her in. "Especially Joe."

Berniece also had the opportunity to meet the Strasbergs who visited with Marilyn in her bedroom while she rested. After they left, Marilyn was upset over a discussion they engaged in about photos of her that the Strasbergs liked, but Marilyn was displeased with.

"Her opinion of them [the Strasbergs] seemed to vary," Berniece said. "This time she was peeved when they left. And she was disappointed."

Berniece was shocked to learn of Marilyn funding the Strasberg trip to Japan with her AT&T stocks.

Berniece enjoyed meeting Joe while she was there, who visited daily at dinnertime sometimes accompanied by friend George Solotaire. She described Joe as "charming," and was tickled when he presented her with an autographed photo on her departure. The four would savor Italian meals prepared by Marilyn's maid Lena Pepitone, and would enjoy conversation and tea after dinner. Berniece thought it ironic that Joe later became a Mr. Coffee spokesperson since he now avoided coffee because of his gastric issues, a far cry from his earlier days when he was a coffee fanatic.

Following their cups of tea and company together, Berniece and George would retreat into the den to watch television and offer Marilyn and Joe some time to catch up alone.

"Joe acted as if he were still in love with Marilyn," she said.

She noted how Joe was also extremely astute and vocal when analyzing Marilyn's finances. After discarding a tea bag into the garbage one evening, he spotted a delivery bill for wines and household supplies and was angered by the discrepancies. The bill totaled to nearly double.

"Doesn't someone check these things when they are delivered?" he boomed.

"I don't think that's any of your business," Marilyn retorted, though she admitted to Berniece later that she had been cheated on many of her bills.

Berniece fretted because her background was in bookkeeping and she wished she could have assisted Marilyn more with her finances. Marilyn confessed she had not been reviewing her expenses with May Reis.

One of the conversations between Marilyn, Joe and Berniece focused on the possibility of Marilyn purchasing a home. In 1955, Marilyn told writer Maurice Zolotow of her interest in a home purchase in Brooklyn.

"I've fallen in love with Brooklyn," she said. "I'm going to buy a little house in Brooklyn and live there. I'll go to the Coast only when I have to make a picture."

Marilyn led Berniece to one of her windows, like a princess high above in a tower, and they peered down together at a house below. The home appeared miniature with a postage stamp square of grass around it.

"I'd love the privacy of a house," she said. "It would seem more really mine. I could have fun decorating it. I loved decorating the house in Connecticut."

Marilyn had always lived in rented properties including hotels, and seemed to seek a permanent landing pad that she could call her own.

Both Berniece and Joe pitched Marilyn about the pros of owning a home in California with Berniece suggesting that Marilyn could have a larger yard. Joe amazingly contributed that she could have a "better place to live for making pictures."

Joe brought their attention back to the home Marilyn ogled over down below, likely one of the properties close to Sutton Park overlooking the Queensboro Bridge. He asked Berniece for a guess on the tab for a place like that in New York.

"It would be astronomical!" Joe exclaimed, telling Berniece her guess of $500,000 was around $50,000 too conservative.

Marilyn's plan was never to be a permanent resident of California again. The taxes were too exorbitant and she only later planned to have the home in Brentwood as a place to rest her head while she filmed her movies in Hollywood. She did not wish to stay at hotels anymore. May Reis (who ceased her employment with Marilyn in 1961), Ralph Roberts, Pat Newcomb and Hattie Stevenson (her housekeeper also known as Hattie Amos) all attested to this. Marilyn also filed her final income tax return in New York in April 1962.

It was Dr. Greenson who would convince Marilyn to finalize the purchase in California, with a miniature version of his hacienda. Yet the doctor would state in 1966 that Marilyn was not interested in domiciling in California but New York.

Following Berniece's two-week visit that July, Joe travelled abroad for his job with Monette from August through November. Marilyn voyaged back and forth between New York and California, first hiding out at the Chateau Marmont and then renting an apartment on Doheny Drive under the alias of "Marjorie Stengel," who had worked as a secretary for both Montgomery Clift and Marilyn.

Marilyn spent time in talks with Fox. The studio reminded her that under her current contract she had two more pictures to film with them. On the West Coast, her relationship became more entangled with Romi, who she began seeing during the filming of *Let's Make Love*.

Dr. Greenson was one of many who took Marilyn under his wing in an unhealthy, unethical and domineering way. Marilyn, as she did with Natasha Lytess, Drs. Hohenberg and Kris, the Greenes and Strasbergs, repeated a harmful pattern of permitting her paid gurus one-way tickets into the depths of her soul. They opened their homes where Marilyn would stay, dine and vent, never leaving her problems at the door. Instead, she confided in people who only took what she offered them and then performed emotional cardiac surgery on her in return. They twisted her in a way that manipulated her whole being. In all of these cases Marilyn instead integrated into their families, as she had done so easily with friends and family members of Gladys as well as the families of her ex-husbands. Though outside of Arthur, her exes and their families had no plans to exploit her. Those who became substitute families who she paid, never had honorable intentions.

She became more increasingly co-dependent on Dr. Greenson and vice-versa. Marilyn was afraid to make a move without the doctor, engaging in therapy sessions with him at his home. Later he made house calls to Marilyn's home. He grew more enamored and possessive over the feather in his cap, Marilyn, his star patient. Dr. Greenson insisted his brother-in-law Milton Rudin become her West Coast attorney and her agency representation. Her recent agent MCA (Music Corporation of America) was kicked to the curb.

Romi also mandated she hire Eunice Murray, a matronly woman who was his friend. Although she possessed no medical training, Eunice held a strong interest in psychology and working with those who she could emotionally dominate. Marilyn became one of those people. "Mrs. Murray" was how Marilyn respectfully referred to her employee, whereas Eunice always called Marilyn by her first name, never "Miss Monroe." She evolved into another older female in Marilyn's life who wove a detrimental and controlling web tightly around her. Eunice could have easily been compared to the likes of Natasha Lytess, May Reis, Paula Strasberg and Drs. Hohenberg and Kris. Eunice became a more intimate companion as a housekeeper, pill keeper and simply a keeper of Marilyn Monroe.

On December 23, Joe joined Marilyn for the holidays, helping her to decorate her apartment for Christmas with Mexican accents. He filled her refrigerator with caviar and champagne. The Greensons invited Marilyn and Joe to enjoy Christmas dinner with them. In spite of Joe's reluctance to attend, he accompanied Marilyn. The couple then spent a quiet New Year's Eve together (though reportedly by some accounts Joanie Greenson and her boyfriend crashed their private party for two and roasted chestnuts by the fireplace with Marilyn and Joe).

Perhaps it was Joe's own treatment with counseling, which caused him to partially let his guard down with Marilyn's keepers. As their marriage disintegrated, Marilyn suggested Joe seek help for his character traits and own insecurities. He did so following their divorce and he credited Marilyn for having saved his life by suggesting he seek counseling. Joe attended psychotherapy briefly and then discontinued it, as most healthy people do once they are feeling better. Marilyn's emotional captors, on the other hand, convinced her that it was necessary for her to perpetually remain in therapy. In the cases of certain members of her team such as Greenson and Strasberg, Joe held an unusual naïveté about their places in her life, not recognizing the stronghold they strangled her with.

It may have Joe's predisposed worshipful attitude towards the medical profession where doctors have often been treated as demi-gods that tainted his perspective. Doctors worked with Joe throughout his career to assist him with the various tolls that sports had taken on his body over the years, as well as with caring for his stomach ulcers. Then of course, medical professionals analyzed him while he battled depression when he was in the military. Joe took their word as gospel for his own care, and maybe put a similar trust in the ones that abused Marilyn. He had not recognized the wrong they were doing, with Payne Whitney an obvious exception. His shyness in this area was uncharacteristic when compared to the other areas of his life, especially his fiscal sense, in which he reacted like a frenzied Piranha towards any affronts.

Unfortunately for Marilyn, psychotherapy became a lifestyle, not a temporary solution to help her through her tough seasons of her life. Of course, those who were "treating" her never promoted ceasing the program, because they enjoyed the benefits of a regular check on her payroll.

"Friends," who were also on the payroll as employees considered Eunice as Dr. Greenson's "plant." She dictated to Marilyn like her predecessors, directing to her how she should conduct business for example. Marilyn's dearest employee friends like Pat Newcomb, makeup artist Whitey Snyder, and Ralph Roberts, were dismayed by Eunice Murray's presence. They noted she eavesdropped and spied on Marilyn, reporting Marilyn's every move back to Dr. Greenson.

Though in her book Eunice alluded that Marilyn asked her to find her dream house, by other accounts the creepy and invasive housekeeper was said to have located unsolicited by Marilyn, what would become Marilyn's first and final home in January 1962.

The small Spanish hacienda was atypical of the palatial homes many stars of her day lived in. It was located in a quiet cul-de-sac on Fifth Helena Drive. The Helena Drives, known as the "numbered Helenas," jut off of South Carmelina Avenue. South Carmelina is one of the arteries from San Vicente Boulevard, a main thoroughfare.

The home itself was guarded with an imposing high surrounding wall and was twenty-three hundred square feet. A small garage connected to the home and there was a diminutive adjacent guesthouse and a kidney-shaped pool in the rear complementing the residence.

Marilyn sought Joe's insight on the potential purchase, which he considered a match for her needs and an excellent buy. With a down payment of $42,500, Marilyn mortgaged the rest at $320 monthly with an agreement of fifteen years at six-and-half percent interest.

Eunice also patted herself on the back in her book for Joe approaching her, she claimed requesting her to remain with Marilyn throughout the remodeling project.

"It's a good deal if she has someone like you to help her," Joe allegedly told the "prodigal" housekeeper.

Eunice took a strong stance in assisting Marilyn with remodeling and redecorating the home. She subcontracted her son-in-law Norman Jeffries as a handyman, and he tended to the various needs around the home. Often Eunice would stay the night in one of Marilyn's spare bedrooms and simply further entrenched herself in Marilyn's life.

One of the focal points of the home's outdoor entry that has been debated as an omen since her death is a tile that remains at the home as of today. "CURSUM PERFICIO," it reads, which translates from Latin to "I complete the race," or "my journey ends here." Many have viewed it as a subliminal message that Marilyn herself was attempting to convey of plans to end her life, although the tile was installed during the home's original construction thirty years prior. A small minority has looked at the positive behind the message and that Marilyn seemed to be planting her roots and on the way to finding herself, while some counter that Marilyn never paid attention to the meaning of the tile.

As life appeared to fall into place for Marilyn, those on the outside did not know how some facets of her existence were truly and actually falling apart. She grew more dependent on Dr. Greenson, who further encouraged Marilyn's dependence on sleeping pills and alcohol.

Many of the drugs that Marilyn was on including Nembutal (a barbiturate now even used in capital punishment proceedings) are suggested for short-term use. Dr. Greenson was definitely versed in the duration for the drug use as someone in his trade for many years that also grew up around a pharmacy. Drugs like Nembutal, one of the ones responsible for killing her, lose their efficacy after two weeks and of course can become habit-forming. Yet the doctor continued Marilyn on this drug and a slew of others.

Chloral Hydrate (not currently approved by the FDA in the United States or EMA in the European Union, though clinicians still use it, is a Schedule IV drug because of its high physical dependency) was another one that was attributed to her demise. That drug also increased bowel symptoms, which in turn triggered colitis issues for Marilyn and necessitated other medications to balance the side effects. Dr. Greenson and his sidekick Dr. Hyman Engelberg initiated a pharmacological battle within Marilyn's body.

Betty Robin was an assistant of Marilyn's that claimed Milton Rudin suggested she work for the star. Betty said she did so the final eight months of Marilyn's life (her work for Marilyn would have commenced in January 1962).

Betty, although recommended by an "insider" connected to Dr. Greenson, did not appear to cater to the doctors. She instead acted as an impartial witness to the activities in Marilyn's life.

During an interview years after Marilyn's death, Betty said that she did not believe Marilyn committed suicide and that she instead had a "bad habit."

"She had a very large table next to her bed. She had a stock of pills there," Betty began.

Betty continued to say that she believed Marilyn "did not voluntarily take her own life."

In terms of friends, Betty described Marilyn as "a friendless, wandering person. The only people that surrounded her were people that she paid. And she paid my salary."

Betty noted two exceptions -- Joe and Joey.

"The only person who would come to see her would be Joe DiMaggio," she said. "He would come with love or his son."

Betty named another friend not on the payroll who was not set out to exploit Marilyn and that was writer and poet Carl Sandburg, who Marilyn would see in New York.

Betty said that Marilyn kept to herself, that she hardly went out, would eat steak for dinner at home, was quiet overall, never smoked and rarely drank alcohol then -- outside of sips of champagne.

In 1962, Marilyn would additionally form a liaison that would haunt her in her final months and beyond the bounds of her earthly life.

Though some will allege that Marilyn had entwined relationships with both Bobby Kennedy and the President of the United States John F. Kennedy, the author of this book believes there exists little evidence and a ton of propaganda to sustain romantic entanglements between either of the brothers. Accounts on this subject vary, most based on hearsay and range from author to author. Some writers have factually based proof swinging the pendulum to the side that there were no relationships. This is a topic that Sarah Churchwell airs out in her biography *The Many Lives of Marilyn Monroe*, displaying both sides of the coin.

Some have said the relationships Marilyn had with the Kennedy brothers began in 1961.

Although Marilyn biographer Donald Spoto, one of the most reliable of all the biographers that Sarah Churchwell dissected, leaned towards the idea of a "few brief encounters" between the President and Marilyn, this author disagrees entirely with Donald Spoto on the topic of an affair between JFK and Marilyn.

This author sides with Donald Spoto's take on Bobby Kennedy, when he wrote that there are "unfounded and scurrilous accounts" of their love affair and the pair "never shared a bed."

This author will not disagree however, that the Kennedy brothers were enchanted with Marilyn. She was Marilyn Monroe after all, what man was not intrigued by her? She was beautiful, charming, intelligent, sweet, humorous and fun.

Much of the Kennedy brouhaha started with the gossip columnists and shortly following Marilyn's death with the publication of Frank A. Capell's *The Strange Death of Marilyn Monroe*. This booklet outed a number of the sycophants surrounding Marilyn such as Dr. Ralph Greenson, the Strasbergs, internist Dr. Hyman Engelberg, Arthur Miller, Norman and Hedda Rosten, Eunice Murray and even Pat Newcomb. He pointed a finger at Pat because of her "influential friends in Washington," namely Bobby Kennedy. Much of the conspiracy in this account lies with Bobby Kennedy, his attack against Communism and how those surrounding Marilyn as closest advisors were teeming with Communist ties. And of course, the book alludes to Bobby Kennedy's tie to Marilyn's demise.

After Marilyn's death and before Bobby Kennedy's assassination in 1968, Dr. Greenson engaged in a conversation with a caller in a recorded conversation.

They talked about Marilyn's passing and Romi stated: "I can't explain myself, or defend myself without revealing things that I don't want to reveal. You know, you can't draw a line and say, 'I'll tell you this, but I won't tell you that.' It's a terrible position to be in to say, 'I can't talk about it because I can't tell the whole story.'"

After a pause in the conversation, Dr. Greenson interjected with the word, "Listen."

"Yeah?" the male caller on the other end volleyed back.

"Talk to Bobby Kennedy," Dr. Greenson replied matter-of-factly.

The author of this book believes that as Dr. Greenson had exhibited in all phases of his work with Marilyn during her life, his projection of his culpability in his role in Marilyn's death onto another target, Bobby Kennedy, was typical.

As it has been par for the course in the death of Marilyn Monroe, those present in the room when the police arrived have appeared more bumbling and incompetent in their testimonies than the Keystone Cops, in the sense that their corroborated stories have changed over time. Accounts from Drs. Greenson and Engelberg and Eunice Murray grew looser and more separate from one another over the years. Their stories when police first interrogated them on the warm August 1962 night in Marilyn's bedroom began their evolution from then on.

Eunice Murray's account vacillated in terms of her hand in Marilyn's passing. She never wavered in her book about Bobby Kennedy's lack of involvement in Marilyn's death. Since Eunice lied about all else her defense of Bobby Kennedy seemed out of place, which actually makes it appear more legitimate since Dr. Greenson tried to pin the blame on the Attorney General.

Eunice said that Bobby Kennedy visited Marilyn's house in June for a tour and was not there on her final day of life. She attacked Robert Slatzer's account that Bobby Kennedy stopped to Marilyn's that day and that witnesses at an afternoon card party watched him enter Marilyn's property carrying a black doctor's bag. Eunice would admit in her book that no card party could have taken place at the particular residence where it was claimed, because the purported host family was not even home until midnight that night.

A frustrated Eunice was apparently overheard making a confession after she was off camera when interviewed for the 1985 documentary *Say Goodbye to the President*. She had stated on camera that Bobby Kennedy was in the home on August 4 (which varied from her book).

She was said to say, "Why, at my age, do I still have to cover up this thing?"

While some consider her statement an admittance to covering up the Kennedy tracks, could Eunice have meant she was suppressing evidence to protect the memory of her friend Dr. Greenson who died in 1979, for Dr. Engelberg (who was the last to pass away in 2005) and to guard her own reputation? Eunice carried her secrets to the grave in 1994.

Following Marilyn's death, Robert Slatzer made it his life mission to throw the blame for Marilyn's death on the Kennedys beginning with his book *The Life and Curious Death of Marilyn Monroe*. Robert Slatzer threw himself together with Marilyn for a few photos in Niagara Falls and later made claims until his own death in 2005 that he was briefly and secretly married to Marilyn. He alleged the marriage was annulled within a few days because of pressure from the studio. He later emerged with false claims to have been one of Marilyn's closest confidants up until her untimely death. Marilyn was gracious to him when they met during her filming of *Niagara*, spoke with him and took a few photos. According to newsman George Carpozi's book, Marilyn once mailed Robert Slatzer a book to borrow, Kahlil Gibran's *The Prophet*. He in turn mailed the book back to her at the studio while she was filming *Gentlemen Prefer Blondes*. Those are the two only known personal connections between the two.

Yet Robert Slatzer and B-movie actress Jeanne Carmen cooked up madcap scenarios about Marilyn after her death, claims that have been proven untrue. It was Robert Slatzer who borrowed from the Frank Capell book, plus Norman Mailer's *Marilyn* to doctor his fabrications. During Marilyn's lifetime, author John Gilmore said Marilyn became aware of a story written in *Confidential* magazine in 1956 long after her Kahlil Gibran book was returned. It was one that the creepy Slatzer had endorsed and claimed he and Marilyn romped in the hay together in Niagara Falls. He alleged the phone was ringing off the hook from Joe while the rendezvous took place. Marilyn was horrified when she learned of this copy and those around her informed her to ignore it, in the days before sensationalist publications faced legal action from celebrities.

Both Robert Slatzer and Jeanne Carmen elevated themselves to the level of secret keepers for Marilyn and alleged that the two Kennedy boys were in sexual relationships with her. The duo claimed Marilyn chronicled the conversations from her lovemaking sessions in a red diary that was confiscated after her death and has never resurfaced. They swore Marilyn was privy to major governments secrets they had shared with her in their pillow talks. These range from the Bay of Pigs to Roswell. They concocted a hoax that Marilyn planned to reveal secrets to the press in a bomb-dropping conference on Monday August 6. Robert and Jeanne said both Kennedy brothers had promised to marry Marilyn and they jilted her, with the news conference her revenge (though Marilyn did not have a conniving or vengeful bone in her body). They claimed the brothers had a hand in killing Marilyn on August 4.

Robert Slatzer stirred the pot with a series of books, reeling in detective Milo Speriglio for the ride. Slippery Slatzer falsely cashed in as an expert and friend of Marilyn's (and claimed copyright over many of her personal photos), which dishonestly earned him dollars, endorsements and accolades for his invented connection to the screen siren.

Marilyn Monroe biographer Ernest Cunningham referred to Robert Slatzer in the book *A Marilyn Mosaic* as "the main villain of the Marilyn Monroe story."

"He is the single worst thing that ever happened to Marilyn Monroe," Ernest vented about the reporter turned book author and fraudster. "Stories that rob Marilyn Monroe of the love and respect that she deserves. These include the cheating and the promiscuity, the fairy tales of Presidents and politicians and Mafiosi, the visits from beyond the grave, the mysteries of flying saucers, the multiple and ever-evolving stories."

It was Marilyn herself, not Robert Slatzer, Jeanne Carmen, Frank Capell, or Norman Mailer, who first revealed about her meeting with the Attorney General. She wrote to her former stepson Bobby Miller to tell him of a dinner party she attended at friend and actor Peter Lawford's home, where she first met Bobby Kennedy on Wednesday February 1.

Apparently, she was asked to attend because Peter Lawford, married to Bobby's sister, asked the Attorney General if there were celebrities he would like to meet at the dinner. Marilyn wrote to her stepson that Bobby wished to meet her. Marilyn was seated next to the Attorney General and Kim Novak was on his other side (assumedly, he probably requested to meet her as well). Marilyn pressed Bobby with many questions about Civil Rights.

"He is very intelligent, and besides all that, he's got a terrific sense of humor," Marilyn wrote to Bobby Miller. "I think you would like him."

Marilyn also penned, "And he isn't a bad dancer either."

Marilyn said the Attorney General joked with Marilyn because of the quantity of questions she asked on the topic of Civil Rights and he wanted to know if she had been attending meetings.

Marilyn following a stage performance that she attended with the Strasbergs, in 1962. From a slide in the author's collection.

"I laughed and said 'no,'" she wrote, "'but these are the kind of questions that the youth of America wants answers to and wants things done about.'"

The Civil Rights topic was extremely important to Marilyn and she said Robert Kennedy offered to mail her a letter summarizing his responses.

"Last night I attended a dinner in honor of the Attorney-General, Robert Kennedy," she acknowledged to her former father-in-law Isidore Miller too.

She still affectionately referred to Isidore as "Dad" in her correspondences to him on that same day. He often signed letters with that title too. He and his wife had a genuine love for her.

"He seems rather mature and brilliant for his thirty-six years," she continued, "but what I liked best about him, besides his Civil Rights program, is he's got a wonderful sense of humor."

Later that day, Marilyn flew to New York where she spent a few days with Lee and Paula and to discuss the script for *Something's Got to Give*. It was her next film and the script was still being written.

Isidore mailed a letter to Marilyn in New York about arrangements he had made for a room for her at the Saxony Hotel in Miami Beach where she was planning to jet and visit with him for a few days. It was a fancier hotel next to the one where he was staying, The Sea Isle.

Pat Newcomb and hairstylist George Masters joined Marilyn in Miami, where she arrived on February 17. She spent three days entertaining her former father-in-law and then left $200 in the pocket of his overcoat. He learned of this gesture after her departure and objected to it. Marilyn looked out for the widower with love and respect and believed he reciprocated.

On February 21, a photographer captured Marilyn leaving from the front entrance of the Yankee Clipper Hotel a lavish venue in Fort Lauderdale designed to emulate the look of a cruise ship. That same day, the Yankee Clipper Joe was photographed planting a kiss on Marilyn's lips, as she was ready to depart from Miami International Airport. Joe was in Fort Lauderdale again working with the Yankees at training camp, this time in this city.

It is the last known photograph taken of Marilyn and Joe.

Marilyn was about to fly to Mexico and before she did, Joe sent her off with $5,000 to help purchase furniture for her home while she visited there.

Eunice Murray joined Marilyn, George and Pat and the group stayed for eleven days. After Mexico City, they visited Cuernavaca, Toluca, Taxco and Acapulco. In addition to furniture shopping, Marilyn met with business people, toured an orphanage and befriended Fred Vanderbilt Fields and his wife Nieves.

Marilyn appeared relaxed in Mexico and both Pat and Eunice recalled took no medications during her trip and functioned beautifully without them, even enjoying a full and restful sleep. Instead, she twirled around, modeling her new svelte figure to the press in a light green Pucci dress. Pucci was her favorite ready-to-wear Italian clothing designer, and she had been photographed wearing Pucci garb for close to a year.

Photographers snapped her too in a dress, another evident favorite, a black cocktail dress with a chiffon bodice adorned with foliage and sequins. She wore it in *Let's Make Love*, and on numerous special occasions such as for the David Di Donatello Awards Ceremony, when Nikita Khrushchev visited Fox from Russia, and when a Mariachi band serenaded her in Mexico. This dress eventually sold at the 1999 Christie's Auction for $79,500.

It was beneficial for Marilyn to be separated from Dr. Greenson. Eunice was unfortunately still there as Romi's watchdog. George Masters described Eunice as a "very weird woman."

"She was terrifically jealous of Marilyn," he said, "separating her from her friends like a divisive person."

Her return to California sadly returned her to the Drs. Greenson and Engelberg prescription abuse cycle. Eunice referred to their injected concoctions as "vitamin shots," which included barbiturates like Nembutal and the famous Mickey Finn knockout drops, Chloral Hydrate. The ill effects of these drugs continued to become more noticeably adverse on Marilyn's comportment.

One such occasion of a display was the Golden Globe Awards, where Marilyn was scheduled to receive her award as "World's Favorite Female Star" from the Hollywood Foreign Press Association. Pat Newcomb had suggested that a Mexican Screenwriter they had been introduced to on her trip, José Bolaños, should be her escort. This, Pat said, was to show goodwill to Mexico following their stay. Marilyn had proposed her favorite standby, Sidney Skolsky.

That night, Monday March 5, Marilyn teetered into the affair with José, ten years her junior. She shimmied in a skintight emerald-colored sequined gown that took seven hours for Fox seamstresses to sew her into.

"Her dress was so tight, she could hardly move," Susan Strasberg who was there reported. "Some people in the room stood on chairs, just to get a look at her, like kids. I'd never seen stars react to another star like that."

The green Norman Norell gown would remain in Inez Melson's possession after Marilyn's death, until she received a letter from Lee demanding she hand it over. Inez also had in her keeping the dress that Marilyn wore to sing "Happy Birthday" to JFK. The "Happy Birthday" dress and a Rodin statue were more of Marilyn's things he ordered be sent to him. Marilyn's green gown would be consigned for sale with Christie's in 1999, at a price of $96,000. Her award from that night sold at a final hammer price of $189,000.

José loyally stood by her side throughout the evening, holding her arm while her fingers intertwined with his as she held his hand. They were caught leaning into one another as they spoke in hushed tones and danced closely. Rumors flew of Marilyn having a spicy Latin lover, though this was far from truth. José departed shortly after the dinner.

All eyes and lenses were on her, as she kept her gaze and attention focused towards the presentation, becoming evidently fuzzy from her beverage, likely champagne or Sherry which was another favorite, that she sipped from a cordial glass. Her drink mixed with the unknown injected cocktail the doctors hopped her up with that day.

Still radiant and beaming yet droopy-eyed at moments, Marilyn received her call to the stage. She embraced her award, before snuggling into the arms of presenter Rock Hudson, looking up at him adoringly. She was photographed with her mouth agape in one of her electric smiles as she proudly cradled her award.

Susan Strasberg enviously watched from a distance, and later presented a jealous commentary about Marilyn.

"Even drunk, barely in control, overly made up, she still exuded innocence and a vibrant life force that surrounded her like an aura," Susan commented.

Susan said Marilyn hardly arrived to the stage, and when she spoke her voice was slurred during her acceptance speech, which she said was uttered in her whispery parodied voice of all of her onscreen characters.

"Watching her weave in front of the microphone like a hypnotized cobra," Susan said, "I tried to reconcile that befogged woman with the clear-eyed, agile-witted, sensitive person I knew was hovering just beneath the surface."

Judy Garland excitedly greeted Marilyn and the two longtime friends embraced. Like Marilyn, Judy herself was trapped into the vicious pill merry-go-round similar to the ones that the Greenson and Engelberg team were advocating for Marilyn.

A crush of fellow stars and fans greeted Marilyn for photos, autographs and to simply be in her space.

The news of Marilyn's demeanor was alarming enough for Joe, who conversed with her daily by phone. He jumped a plane to Los Angeles for a personal well check.

Although Dr. Greenson had invited Joe into his home for a Christmas dinner, Joe's first instinct to refuse the invitation for both he and Marilyn should have been followed. Now that Dr. Greenson had gained Joe's trust, the doctor was, behind closed doors, encouraging Marilyn to rid her life of both Joe and Frank Sinatra (although Frank was also one of his patients, and like all other additionally likely receiving dirt on Marilyn).

Joe found Marilyn at Dr. Greenson's residence the following day. An intern who was there witnessed something that made him uncomfortable before Joe's arrival, which was to find that Marilyn was "in residence" at the doctor's home. Dr. Greenson claimed to the intern he sedated her due to an emotional collapse. Marilyn resting upstairs in Dr. Greenson's personal home alone disturbed the intern and then he said the situation progressed in creepiness.

There were two interns interviewed who were never named in Donald Spoto's book. They were both in private practice at the time of their interview with the author. They reported that Joe arrived and Marilyn requested to see him after learning of his arrival. Dr. Greenson disallowed the visit, while Marilyn caused a stir upstairs in a way one of the practitioners described, "like a person confined in a hospital against her will who wanted to see her family or her visitors."

Dr. Greenson attempted to coerce Joe, by speaking with him downstairs about Marilyn's situation. Marilyn's upset escalated upstairs. Joe, having already emotionally conquered the Freudians at Payne Whitney, also did not accept the bill of goods and smoke and mirrors Dr. Greenson presented to him. Joe pushed his way past the doctor and headed upstairs.

What shocked the former intern and now prominent doctor the most as Romi Greenson's charge, a point that further added to the loss of admiration for the man who was then his mentor, were Dr. Greenson's last remarks on the subject of Marilyn. He considered them the icing on the cake.

"You see," Dr. Greenson told him, "this is a good example of a narcissistic character. See how demanding she is? She has to have things her way. She's nothing but a child, poor thing."

Donald Spoto editorialized that it was Dr. Ralph Greenson, who was the narcissistic one, projecting his personality flaws onto Marilyn -- a correct assessment.

Marilyn waited as the script continued to be prepared for *Something's Got to Give*, already way behind schedule and racking up the budget, although the picture had not even begun filming.

On March 15, Marilyn was hit with a high fever and chills from a virus. Pat Newcomb stuck by to help tend to Marilyn, while Dr. Greenson insisted Marilyn must increase Eunice Murray's pay, based on what Eunice reported to him as an increased workload. After a lambasting from the doctor, Marilyn subserviently apologized to Eunice, offering her twice her salary and retroactive compensation. Eunice asked Marilyn for signed blank checks as well for son-in-law Norman and his brother Keith to perform work around her home, an action Marilyn declined.

Though still battling her virus, at the end of March claims exist (though some deny) that Marilyn headed to a special event at Bing Crosby's home honoring President Kennedy. Other celebrities including Judy Garland and Bob Hope were said to be there. Here it was rumored that President Kennedy bedded Marilyn and presented his personal invitation for Marilyn to sing at his birthday gala. To the contrary, there was not an affair between the President and Marilyn and the invitation to sing came from his brother-in-law Peter Lawford.

Although a letter would come to Marilyn from their sister Jean Kennedy Smith, referring to Marilyn and Bobby as "the new item" hoping Marilyn could accompany Bobby when he visited east. Those close to Marilyn denied a relationship with the Attorney General. People like Susan Strasberg would claim one existed between Marilyn and JFK.

Ralph Roberts said that Marilyn approached him to inquire if he had heard about the rumors of having an affair with Bobby.

"It isn't true," Marilyn mused. "Anyway, he's so puny. Bobby is trying to break up MCA [her former talent agency] and he asked me to help him."

"She loved helping to do something like that," Ralph said.

It is known that Marilyn declined an invitation to a dinner hosted by Robert and Ethel Kennedy in June for Peter and Pat Lawford, with a famous telegram that she sent indicating she was unable to attend and "involved in a freedom ride protesting the loss of the minority rights belonging to the few remaining earthbound stars."

"After all," Marilyn wrote to them on June 13 less than two months before her death, "all we demanded was our right to twinkle."

Had Marilyn been so anxious to see the Attorney General and of course was close to the Lawfords, would she not have made sure she cleared her schedule for this event?

There was still a wait as the script for *Something's Got to Give* was finalized. Marilyn met with higher-ups at Fox and studio doctor Lee Siegel, who charged her up with a cocktail in her arm similar to the one mixed by Dr. Engelberg.

Marilyn was set to be the shining star in this film, yet was compensated meagerly though she was ranked high on the pecking order. While Marilyn was contracted for $100,000, co-star Dean Martin and director George Cukor were set to receive $300,000 each. Supporting stars Cyd Charisse and Tom Tryon were slated for $50,000 and $55,000 respectfully. Marilyn planned to be patient because she was committed to one more Fox film after this one and was then a free agent by spring of 1963.

On April 10 and 11, there were costume and makeup tests shot. Marilyn looked angelic with her hair pillow white and the footage radiated her mature and demure beauty and elegance. The film was an adaptation from the 1940 film *My Favorite Wife* starring Cary Grant and Irene Dunne. Marilyn played a wife and mother who was stranded on a desert island for five years, and returned after her family believed her dead and declared her legally so. Dean Martin as her husband was ready to marry Cyd Charisse's character, an action that Marilyn's character Ellen's return put the brakes on.

Ready to hit the ground running and begin filming, Marilyn awoke on the first day of shooting April 23, with an excruciating headache, laryngitis and difficulties breathing. She was diagnosed with acute sinusitis. The Fox crew was annoyed and shot around her.

Marilyn appeared refreshed a week later on April 30 and worked for seven hours straight with a 101-degree temperature, the sinusitis still lingering. Marilyn collapsed into bed at the end of her first workday after four o'clock, and the next day, Dr. Engelberg declared her too ill to work. The studio sent Dr. Siegel, who confirmed her condition, indicating he would not suggest even the film's Cocker Spaniel work if his health was like Marilyn's. Dr. Siegel concurred she must not exert herself for the remainder of the week.

The footage that Marilyn shot on this film when she was healthy enough to work was brilliant and reflected her luminous exquisiteness. Her interactions with the children in the film were emotional and sensitive as Marilyn found her way through the scenes. Her imitation of a Swedish accent was not only well crafted, but also endearing. Her comedic timing was sheer perfection and though the Strasbergs and others always tried to feed her otherwise, her gifts were truly innate. Marilyn's scene with the dog "Tippy," who she named in tribute of her childhood canine companion shot by a neighbor, was euphoric. Marilyn's love of dogs was evident as she interacted enthusiastically with her onscreen pet.

The crew juggled her schedule and Marilyn attempted to stay abreast of the regular script changes with Paula. The studio obnoxiously sent script changes via messenger to her home often close to eleven in the evenings. The studio appeared to be harassing Marilyn with various versions of the script, attempting to trick her that changes were not made when they were and vice-versa -- pranks Marilyn did not fall for.

A mix of unidentified drug blends she received regularly further weakened Marilyn's immune system and hindered her recovery from the virus. Marilyn made an attempt to work on May 7, only to be sent home with the chills.

Over that weekend on Saturday May 12, Paula and her sister Bea visited to dote on Marilyn with soup, and Joe also stayed the weekend to care for her.

"Joe was really the only one in her life then," Ralph Roberts told Donald Spoto, "and that gave us hope, for the rest of us knew there was something terribly wrong in Marilyn's relationship with Greenson."

Dr. Greenson's brother-in-law Milton Rudin who Ralph Roberts referred to as "Rudy," also questioned the doctor about his conflict of interest. Yet as the doctor's relative "Rudy" would always be Romi's advocate and on his side no matter what, tarnishing his relationship with his legal client.

Marilyn's chemical and emotional dependence further deepened with the doctor and she was devastated to learn Dr. Greenson and family headed for a trip to Switzerland and Israel on May 10 for five weeks. He left a prescription of Dexamyl, an amphetamine and sedative mix (the same one Milton Greene had ordered for her while filming in England), as a babysitter while he was away.

Before he left, Dr. Greenson suggested that Marilyn fire Paula. Marilyn dismissed Eunice Murray instead as she had grown agitated with her intrusiveness.

When Marilyn rid of Eunice Murray while Dr. Greenson was safely away, her condition improved and she returned to work for several productive days. The next day however, the studio was in an uproar about Marilyn's departure to New York, where she was scheduled to perform for the President's birthday gala.

For more than fifty years since this event, many biographers have erroneously reported "facts" about the Presidential gala on Saturday May 19. The purpose of the event was to raise funds to counter the Democratic National Committee's 1960 deficit. More than 15,000 people packed into Madison Square Garden in New York that night at $100 to $1,000 a ticket.

One online myth buster in this department who must be commended for an accurate and detailed account of the evening is historian Carl Anthony. He does an admirable job outlining the event, to show that there was truly no proof of a secret love liaison between Marilyn and the President that evening or any other.

Sadly with the advent of the Internet comes the endless stream of mistruths and doctored photos that can be disseminated about anyone or anything at the stroke of the keyboard and touch of the button. And unfortunately once someone reads something on a website, especially if a news site, they automatically assume it is legitimate.

The case of Marilyn and the Kennedy boys is a classic example of this applied into practice.

The story typically reads that Marilyn sang seductively to JFK, as if it was only the two of them in the entire building. Also, that Jackie Kennedy purposely eschewed the festivities because Marilyn would be present, although it was the President's birthday.

Truth be told, it was not the President's birthday, only an advanced celebration of his birthday ten days ahead. Some biographers will mention that while others will either purposely or irresponsibly and inadvertently ignore that detail.

Jackie was at a horse show that day and horses were one of her lifelong passions. The Kennedys had a retreat residence in Loudoun County Virginia in Middleburg. They leased "Glen-Ora," an estate property on four 400 acres and then purchased their own thirty-nine acre tract of property "Wexford," where they eventually built their own home. It was an area known for fox hunting, where Jackie Kennedy showed horses and participated in the activity of pursuing foxes. Caroline and John, Jr. (aka "John-John") spent time there as well, which permitted some normalcy for "Camelot" out of the public eye.

That day, she participated in a horse show at the Loudoun Hunt Horse Show. Decked out in equestrian gear, photos show the First Lady in action jumping with her horse and then later quietly riding on horseback with John-John on her lap. Caroline trotted on her own horse alongside of her mother.

A photo caption from that day read, "First Lady in Horse Show -- Mrs. John F. Kennedy clears a jump as she competes in the Loudoun Hunt Horse Show today. The First Lady is riding Minbrene which she jointly owns with Mrs. Paul Fout."

Another stated, "Mrs. Kennedy As Horsewoman -- Mrs. John F. Kennedy visited the Loudon Hunt Horse Show in Leesburg today and was a surprise participant. Mrs. Kennedy is mounted on Minbrene in which she competed in several classes. Minbrene is owned jointly by Mrs. Kennedy and Mrs. Paul Fout."

Jackie, well beyond the President's death, continued horseback riding and fox hunting, even procuring a weekend estate in Bernardsville New Jersey to engage in two of her favorite hobbies. Many photos exist over the years in varying locations with Jackie fox hunting while gracefully positioned on horseback.

Some commentators have downed the idea that Jackie could have seriously been interested in the horse show and was only using it as a way to pacify herself about the love affair between Marilyn and her husband.

This idea is totally false. For Jackie Kennedy had an affinity for her retreat area and spending time out of the public eye with her family. She enjoyed equestrian pursuits and absolutely despised enormous political events. Her absence had absolutely nothing to do with Marilyn, especially since Marilyn had nothing to do at all with JFK in a romantic capacity.

And why has it never been scrutinized that Lady Bird Johnson also did not attend the birthday gala with her husband the Vice-President? Susan Strasberg alleged in both of her memoirs that Lyndon Johnson stuck his hand up her skirt at the party after the gala, trying to encourage her to sit on his lap, while no biographer has noted that anyone pawed Marilyn that night.

Another connection can further verify Jackie Kennedy's lack of suspicion or concern over her husband's connection to Marilyn Monroe.

Approximately a week prior to the gala at Madison Square Garden, Jackie Kennedy played hostess at the White House, a role she did enjoy. The President and First Lady held a dinner on May 11, 1962 for French Minister of Culture Andre Malraux. Many talents in the arts were present including Arthur Miller, who Jackie insisted sitting at the same table with (Susan also placed herself at this event with Lee and said the two did not utter a word to each other the entire ride home to New York).

However, following Marilyn's death and his release of the play *After the Fall*, Marilyn garnered a posthumous ally the world would never suspect: Jackie Kennedy herself.

Like many, Jackie was disenchanted because it was obvious that Arthur modeled his self-destructive female lead after Marilyn. According to the book *America's Queen: The Life of Jacqueline Kennedy Onassis*, when Jackie was asked to support the American Theater she refused to participate.

She asked the person who coordinated a meeting to discuss the theater, "Tell me something, you are currently doing a play by Arthur Miller, is that correct?"

When "yes" was the response Jackie replied, "I won't have anything to do with that theater because of the way he [Arthur] treated Marilyn Monroe."

Why would Jackie have defended her after her death if she suspected Marilyn had slept with her husband?

As historian Carl Anthony had also so aptly pointed out in his writings about the purported fling between Marilyn and the President, while heading up *George* magazine, JFK Jr. considered the idea of Madonna on the cover as Marilyn copying the "Happy Birthday" theme.

The idea to recreate a Marilyn Monroe birthday tribute became reality for JFK's junior. In 1996, *George* magazine in honor of President Bill Clinton's fiftieth birthday featured Drew Barrymore on the cover as Marilyn's extraordinary look-alike instead.

"Happy Birthday, Mr. President," was prominently typeset underneath Drew's picture.

Had the idea of Marilyn Monroe been such a sore spot for his family, would JFK Jr. have so creatively embraced the idea of offering that homage to President Clinton? As classy and graceful a person John F. Kennedy Jr. was, it is highly unlikely if the President's degree of separation to Marilyn was so harmful to his family fabric that he would have approved this cover.

Much of the night that Marilyn performed for JFK has become the centerpiece for tabloid trash and sensationalized documentaries. Both types of media have interpreted their pieces as exposures of an illicit and blatantly flaunted relationship between Marilyn and JFK. Details reported from that event have also been doctored in such a way that it slants towards a romantic connection between the two, when in effect the evidence of a lack of affiliation has become so buried underneath the lies.

What is known is that Marilyn was stunning and glamorous in a manner that has become historic. Gowned in a sheath dress elegantly crafted by fashion designer Jean Louis, which has often been described as "skin and beads," the dress was flesh-toned, backless and then encrusted with crystals. As Marilyn had been with so many other affairs, she was literally sewn into this gown.

When this gown was sold at the Christie's Auction in 1999, it was placed on a dress form. When it came time for the hammer to begin falling on this item, the spotlight hit it, as if Marilyn was wearing it again on May 19, 1962. The crowd in the auction house gasped, marveling as Marilyn's voice wavered over the sound system singing "Happy Birthday" to the President once more. The auction excitement arrived at a crescendo with the dress selling for close to $1.3 million.

Most of the time the footage shown now of Marilyn's song has become spliced together in such a way that it wrongly leans towards an open flirtation between the President and Hollywood's golden goddess that night.

Often swept under the rug was how it was a star-studded event with Jack Benny as the emcee, followed by other Tinseltown favorites. Ella Fitzgerald, Jerome Robbins, Henry Fonda, Maria Callas, Eric Ambler aka "Eliot Reed" and Peggy Lee, kicked off the lineup.

Marilyn was featured in the middle of the program, not in the beginning or end as is often falsely alluded to.

Peter Lawford, Jimmy Durante, Eddie Jackson, Bobby Darin, Mike Nichols, Elaine May and Diahann Carroll, rounded out the entertainment roster, with Henry Fonda appearing again in the second half of the show after Marilyn performed.

Harry Belafonte was another celebrity photographed, though he did not perform. Vice-President Lyndon B. Johnson and Presidential Advisor Arthur Schlesinger were also in attendance, as well as some members of the Kennedy Clan, Bobby, Ethel Kennedy, Eunice Shriver, Pat Lawford, Jean Kennedy Smith and Steven Smith were present.

Before Marilyn's appearance, Peter Lawford took to the stage. Though, like other documentation of the evening, much of the events have been edited and sensationalized to falsely piece together a sordid tale of lust between Marilyn and the President. What is often emphasized is Peter's introduction to Marilyn, which some, again have incorrectly interpreted as an eerie prophecy of murder conspiracy theory or even a death wish on Marilyn's part.

"Mr. President, the *late* Marilyn Monroe," Peter quipped as she stepped up his side.

As someone who was a friend, Peter was joking about Marilyn's notoriety for tardiness, and he did not have a previous knowledge of her upcoming death.

The full dialogue from Peter Lawford, however, took place as follows: "Mr. President, on this occasion of your birthday, this lovely lady is not only pulchritudinous, but punctual. Mr. President -- Marilyn Monroe."

The spotlight swung towards the rear of Peter's shoulder, while the audience cheered and no Marilyn emerged.

"A woman," he continued feigning frustration, "whom it truly may be said, she needs no introduction. Here she is."

No Marilyn again and instead a short drum roll. Some laughter emanated from the audience.

"But I'll give you an introduction anyway," Peter stated, "Mr. President, because in the history of show business perhaps there has been no one female who has meant so much, who has done more..."

The crowd began to explode into a roar as Marilyn emerged, running out as if on her tiptoes and as quickly as she could be carried in her stiletto heels, the restrictiveness of her gown also slowing her down. A white ermine cape was draped around her shoulders. She reflected the epitome of glamour her head piled high with her sweeping bouffant hairstyle and dangling sparking jeweled earrings to complete her outfit.

"Mr. President, the *late* Marilyn Monroe," Peter said.

He took her fur and after revealing her gown, the crowd let out a collective gasp in amazement at her loveliness. Many knew at this point it was an extremely historic moment. Marilyn did as well.

She flicked the microphone with her finger and then the orchestra tuned up. She peered out into the audience, shielding her eyes, while squinting slightly from the lights glaring into her face.

"Ha..." she began timidly.

And then the affective, sensual version of the song:

"Ha-ppy biiirthday tooo yoooou,"
"Happy birthday tooo yoooou,"
"Ha-ppy birthday, Mr. President," (sung with a pouty emphasis on the words "Mr. President.")
"Happy birthday, to you..."

The piano tinkled as Marilyn continued with some special lyrics:

"Thanks Mr. President,"
"For all the things you've done,"
"The battles that you've won,"
"The way you deal,"
"With U.S. Steel,"
"And our problems by the ton,"
"We thank you, so much..."

Swinging her arms in a gesture to encourage audience participation, Marilyn urged the crowd next with an, "Everybody, Happy Birthday!"

Lee Strasberg later tried to steal Marilyn's thunder as he did all else that he took from her, claiming he was the one who taught the technique in singing "Happy Birthday" the way Marilyn did that night. Susan's memoirs refute this otherwise -- she complained that her mother thought Marilyn's version of the song was too sexy and Lee was so upset he did not attend the Presidential gala. Though Lee never mentioned her name in the section of his book *A Dream of Passion*, it is obvious he is referring to Marilyn's example.

"Let's say the actor take a song as simple as 'Happy Birthday,'" Lee wrote. "Instead of singing it in his usual way he starts by singing, 'Hap—py—birth—day...' 'No,' I say 'Not quite that way, just take each syllable and give it a full value –- 'Haaaaaaaaaaaaaaaap.' Take your time: check to see without moving that you are relaxed; check with the brain. Take new breath into the lungs, then the same thing with 'py:' 'pyyyyyyyyyyyyyyyyyyyyyy.' Commit yourself, make the sound. Then: 'Birrrrrrrrrrrrrrrrrrrth.'" Each sound is equal for no special reason, just to show that the sequence of the melody does not tire you, but you have control of it."

Marilyn lightly jumped up and down after her song while conducting the orchestra with her arms as a chorus of "Happy Birthday" repeated and a monstrous three-tiered cake was carried out for the President.

Most news and documentary outlets always switch what happened next for effect and to continue with the relationship spin to President Kennedy at the podium stating, "I can now retire from politics after having had 'Happy Birthday' sung to me in such a sweet wholesome way," as if Marilyn was the one and only performer crooning to the President that night in a private serenade.

What many fail to reveal, sweep under the rug, or simply are unaware of, are the President's remarks just prior to that line, which give the full picture of his gratitude to those all who appeared at the event not only Marilyn. This clip has been easily found on sites like YouTube.

"I got a telegram tonight," the President began, "which said, 'In honor of your birthday, I believe that you should get a rise in pay.' Signed Roger."

"And then," JFK continued, "it said, 'P.S., my birthday's next month.'"

The audience chuckled.

"But we are grateful to them," he said, "to Bobby Darin, and to Miss Carroll who was going to come, and to Miss Monroe," he gestured towards the rear of the stage, "who left a picture to come all the way East..."

Then the famous line overused in many documentaries erroneously as the start of his remarks, "And I can now retire from politics after having had 'Happy Birthday' sung to me, in such a sweet, wholesome way."

The crowd hollered in agreement.

The wheels of gossip began further turning and have not stopped since May 19, 1962. Hopefully, the account in this book will aid in derailing the rumors permanently.

When Marilyn died and prior, Joltin' Joe developed a strong hatred of the Kennedys and anyone affiliated with their clan. That included the Lawfords, as well as a further deepened hatred towards Frank Sinatra. As Joe had been in anguish when throngs watched Marilyn's skirt fly high above her head while filming *The Seven Year Itch*, he was convinced she had been a plaything of what he thought was a dangerous element.

"If one of those Kennedys had showed up," he allegedly remarked to none other than Walter Winchell about what would have happened if any of the above had crashed Marilyn's funeral, "I would have taken a baseball bat and bashed in their faces. All of those sons-of-bitches killed Marilyn."

Joe had his opportunity to confront Bobby Kennedy and did so without a bat, when both attended Mickey Mantle Day on September 18, 1965. Joe escorted Mickey Mantle's mother to the microphone.

Bobby Kennedy ambushed the dignitary lineup with a run from the dugout to center field as Joe was introducing "The Mick." Bobby made a beeline for Joe and Joe stepped away and back from his handshake. Instead of bludgeoning RFK over the head with his Louisville Slugger, he slugged Bobby with what was known as his "Sicilian stare" -- Joe's evil eye. Recipients buckled in distress over Joe's glare. Bobby uncomfortably moved down the line to shake the hand of the next person.

Joe once additionally required convincing to attend a charity gala at the Kennedy Center after reassurance that no members of the Kennedy family would be present.

On May 19, 1962 there was no private rendezvous for Marilyn with the President and Bobby, in spite of a photo that has been circulating and published since minimally the 1980s of the three. They appear in a cropped version of the photo standing in a corner as a lone threesome. In 2010, further outrageous claims emerged that this was a new photo that had been recently discovered and hidden to protect Jackie from emotional harm (the photo was first published while Jackie was still living).

The photo is snipped ad nauseam to support the cooked up theories of a love triangle, slighted Kennedy wives and Marilyn tossed around like a slab of meat between the two brothers.

In actuality the photo of Marilyn and the brothers when in its expanded version, shows Marilyn amongst a crowd. Historian Arthur Schlesinger was visible and joining into the conversation. Other partygoers including Harry Belafonte are noticeable in the distance.

Other photographs display some of the additional famous guests that night that the President mingled with like Diahann Carroll and Jack Benny.

Marilyn too was pictured with various people during the evening and was not kept sequestered in some closet by JFK and RFK. Among them were Maria Callas and Peter Lawford.

Marilyn had a date as well whom many fail to highlight as having had any importance that evening -- that was Isidore Miller. Marilyn thought he would enjoy the affair and he was her escort. As she always had, Marilyn doted on her former father-in-law, ensuring he was nearby throughout the evening and adoringly caring for him. She retrieved food for him and made sure he was seated comfortably. Photos show the back of Marilyn's head in the distance with Isidore next to her, in a photo where JFK was pictured speaking with Jack Benny and sister Eunice. Another picture was a panoramic style shot of Diahann Carroll singing at the after-party at the lavish Manhattan home of Arthur and Mathilde Krim. The crowd was seated and on one end in the corner was Marilyn, sitting with Isidore in her proximity, while on the other side of the group sat President Kennedy, smiling as he listened to Diahann Carroll's performance.

Marilyn's innocent candor about the entire evening was included in her final interview in *LIFE* magazine, published one day before she died. She had concerns about her etiquette in meeting the President.

"I was honored when they asked me to appear at the President's birthday rally in Madison Square Garden," Marilyn said. "There was like a hush over the whole place when I came on to sing 'Happy Birthday,' like if I had been wearing a slip I would have thought it was showing, or something. I thought, 'Oh, my gosh, what if no sound comes out!'"

"A hush like that from the people warms me," she added. "It's sort of like an embrace. Then you think, 'by God, I'll sing this song if it's the last thing I ever do. And for all the people.' Because I remember when I turned to the microphone I looked all the way up and back, and I thought, "That's where I'd be, way up there under one of those rafters, close to the ceiling, after I paid my two dollars to come into the place."

Then Marilyn described the event where she was photographed with JFK and RFK, and shows how she had only met the President that very evening for the first time: "Afterwards they had some sort of reception. I was with my former father-in-law, Isidore Miller, so I think I did something wrong when I met the President. Instead of saying, 'How do you do?' I just said, 'This is my former father-in-law, Isidore Miller.' He came here an immigrant and I thought this would be one of the biggest things in his life, he's about seventy-five or eighty years old, and I thought this would be something that he would be telling his grandchildren about and all that. I should have said, 'How do you do, Mr. President,' but I had already done the singing, so well you know. I guess nobody noticed it."

The next day Marilyn was back in Los Angeles, where Eunice Murray like a pesky cold, showed up to Marilyn's home. Marilyn had paid her in attempts to cut the apron strings though to no avail. Marilyn swept the situation and her feelings under the rug and acquiesced. A part of her was relieved that "Mrs. Murray" was there to help her readjust to her return.

Although President Kennedy did not recognize what Marilyn had thought was a blunder, the studio brass at Fox had considered Marilyn's actions in performing for the President and leaving the film after so many absences although she had been gravely and legitimately ill, as an inexcusable grievous mistake. Three days prior to her appearance in New York, Fox forwarded a breach-of-contract letter to both MCA and Milton Rudin for failure to work.

While *Cleopatra* drained Fox's bank account more than any other production nearly bankrupting the studio and its star Liz Taylor was filled with her own childish antics on the set (while Liz was slated to receive ten times the amount as Marilyn), Fox made Marilyn the example.

Dean Martin now battled a cold, and was asked to not be in close contact with Marilyn because of her own immune system weaknesses. Later, Dean ended up home for a few days to recover and Marilyn worked on other scenes.

Wednesday May 23 would emerge as another day to cement Marilyn in history. They filmed a scene where Marilyn was to pretending she was skinny dipping in a pool. Her flesh-colored bikini top to emulate her nudity presented difficulties and looked artificial. The bra strap was visible across her back in one shot when Marilyn was drying off on the edge of the pool. Easily solved, Marilyn removed the suit entirely and a rear image of her uncovered back was shot. Marilyn truly skinny-dipped in the pool.

Then it was Marilyn who suggested the brilliant next plan, which was to photograph her nude. She frolicked in the water then cuddled up in a fluffy blue robe for her exit. The swimming pool set soon became the most popular spot on the lot and two freelance photographers joined in on the action, capturing an overjoyed Marilyn as she relished in the attention she was receiving. Marilyn appeared even more beautiful than she ever had, her body more trim since her gall bladder removal, yet still feminine and signature Marilyn.

The crew and director George Cukor rejoiced after the long day, while Marilyn's body was shown from many angles, though still tastefully without frontal nudity.

The following day, Marilyn's health was precarious again, her ear aching from the arduous shooting from the previous day. On Friday, May 25, Marilyn shot her scenes with Cyd Charisse, Marilyn acting out the sequence in a Swedish accent. Her health condition was beginning to intensify, a fever surfaced, as well as discharge from her ear.

By the weekend, Marilyn had hit her sickbed again. With a fever of 102, she called out ill on Monday and then reported back on Tuesday May 29 for scenes with Dean Martin. The next day was Memorial Day and neither the cast nor crew worked. On Thursday, May 31, she filmed her scenes with Wally Cox.

The day after that was Marilyn's birthday, June 1, 1962. She did not realize it would be her final day on the Fox lot, nor her last scene to ever be filmed in a motion picture. She acted with both Dean Martin and Wally Cox.

Reaching age thirty-six, it appeared Marilyn had many more years left to enjoy though it would be her final birthday celebration.

Marilyn worked a full day and at 6 p.m. her friend and stand-in Evelyn Moriarty wheeled out a cake decorated with sparklers. A hand-drawn card with a cartoon rendition of Marilyn peeking over her shoulder and reading "HAPPY BIRTHDAY (SUIT)" was on display. Weird Eunice made her way through the celebration and left without a word while Marilyn enjoyed some time and Dom Perignon with Evelyn and Wally Cox before departing the lot with Wally by limousine. She toted her cashmere suit and mink hat that she had worn that day for filming along for the ride.

As the car crossed the gate, unbeknownst to all it would be Marilyn's final exit out of the Fox lot for work.

That evening, Marilyn and Joe spoke on the phone. He was away in Europe on business for his company.

He had sent a telegram earlier in the day from Madrid, which read: "Happy Birthday, Hope today and future years bring you sunny skies and all your heart desires as ever. Joe."

Marilyn dressed in her cashmere suit and fur hat for a charity fundraising ball game at Dodger Stadium between the Yankees and the Angels. The mission of the game was to raise funds to fight muscular dystrophy.

Her final public appearance would be in front of a crowd more massive than any other she had faced at once at more than 51,000 -- she did so with grace and enthusiasm.

Before Angel Albie Gregory jogged with Marilyn out to the field, she was told her speech would be at home plate.

She was still not yet versed on baseball terminology and reportedly replied sweetly and innocently, "Oh, that's wonderful, where's that?"

Yankee Roger Maris also joined Marilyn when she did reach her intended place. The muscular dystrophy cause had been one dear to Marilyn's heart in her past and she asked for support from the audience. Then she clarified she held a neutral stance for the outcome of the game in spite of her Yankees connection.

"I'm for both teams," she gushed.

She threw out the first ball of the game.

Marilyn blew kisses to the crowd, spent time with afflicted kids sitting in wheelchairs, signed autographs and listened to a children's choir perform.

Although her own Joe was absent, Joey reportedly escorted her to the gathering and then she was said to have enjoyed dinner with Wally, Joey and Dean Martin's son Dino. Marilyn returned home after midnight.

Though Dr. Greenson was away, his presence still loomed via a bill waiting for Marilyn at her house that night.

It is not known what triggered a decline that weekend, but Dr. Greenson who was still in Europe, summoned his friend Dr. Milton Wexler to pay a call to Marilyn. Dr. Wexler unlike his pal Romi, was said to have removed Marilyn's arsenal of pills. This was an action said to have traumatized her, due to the vicious cycle of pharmacy items the pair of Engelberg and Greenson had her hooked on.

On Monday Marilyn did not return to work, or Tuesday June 5 when Dr. Siegel from the studio was dispatched again. He observed Marilyn weakened from another attack of sinusitis and a fever once more of 102.

At this stage Fox viewed Marilyn as a star "getting her way."

Though Liz Taylor's poor behaviors on *Cleopatra* had far exceeded Marilyn's, studio executives and director George Cukor decided they must terminate and replace Marilyn after she worked only twelve of thirty-two days.

By Thursday June 7 a jetlagged Dr. Greenson was back in town and fired up. He and brother-in-law Milton Rudin attempted to negotiate with the stubborn Fox on Marilyn's behalf.

Ralph Greenson, one controller attempting to circumcise another, offered to help do away with Paula Strasberg. Once again Paula was viewed as a hindrance and thought her absence would facilitate Marilyn's completion of the picture. Romi assured the executives he could coerce Marilyn into fulfilling "any responsible request."

Executive Vice-President Phil Feldman suggested a consultation with a doctor of their choice to meet with Dr. Greenson to discuss Marilyn's case. Dr. Karl Von Hagen chairman of the Department of Neurology at the University of Southern California was their idea. Romi refused and countered with his suggestions -- a deal was not reached.

Romi was directing Marilyn's every move by now in her personal life and career, his grip becoming increasingly worse. Even with a contract that now permitted her creative freedom, the captors around her were limiting Marilyn's potential in her projects. The Strasbergs shut her from *Rain* and also *Breakfast at Tiffany's* (which her friend Truman Capote had written the part of "Holly Golightly" with Marilyn in mind). The therapists, both Drs. Greenson and Kris, rejected the idea of Marilyn starring in *Freud* in a role that Susannah York eventually took and director John Huston proposed Marilyn star in.

The reason? Anna Freud rejected the project and Marilyn would be playing a girl writhing in bed similar to what happened to her during "The Surgeon Story" session with Lee and Dr. Hohenberg. It hit too close to home. Marilyn was not allowed because she would be committing treason against Freudianism.

"I can't do this because Anna Freud doesn't want a picture made," Marilyn said. "My analyst told me this."

With the group at Fox, here was Romi attempting to oversee the entire chessboard of Marilyn's life. And the game was not in Romeo's favor.

The doctor was losing control and had his own tactics of convincing Marilyn to fill "responsible requests." Earlier in the day before the meeting, though it has often been written off as a fall in the shower, Dr. Greenson took another controlling step that most emotional abusers eventually escalate towards -- physical violence. He struck Marilyn across the face during a verbal altercation, leaving her black and blue and lacerating the bridge of her nose. Perhaps, he was also angry with her for dismissing Eunice while he was away. As his co-dependent in the situation and obviously intimidated by him, Marilyn covered for the doctor. He would have been subject to disciplinary action and public condemnation for acting in such a manner. He probably also pointed it out to Marilyn and like a typical abuser blamed her actions as the reason he struck her. He already had blamed her for his poor behaviors. He coerced her into hiding the truth through guilt-trips, threats, blackmail and other means -- from there Marilyn told the press the injury was the result of her own clumsiness.

Marilyn visited plastic surgeon Dr. Michael Gurdin who performed x-rays under the alias "Miss Joan Newman," a name obviously formed in ode to Romi's daughter Joan and his book *Captain Newman, M.D.* Marilyn was also reading the novel around the time of her death.

Though Dr. Gurdin reported no fractures, nevertheless he documented the swelling of her eyelids and face. A modern day inspection by medical professionals of the x-rays, which sold in 2013 at auction for $25,600, has uncovered a hairline fracture at the tip of Marilyn's nose from the blow.

One of Marilyn's hairstylists Sydney Guilaroff stopped to see Marilyn at her home after she was fired from Fox. She was leaning on the arm of Dr. Greenson, who Sydney described as holding a withering gaze "betraying a deep hatred for me."

After Marilyn threw her arms around Sydney in the midst of her upset, Sydney described the doctor's reaction as "almost violent."

Dr. Greenson pulled Marilyn away from her hairdresser and chastised her as they headed into her home.

"You're under treatment with me," he heard Romi roar. "You must never see this man again."

It was the last time that Sydney would see Marilyn. In less than two months, Marilyn would be dead.

The following day after the melee with Dr. Greenson, Marilyn received another slug, this time figuratively from the studio. They officially fired her then filed a $500,000 lawsuit against her.

The press had a field day ignited from the studio trashing her to the media about her insolence and unprofessionalism. Many writers chimed in with slanderous puff pieces to aid the studio in its cause.

"No star is bigger than the studio," Fox gloated.

Lee Remick who had two films left in her contract like Marilyn and shared the same dress size, was ordered to the set for pictures in Marilyn's costumes.

However, the studio did not expect a champion for Marilyn waiting in the wings. That same night Dean Martin announced he would not work with Lee Remick and quit the film. Though the tales over the years have alleged that Dean Martin was threatened with a suit for his action and then returned the threat like a grenade, some recent stories have come to light that he would work again, if a "suitable replacement" for Marilyn were located.

Marilyn look-alike Edie Adams, another star that also wore the same dress size and impersonated Marilyn, was also supposedly considered. However, Milton Rudin frightened the studio away with cease and desist tactics for stealing Marilyn's image through the use of an impersonator. His harassment caused Edie to give up her Marilyn impersonation gig altogether after subsequent legal threats of the same manner.

While Marilyn was now out of work, Pat Newcomb worked to occupy her with other activities, including some photo shoots, which would be cemented into Marilyn Monroe legend.

The first session was to be featured in Vogue and ran a course for three nights with various studio and indoor poses, ending on June 25. Bert Stern was the photographer who would later allege there was a romantic attraction between the two.

The next session was shot with photographer George Barris, another three-day marathon in which Marilyn romanced the camera for photos intended for *Cosmopolitan*. She had planned to work with George on her autobiography he said, in what she prefaced would be "the first true story." Obviously, she never intended for the book project to go forward that Milton Greene released after her death.

Receipt from the author's collection, of a purchase of champagne, less than two months prior to Marilyn's death.

One of their locations was Santa Monica Beach, where he witnessed a Marilyn with a "zest for living," who enjoyed champagne and romping in the chilly Pacific.

On Wednesday July 18, George Barris stopped by with the photos for her inspection. There was no mood of anything foreboding that he interpreted and in only over two weeks she would take her last breath.

"There is now and there is the future," Marilyn told him as he departed. "What's happened is behind...as far as I'm concerned, there is a future and I cannot wait to get it."

Earlier that month, Marilyn had met with LIFE Associate Editor Richard Meryman for his piece, "Marilyn Lets Her Hair Down About Being Famous."

Allan Grant shot some accompanying photos that displayed Marilyn's range of emotions during the interview -- some pensive, some beaming, and some goofing around while hanging from one of her ceiling beams.

During Marilyn's interview, she spoke candidly about the demands the studio placed on her, interjecting with anecdotes and peppering their chat with random thoughts, life lessons and recollections.

Her interview was slated to appear in the Friday August 3 edition.

As Richard headed out the door she requested, "Please don't make me a joke," of the upcoming article.

He turned as he walked down her driveway then looked back at her -- she waved and called after him, "Hey, thanks."

In between her two photo sessions and perhaps the reason Marilyn appeared more solemn in some of the Bert Stern photos and more celebratory in the George Barris pictures, was that the studio reneged on Thursday July 12 with their attack against her. They reinstated her with a $1 million deal -- $500,000 for *Something's Got to Give* and then another for what would be the film to round out her obligation to Fox.

There were several caveats during the renegotiations -- both Paula and Pat Newcomb were forbidden from the set and Fox requested that Dr. Greenson be removed as a negotiator (of course there was Milton Rudin who he spoke freely with). Marilyn agreed to the terms and in turn demanded that the screenplay be tailored to her liking and Jean Negulesco from *How to Marry a Millionaire* replace George Cukor. The studio reluctantly accepted both requests. The studio also withdrew its lawsuit (though the studio sought compensation from Marilyn's estate after her death, since the film was never completed due to her passing).

This meeting proved a victory for Marilyn and filming was scheduled to resume in September. Her contract was made official on August 1 only a few days before her death.

Marilyn's unexpected demise would interrupt the film's completion and it was shelved. The 1963 remake of the remake entitled *Move Over Darling* starred Doris Day and James Garner.

While certain facets of Marilyn's life were resolving, she was still cloudy in the Greenson and Engelberg haze. Both continued prescribing her an array of drugs. From sedatives to medications to calm her colitis to antianxiety medications, to her "vitamin" shots, Marilyn's body continued to be controlled by the "team" with their prescriptions.

On her final full weekend of life Saturday July 28 and Sunday, July 29, Marilyn spent time at the Cal Neva Lodge on the California Nevada border. The visit was documented in final photos of her with Peter Lawford, Buddy Greco and Frank Sinatra. Stories have surfaced about Marilyn having been subjected to gang rape by mobsters while there, which the author of this book believes to be totally false. With the Kennedy story determined to be bunk, it would have been improbable that the mafia supposedly retaliated by using Marilyn as their sex slave as revenge against the President.

What has been noted in several places is that Joe DiMaggio also visited Lake Tahoe that weekend where the Cal Neva Lodge is located. He apparently received an urgent call from Marilyn that evening while at a Mitzi Gaynor show. Some reports have noted a visual standoff between Joe and Frank Sinatra, while others that Marilyn overdosed at the lodge and was revived by Frank and Peter with copious amounts of black coffee.

In the week that followed, Marilyn made some extremely confident and life-changing decisions. That Tuesday July 31 author Donald Spoto has written that she contacted couturier Jean Louis's assistant Elizabeth Courtney for a gown design. This gown she intended was for her second wedding to Joe the following week on Wednesday August 8.

Marilyn made some purchases to spruce up the grounds around her home for the special occasion. She stopped to Franks Nurseries and Flowers on Wilshire Boulevard to purchase a bevy of plants. Petunias and several varieties of Begonias, tomato plants and citrus trees (lime, lemon and Valencia Orange) were several of the types of greenery and color she envisioned. Marilyn loved to garden and racked up a bill of close to $160 for the plants. She would never place them in the ground -- they were delivered the day of her death and were still in their pots when police and photographers tromped around the scene.

Whatever involvement Joe held during the Cal Neva weekend, he initiated some major moves too.

"Joe left us on August 1, 1962," Val Monette his employer reported. "He told me he had talked to Marilyn and thought she had finally agreed to leave the movies and remarry him and move with him to San Francisco."

According to Morris Engelberg, Joe told his friend Joe Nachio to keep his calendar open for early August and to come to California.

Less than a year prior, Marilyn had sent Joe a telegram signed "Mrs. Norman," addressing him as "Dear Dad Darling," in her usual playfulness. She informed him that after her plane had some trouble she "thought of two things, you and changing my will."

"Love you more than ever, I think," she ended the message with.

Marilyn told sister Berniece she had planned to change her will and was scheduled for an appointment Monday, August 6. Naturally that appointment would take place with Milton Rudin, who shared secrets with Romi.

That day "Mrs. Murray" announced her plans to take a month-long vacation beginning on August 6. In her usual non-confrontational manner, Marilyn wrote her housekeeper a check for the rest of the month, a severance pay of sorts, informing Eunice to not return in September.

Hattie Amos most known as Hattie Stevenson was Marilyn's housekeeper the last four years of her life in New York. About two days before Marilyn died, Hattie testified in an affidavit she supplied following Marilyn's death that Marilyn, who had instructed Hattie to regularly clean her home in New York even while she in California, asked her housekeeper to come to California to stay for approximately the next month. Marilyn would then return with her housekeeper to New York. It was within this timeframe that Marilyn fired Eunice Murray and was making alternate arrangements to begin her future with Joe.

Marlon Brando stated in his autobiography that he and Marilyn had caught up on the phone a few days before her death and he perceived her mood as upbeat, not someone he would have expected to take their own life as is often reported. He additionally noted that Marilyn expressed her dissatisfaction to him about the Strasbergs.

Although some reports have had Marilyn firing Dr. Greenson, he was at her home on Saturday August 4, her final day alive.

Pat Newcomb and Ralph Roberts were apparently in support of his termination, and Marilyn allegedly relayed to Pat that she was angry at the doctor not only for the abandonment with his trip overseas while she contended with the Fox issues but also the physical abuse and his attempts to place a wedge between she and Joe.

Ralph Roberts said that Dr. Greenson threateningly told him there was "not enough room for both Ralphs" in Marilyn's life.

It appeared Marilyn agreed and was ridding herself of the Ralph she thought the most suitable to go, and that was not Ralph Roberts, the one Romeo suggested she rid of. If Dr. Greenson had not been manipulative and able to give a relaxing massage instead of a punch in the kisser, perhaps he would have stood a chance.

While Marilyn demanded both he and Eunice leave on August 4, the two still lurked there.

The evening prior Marilyn and Pat dined together and then returned home. Marilyn's *LIFE* interview was released publicly the day of their dinner and had been excellently embraced -- she had much to look forward to.

Marilyn did not sleep well the night of August 3 and invited Pat, who was nursing a case of bronchitis, to sleep in the guest room. Marilyn was allegedly annoyed at Pat though after Pat slept soundly until noon while Marilyn struggled again overnight with her usual insomnia. Marilyn spent her final day puttering around the house in her white hooded terry cloth bathing robe, the one she had worn in her photo session on Santa Monica Beach with George Barris (that robe later sold at Julien's Auctions in 2009 for more than $100,000).

The accounts throughout the day have varied, though it is known Dr. Greenson spent a considerable amount of private time with Marilyn on August 4. Perhaps he was trying to save himself and make her change her mind, though he alleged that he stayed because she was distraught.

A call came in at about seven in the evening from Joe Jr. When interviewed by police on August 10, Joey said he called Marilyn collect from Camp Pendleton, after twice trying to unsuccessfully reach her earlier in the day. Once was at 2 p.m. and the other time at 4:30 p.m. He overheard Eunice tell the operator both times that Marilyn was "not in." Obviously Eunice lied, since Marilyn was home all day. The two spoke for about ten minutes. Her former stepson who was soon to be future stepson, was now twenty-years-old. The seventh inning of the Baltimore Orioles versus the Anaheim Angels game was on in the background at the time he reached Marilyn. He described Marilyn's mood as cheerful and alert, especially when he relayed he had broken an engagement to a young woman named Pamela, who Marilyn advised him that he should not be involved with.

Morris Engelberg's biography also revealed that Joe Jr. later said Marilyn excitedly told junior her wedding gown was ready for pickup on Monday. She told him she looked forward to marrying his father again.

A story was concocted about another phone call between Marilyn and Peter Lawford just before she died. He asserted she sounded drugged, though the call was later revealed an invention for a biography ghostwritten by his fourth wife. Though stories emerged also of individuals at a Hollywood Bowl concert apparently also concerned for Marilyn's well being, none of them personally checked on her, as upset as they allegedly said they were in their tales that they knew she was dying. Some claimed to have called Eunice. These fabrications also appear unlikely and just people looking to jump on the Marilyn death bandwagon, which continues to grow with a long list of freeloaders.

While rumors swirled that Marilyn was set to marry José Bolaños, those were also untrue. Nor was it correct that her Golden Globes date spoke to her on that final day.

What is known is Eunice Murray remained at Marilyn's home for what was intended as her final day of employment with Marilyn. Marilyn, she reported, said goodnight to her and then quietly closed her bedroom door.

Chapter Six – Love Beyond Life

At 4:25 a.m. on Sunday August 5, Sergeant Jack Clemmons of the West Los Angeles Branch of the Los Angeles Police Department picked up the ringing phone at the department's front desk.

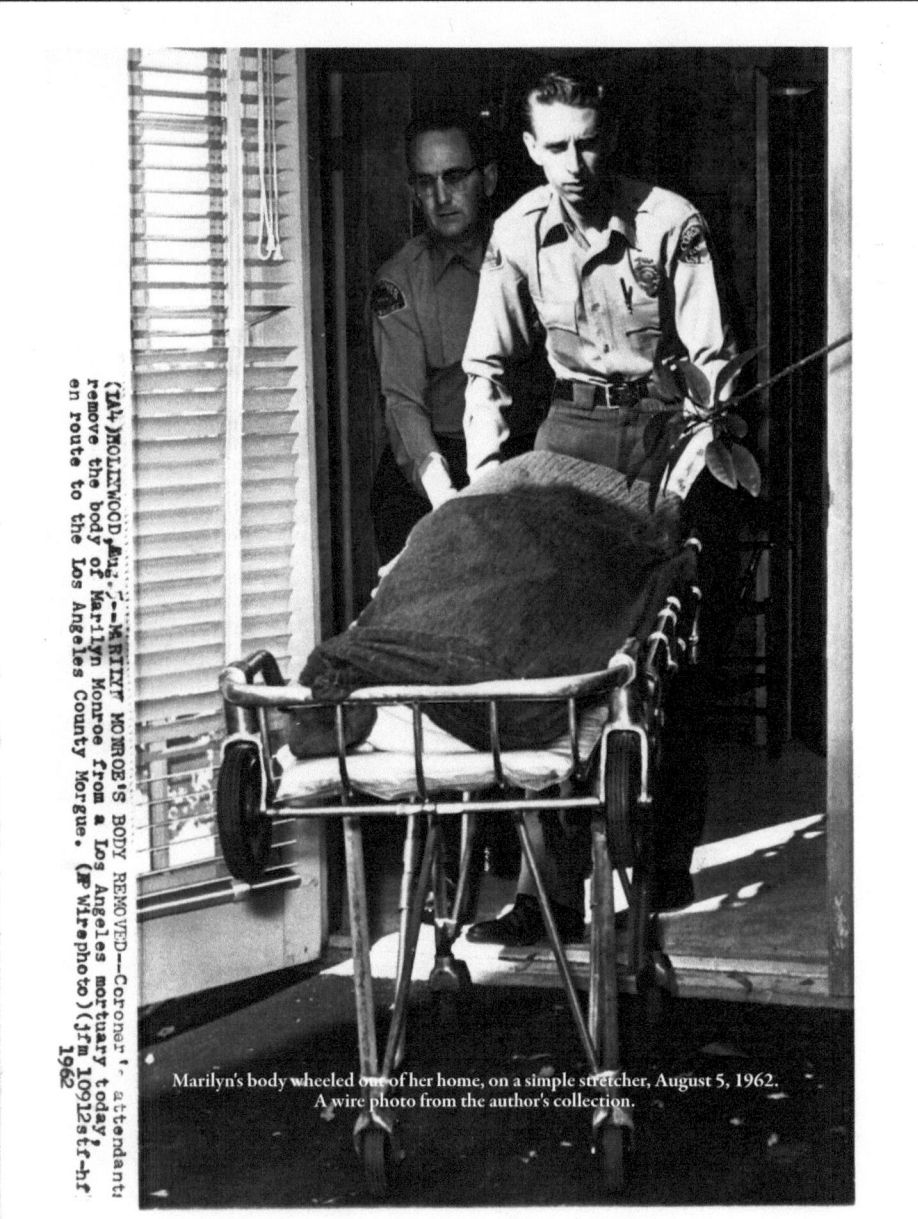
Marilyn's body wheeled out of her home, on a simple stretcher, August 5, 1962.
A wire photo from the author's collection.

"Marilyn Monroe is dead," the male voice, which was that of Dr. Hyman Engelberg asserted, "she committed suicide."

The sergeant raced into the dawn, responded to the address given and entered the bedroom. He found a woman lying in a swan-like position on her belly on a nondescript mattress minus a bed frame in a cluttered bedroom. There was a sheet draped over her body. Her hair was matted in the back and appeared greasy and her body and face mottled with spots.

Although she did not appear to be the celluloid goddess of the big screen, the sergeant recognized the actress Marilyn Monroe as the deceased. He questioned the trio in her room, Drs. Greenson and Engelberg and Eunice Murray. He found their behaviors suspicious, from the looks in their eyes, the snappiness and evasiveness in the tones of their voices, Eunice washing sheets and emptying the refrigerator and their allegations that they had first discovered Marilyn's body at midnight, over four hours prior.

Joe makes final arrangements for Marilyn's funeral -- which was held on the day that they had planned to remarry – August 8, 1962. UPI News Photo, from the author's collection.

HCP030605-8/6/62-HOLLYWOOD: Joe Dimaggio, former husband of Marilyn Monroe, leaves Westwood Village Memorial Park after making arrangements for the funeral of Miss Monroe who was found dead here 8/5. The actress who apparently died from an overdose of sleeping pills will be buried 8/8. UPI TELEPHOTO

The question remained, why had it had taken four hours to call? Dr. Greenson replied they required permission from the studio publicity department. Later, Eunice would state she found Marilyn at three in the morning and not midnight. The conflicting accounts would vary as time marched on.

Though the circumstances surrounding Marilyn's death still swirl with questions and controversy, the author of this book does not believe Marilyn took her own life. This author asserts she lost her life instead against her will through an overdose of medication for a greater cause, because the Freudians and the Strasbergs were losing her.

Her Last Will was to be rewritten that Monday to exclude her doctors, acting coach and others connected to her New York life. She planned to craft the will she wished to create to her specifications and to include a person who had never been on any of her previous wills, her future husband for the second time Joe DiMaggio. Joe was on his way to see her on August 6 as well, and those on the current will would lose out entirely if she was not stopped dead in her tracks, literally.

As mortuary employees removed Marilyn from her bed, she was laid on a stretcher. This was not a simple task since rigor mortis had already set in. With her corpse stiffened, the timing of Marilyn's death was estimated between nine o'clock until midnight the night of August 4, shortly following her conversation with Joe Jr.

Marilyn the world's greatest glamour queen was strapped to the gurney and wheeled out of her home. A generic woolen blanket covered her body. From her home she was transported to her next stop, the Office of the County Coroner.

Dr. Thomas Noguchi, who became known as the coroner to the stars ranging from Natalie Wood to Sharon Tate to John Belushi to Janis Joplin to Bobby Kennedy and more, performed the autopsy. Even with his skills, autopsying her was not an easy task.

"For an instant," he wrote in his memoirs, "I couldn't grasp the fact that I was looking at the face of the *real* Marilyn Monroe. It was the first time in my young professional life that I had been emotionally affected by a decedent on an autopsy table."

He remarked about his attempts to refocus and his Buddhist upbringing about life after death.

"But no one," he continued, "professional or not, Buddhist or not, could have been unaffected by the sight of the beautiful Marilyn Monroe, so untimely dead. I couldn't help thinking that here, before me, was a person so incredibly fortunate in every way -- from the endowment of an astonishing beauty to the talent and drive that had transported her from the ranks of factory workers to a woman who walked with presidents. All gone, so young."

Next-of-kin Berniece was notified. Berniece could not muster the heart and strength to identify Marilyn's body nor could Inez Melson, who was also reached as Marilyn's business manager and Gladys's guardian.

He would come to her rescue again. While Joe was at an Old Timers event with brothers Dom and Vince, sister Marie rang him with the horrendous news. A distraught Joe flew down to Los Angeles that evening, apparently refusing to speak to the press after he debarked. He checked into the Santa Monica Fairmount Miramar Hotel and sobs were reported to have wavered from his room.

Reporters tracked down Marilyn's first husband Jim Dougherty, then a police officer with the Los Angeles Police Department, on duty in his squad car.

"I'm sorry," he choked back without another reply.

Arthur declined to comment at all.

The next morning, Joe nervously took a deep breath as he followed an attendant into a room with fifty walled compartments. The gentleman, who had escorted Joe, slid the drawer out of Crypt 33 and removed the white sheet. There Joe saw his love, hair now slicked back following the autopsy, which had damaged her skull.

Joe was unaware that the day before, photographer Leigh Weiner stopped by to the morgue and captured Marilyn's toe tag number 81128, in a photo exposing her foot in the drawer. The photographer did not stop there and allegedly took a series of photos of Marilyn's dead body, over five rolls. He later said it was one of the most upsetting moments of his career and turned in all of his photos to *LIFE*. The publication had only released her interview two days prior. The magazine supposedly rejected the morgue photos, though the toe tag one has been published.

Joe, who had been shaking as he made this final walk down the cold fluorescent-lit corridor, began gasping for breath now while he viewed her. He noted the red blotches on her face, while answering the attendant's questions as calmly as humanly possible under such emotional circumstances. Yes, this body in the metal drawer was in fact his beloved. What a traumatic experience it must have been for Joe to not only identify the corpse of the one he loved the most, but to also have seen her in the condition she was, following the violation from the coroner's tools.

An excess of Nembutal and Chloral Hydrate found in her system was considered responsible for Marilyn's death, which was ruled as a "probable suicide." The "Suicide Prevention Team," which was headed up by Dr. Robert E. Litman, was formed on the advent of Marilyn's death and never convened for any other case. Dr. Litman was a friend and colleague of Dr. Greenson's and let the doctor off the hook for the death of Marilyn Monroe.

Certain toxicology tests were never conducted that should have been. Dr. Noguchi said that as a junior member of the staff, he had asked for all of Marilyn's organs to be tested and they were not. His superiors told him nothing more was required based on the liver analysis. The coroner wished he had been more determined in his stance.

Although Marilyn was not tested for Phenergan, this was a drug she was also prescribed on August 3. She had ingested one pill prior to her death, according to an accounting of the prescriptions found at the death scene. This is a drug with "black box" warnings that can stop one's heart especially when mixed with other drugs. This author believes the drug contributed to Marilyn's demise per her own investigation. Marilyn's system was not as acclimated to Phenergan as to the other medications that she ingested regularly like Nembutal and Chloral Hydrate. Dr. Noguchi noted that drugs taken regularly pass through the system with fewer effects because of tolerance. Phenergan was not a drug that she took regularly. Noted as an antihistamine, an anti-nausea medication and sedative, Dr. Engelberg, a cardiologist by trade, actually prescribed this drug for Marilyn on August 3 for "sleep." Marilyn was dead the next evening.

Phenergan and Nembutal were drugs both used in MKUltra experiments.

This author feels that verdict of "probable suicide" leaves the door open for other possibilities and the Strasbergs and the Freudians were let off the hook for their participation in the death of Marilyn Monroe. These parties have since inherited her items and finances -- both should truly be classified as "blood items" and "blood money." Marilyn had planned to ax these parties from her will and instead they axed her from this world.

Marilyn's items are now in the hands of many collectors, some who cherish them (including several items owned by the author of this book, in an attempt to rescue and preserve Marilyn's legacy), others who simply enjoy having a piece of history and others who have purchased them for investment and resale purposes.

The author of this book can vouch however, that sadly with the sale of her personal effects, Marilyn's items have ended up in hands of some who have no idea how to properly care for them. The author of this book has personally been shipped Marilyn's dresses, which were sent in two plastic grocery bags that floated carelessly around in a Priority Mail Box. Many collectors do not handle her items as they should because they are not museum professionals -- even some museum professionals do not care -- the author witnessed one museum curator throw one of Marilyn's garments casually onto a chair right after winning it at auction. Others have handled Marilyn's items with bare hands while placing them on display and damaged them.

A wire photo from the author's collection, released the day that Marilyn's body was found.

This has been the fate for many Marilyn belongings. Her things have ended up at times in a circuit for sale and then resale, being tossed around in ways that are demeaning to an American legend. Some are placed into the hands of individuals not properly versed in how to handle them correctly.

Not to mention that after their thirty-seven years in storage in an environment that was not climate controlled, courtesy of the Strasbergs, Marilyn's belonging suffered the ill of effects of floods, heat, cold, moths, vermin, theft and more. Many of her belongings are now rust-stained or with moth holes and all with the musty odor of the storage unit. Marilyn's items were never intended for sale -- in the 1961 will it was specified that Lee distribute these items "to his sole discretion, among my friends, colleagues, and those to whom I am devoted."

Lee toyed with the idea of a museum, though that never came to fruition and would have been the best solution since he did not plan on distributing them. The items would have remained together and not been scattered throughout the world.

To boot, a whole other market has evolved from the multiple auctions of Marilyn's belongings especially on eBay. Counterfeit items are up for auction on a daily basis with fake certificates of authenticity. This has also sadly occurred with Joe DiMaggio items, though not to the same degree. Validating these items falls on deaf ears with eBay, which at one time had a security department open to complaints, a department that has since been downsized. Their customer service group is difficult to reach. At the end of the day, eBay is also about the bottom line. For buyers, it is a case of "Caveat Emptor" -- "Let the buyer beware."

For those looking to purchase, whether it be an autograph or an article of clothing, it is important to carefully research the provenance. Since those have become tainted with many sources thought to be legitimate, buyers must be savvy and research into the provenances even deeper.

For example, who would guess that Bebe Goddard faked items with claims that they belonged to her own foster sister? Bebe purposefully engaged in selling phony Marilyn Monroe items to make a quick buck before her death.

Some have said strife existed between the two, because Marilyn and Grace borrowed details from Bebe's life story to make Marilyn's life story for studio biographies more interesting. Bebe had reportedly suffered abuse and neglect as a child, while living with her mother in Texas. Whatever the strife was between the two, it is possible it was one reason why Bebe decided to go forth beginning in 1996, to write a letter to a memorabilia fraudster and thank this party for permitting her to be a "rip-offer," instead of "rip-offee for a change." Maybe she considered Marilyn her "rip-offer." One would suspect items from Bebe would be legitimate, however never trust them. Bebe even suggested to the seller in her letter to dab Marilyn's items with Chanel No. 5, Marilyn's favorite fragrance, to give the appearance of validity that the fake items had belonged to Marilyn. Longtime collectors of authentic Marilyn Monroe memorabilia will know that no perfume will be present on Marilyn's true belongings at this stage, only the stale scent from the storage unit.

Marilyn was first sacrificed in the flesh -- then it was those who sought financial gain that cannibalized her legacy. Rather than keeping Marilyn's items together for a museum, Marilyn's lifetime has been instead dissected on the auction block, piece by piece.

There was something sinister behind her death, which did not check out as someone who truly wished to take her own life. There were vultures angered that she had planned to marry Joe again, as they would lose everything they could benefit from her when she did. With Marilyn's proceeds and royalty payments set up in a rolling manner, these parties would eventually cash in over the long-term, a benefit Marilyn never had the opportunity to enjoy. While Marilyn spent her life working tirelessly on her films, those who never knew her now financially profit from the fruits of her labor.

Though the Greenson family was never officially on her will, they certainly profited. The Greensons illicitly looted items from Marilyn's home following her death. One such item was a Pucci blouse, pictured in Marilyn's room right after she died and neatly folded in a pile on the floor that was photographed in her bedroom before the house was sealed. The exact blouse, which Marilyn had been pictured in for a series of photos before her death, sold at auction in 2010 for close to about $3,000. The auction catalog asserted that Marilyn had gifted it to Dr. Greenson's daughter Joanie. How could it have been gifted to the Greensons when it was pictured in Marilyn's home in photographs of her bedroom at the time of her death? With it having been taken from the death scene, the proceeds the Greensons reaped from that item sale are literally classified as "blood money." The removal of items from the scene of Marilyn's death, also points to the fact that those who were her keepers realized her personal effects and income would yield significant monetary worth in the future.

Joe reached out to Whitey Snyder the day after claiming her body. In 1952 after Whitey made up Marilyn's face following her appendectomy, she asked him if something was to ever happen to her if he could promise her to prepare her visage for the next life. Whitey gathered his courage as he approached her body at the mortuary, stunned at first by the vision on the steel table.

Joe and Whitey always held a mutual respect for one another. While Joe had been vexed about many men who Marilyn worked with, Whitey as her personal makeup man over her entire career had one of the most intimate of jobs, and Joe never batted an eye over it. In fact, Whitey and his wife often dined with the DiMaggios. It was Whitey who in turn while filming *River of No Return* in Canada had proposed to Marilyn as they rode a train together and passed a mountain range, that she might like to escape into the mountains with Joe and start a family. In Whitey's eyes, he had the foresight that Joe could and wanted to offer Marilyn a loving and stable home.

Joe asked Whitey if he could make Marilyn look as gorgeous as she had when she was onscreen. Whitey assured Joe he would.

"Whitey Dear, While I'm still warm," Marilyn had reminded her friend of their deal, with a money clip as a personal joke between the two.

What had been chuckles friend to friend, was now a promise made and about to come full circle.

Whitey hesitantly touched Marilyn's cold forehead, afraid if he did not make contact he would run in the other direction. Then he worked as he always had, once he was more at ease, as if it was one of the moments she used to doze off during the hours he applied her makeup. He convinced himself she was only napping as his brushes gracefully swept across her face, with his army of colors to revive her looks while she caught winks in her forever slumber. Soon, the haggard-looking corpse disappeared and he saw the beauty once again emerge.

She was outfitted in her Green Pucci Dress that she so proudly wore in Mexico, her ensemble accented with a green scarf. Her body had been lifted into a special bronze casket lined with satin. A false bosom was created since the autopsy destroyed the famous figure. Her hair, now appearing stringy, had also been ruined during the investigative procedures. Her mane was already susceptible to thinning and breakage from the years of color treatments and one of the wigs she wore in *The Misfits* was adapted for her burial. She had become accustomed to wearing falls as it was to add fullness to her damaged tresses. A wig would have been nothing new or different for her at this point.

As Whitey departed, Joe returned and thanked him.

The following morning, Whitey arrived early with plans to touch up her makeup, only to find Joe still loyally seated by Marilyn's side where he had left him, having stayed the entire night in a silent vigil.

While Joe still carried a torch for her, she had done the same for him. Located in her bedroom on August 6, was a note she had started to pen to him.

"Dear Joe," she wrote, "If I can only succeed in making you happy -- I will have succeeded in the bigest (sic) and most difficult thing there is -- that is to make <u>one</u> <u>person</u> <u>completely</u> <u>happy</u>. Your happiness means my happiness."

Still believing the Kennedys, Frank Sinatra, the Lawfords and Hollywood overall were responsible for her death, Joe insisted services be open for invited guests only and all others especially those mentioned, be barred from entry. This led to an outcry from those shunned, some questioning how the President's family could be disallowed. Her other former husbands, Jim and Arthur, were not in attendance at the services. Berniece reiterated to the inquiring press that services were private and Berniece, Inez, and Joe issued a statement indicating that Marilyn sought privacy in life and they hoped to give her a quiet sendoff in death. Marilyn personally was never fond of the large Tinseltown funerals and they wished to abide by her views. Columnist Jim Bacon, who knew Marilyn during her lifetime, reported erroneously that details for her desired burial were in her Last Will.

A heartbroken Joe, as he is escorted into Marilyn's funeral.
AP Wirephoto from the author's collection.

As savvy as he was with some details, Joe did not recognize he had shut out the wrong group. The true enemies were still within the confines of her funeral services and Joe had been snowballed by their shenanigans. Lee Strasberg amidst the crocodile tears delivered the eulogy. Carl Sandburg had supposedly written the eulogy, though some of the wording is pure Strasberg. Joe had initially asked Carl to speak, except the poet and dear friend of Marilyn's was unable to attend due to his own frail health. Eunice Murray was there and so were Dr. Greenson and his family. Photos show the doctor staring into the distance, a deranged, calculating and guilty look in his beady eyes.

The afternoon of her funeral scheduled on August 8, at 1 p.m., a car from the funeral organizers chauffeured Joe and Joe Jr. to the Westwood Memorial Park for the event. On the way to there, Joe broke down in tears and took his son's hand in his own. In his later life, Joe Jr. attested that during his lifetime, he never remembered a gesture that brought father and son closer to one another ever.

A.J. Soldan, of the Village Church of Westwood oversaw the services, reading from the twenty-third Psalm and book of Amos. An organist also played one of Marilyn's favorite songs, Judy Garland's "Over the Rainbow."

As it was time to say "goodbye" Joe, who was dressed in a gray suit, stalled to allow the other mourners to depart from the chapel. He placed a small nosegay of pink roses in her hands sobbed and uttered, "I love you" three times in a staccato tone, while kissing Marilyn on the forehead. Joey in his Marine Corps uniform stood at attention solemnly by his father's side, also grief stricken.

For Joe, it was the day that he and Marilyn had earmarked for their remarriage, and instead he had coordinated funeral services to lay his true love to rest.

The pallbearers wheeled Marilyn's casket from the chapel in the Westwood Memorial Park to a hearse and drove the short distance within the complex from the chapel to the area of the cemetery where she would be forever encased. She was laid to rest on the same grounds where her precious Ana Lower and Grace Goddard had also been laid down for their eternal sleep.

The walled area where Marilyn rests is now filled with those who have passed on. In those days, the wall was still fairly vacant. Pinkerton Security Guards and Los Angeles Police Department Officers advised the public and members of the press, outside of two photographers Leigh Weiner and Gene Anthony who were permitted to walk freely within the mourners, they were required to stay behind chain-link fences and walls. Some watched from atop the offices buildings surrounding the complex.

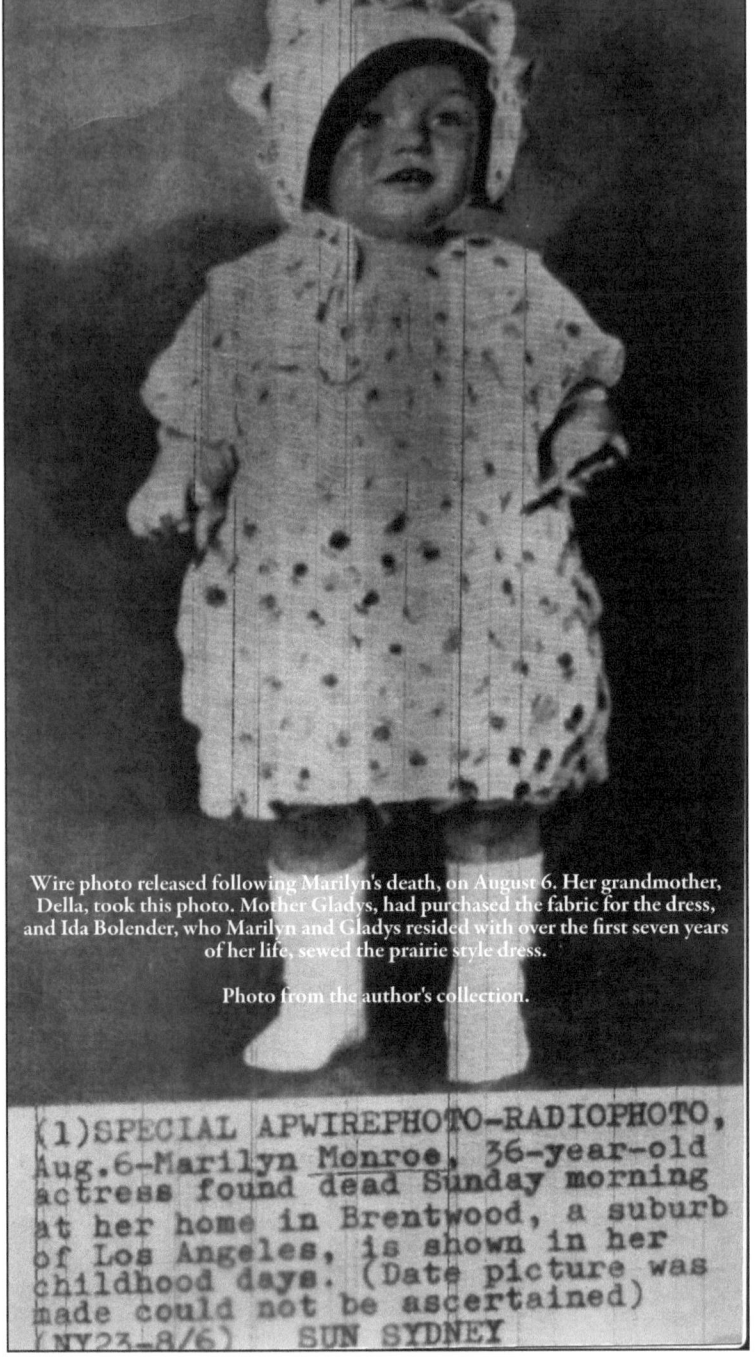

Wire photo released following Marilyn's death, on August 6. Her grandmother, Della, took this photo. Mother Gladys, had purchased the fabric for the dress, and Ida Bolender, who Marilyn and Gladys resided with over the first seven years of her life, sewed the prairie style dress.

Photo from the author's collection.

For onlookers, it appeared like a day at the races. Their arms hung casually over the wall, many of them were smiling, smoking cigarettes and bedecked with fashionable sunglasses.

Temperatures skyrocketed to ninety-three that day while the crowd of about 1,000 waited outside and about thirty-three privileged invitees remembered Marilyn from within the gates.

A small curtain covered the square cavern in which Marilyn's casket would be inserted and a somber procession followed the hearse, flanked by the guards. After the hearse arrived, Marilyn's coffin was wheeled over and slid inside its cubby, while the mourners sat for a short graveside service.

In front of the crypt the minister stated after reading the Lord's Prayer, "We are gathered here today to pay tribute to a grand, great woman. The going away of Marilyn Monroe caused great sorrows and was felt in the heart of millions..."

He continued, "She was a wonderful friend, God. I'm not complaining that you took her, I'm only grateful we had her."

In addition to Joe, the press reported invited mourners as: Berniece, Joe Jr., Inez Melson and husband Pat, Lee and Paula, hairdresser Sydney Guilaroff, Whitey Snyder and his family, Anne and Mary Karger, Pat Newcomb, George Solotaire, Eunice, Dr. Greenson and family, hairdresser Agnes Flanagan, maid Florence Thomas, Sam and Enid Knebelcamp (who had been Marilyn's guardians in childhood and were relatives of Grace Goddard), chauffeur Rudy Kadensky, attorney Aaron Frosch, attorney Milton Rudin, Walter Winchell, May Reis, Richard Diebald (a neighbor from New York), Ralph Roberts, Lotte Goslar (one of Marilyn's early movement teachers), Pearl Porter (another hairstylist, also known as Pearl Porterfield, a colorist who worked on both Marilyn's and Jean Harlow's hair) and E.S. Goddard (the initials for Ervin Silliman Goddard, Marilyn's foster father, Doc).

The day of Marilyn's funeral, which was heavily guarded, and attended by a small group of invited guests. Joe was one of the coordinators of the services. UPI Wire Photo, from the author's collection.

Though friends like Frank Sinatra, Shelley Winters, Clifton Webb and Jack Benny were uninvited they had a presence by osmosis because of the flowers they sent. Some reports have placed characters like Sinatra at the scene -- no photos exist of Frank Sinatra lurking in the wings even with the many photographers on scene.

There was an outcry from those banned from the services, Peter Lawford yelling the loudest. Pat Lawford had flown in from the Kennedy compound in Hyannis Port Massachusetts, only to learn she and her husband were excluded from the event.

"Marilyn had lots of good friends here in town who will miss her terribly and would love to have attended her final rites," a plaintive Peter bellowed to the papers.

He told reporters that he had been acquainted with Marilyn since 1949 and "loved her dearly."

Another unnamed star threw inaccurate retaliatory barbs at Berniece.

"Some of the people at the funeral barely knew Marilyn," the one unknown person griped. "Her half-sister, who apparently is in charge of inviting or barring guests, only met Marilyn once in her whole lifetime, last summer."

Continuing on their slighted tirade, this person jabbed, "I think it's a shame Marilyn's friends could not be there to pay their final respects."

Arthur Jacobs, who had been one of Marilyn's longtime publicists, commented, "About half of the people in there would not even be there if Marilyn had anything to do with the invitations -- a lot more of her friends would have been there."

An unidentified spokesman for Joe stated, "If we would allow the Lawfords in, then we would have to allow half of the big stars in Hollywood. Then this whole thing would turn into a circus. I hope Marilyn's friends understand this."

Milton Rudin, who was in attendance, questioned Joe for barring "important people" from partaking in the final goodbyes.

"If it wasn't for them, she'd still be here," Joe snapped back.

George Solotaire in the midst of the upset suffered a small heart spasm and was taken to rest in the cemetery office, before he was escorted to his waiting limousine.

Many have said that Joe letting down his usual expressionless guard in favor of noticeable tears and grief was the most notable and sincere gesture of all. Though publicly most of his lifetime he appeared icy and could be jagged in terms of his personality, there was an obvious and deep sensitivity that he finally permitted the world to glimpse before retreating once again into his protective shell.

After the invited guests departed including Joe and Joe Jr., pandemonium commenced. After about the 200 remaining fans thought they had their cue, they jumped over the wall, trampling grass and flowers on surrounding graves as they tore towards Marilyn's crypt.

Large floral arrangements, that surrounded Marilyn's crypt, including a rose-filled heart from Joe, were soon dismembered and torn to shreds by the crowd. Guards protected Marilyn's vault, not yet sealed, from the melee, fearful of a possible pilfering while her flowers were destroyed.

Some onlookers were dismayed and expressed their disgust at the rioting.

"It's silly to leave them [the flowers] here," one defensive plunderer hissed, "they'd just die."

After the throng of rose stealers dissipated and Marilyn's coffin was officially cemented in, Joe returned that evening at 5:30 p.m. with a friend. He did not exit the vehicle and he mourned Marilyn quietly from a distance.

The Friday following the funeral (two days later), Joe stopped to the Westwood Memorial Park before heading for a jaunt to Coronado and Mexico to seek some relief from the constant press about her death and the bombardment of speculation already commencing.

Joe wished to say goodbye, yet her crypt was jammed with fans visiting to pay their respects. Guy Hockett, the managing director of the cemetery, advised the crowd that Joe was nearby and hoped to visit with Marilyn. Unlike the crowd on Wednesday afternoon, this group of about thirty stepped back and dispersed to permit Joe his time with Marilyn.

According to Morris Engelberg's book, Joe took a trip to the Westwood Memorial Park once with sportswriter Arthur Richman, who handled media relations for both the Yankees and the Mets. It was after midnight following a sports dinner and the two stood silently in the night for a brief visit.

Joe's friend Dr. Rock Positano shared about a trip to Westwood in the book as well a few years before Joe died. Joe remained in their car and instead sent his friend out on an intelligence-gathering mission. Joe requested to know what the area around her crypt looked like. The doctor reported to Joe that he saw Marilyn's crypt and a stone bench, which was dedicated there on August 5, 1992 by the fan clubs "All About Marilyn," and "Marilyn Remembered."

"Rock," Joe told him, "a guy has been waiting for thirty years to get a picture of me visiting her. It's worth $10 million. Let him wait."

On August 4, 1962 not only did Marilyn Monroe physically die, a part of Joe DiMaggio did as well. She had enriched his life for more than a decade and even during the periods of separation. Of course the two fought bitterly at some moments, in the end though they made their way back to one another and never stopped caring for each other. Their hearts and souls finally connected into a deeper, more mature and grounded type of love. Their souls became entwined with one another. It was a rare type of love that many dream about and only a few are truly blessed to find. For the remainder of his time on this planet, Joe never stopped caring either and did so in his dignified fashion.

Joe mourned her physically from the distance for the rest of his days. Though it is known he paid several clandestine visits to her crypt, he grieved and visited her closely in his heart forever.

For the next six weeks following her death, Joe hid in his home in San Francisco. Already sullen at times naturally, he now was easily curt especially towards those closest to him because of the rawness he was now experiencing to the depths of his core.

Unlike Jim Dougherty and Arthur Miller, for Joe Marilyn was off limits in terms of public commentary. He would thwart any attempts to pry for information and was not fooled by veiled attempts from those who feigned they would talk baseball only to segue to the topic of Marilyn. While Jim and Arthur would write books and of course, Arthur vented his frustrations too about Marilyn in his "tribute" *After The Fall*, Joe continued his quiet vigil for the remainder of his days for the one he loved. Though always the shrewd businessman, true love could never be bought and even as $50,000 was dangled in front of him for a *McCall's* interview about his life with Marilyn, Joe did not bite the bait -- he was never a sellout. Joe was known to storm out of events when they turned into an inquisition about Marilyn.

A grief-stricken Joe, cannot mask his sadness on August 8, 1962, as he says his goodbyes to Marilyn. Photo from the author's collection.

Marilyn found it romantic how William Powell had flowers delivered weekly to Jean Harlow, the platinum Hollywood predecessor she had admired since she was a child and to whom she was often compared to while she was alive. As she had requested from Whitey the makeup application, she asked Joe if he outlived her if he could also have flowers delivered to her grave in the same manner. It was a promise that Joe kept too. Like Joe did for Marilyn at the time of her funeral, William Powell also sent his Jean to her eternal rest with her favorite flower and placed a gardenia bloom in her hands. As the herd mangled Marilyn's flowers, ironically groupies also stole flowers from Jean Harlow's mausoleum following her service.

Twice weekly and as late as 1982, delivery man Jim Pierce of Parisian Florist, the florist that Joe had contracted out for the task right after her death, would approach Marilyn's pink marble crypt with a bouquet of a half a dozen roses accented with baby's breath and ferns. Joe had spent in the thousands on flowers by this time with the red long-stemmed roses for Marilyn tallying to $3 per bloom around the twentieth anniversary of her death.

At the end of August 1982, a mutual friend of Joe's and Bob Alhanati, a co-owner of Parisian Florist, reached out on Joe's behalf to request the flower delivery be ceased without explanation why. When the press attempted to reach Joe they were unable to. A reporter reached his sister Marie and she refused to specify.

In Ernest Cunningham's book *The Ultimate Marilyn*, the author stated that Joe ended flower deliveries, "reasoning that the money could be put to better use by the children's charities that Marilyn had helped to support."

Richard Ben Cramer author of *Joe DiMaggio: The Hero's Life* told CNN in an interview in 2000 that Joe stopped the flower deliveries because, "people were stealing his roses."

The opportunist Robert Slatzer however reached out to the press in a superman attempt, claiming that he "will see to it she has flowers forever."

The man who generated the fake husband claims also falsified, "I've been giving her flowers for sixteen years. She loves them. She deserves them."

An online Australian publication *The Age* would report Robert Slatzer had the largest floral tribute for Marilyn at her crypt on the fortieth anniversary of her death, though no further report of flowers from him has surfaced. It was also the slimy Robert Slatzer who would report another ominous person enlisted him, and he joined Anton LaVey founder of the Church of Satan, at Marilyn's crypt on the eleventh anniversary of her death. They supposedly held a séance in 1973 with Robert claiming after she was "summoned," Marilyn appeared to them and walked by vanishing into mid-air afterward.

Joe lingered in his silence about his Marilyn, feeling that standing on a soapbox would only violate her further. He continued to live, though he was no longer alive technically in many ways. Over the years, his relationship with Joe Jr. would further deteriorate with some feeling only Marilyn could have bridged the gap to keep father and son together. With a spirit of wiping people from his life easily when he was offended, which was often, Joe was constantly in fights with various individuals even cutting his own siblings out of the picture.

"Where have you gone Joe DiMaggio?" was the question Paul Simon posed in his song "Mrs. Robinson."

When Joe ran into the singer in the '70s in New York, he expressed his consternation -- first, over the songwriter using his name without permission and royalties and then for a greater reason.

"What I don't understand," Joe responded, "is why you ask me where I've gone? I just did a Mr. Coffee commercial. I'm a spokesman for the Bowery Savings Bank and I haven't gone anywhere."

Yet Joe's heart disappeared as he accepted his accolades and awards as the "Greatest Living Player" in 1969 and was the recipient of the Presidential Medal of Freedom in 1977. Joe received these honors alone. Already a loner by nature, he continued on his solitary odyssey of money making from marketing his own image. In between games of golf and an active lifestyle as a living Yankee legend, Joe's home base was Hollywood Florida where he relocated in lieu of San Francisco, because the climate quelled his progressing arthritis. While Marilyn was frozen in time at age thirty-six, time of course marched on for Joe. He shunned painkillers for his aching bones. Though still a handsome silver-haired gentleman, the effects of aging continued to take their toll. Osteoporosis diminished his height, a pacemaker kept his heart on track and his left eye battled consistent tearing from a case of dry eye in his last years.

Joe became a bat-signing machine, garnering up to $350,000 per memorabilia show (and $3 million to autograph 1,941 bats, in commemoration of "The Streak") in between life as the token retired baseball dynamo and honored guest at many black tie affairs and parades. Joe also worked as Vice-President and coach for the Oakland A's and was on the Board of Directors for the Baltimore Orioles.

Joe was a doting grandfather and great-grandfather and enjoyed the company of those in his inner circle who surrounded him in his final years. At the end of the day though, he had no love to come home to as he had hoped he could with Marilyn when they married for the first time and after they anticipated marriage for the second time. Had she lived, it is most definite Mrs. Marilyn DiMaggio would have proudly been on her husband's arm as he was bestowed the many special honors, adoringly standing by with a loving smile.

Joe also had a renewed interest in Marilyn both personally and professionally the second time around. It is clear that he would have been there for her in whatever way he could have.

Sometimes even in Joe's final years, Morris Engelberg who knew him well those last sixteen, wrote in his biography about Joe that Joe would occasionally stop suddenly and drop his head in the middle of a conversation.

When asked why, Joe would reply, "Don't you know? Don't you know?"

It was in those moments, that his grief over Marilyn would unexpectedly sideline him.

All of those dreams were stolen from both Joe and Marilyn on that August day in 1962 when the world lost her. He would not have a significant other to rejoice in these special moments with. It is likely Marilyn could have lived a long life, as outside of her grandmother Della, the females in her direct family line including her mother have mostly survived beyond their seventies. If that was the case, Marilyn and Joe could have hopefully aged gracefully together. Instead, Joe lived every day of those almost thirty-seven years silently missing her, wishing the outcome could have been different and anticipating the day when they would be reunited again.

One journalist wrote when both were still living, and after they had separated: "Like her, he was lonely. Like her, he was famous, and surrounded by people who offered their time, presence, laughter -- but seldom their love."

It was Joe who founded in his elder years in 1992 the Joe DiMaggio Children's Hospital in Hollywood Florida because of his lifelong love of children. It was a strange irony since his relationship with Joe Jr. was so strained. Joe funded the hospital expenses in a medical center where any child, no matter their family's income level, would be eligible for treatment. In addition, Joe spent those later years visiting children who were patients there, offering pep talks to older kids, shaking hands with their family members and being photographed cradling small babies. This would have made Marilyn smile, as causes with children and even visits to children's hospitals and orphanages, was a service she often performed in many communities wherever she traveled and lived. Perhaps it was Marilyn in his mind when he chose to spearhead this effort.

Marilyn remained publicly a taboo word because as he did with her in the flesh, he strongly guarded her memory in death. He was ready to pounce on any offender who slighted her or attempted to press for information about her.

It is not often publicized who Joe dated and if he did in the years following Marilyn's death. Joe was an extraordinarily private person. Actress Mamie Van Doren, vibrant blonde actress and an avid baseball fan, described her encounter with Joe in 1965 on her blog. The two spent an evening together at her home, she has written, enjoying some dinner and chocolate almond ice cream.

"I could sense an undercurrent of melancholy," she said of her visit with Joe, who stopped to Mamie's in Los Angeles on his way to Hawaii to visit a friend who was ill.

"He spoke wistfully of Marilyn and his career," Mamie wrote.

Mamie shared her stories about Marilyn with him, including the time the two met up in the Russian Tea Room in New York. Mamie has claimed that Marilyn did have an affair with JFK.

The two exited to Mamie's patio, where Joe intended to smoke a cigarette. Mamie, who has been openly candid about the loves in her life on her blog, said instead of a cigarette Joe kissed her. Though Mamie rarely spares the details of her romantic life in her writings, she only mentioned nothing more than a kiss from Joe, which would be typical of this man who was always a gentleman that conducted himself with classy decorum.

"As we did," she said of the kiss, "I couldn't help wondering if he was thinking of me or Marilyn."

Not every encounter with women was as pleasant or welcome as the one Mamie described about her time with Joe. One night at a supper club in 1966, a drunken woman stumbled over to him and then became angered when Joe did not invite her to sit at his table.

"All right, I guess I'm *not* Marilyn Monroe," she slurred.

Joe attempted to ignore the dig, which she repeated to incite a reaction. Joe was now ready to explode.

"No, I wish you were, but you're not," he fired back.

The woman retreated after realizing she may have committed an offense and then asked, "Am I saying something wrong?"

"You already have," Joe snapped before requesting, "Now will you please leave me alone?"

It was also evident Joe cherished Marilyn's memory so deeply because in the family's San Francisco home, along with his portrait hanging on the wall, there was also a painting of her directly facing it. When the earthquake struck the family home in 1989 devastating it, Joe flew to San Francisco and the pictures were still hanging. In addition to seeking out his sister Marie, who was among the missing and safely at a home of a friend, he dragged out a garbage bag, which was later revealed reportedly to have contained a stash of $600,000 cash.

He revered Marilyn so greatly that among his refusals of pieces people requested to autograph were Mr. Coffee items or any Marilyn Monroe memorabilia. It was reported less than a year after his death that his signature on first edition of Playboy in which Marilyn's "Golden Dreams" photo appeared, sold at auction for $40,250. The author of this book does not question the occurrence of the auction yet distrusts the validity of the signature. Joe possessed such a deep respect for Marilyn that signing a piece of memorabilia with a nude photo of her would have gone against everything he believed in. Not to mention, the sight of Marilyn scantily clothed was upsetting enough for him. A nudie photo though he obviously knew they existed would have sent him into orbit. Marilyn's name itself was off-limits in terms of public mention -- to sign a piece of Marilyn ephemera would have been against Joe's personal moral code.

There were of course highlights to Joe's later life. Becoming a legend had its privileges. In 1987, President Ronald Reagan invited Joe to a White House dinner honoring Russian leader Mikhail Gorbachev.

On the receiving line, the greeter asked Joe how he would like to be introduced.

"Just Joe DiMaggio," Joe replied humbly.

President Reagan turned to the Soviet chief and commented, "This is one of our greatest players in the United States."

Though President Reagan obviously revered Joe, for the first time, Joe turned the tables on his protocol for signing baseballs and asked the President and Mr. Gorbachev to sign one for him. His granddaughter Paula now apparently cherishes the ball.

"In my life that's the only time I ever asked anybody to sign a baseball," Joe said. "But I was a witness to history."

President George H.W. Bush invited Joe and Ted Williams to the White House for a special dinner in 1991 and flew the baseball stars in Air Force One. The President and son Jeb played golf with Joe as well in Florida. President George W. Bush and Joe met at a dinner in Texas once and Joe was amazed by the resemblance between father and son.

Joe was not awestruck for long over Presidents or anyone else for that matter. It had been those around him who venerated Joe and still do. In some cases, Joe did not respond warmly. One example was President Bill Clinton who attempted to connect with the Yankee Clipper several times such as when Joe was hospitalized. He was unavailable to speak to the President. Joe it was known held a disdain for President Clinton's politics and the Monica Lewinsky scandal. It was Morris Engelberg who admitted in his book that he declined the President's phone calls on Joe's behalf, especially when Joe was gravely ill and intubated.

"As DiMaggio's health surrogate," he said, "I was empowered to make the decision, and I did."

Morris deduced that Joe rejected the President when he was well, so he would surely not have wished to hear his voice when he was ill.

According to Richard Ben Cramer the author of *Joe DiMaggio: The Hero's Life,* Joe first snubbed President Clinton in 1998 when *Time* magazine celebrated its seventy-fifth anniversary at a dinner. President Clinton requested that Joe sit at his table. Joe told the President that he had a previous seating commitment with Henry and Nancy Kissinger to excuse himself from the overture.

"Joe detested Clinton," he said, "because he was a Democrat -- and Joe hadn't admired any Democrat since the Kennedys had soured him on the party, and, he thought Clinton was soft, self-indulgent and a phony."

Morris Engelberg also wrote in his biography of Joe's disdain about the President as well as Hillary Clinton.

"Look, I can see his nose growing," Joe commented to Morris who reported in his book that Joe said that as the two watched President Clinton speaking on television.

Joe surmised to Morris that the President and his spouse owned a particular newspaper in order to receive such favorable reporting.

In 1995 it is said, one of President Clinton's aides asked Joe when the two were both in Camden Yards in Baltimore to witness Cal Ripken break Lou Gehrig's streak, if the President could shake Joe's hand. Joe declined the request. The President had shaken Joe's hand once before and he thought a second time was excessive. The aide then asked if Joe would be interested in sitting with the President and Joe also turned down the invitation. Joe was apparently pleased to have shown a cold shoulder towards President Clinton.

Ironically and what would most likely be to Joe's chagrin, the Joe DiMaggio Children's Hospital Foundation scheduled the presentation of the Joe DiMaggio American Icon Award on January 24, 2013. The inaugural award is in honor of what would have been Joe's 100th birth year. CBS News in the Hollywood Florida area reported that the vice-president of the foundation said that they were looking for people in the same realm as Joe and "we believe President Clinton certainly transcends the world politics. He's done so much through the Clinton Foundation around the entire world."

Current day baseball heroes are also awestruck over Joe's achievements.

New York Yankee Shortstop Derek Jeter, who plans to retire from the game in 2014, once said, "Joe DiMaggio has a song. That brings it to another level."

Not to mention he was an inspiration to the protagonist in Ernest Hemingway's book *The Old Man and the Sea.*

It has been reported that Derek Jeter, retired New York Yankee Daryl Strawberry and David Cone (who played for the Yankees from 1995 through 2000 and retired from baseball in 2003) were nervous to speak to Joe or ask for an autograph. David Cone admitted to purchasing one dozen signed Joe DiMaggio baseballs rather than approaching him for a signature.

Joe was still a presence beyond his name, which those around him recognized. Joe continued to radiate his elegance and carriage that he had in his earliest years. His poise was one that commanded respect as he smiled in front of crowds retelling stories of his younger days. Joe was still sharp, moving slightly slower, yet remaining animated when he talked about those nostalgic times. Though he was older, those around him reveled in the underlying spirit of the upright, proud and silent dark-haired champion who blessed the dreams of baseball fans in New York and beyond. They greeted him at events where he graced his presence with extensive standing ovations.

Joe had outlived most of his ball club compatriots after having watched his friends like Lefty Gomez and his mentor Lefty O'Doul predecease him. Even his Yankee successor Mickey Mantle, seventeen years his junior, passed away from inoperable liver cancer. Not even a liver transplant saved "The Mick."

Marilyn had Dr. Hyman Engelberg pronounce her dead and Joe ironically had his own Engelberg at his deathbed. Unlike Dr. Engelberg who was there with Marilyn, Morris Engelberg spent the last sixteen years of Joe's life with him and was there when he exhaled his final dying breath and said his last words.

Morris became Joe's attorney after renegotiating his Bowery Savings Bank contract. Joe described Morris in his will drafted in 1996 as his "dear friend and attorney." It was Morris who was appointed Joe's "Personal Representative" of his estate as well as his Trustee.

As there were those surrounding Marilyn who exploited her, while some have described Morris like a son to Joe, others have viewed him like those who enveloped Marilyn, as his handler and controller.

Like Aaron Frosch who laid claim that he never charged a fee to Marilyn for legal services, Morris Engelberg would state the same. Yet, in 2000 as the "estate" of Marilyn Monroe would do, Morris Engelberg would attempt to sell items of Joe's at a Christie's Auction. He has also been criticized for his spilling his beans book about Joe in his book *DiMaggio: Setting The Record Straight*, which some have accused to have been another attempt to profit further from Joe's memory.

However Morris was also able to document through photos how he became a part of Joe's family. Morris, who was frequently pictured with Joe in those last years, ended up in family photographs with Joe and his brother Dom and even in a family photo posed with Joe and his grandchildren and great-grandchildren. The grandchildren endorsed Morris's biography.

Morris unleashed his book after enduring a firestorm of criticism from various publications following Joe's death, among them the *Daily News, ESPN* and *Vanity Fair*. The blaze began to smolder following the small embers that Pulitzer Prize winning author Richard Ben Cramer began planting because of his own book and launch of a direct attack against Morris.

Richard Ben Cramer, who ironically also died in 2013 from lung cancer, the disease that took his subject Joe DiMaggio, began looking into the Yankee legend in 1995 while Joe was still alive and well. Joe was not fond of the idea of this biographer's book and made that evident to him.

The author of this book has evaluated both Richard Ben Cramer's book *Joe DiMaggio: The Hero's Life* and Morris Engelberg's work. As a journalist, this author must straddle the line of impartiality and report the truth. At the same time, the author of this book like Morris Engelberg is to Joe DiMaggio is a longtime fan of Marilyn Monroe, the preferred biographer and press representative for Marilyn Monroe's cousins on William Hogan's side of the family and a distant relative of Marilyn's herself (an exciting find after years of admiring Marilyn since girlhood). This author with her own experiences in challenging the "estate" of Marilyn Monroe long before forging the relationships with William Hogan's descendants, in the eyes of some may not appear unbiased. After many years though this author will and can counter her detractors impartially because she has still employed a critical eye in evaluating Marilyn Monroe's legacy and has studied the facts about her life since childhood. Marilyn Monroe is a subject, in other words, that this author is very well versed in.

After reviewing both books, Richard Ben Cramer came across in some instances as a curmudgeon with an ax to grind with Morris Engelberg and Joe himself, because he was unable to penetrate the DiMaggio wall. He appeared as almost jealous and looking to destroy the bond that Morris and Joe forged. Though Morris Engelberg asserted that Joe permitted him to write his biography at the same time this can be viewed as hearsay because Joe did not endorse any book written about him during his lifetime (except his own of course) and vacillated in 1989 about writing his own story because of the pressures of writing about Marilyn. No one but Morris and Joe will ever truly know what happens behind closed doors with two friends and what may have happened with a handshake. Of course his grandchildren may have witnessed the conversation. It is knowledge that Morris has remained a spokesman for the family.

What is known is Richard Ben Cramer flaunted his Purple Heart in the battle, the cease and desist letter he proudly published in the back of his book penned by Morris Engelberg's firm. He considered Morris an opportunist who took control of a dying man and painted a scathing picture of Joe's friend and attorney. The letter from the firm hammered in the fact that Joe did not support Richard Ben Cramer's biographical efforts.

The writing in the Richard Ben Cramer book was entertaining at times and conversational, a style not utilized by this author who prefers more of a formality and journalistic feel in her writing approach. Richard Ben penned the book as if he was one of a bunch of guys chatting about Joe's life over a few drinks. In this author's eyes, he overused ellipses and started too many sentences with the word, "anyway" followed by a comma, again signifying as if he was savoring some stogies and drinks while talking about DiMag with some pals in a bar. Referring to women and Marilyn as "broads" was another technique that gave rise in his writing style and especially how he attempted to describe Joe's sexual romps with Marilyn was a bit lurid ("God, he never wanted to jolt anybody like this girl," was part of one description, which would have sickened both Joe and Marilyn).

This author's two cents about the Morris Engelberg portrait -- he provided a more sensitive and accurate view of Joe and filled in many gaps left by Joe's silence about Marilyn and Joe Jr., as well as the brokenness Joe truly experienced over her death. Morris discussed the fractures in Joe's other relationships, such as with Dom and sister Marie. Though some of Morris's motives have been questioned by third-party sources via news publications, Morris's reverence of Joe was evident and his portrait of the Yankee Clipper appeared honest and sincere in the book.

The Jerome Charyn book, *Joe DiMaggio: The Long Vigil*, is a third book of similar caliber that appears a regurgitation of the Richard Ben Cramer book, though Jerome Charyn offered a more sympathetic view towards Joe in his portrayal than Richard Ben Cramer. That author still slammed Morris except with less of a vengeance than his obvious inspiration Richard Ben Cramer.

Jerome Charyn's commentary about Morris portrayed some sympathy. Morris was born as a fatherless child (his dad passed away from an aneurysm before his birth) who had coveted Joe as a father figure since his childhood. Morris did admit early in his book, which he dedicated in memory to both his mother and Rosalie DiMaggio, that he dreamt of Joe having been his father as early as the age of eight.

"Morris, don't even think such a thing," his mother replied to him. "DiMaggio? He's Italian. You're an orthodox Jewish Boy."

Morris like Dr. Henry Kissinger who wrote the forward to his book, were both star struck in their youth by baseball hero Joe DiMaggio. Morris's devotion to the Jolter held such fortitude as a Brooklyn boy residing in Dodger territory, he pasted number fives on his clothing without fear of backlash.

Morris challenged both of these authors with threats of lawsuits, which he never followed through with. Could the warnings have only been to keep these authors quiet and could their portrayals of him have held some kernel of truth?

As someone versed in Marilyn more than Joe, this author finds Richard Ben Cramer's portrait less believable and sensitive than Morris's because of the sources that Richard Ben Cramer utilized to sum up certain happenings in Marilyn's life including Anthony Summers's biography, a work that this author personally steers from.

His book *Goddess: The Secret Lives of Marilyn Monroe* was sensationalized and banked on the testimony of Robert Slatzer and Jeanne Carmen, well-known Marilyn Monroe piggy backers who ameliorated their personal relationships with her in order to bring themselves closer into the limelight. Robert Slatzer cuddled close to Marilyn, to invent a romance. Though Marilyn did loan him a book once, so what? Marilyn offered her reading suggestions to many. Jeanne Carmen claimed to have been a pill buddy of Marilyn's and many a biographer since, have also removed her from the picture. Jeanne allegedly resided near Marilyn on Doheny Drive in 1961 and yelled for Marilyn to come join a noisy party of which she played hostess to. Marilyn declined the invitation instead, though of course Jeanne invented this elaborate friendship between the two. Neither of these sycophants was in Marilyn's last address book either. The only "picture" Jeanne had of she and Marilyn "together" was not a photograph, but a painting of the two of them outfitted in towels on their bodies and heads as if they had sat in a steam room together. It was an artist's rendition of Marilyn with her "best friend."

Richard Ben Cramer asserted that Joe spied on Marilyn at the end of her days with wiretapper Fred Otash and that Joe was the one who busted Marilyn's nose, not Dr. Greenson. If he regurgitated this nonsense, how much more sloppy investigative work did he perform to generate these writings? Unfortunately, biographer Jay Margolis also ran away with the Fred Otash and Joe affiliation likely thanks to Richard Ben Cramer's bunk on the topic.

The wiretapper and Joe were never affiliated. Fred Otash as well was another freeloader on the Marilyn bandwagon for his claims that he listened to Marilyn and the President in bed. How much did Fred Otash receive for his television appearances, which perpetrated fabrications about an American Movie Legend and an American President?

Richard Ben Cramer's book, which has become a resource about Joe like the Anthony Summers book has become for Marilyn, is sadly sensationalized in some ways. Part of the reason is the analysis this author has also done of outside sources and review of outside news reports versus his statements. He has crafted his account to slam Morris Engelberg in every way possible in means that it appears purposely veers from the truth (for example blaming him for insulting politicians and causing a dispute about the naming of a New York roadway after Joe, when the politicians involved already had a longtime feud per newspaper accounts).

However, the author of this book offers constructive criticism as well about some of Morris's stories about Marilyn in his book. He and co-writer Marv Schneider apparently attempted to recreate Marilyn's life and used bunk sources such as Robert Slatzer, plus gratefully acknowledged him in their book for his personal interviews. Robert Slatzer was a man who chose to defame Joe in life and having used him as a source seems like a slap in the face to Joe's memory. Whether it is Morris or his co-writer who chose to refer to this unreliable source, it still infers a lack of responsible journalism since he is a well-documented phony. As an example, their book asserts that Marilyn and Robert Slatzer were secretly wed October 4, 1952 because he likely told the authors so. Yet evidence shows otherwise including a check Marilyn wrote to Jax, her favorite clothing store, which documented that Marilyn was busy that day shopping with Natasha Lytess. How could Marilyn have participated in that marriage in Mexico if she was in Los Angeles that day? Robert Slatzer again was the downfall in the aftermath of Marilyn's death, creating colorful tales of times with the Kennedys. How Robert Slatzer could have even appeared in the book makes their reconstruction of Marilyn's life and last days unbelievable in some ways.

Morris Engelberg also cited Lena Pepitone as a source to reconstruct Marilyn's and Joe's love story. Though Lena was a valid person in the last years of Marilyn's life she released a biography in which she too fabricated her story about her dealings with Marilyn. She elevated herself to the level of "confidante" when she was simply Marilyn's maid and cook. The relationship according to witnesses including Marilyn's sister Berniece (whose book came out following all the jabber among the con artists) demonstrated Marilyn's relationship with her maid did not extend beyond professional.

The writers of *DiMaggio: Setting The Record Straight* also interviewed Jeanne Carmen, another strike against their "setting the record" when it comes to Marilyn. Jeanne laced the writers with her stories of offering to teach Marilyn and Jayne Mansfield golf on Sunday August 5, the day Marilyn's body was found, Another unlikely tale since Marilyn already had golf pointers from Joe and also it is known, spent no time with Jeanne Carmen. Plus Marilyn was not a fan or friend of Jayne. To Marilyn's dismay, Jayne visibly attempted to flock around and photobomb Marilyn at an Actors Studio benefit in the 1950s with Marilyn, obviously and uncomfortably captured in photos shying away from Jayne.

Yes, Joe was skeptical of Marilyn's relationship with the Kennedy brothers. Affirmative, Joe grew to despise Frank Sinatra by the early 1960s and blamed him for the death of the love of his life. In both cases, Joe barked up the wrong trees and was totally off in his conclusions. He allowed in the therapists and acting teacher Lee Strasberg, though in his earlier days he was spot-on in suspecting Natasha Lytess as a bloodsucker.

Did he simply wish to acquiesce to Marilyn the second time around and accept those around her, who emotionally held her captive, and closed his eyes enough to miss that the therapists and Lee Strasberg, were actually the ones who took the life of his beloved? This author believes so.

Now back to Morris.

The *Daily News* reported that while Joe was alive Morris betrayed his attorney-client relationship, leaking to others secrets about Joey and referring to Joe as "extremely cheap, will never go into his pocket to pay for a meal."

Morris also complained, per a *Daily News* story that Joe's frivolity extended to Morris's daughter's wedding, and that Joe did not bring a gift.

Richard Ben Cramer was the source of these shocking stories, which could be questionable.

When asked during an interview how proceeds are still made from Joe's legacy, he revealed to CNN in 2000: "The organization that marketed DiMaggio for the last few years of his life was called Yankee Clipper Enterprises. That organization was structured and operated by a lawyer in Hollywood Florida, Morris Engelberg, and it's he who sits on Joe's vast pile of money. The heirs in Joe's will were his 'granddaughters'-- actually not blood relations but women whom Joe Jr. had adopted when he married their mother thirty years ago. But the granddaughters only enjoy the interest from Joe's trust. The trust itself and the tens of millions which Joe had piled up are all under the control of Mr. Engelberg (who, of course, drafted the will)."

Morris was sued by one of his former partners for breach of confidentiality in the matter of Joe's estate too and was accused by the plaintiffs of fleecing Joe's heirs of close to $2 million to avoid estate taxes. The former partner Rick Leone said that Morris badmouthed him to clients after he purchased a portion of Morris's accounting and law firm. He accused Morris of exercising the "generation-skipping tax," as he did with Joe's family, which would avoid the tax while placing fewer dollars in the beneficiaries' pockets. Otherwise, Morris would not have received his cut.

"Once reason an attorney, who is also a trustee might choose to pay the generation-skipping tax would be so the attorney would not lose his trustee's fees," Rick Leone explained to *ESPN*. "The attorney would be willing to sacrifice the interests of the beneficiaries for his own personal gain."

Morris denied the allegations, replying if there had been an issue Joe's grandchildren would have sued him. Joe's relatives to the contrary and namely his grandchildren have spoken highly of Morris when they were interviewed.

Morris added that, "He [Joe] loved his great grandkids more than his grandkids," and that Joe had concerns if his granddaughters passed away monies would skip his great grandchildren because the husbands of his granddaughters would inherit them. Morris insisted that it was Joe who wished for the funds to be placed in trust.

The *Daily News* explained that Morris was entitled to "reasonable compensation" under Florida Law as a trustee administering trusts. In 1999, Joe's estate was estimated at $30 million and when marketed for the use of his name and license that number increased.

A document secured by the *Daily News* drafted by attorneys for Lee Kushner attorney one of Morris's former partners who engaged in litigation with Morris, stated that Morris refused to accept deals on Joe's behalf while he was alive in order to cash in on Joe after he passed. He alleged that Morris accepted pieces of signed memorabilia by the hundreds in lieu of payment from Joe. Morris has been known to say it was Joe who made the decision to hold off sales of memorabilia until after his death to bolster the trust accounts that he designated to his recipients.

Joe, signing autographs in his military days.
From the collection of Pauline and Georgie Riggio.

Les Kushner's lawyers wrote, "Purportedly, none of the items received were reported on his [Morris's] individual tax returns even though he has received these items in lieu of fees."

Other court documents that the *Daily News* acquired have stated that Morris filed an invalid will for one of his clients Bertha Behrman, founder of Madame Alexander dolls. Morris was removed as executor with a $100,000 settlement at the end of the case and the client's daughter taking over the estate.

When *CNN* asked author Richard Ben Cramer why Morris Engelberg refused the naming of a park in Joe's name in San Francisco, he replied: "Morris fought with San Francisco, insulted the Mayor of New York and soured literally hundreds (or thousands) of people who loved Joe because Morris wants absolute control of Joe's legacy. It's not too far to go to say that now Morris Engelberg thinks he owns Joe DiMaggio, or is Joe DiMaggio -- or somehow he's working out his own personality problems."

However, news reports counter for example that a war was already ongoing between the Mayor of New York and Governor of New York over relocation of Yankee Stadium and which highway to rename in Joe's memory.

Is it possible Joe's relationship with accepting Morris Engelberg to handle his affairs so deeply was a reason why he was unable to discern that the Freudian and Strasberg crews were overtaking Marilyn?

There are conflicting stories about Morris and his relationship with Joe. The writer of this book has documented the evidence and is allowing the reader to make the final verdict on the relationship.

It was also Morris Engelberg, who had according to some, developed a hatred of Dom DiMaggio after Joe cut Dom off because of bad blood between them. By Morris's own account, it was he who tried to smooth over old wounds and backs up the account with a photo of Joe, Morris and Dom in the book.

Morris additionally confessed in his book how upset he was by the rift between Joe and his sister Marie. Joe often vented to Morris about his sister, who he accused of selling memorabilia on display in their San Francisco home and once taking three bottles of Scotch from Joe's liquor cabinet to gift to her daughter. However, Marie gave her life to the family throughout their lives as a matriarch. Joe frequently grew irritated with his elder sister when she did not stock their home in San Francisco with groceries, even as a woman in her eighties. When Morris asked after Marie one day who he knew had been ill, Joe shocked him by revealing that Marie had died two weeks prior. After that, not another word was said about her.

Another source cited that Morris told Joe's grandchildren they could invite Dom if they wished to Joe's memorial service at St. Patrick's Cathedral. Morris apparently did not wish Dom to go (Dom did not appear to be there) and was also not the most keen about including Joe's friend restaurateur Dick Burke or even Joe Jr.

Some have spoken of Morris as replacing Joe Jr. as a son figure. Morris countered in his book that following Joe's death he took Joe Jr. under his wing, temporarily moved him to Florida and tried to look after him for three months. The two could have been brothers based on their closeness in age with Morris three years older than Joey. Morris also commented positively about junior in an article following his death, putting to rest that he died from drug abuse (which Richard Ben Cramer cited the death was from a drug overdose) and instead suffered from asthma.

Morris said he found Joey likeable, loving and generous with hugs unlike his father, who was reserved with physical touch. The two took in sports events together and dined out, though junior barely touched his food and instead relied on liquid nutrition (in other words mugs of beer). He was apparently embarrassed to eat in public because of his missing teeth (which his natural teeth were gone, and his replacements were often lost, because he threw his dentures at people who annoyed him).

Joe's granddaughter Kathie Stein on the other hand praised Morris Engelberg, while many old friends such as Phil Rizzuto said they had been circumcised quickly from Joe's life. *Vanity Fair* classified the attorney as a "praying mantis of a man."

DiMaggio: Setting The Record Straight sets the records straight on many of the final details of Joe's life. It was Morris who basically described himself as the one who became Joe's errand boy, and performed chores, he said, as a labor of love and friendship and above the scope of his role as attorney. For example, he was the one who purchased Joe's bagels for him at six in the morning, assisted Joe when he had difficulties with his cable television and screened restaurants Joe wanted to try to ensure they did not have Marilyn's picture hanging in the men's room.

Morris continued in this role for sixteen years in what was described as Joe's "guardian and gatekeeper."

Though some have considered Morris Joe's advocate, detractors have viewed him negatively as the man who would continue to oversee Joe's image for profit following his death.

Yet, it was also Morris who would temper Joe's temper, especially on Joe DiMaggio Day in September 1998. Joe nearly blew a gasket when he was made to wait at Yankee Stadium the day the Yankees were scheduled to present the Clipper with replicas of his World Series rings that had been stolen. Joe nearly left because he was agitated from the heat and the wait. Morris calmed him down enough to accept the gift and ovation from the crowd. To boot, when Joe Torre took Joe to the microphone, it did not function properly so no one also sadly heard his speech that day. Following the presentation, Joe verbally tore into Yankee Marketing Representative Deborah Tymon and she broke into tears.

A "close associate" not named in a *Vanity Fair* article claimed Joe suffered from Stockholm syndrome from Morris's influence. Many of Joe's friends and confidantes feared revealing their names in multiple articles following Joe's death, in anticipation of litigation from Morris when they came forward with their gripes about him.

"A lot of people don't like me," Morris volunteered to the *Daily News* in April 1999. "Know why? I protected Joe for sixteen years."

One friend who was irritated was Bert Padell, Joe's business manager in the 1970s and 1980s, stating he was one of many whose well wishes and final goodbyes were never conveyed to Joe.

"Fifteen times I called Morris," Bert said. "I wrote letters to Morris. When Joe was really sick, I called Morris at least twice a week, and he never got back to me."

"I knew him [Joe] since 1948," Bert emphasized then exclaimed. "Since 1948!"

Morris was Bert's replacement after the two had a falling out.

Like Marilyn, Joe was accordingly becoming annoyed by decisions made around during his last year, which he said did not involve his input. One party consulted for a *Daily News* story the month after Joe's death said that Morris's brother approached an entertainment company, possibly Walt Disney, about utilizing Joe's name and image. The anonymous source said this action led Joe to grow furious and that his anger was described as a "ten and a half" on a scale of one to ten. Morris denied the allegations though he did admit that he approached another company about an animated cartoon series with Joe's consent.

"I never started a deal without him," Morris told the *Daily News*.

Norman Brokaw who was then CEO of the William Morris Agency and a friend of Joe's recalled discussing Disney over dinner with Joe before his death. Joe frequently discussed his business with Norman and sought his advice and second opinion.

One longtime unidentified friend said although Joe was seething, his illness hindered him from his usual feistiness in emotionally tackling the likes of those who attempted to overpower him in the past.

That friend told the *Daily News*, "Joe was eighty-three years old. He was frail and sick and wasn't anywhere near the tiger he used to be."

Following Joe's death, Morris arm-wrestled with and sued politicians who sought to name parks and roadways in Joe's name. In Hollywood Florida, Morris downed the idea that the mayor had of naming the Presidential Circle in town after Joe (though there is Joe DiMaggio Park, a twenty-acre recreational area, situated in Hollywood's Harbor Islands, the neighborhood where both Morris and Joe resided).

"I control the license and use of Mr. DiMaggio's name in perpetuity as long as I am alive," Morris responded.

Morris downed the idea of the park in San Francisco, his reasoning was "San Francisco wasn't right for Joe DiMaggio," though Joe had lived there through his childhood, some of his adult life and requested his funeral service be at the parish where he attended in his youth and also married Dorothy.

The Joe DiMaggio Playground now exists in North Beach, and is 110,000 square feet and comprised of a children's play area, sports courts and pool building. A 2012 bond was allocated for $5.5 million for improvements to the spot, which will also eventually be the site of the future North Beach Branch Library.

Other cities have named recreational areas after Joe too. Clearwater Florida has the Joe DiMaggio Sports Complex with four multipurpose fields and two baseball fields. In his birthplace Martinez California, the softball complex is named in Joe's honor.

Morris accepted New York Mayor Rudolph Giuliani's suggestion to rename the West Side Highway after Joe following his death. On the contrary, he slammed New York's then-Governor George Pataki when he proposed renaming the Major Deegan Expressway in Joe's memory.

"Governor Pataki should be made aware that there cannot be anything named after Joe DiMaggio anywhere, without my approval," Morris replied in his correspondence to the Governor.

As Joe spent ninety-nine days hospitalized from battling pneumonia and dealing with the "funny cells," his euphemism for the cancer in his lungs, Morris continued to tend to Joe's needs. As Joe led the charge in controlling the press after Marilyn's death, Morris was the media liaison for Joe in those final months.

When Dom sought answers about Joe's health, which took a turn for the worst after he contracted pneumonia, Morris invoked the attorney-client privilege. This incited Dom who referred to Morris as a "phony, liar and control freak." The dispute nearly escalated to a fistfight outside of Joe's hospital room. It took the family six weeks to determine the cause of Joe's true health woes. The head of the hospital Frank Sacco, kept Dom apprised of Joe's health.

Morris on the other hand told the *Daily News*, that he was only enforcing Joe's "privacy orders," keeping them as well from Joe's only surviving brother.

"We had our scuffle in the hallway," Morris told the *Daily News*. "Dom wanted to know what was wrong. But I couldn't tell him. Joe made it totally 100 percent clear."

Another person who said he was concerned about Joe was Barry Halper. After reaching out, he was greeted with an accusatory letter from Morris citing Barry for stealing Joe's 1951 World Series ring. Barry said he purchased it from a dealer after Joe gave the ring away to a friend and who sold it. Barry said Joe offered a note authenticating that the ring had been his.

Barry Halper has been referred to as the "Bernie Madoff" of collecting, with some of his items now considered forgeries. In fact, it was Barry Halper who was the mastermind behind the 1953 Playboy with "Joe's" signature. It was noted in Barry's obituary as a feather in his cap in 2005, yet this item was counterfeit. Barry Halper was like all of the Marilyn Monroe memorabilia cons that cash in on her legacy, while he defamed the legacies of numerous sports legends.

Following Joe's death, Morris on the other hand, was spotted wearing Joe's 1936 World Series ring at his funeral and an unnamed family member reportedly confronted him.

"Joe said I could have the ring for one year," Morris replied.

The *Daily News* cited that when Morris was asked if he had recommended return of the ring to the family, he replied, "If you want it back, it's yours."

While Morris would release the positive points of Joe's battles with cancer, Joe was in essence considered terminal beginning in September 1998. Joe began spitting blood (which Joe apparently penned as well in his diary entries as early as a 1992), while still maintaining his outer strength for the public, and asked Morris not to disclose the true breadth of his condition with anyone.

Joe had surgery to remove a spot on his lung at Memorial Regional Hospital on October 12, a known cancer center in the Southeast Florida area. He was not registered under his own name for privacy reasons. The surgery was successful but the prognosis poor. His doctor noted that the cancer had spread to the carina nerve of his lower respiratory tract, which would have been impossible to reach without removing Joe's lung.

Morris had a scare three days after Joe's surgery when he arrived to the hospital and found Joe's bed empty. Joe, who had been comatose after his operation, was moved to another room and surprisingly was recovering well. Those last months were up and down with progresses and hindrances. However only a couple of days later, Joe suffered a setback with the collapse of right lung and accumulation of fluid in his left. Joe was placed back on the respirator after Morris gave his consent as Joe's health surrogate. In the meantime, Morris reached out to Joe's granddaughters, to alert them to their granddad's turn of health.

Unfortunately, hospital staff began gossiping and news of Joe's physical condition started to leak to the papers. Morris said he refused to use the word "cancer," and instead told the media he had pneumonia.

Side effects began kicking in -- Joe started to suffer from what is defined as "hospital psychosis," a condition patients can deal with temporarily following extended periods in a medical center. Joe turned combative and started to rip out his tubes. Between those issues and the prowling media, soon security was stationed outside of his room, on twenty-four hour shifts.

Morris visited Joe on a daily basis, and often he was incoherent and in a deep sleep. The nurses would instruct Morris to not disturb him.

It was around this point in the timeline when Dom and Morris argued in front of Joe's room. The brothers were still estranged from each other. That was when Morris referred Dom to Frank Sacco. From then on, Dom and wife Emily visited Joe a few times weekly to Morris's chagrin.

In mid-November, Joe contracted a bacterial infection and massive doses of antibiotics were administered. The drugs backfired and began to kill off beneficial bacteria. A gastroenterologist was then called in on the case. Eventually, the team found an antibiotic that cooperated and the fever Joe fought and his health overall began to stabilize.

Joe celebrated his eighty-fourth birthday in the hospital that year and Morris arranged a private celebration with members of the hospital staff, his grandchildren and great-grandchildren and Dom and Emily. Joe was coherent now and watching television regularly. He grew upset when he saw a false news report that he was hospitalized for a heart attack. Unable to speak and still intubated, Joe's angst was evident in his eyes. Morris assured Joe that inaccurate news would be rampant about his health because the real story had not been disclosed.

Dr. Earl Barron began to keep the public apprised of Joe's physical condition and released optimistic reports. The doctor confirmed Joe's cancer, though stated he was recovering well.

During the early part of December, Joe's infection further subsided, and visitors including nephew Joe, Yankee owner George Steinbrenner, friend Martha Lee and pal restaurateur Mario Faustini, were among those who visited him in the hospital.

Joe was well enough to express to Morris his fears about Dom. He worried that Dom was attempting to pull his estate away from his granddaughters. Joe had overheard Emily, who he had supposedly referred to over the years as the "Barracuda," insulting his grandkids, because they were adopted into the family and were not blood.

Dom and Emily, again to Morris's annoyance, attempted to intervene in Joe's health matters. They informed Morris they were bringing in their own healthcare professional to evaluate him and planned on transferring Joe to another facility. Morris advised Joe's doctor, who said he would gladly speak with their consultant. Dom's specialist was satisfied with the treatment Joe was receiving and the shift to Dom's care never materialized.

Joe's health suffered another blow with a subsequent bacterial infection -- the doctors believed he would not pull through. Morris called a meeting with the granddaughters, Dom and Emily, Joe's close friend Joe Nachio and one of the doctors. Dom insisted he would be the one to make funeral arrangements, which upset Morris. Joe's granddaughter Paula told Morris to allow Dom to do so and she said she hoped Dom would "eventually go away."

After lunch, they all began their goodbyes. It was December 11, the same day that Morris's father died. He said he held Joe's hand and begged him not to die that day --- he surprisingly felt a squeeze.

Later that afternoon, Joe was amazingly out of bed, sitting up in a chair and reading a newspaper.

Joe soon asked to go home. Morris recalled that the only point he and Dom agreed upon, was that Joe should have the comfort of dying at home, not a hospital.

Joe left the hospital incognito in a Joe DiMaggio Children's Hospital van on January 19, 1999. Once the press caught wind of his discharge, they rejoiced over a possible recovery.

Joe was returned to his secluded and luxurious community in the Harbor Islands section of Hollywood Florida. When Morris arranged for Joe to be home, Joe surprised Morris by asking where his home was. His mind was now slightly slipping. Morris and the staff equipped Joe's downstairs den with a hospital bed and neuro-chair for comfort. From there, he could have a view of boats floating by. A security officer was stationed around Joe's home daily to keep away lurking paparazzi. Nurses attended to Joe's grooming and a cook prepared him gourmet fare to eat.

Fan mail from those wishing Joe a strong recovery came in and Joe continued to sign baseballs. His signings were not with the fervor that he had previously -- his average in better health was 300 an hour -- now, it was barely nine. He grew weary and his body needed rest. A few of these balls were auctioned off after his death, though most were kept by his family and close friends and donated to the Joe DiMaggio Children's Hospital and other significant places.

The relationship between Joe and Joe Jr. remained strained even as Joltin' Joe's health remained precarious. The television program *Inside Edition* interviewed Joey for a segment that was broadcast on February 11. Joe the son apparently received $15,000 for his appearance on the show. Morris said after the Joe's death, Joey turned down a lucrative offer to write a tell-all book about Joe.

When asked why he did not rush to his father's bedside, junior replied, "You know, I never got the words, 'Come now,' or I would've been there in a flash. I love him and just all of the things that are felt, but never said, between people. When he wants me there, I'll be there."

Father and son never reconciled and Joe never summoned for him. However, it was impossible to reach Joey -- he refused to have a phone and chose to live his life like "a bum" -- his own words.

Joey's cousin Joe T. DiMaggio, one of the benefactors on the Yankee Clipper's will, was careful to apportion money to Joe Jr. He feared Butch would spend it on booze and drugs.

When Joltin' Joe could spend time with junior, he truly attempted to help him according to Morris. When Joe visited he San Francisco area, he would outfit him and take him to the dentist.

Joe T. and his wife Marina helped Joe Jr. after he had been riding a bicycle drunk and fell and broke his hip and ankle. The Yankee Clipper attempted the same, even offering to bring his son to his friend Dr. Positano in New York, though junior refused the offer.

As Joe passed his final days without his son, he was still able to relish some sun in his yard and enjoy the glittering stars as he sat outside in the evenings. Sometimes he could remove the tracheostomy for short periods.

One night, Morris said Joe looked into the sky and told him, "Morris, soon Marilyn and I will be together again, up there."

He verbally repeated this thought several times before his death and stunned Morris each time he did so.

Morris was also surprised to walk in on Joe one morning as he threw a baseball from his bed. Hurling the ball was done weakly and in anger over Dom, who had cut a deal with a memorabilia dealer without Joe's consent while Joe had been hospitalized. According to Morris, Dom forged Joe's signature on the balls. He expected fury from Joe at Dom's next visit though Joe to his surprise did not address the issue.

In his final week of life, George Steinbrenner visited the Yankee Clipper who was now wheelchair bound, yet still the picture of grace. The man who shunned painkillers for his arthritis now relied on morphine to suppress the aching. A sign had been placed at Joe's bedside to inspire him to continue on a path of strength -- it read "April 9 Yankee Stadium or Bust." Joe had been invited to throw the first ball at the stadium and George mentioned the invitation again when he visited Joe five days before his death.

"He just smiled," George recalled to reporters.

Morris said at that last visit, George had difficulty holding back his emotion and as soon as he rushed through Joe's front door, burst into tears.

Morris began to call Joe's friends for their final visits. Dr. Rock was one, though he was too upset to come. This was supposedly to the dismay of Joe's granddaughters and friend Joe Nachio. Morris said he could understand Rock's reasoning.

Morris claimed that Joe rebuffed Barry Halper, though Barry would have more likely pinned the blame on Morris.

While Richard Ben Cramer recounted Joe's last moments as fully orchestrated by Morris, even down to coordinating his final breath on the respirator backed with a constant supply of morphine suppositories and theft of Joe's 1936 World Series ring from his finger, Morris's book painted a different picture of that day. He also shared his version of the scenario with the ring.

Morris said the 1936 treasure spent significant time on his finger for two occasions. First when Joe was outfitted with a pacemaker and then after he was admitted to the hospital in '98 for cancer treatment. He said that both times, Joe voluntarily handed the ring over to Morris. Again, Joe's grandchildren and his nephew Joe T. supported Morris's book -- if they had an issue it has since likely been resolved.

Morris said about a half-hour before Joe's death, he removed the ring from his finger to place on his. He had to run home for a jar of Vaseline to slip it back on Joe's finger. He said after he did, he wiped off the Vaseline and then placed it back on his own finger. He wrote nothing further about the ring in his book.

Only a few days prior, his granddaughters had Joe's last rites administered. Joe Nachio was called and made his final voyage to his dear pal. Joe spoke to his friend on the phone though Joltin' Joe's words were garbled.

Some reports have Dom at Joe's bedside -- *People* magazine for one counted him in -- Morris did not and said that Dom departed for a luncheon that day and never returned. In Richard Ben Cramer's book, he alleged that Dom was there the day prior on March 7, though he did not place him there at the moment of Joe's actual death.

Richard Ben Cramer claimed that Dom, who he interviewed for his book along with Emily (Marv Schneider, Morris's co-writer, did not mention Dom and Emily in his acknowledgments), was upset when Morris began to initiate the proceedings the day prior.

As they began to wean Joe from respiration, Dom apparently screamed to the staff, "You're killing him!" According to that account, the staff cranked back on the juice to stabilize Joe's heartbeat and then the following day (without Dom) after Morris gulped down his dinner, the group started the process of exiting Joe from the world. Richard Ben Cramer also placed DeJan Pesut the butler on the scene (does the old statement, "the butler did it," count in this scenario?). Granddaughter Kathie and her brother-in-law Jim, according to this account, sniffled in the background, as Morris was the conductor. DeJan he said stated, "Joe, you leaving us," as "Ave Maria" softly played. Javier Ribe the nurse held his hand and Joe passed in a morphine stupor. Joe's body was prepared for departure and Morris yanked off Joe's 1936 World Series Ring.

By Morris's account, the scene was much different. Nurse Javier Ribe, Joe Nachio, Kathie, Jim and Morris were all present. Midnight came and went on March 7, which was a relief to Morris as that is his birthday. He feared Joe dying that day as he said he did on the date significant for his father.

Morris said early on March 8, 1999, Javier held Joe's hand, Kathie and Morris the other and Jim who was weeping profusely, held Joe's feet.

"His face was radiant the moment he died," Javier told *People* magazine of Joe's last minutes. "He looked as young as the first picture I remember seeing of him. So peaceful, so peaceful."

It is said in Morris's book as Joe exhaled his last breath, he removed his tracheostomy tube and articulated in a whisper his anticipation for his upcoming journey: "I'll finally get to see Marilyn."

It was 12:12 a.m.

"Did he just say what I think he said?" Javier asked shocked.

"He sure did," Morris replied affirmatively.

After he died, Morris also said he also located Joe's false teeth and hurled them into the nearby Intercoastal Waterway for fear they might end up in an auction house as Barry Halper had done with Ty Cobb's dentures (also cited by some as counterfeit memorabilia).

"DiMaggio, the consummate gentleman on and off the field, fought his illness as hard as he played the game of baseball, and with the same dignity, style and grace, with which he lived his life," Morris announced to the press in the wee hours.

As Joe wished for a quiet remembrance at Marilyn's life celebration he also apparently requested the same for himself at his funeral.

There were naturally some tributes above and beyond the Yankee Clipper's request. The flag at the National Baseball Hall of Fame in Cooperstown was lowered to half-staff, as well as the American Flags at Yankee Stadium including the one by Joe's plaque at Monument Park. A wreath was placed at his plaque in Cooperstown.

In lieu of flowers, the family asked for donations to the Joe DiMaggio Children's Hospital and to the Hospice Care of Broward County in his memory.

Joe's body was flown in a chartered plane to San Francisco with Dom and Emily and two baseball officials, Bud Selig and Gene Budig, which apparently surprised other members of the family and Morris since no other members of the baseball community had been invited.

Dom insisted on an open casket, which Morris immediately declined -- he said he knew how private Joe was. Dom requested "professional pallbearers," an idea Morris additionally nixed. He rounded up those close to Joe for the duty and planned to locate Joe Jr.

Emily told Morris the repast was scheduled at the Bobby Rubino's Place for Ribs restaurant, another idea Morris was not thrilled with though Emily and Dom insisted it must be. It was the venue where the DiMaggio restaurant had been previously and the site where the repasts were held for the last two DiMaggio sisters who passed.

Emily obviously chose not to keep up this "tradition." She had a different idea for the sendoff of the last DiMaggio sibling a decade following Joe's death. When Dom died, his wake and mass took place in Wellesley Massachusetts, which an online source quoted that early in their courtship, Dom tracked down Emily in Wellesley to woo her with an autographed ball.

"He and a friend subsequently drove out to Wellesley," the online source reported. "Emily turned out to be even prettier and more vivacious than he remembered. He [DiMaggio] recalled thinking, 'She's not going to get away from me.'"

The St. Paul Church in Wellesley won out over the DiMaggio family church in San Francisco, and Emily evidently decided against Bobby Rubino's Place for Ribs for the repast after Dom's funeral mass.

Dom disliked the idea of Joe Jr. attending his father's funeral.

"He's nothing more than a bum," Dom allegedly stated.

Morris often heard Joe say the same of his offspring, though he would add, "but he's a good boy," at the end.

Morris said he felt by locating junior, it would be a final gift to Joe.

Joe Nachio, who had known Butch for many years, agreed and said he would assist. After an arduous search, the pair found a man repairing the engine of a car. He was covered with grease and dirt and was toothless. There was a warm reunion as Joe hugged Butch, now a nearly unrecognizable man.

Joe handed Joey money to purchase a suit and clean himself up. The only clothes he owned were those on his body -- one pair of jeans, a tank top and a pair of thong sandals. Though Butch's cousin Joe T. bet junior would be a no-show, he surprised them all by coming by limo, suited up and with his hair pulled neatly into a ponytail.

His conduct also astonished the funeral attendees, as junior quietly assessed the scene and gently involved himself in some conversations during the remembrance.

On March 11, 1999, Joe's funeral mass took place at the Saints Peter and Paul Church in the North Beach neighborhood in San Francisco where he spent his youth and also where about sixty years prior he had celebrated his nuptials with Dorothy. As was Marilyn's funeral, Joe asked that only family and friends be present.

Like that day in 1962, the famous were turned away. President Bill Clinton (who sent a letter with his condolences the day after Joe's death) and actors Jack Nicholson and Tom Hanks, all were apparently informed, "their inquiries were appreciated, but it would be a small funeral for family."

"Joe insisted that his funeral be a private, religious service, and his family is intent on carrying out his wishes," Morris told the *Daily News* of the approximately forty guests in attendance.

Morris was among the pallbearers, with Joe Nachio, nephew Joe T., the husbands of Joe's granddaughters Roger Stein and James Hamra, and lastly Joey.

Those acquainted with Joe, as well as fans seeking to say their goodbyes to San Francisco's legendary son, waited outside of barricades as a motorcycle police squadron escorted his hearse to the church. When Joe's casket was carried into the church, the bells began to ring.

Ann Bonzani was a childhood friend and then eighty-five years old as she watched the procession from behind the barricades. The two played jacks together on the sidewalk of their neighborhood.

"He was so tall and thin and shy the other kids made fun of him," Ann said. "Then he got really good with a ball, and they didn't tease him anymore.

Ray Piccinini was a waiter that worked at a restaurant, which Joe frequented in the 1950s.

"He was very kind," reminisced the former waiter. "He signed autographs."

J.D. Reynolds was another spectator outside of the church. His father Allie pitched for the Yankees when Joe played.

"My dad said DiMaggio was the greatest player he had ever seen," he recollected. "My dad said he had a great record because, when he was pitching, someone would hit one and Joe would run a mile to catch it."

Dom eulogized his brother and Joe's granddaughter Kathie recited the twenty-third Psalm.

Not much was reported on Dom's remarks about his brother, though they have been summarized as words about his achievements and that Joe "never found a life's companion."

While Dom and Emily had sixty-one years of marriage under their belts at the end, Joe craved that with Marilyn.

Dom was incorrect -- Joe had found that companion -- Marilyn remained in his heart forever. The lack of a regular lady on his arm until the end of his days reflected the adoration Joe held for Marilyn. It did not signify his lack -- what he lacked and yearned for was the ability to hold Marilyn again.

As the motorcade exited to bring Joe to his final resting place at the Holy Cross Cemetery south of San Francisco, he received his final applauds.

"Bravo!" fans exclaimed and clapped when the hearse carried Joe to his eternal home.

There would be other memorial services for the great ballplayer, which were held by family and friends around the country who wished to celebrate Joe.

The City of Martinez, the town where Joe was born, planned a service on March 20.

On March 26, Joe's four great-grandchildren led a memorial service for him at the Joe DiMaggio Children's Hospital. Over 300 attendees, including Florida's Governor Jeb Bush, were there to pay their respects to Joe. Various members of the Yankees like Phil Rizzuto, Reggie Jackson, Clyde King, Phil Linz, Tom Tresh and Stan Bahnsen also attended.

Sisters Vanassa and Valerie Hamra and Kendahl and Mitchell Stein shared their memories.

"We also looked up to him, but not as a legend," said Kendahl. "We looked up to him as our great-grandfather."

They knew him most fondly as "Big Joe," and he was the man who made them smile on Thanksgivings when he fed turkey to their pet cats.

Dom also attended the memorial though he made no comments about his sibling.

There was another major memorial service, this one in New York City. It was open to the public on April 23. Morris assigned the organization of this event to Dr. Rock. He had become a close confidante and was one of Joe's five male friends who would eat dinner with Joe when he returned to New York. Outside of the young doctor, the other men were senior citizens who ogled over Joe. Dr. Positano nicknamed that quartet "the Bat Pack."

Dr. Positano was only thirty-one years old when Joe befriended him and forty when he was asked to organize the memorial service.

It was Morris who despite Joe's wishes to keep services contained to family, believed that the small family funeral was not enough -- there were many others who wished to say goodbye.

"So I decided he deserves a send-off in New York," Morris said, remembering Joe had told him that the best thirteen years of his life were spent in New York when he was a Yankee. "So I call up Rock. Rock is Catholic, I'm Jewish."

Morris told *The New York Times* he suggested to Dr. Positano, "'Let's do something at St. Patrick's Cathedral. I don't know where to start.'"

He admitted to the publication, "Rock's a newcomer, but he knows New York, all the right people. He knows how to plan these things. Rock is all over the place."

Those that he knew and invited to Joe's memorial service who many were Joe's high-profile friends included: Henry Kissinger, Mortimer Zuckerman, Mayor Rudolph Giuliani, Woody Allen, George Steinbrenner, Yogi Berra, Michael Bolton, Bobby Brown, Joe Piscopo, Bryant Gumbel, Bob Costas, Phil Rizzuto, Yogi Berra and Ralph Branca of the Brooklyn Dodgers. President Clinton was not in attendance.

There were many unknowns holding their own vigils for Joe outside.

Teammate Dr. Bobby Brown was one of the speakers, as was Mayor Giuliani. Joe's granddaughters also attended the event, which lasted an hour and focused on his achievements. Both Bobby and the Mayor predicted Joe's 1941 record would remain untouched for all time.

"I would suggest that rarely was there ever seen such consummate skill, grace, power, speed, and dignity in one person," Bobby said. "I know Joe is in heaven. I suspect there's a committee up there right now trying to determine when to retire his number."

Program from service for Joe from the author's collection.

The New York City service was held at St. Patrick's Cathedral, and Cardinal John O'Connor, said regardless of the illustrious guest list the service would be "simple."

Though the Cardinal asked the attendees to show "gratitude to Joe DiMaggio by your applause."

A thunderous roar rang across the cathedral and the crowd offered Joe's memory a standing ovation.

Two days later on April 25, Paul Simon was scheduled to perform his song "Mrs. Robinson," when the granite and bronze monument for Joe was unveiled at Yankee Stadium.

Joe was temporarily laid to rest in a mausoleum where his parents were entombed in the Holy Cross Cemetery in Colma California. His burial site was fashioned as he slept with Giuseppe and Rosalie and now Joe slumbers forever in a handsome, black marble mausoleum with its own special marker. On it is etched, "Joseph Paul DiMaggio," his birth and death dates and the words, "Grace, Dignity, And Elegance Personified."

As thousands of fans that adore Marilyn leave flowers, cards and lipstick marks on her crypt plus often chisel away at its front so it must be replaced from time to time, Joe's final resting place has not been defaced though fans leave their gifts. Joe DiMaggio followers leave behind balls, bats, cards, pictures and floral tributes. Marilyn's plaque, which is replaced each time her stone is, is simply recognized as "Marilyn Monroe 1926-1962," though she often joked her epitaph should have read, "Here Lies Marilyn Monroe, 38-23-36."

Not all of the tributes for both are positive. One of the more recent betrayals to both Marilyn and Joe's legacies was June Elpine, a lady who referred to herself as "June DiMaggio."

In 2006, June released a book co-written with radio host Mary Jane Popp. In it she claimed to have been Joe's niece and Marilyn's best friend for eleven years. She said she was the daughter of Tom and Lee DiMaggio. Though June was able to furnish some previously unpublished photos of Marilyn and Joe with Tom and Lee, it was unclear if June was actually present when the photos were taken (there were no photos of June with Marilyn or Joe, though she did furnish one taken in a group with Dom). Many versed in the life of Marilyn have challenged her stories.

She alleged that she knew Marilyn was murdered and her mother overheard Marilyn being slain while conversing on the phone with her. June said her mother never divulged details of Marilyn's death, because she "wanted her children to live."

June carried the story so far to indicate that she arrived to Marilyn's home the day her body was found and crossed police lines to enter the residence (which in actuality was sealed by then) to retrieve a pizza pan that she had delivered an anchovy pizza on for Marilyn the day before her death (Marilyn ate out with Pat Newcomb the day prior and had nothing in her stomach during her autopsy -- the whole story itself is a fabrication anyway).

She also said she rode in the limousine at Marilyn's funeral with her "Uncle Joe," when it is known that no other DiMaggios were at the funeral except for Joe Jr. (brother Tom and Lee were not there, nor was Joe's sister Marie, who had developed a close friendship with Marilyn when she lived in San Francisco). There was no female in the limo with father and son. Neither "June DiMaggio" nor "June Elpine" was on the guest list of funeral attendees. The only DiMaggios in Marilyn's 1962 address book with names of people she contacted regularly were Joe and junior. June never commented publicly if she had been invited to Joe's funeral though Joe was gone about seven years at this point. Commenting on that topic was an act that could have cleared or implicated her further (it has implicated her further for storytelling for her lack of comments on this subject).

It is an interesting point as well to mention that Tom, according to a blurb from Marilyn and Joe's wedding day in 1954 in the *Long Beach Press-Telegram*, stated he spelled his name differently than his famous baseball-playing brothers -- "Dimaggio," perhaps in order to maintain some anonymity. Why did June not implement the same spelling "Dimaggio," instead of the most commonly known "DiMaggio" then if she was really a close family member?

At the end of 2005, June "DiMaggio" was one of several parties involved with an exhibit on the Queen Mary. There were items on display alleged to have been Marilyn's and claimed to have been so unknown because the collector Robert W. Otto said they belonged to the "private" Marilyn.

The exhibit had its premiere and endorsement a year prior at CMG Headquarters in Indiana, the company that was then licensing Marilyn's image.

The news media, mostly the local CBS affiliate in Long Beach California where the exhibit was held, jumped on the media train. They crowned June as "the last DiMaggio."

There was one last bloodline of Joe's still living at the time -- Dom.

"June DiMaggio is not the biological daughter of my brother Tom," Dom commented when reached in Florida.

While June "DiMaggio" and Robert W. Otto, along with Playboy's Hugh Hefner and CMG's Mark Roesler (who was then the licensing representative hired by Anna Strasberg) sat at a front table at a press conference, there were skeptics in the audience. Mark Bellinghaus, who then owned some legitimate items of Marilyn's purchased at auction houses like Christie's, was one.

One particular item that gave away the fraud was a set of Clairol Hair Rollers that June and Robert the collector claimed had Marilyn's hair wrapped in them. The charade was carried so far that "psychic" James Van Praagh said he was communicating with Marilyn using those very rollers as a conduit to the other side.

The major scam was planned to travel the world. If it had, it would have left false impressions about Marilyn and Joe. Thankfully, the exhibit would never debark from Long Beach. Mark Bellinghaus had recognized the hair rollers were not authentic since he owned some of his own that once belonged to Marilyn, and learned the ones on display were manufactured in 1974, twelve years following Marilyn's death. Whose hair was it that James Van Praagh was then communing with?

Author Ernest Cunningham joined in the fight, filing a lawsuit against the organizers with another Marilyn fan Emily Sadjady. With the combined efforts of these astute individuals, the exhibit was shut down.

To boot, Hollygrove, which had previously been the Los Angeles Orphans Home where Marilyn resided in childhood, was slated to receive a donation from the ticket sales. They never received a dime of the $22.95 per ticket price, which Ernest and Emily in their suit asked that attendees have the ability to receive refunds for.

Neither a representative from the Queen Mary nor Robert Otto cared to comment once the *Los Angeles Times* broke the story on May 31, 2006 about the lawsuit, after thousands of spectators had already viewed the exhibit including the mother of the author (she simply entered to buy a mug at the souvenir shop and was not permitted into the gift shop unless she purchased a ticket. The CMG-licensed mug was emblazoned with a sticker warning on its bottom that in the State of California, lead paint causes birth defects. The author has never used the mug because she knows that lead paint causes birth defects and other issues no matter where one resides).

The suit was settled with organizers, though details of the suit were never disclosed nor were ticket recipients ever given the opportunity of a refund.

June, who the author has verified by a genealogy search, was born June M. Elpine on June 11, 1923 slightly under three years prior to Marilyn's birth. Her parents were Rosetta Louise (aka "Louise" or "Lee") Rovegno and Albert U. Elpine. Lee was born in Washington (her birth record from Tacoma in 1903 specifies she was named "Rosetta Louise Elizabeth" and she was also located on the 1910 census at seven years old). Lee's mother was Swiss and her father Italian. In probability, June's parents divorced as Albert Elpine was listed in a 1948 San Francisco City directory with his spouse Margaret.

On the U.S. Census records for 1930 and 1940, June (listed as "June Albino") resided with her grandmother (with her last name also incorrectly spelled "Rooegno"), a woman who hailed from Switzerland and spoke German. Lee was tracked living with her sister and brother in 1930, reverting to her maiden name "Rosetta Rovegno," according to that census. Lee then worked as a hotel manager. Before marrying Tom, she also used the name "Louise R. Rovegno." Lee died in 1984. Albert Elpine, who was born in Italy, died in 1973 in California. Tom died in 1980.

Lee DiMaggio, it is speculated, married Tom DiMaggio in the 1940s.

If anything, June was a potentially casual acquaintance of Marilyn's during her marriage to Joe. At the time the photos were taken of Marilyn with Tom, Lee, and Joe in January of 1954, days before their wedding (Tom was born on January 12 and the photos were from his birthday), June was more than thirty years in age. She was older than Marilyn in fact, closing in on her thirty-first birthday when Marilyn and Joe married (Marilyn was only twenty-seven).

June asserted to be the only DiMaggio who leaked a story about Marilyn, one detail she stated accurately. Obviously she did not know her "uncle" well enough to recognize that privacy was so important to Joe. He never even penned his own memoirs about his life with Marilyn. Most likely June would have been excised from Joe's life for such an offense, if she had not been already before his death like siblings Dom and Marie were. Joe would have been especially horrified about the tales June told regarding Marilyn's sexual escapades with Hollywood moguls. June made vile claims that Marilyn showered for days after engaging in sexual activities to climb the ladder of fame.

The story of "June DiMaggio" has tragically remained on the radar for close to a decade. Even trinkets from the phony exhibit still float around on eBay occasionally. Charm jewelry of Marilyn's "things," like a tennis racket that had been on display that she never touched, are still sold. June wrote herself into Marilyn Monroe and Joe DiMaggio history much like Robert Slatzer and Jeanne Carmen did.

One of the most recent attacks against Marilyn and Joe's romance hails from *Newsweek*. Though *Newsweek* killed its print editions due to profitability issues (it is said to be reigniting print editions in 2014), the publication emerged with a special edition about Marilyn for February and March of 2014. Sadly, a "lost scrapbook" was released of photos that Marilyn allegedly presented to photographer friend Sam Shaw. Photographer Lawrence Schiller, who had taken Marilyn's picture when she swam nude on the set of *Something's Got to Give*, was the one who claimed Sam Shaw presented him with the scrapbook in 1973. This is the second "lost" item Lawrence Schiller has emerged with, having previously come out with "lost" pictures from Marilyn's nude swimming escapade in 2012.

As a well-versed Marilyn student who has pored over her documents for years, the author of this book immediately noted the handwriting, supposedly written by Marilyn alongside of the pictures, was not Marilyn's. Who then wrote in crayon the "love letters" claimed from Marilyn to Sam Shaw, if this is not Marilyn's handwriting?

Lawrence Schiller said he dined with Sam and Norman Mailer, whose book is not a trusted source (and was the first one this author read about Marilyn). After one of these gatherings, he said Sam told him of an affair with Marilyn. The timeline Lawrence Schiller claims falls in line with Marilyn's time with Joe. The author of this book believes this whole story and the scrapbook accompanying it, is sadly a sham tainting the memories of Marilyn, Sam and Joe.

Another black eye that has been administered posthumously to the love story of Marilyn and Joe evolved from Amy Greene who appeared in an HBO documentary about Marilyn in 2013 entitled *Love, Marilyn*, in which she claimed that Marilyn only planned to marry Joe because he "was good in bed."

First, this idea reflects disrespect for both Marilyn and Joe as if they were shallow human beings and especially towards one another.

This is also a highly impossible fictional hypothesis, as it is well-documented that Marilyn enjoyed her moments with Joe, such as their conversations in their early days together under the California moonlight while they dined on burgers and coffee, to walks in the snow during their secluded honeymoon, to surprise Christmas celebrations, to baseball games, to walks on the beaches of Florida with a fishing pole. If it were only about sex, these shining moments would have never glimmered through. If their relationship only existed between the sheets, Joe would have allowed Marilyn to rot in Payne Whitney, until she rocked in a catatonic fetal position in the corner for the rest of her days. If the relationship never endured, Joe would have never stepped forward to identify her body and handled the final arrangements for the woman who was his one true love. Lastly, he would have never mourned her for thirty-seven years, then rejoiced at the hope of meeting her again, on his dying day.

Joe and Marilyn were alike and so different in so many ways. They have become the stuff for which dreams have been created and love emulated. They each recognized their unique similarities and differences -- and admired and were drawn especially to one another's shy sides.

While Joe was smitten with Marilyn's outward gorgeous appearance, he fell for the loveliness emanating from within, her introversion and her innocent childlike spirit. He was knocked off his feet by the endless stream of love she dished out. Even in those times he would appear to reject her, he could not exist without her dedication and persistence for his heart. When she eventually turned away, it drove him mad and the insane jealousy kicked in.

Marilyn was enraptured with his mere commanding and elegant presence. She looked towards his protective nature as something that she also required for her survival and he warmed her with feelings of safety. She trusted his business sense and his way to see through the smoke and mirrors, qualities she lacked. His honesty was attractive to her. She was sensitive so that outspokenness could also be cutting. In the end, she forgave him for his previously rough nature, embraced the softer Joe even tighter and approached her grave with the desire to please him.

Though they were both flawed in many ways in how they related to one another (as members of the human race can naturally be) and some facets of their relationship were imperfect, eventually they meshed into true perfection and compatibility. It was after the egos, immaturities and insecurities were set aside, that the real love between Marilyn and Joe, always present, had the chance to really radiate.

Marilyn and Joe have now become the true shining example of a match made in heaven since that is where they exist together now.

Following her incarceration in Payne Whitney and after Joe rescued her, writer George Carpozi said, "Joe's the only man Marilyn has ever known, who can rock her in her place -- and I think that, above all else, would be her salvation."

In turn, Marilyn became Joe's salvation. She was a gentle soul who penetrated the heart of a person, who at times in his earlier years could be a mean-spirited ogre and impassable with a cool outer layer, but who in the end was charmed and tamed by the love of his beautiful princess.

In exchange, she taught him and he began to sincerely learn what it was like to set his pride aside. He stepped to the plate of life to become Marilyn's defender and her superman. She warmed his heart and he melted. He was a hero in the stadium to many, but his favorite role was champion to Marilyn Monroe, the beautiful blonde he loved, cherished and adored in a way he never imagined possible with another person.

Author Richard Ben Cramer, though it is evidenced in some ways he truly knew little about Marilyn, aptly summarized the relationship during his interview in 2000 with CNN when he said, "The one real intimacy in his [Joe's] life -- and the great chance he had for some happiness in the *Hero's Life* -- was his relationship to Marilyn Monroe."

Joe has the final say in this book with his private words extracted from his 1982 through 1993 diary entries. They hit the auction block, something that most likely would have made that guarded man shudder. At the same time, thanks to learning about Joe's inner thoughts, historians like the author have been able to assess further how much Marilyn remained at the forefront of his daily life.

"Book people felt me out with questions pertaining to baseball," Joe penned on April 28, 1989, almost twenty-seven years after her death and less than a decade before his.

He had just met with executives from Simon & Schuster about a potential book project.

"Some part of my private life but not too strong on that," Joe pondered. "Will not reveal anything in a negative way towards Marilyn -- only books that have come out on her might have not been truthful."

The ever private Joe would likely cringe to know that his diary hit the auction block, as well as love letters he wrote to Marilyn. He anguished at the divide that he may have caused, writing to her that he was "punishing himself," for potentially causing her pain. "It annoys me no end to think that I have 'bit' your feelings: you of all people, would be the last one I'd hurt! It has never been my nature to do that to anyone, and I'm certainly not going to start now."

He further expressed how it upset him in this letter that many had taken advantage of Marilyn, "a real solid human soul, with tremendous inner feelings."

Joe's friend Dr. Rock Positano remembered a Joe who not only sent the doctor home to change one night when he showed to a restaurant attired in a turtleneck and insisted it was necessary to return with a shirt and tie, he also recalled the man whose policy was, "Never bring up baseball, unless Joe did first, and never, ever bring up Marilyn Monroe."

It is likely with the doctor both were potentially topics that Joe initiated discussions about himself.

Dr. Positano said, "That was the whole thing with Joe, you didn't ask any questions. But if he volunteered information, you just sat there with your mouth hanging open."

There were secrets that the doctor said he will forever keep mum.

It is no secret Joe carried a torch for Marilyn daily and wherever Joe roamed, that light for Marilyn glowed brightly in his heart.

We can only hope that Joe has reconnected with Marilyn -- his true final wishes on starry nights and his deathbed -- and now embraces her in another dimension. Without a doubt then as it is remembered here on earth, their affection for one another can be considered a love for all time.

Wedded bliss on January 14, 1954. Original photo from the author's collection.

Bibliography

Many books, articles and websites have been written and created about Marilyn Monroe and Joe DiMaggio. The list below includes resources the author consulted with to conceptualize this book.

Books

Badman, Keith. Marilyn Monroe: *The Final Years.* New York: St. Martin's Press, 2010. Print.
Banner, Lois. *MM – Personal From the Private Archive of Marilyn Monroe.* New York: Abrams, 2011. Print.
Baty, S. Paige. *American Monroe: The Making of a Body Politic.* Los Angeles: University of California Press, 1995, Print.
Berra, Yogi (with Dave Kaplan). *When You Come To A Fork In The Road, Take It!* New York: MJF, 2001. Print.
Brando, Marlon. *Songs My Mother Taught Me.* New York: Random House, 1994. Print.
Brown, Peter Harry and Barham, Patte B. *Marilyn: The Last Take.* New York: Dutton, 1992. Print.
Buchtal, Stanley and Comment, Bernard. *Fragments.* United States: FSG, 2010. Print.
Carpozi, George. *Marilyn Monroe: "Her Own Story."* New York: Belmont Books, 1961. Print.
Carroll, Jock. *Falling For Marilyn: The Lost Niagara Collection.* Toronto: Stoddart Publishing Company, 1996. Print.
Cataneo, David. *I Remember Joe DiMaggio.* Nashville: Cumberland House Publishing, 2001. Print.
Charyn, Jerome. Joe DiMaggio. *The Long Vigil.* United States: Yale University Press, 2011. Print.
Christie's. *The Personal Property of Marilyn Monroe.* New York:1999. Print.
Churchwell, Sarah. *The Many Lives of Marilyn Monroe.* New York: Metropolitan Books, 2004. Print.
Cohen, Lola. *The Lee Strasberg Notes.* New York: Routledge, 2010. Print.
Cramer, Richard Ben. *Joe DiMaggio: The Hero's Life.* New York: Simon & Schuster, 2001. Print.
Cunningham, Ernest. *The Ultimate Marilyn.* Los Angeles: Renaissance Books, 1998. Print.
Cunningham, Ernest and Bellinghaus, Mark. *A Marilyn Mosaic.* Los Angeles: 2007. Print.
Daily News. *Joe DiMaggio An American Icon.* United States: Sports Publishing Inc., 1999. Print.
DiMaggio, Joe. *Lucky to Be a Yankee.* New York: Bantam Books, 1949. Print.
De La Hoz. *Platinum Fox.* Philadelphia: Running Press, 2007. Print.
Engelberg, Morris and Schneider, Marv. *DiMaggio: Setting The Record Straight.* St. Paul: MBI, 2003. Print.
Farber, Stephen and Green, Marc. *Hollywood On The Couch.* New York: William Morrow & Company, 1993. Print.
Feingersh, Ed and LaBrasca, Bob. *Marilyn: March 1955.* New York: Dell Publishing, 1990. Print.
Franklin, Joe and Palmer, Laurie. *The Marilyn Monroe Story.* Rudolph Field Company, 1953 (Republished Campfire Network Publishing, 2012). Online.
Flynn, Chris. *Faces of Fukuoka.* Japan: Nishinippon Newspaper Co., 1999. Print.
Glatzer, Jenna. *The Marilyn Monroe Treasures.* New York: Metro Books, 2008. Print.
Gilmore, John. *Inside Marilyn Monroe.* Los Angeles: Ferine Books, 2007. Print.
Guiles, Fred Lawrence. *Legend: The Life and Death of Marilyn Monroe.* New York: Stein & Day, 1984. Print.
Guiles, Fred Lawrence. *Norma Jean: The Life of Marilyn Monroe.* New York: McGraw Hill, 1969. Print.
Harding, Les. *They Knew Marilyn Monroe: Famous Persons in the Life of the Hollywood Icon.* 2012. Online.
Haspiel, James. *Marilyn: The Ultimate Look at the Legend.* United States: Henry Holt and Company, Inc., 1991. Print.
Kahn, Roger. *Joe & Marilyn A Memory of Love.* New York: William Morrow & Company, Inc., 1986. Print.
Kazan, Elia. *A Life.* New York: Anchor Books, 1988. Print.
Kennedy, Jason Edward and Miller, Jennifer Jean. *Marilyn Monroe Unveiled: A Family History.* New Jersey: J.J. Avenue Productions. 2016. Print.
Leaming, Barbara. *Marilyn Monroe.* New York: Three Rivers Press, 1998. Print.
Leutzinger, Richard. *Lefty O'Doul: The Legend That Baseball Nearly Forgot.* California: CBPG, 1997. Print.
Margolis, Jay. *Marilyn Monroe: A Case For Murder.* Indiana: iUniverse LLC, 2011. Online.
Martin, Pete. *Will Acting Spoil Marilyn Monroe?* New York: Doubleday & Company, 1956. Print.
Miracle, Berniece Baker and Miracle, Mona Rae. *My Sister Marilyn.* Chapel Hill: Algonquin Books of Chapel Hill, 2004. Print.
Moore, Robin and Schoor, Gene. *Marilyn & Joe DiMaggio.* New York: Manor Books, Inc., 1977. Print.

Morgan, Michelle. *Marilyn Monroe: Private and Undisclosed.* New York: Carroll & Graf Publishers, 2007. Print.
Morgan, Michelle. *Walking in the footsteps of....Marilyn Monroe: A list of her homes and haunts.* 2011. Online.
Murray, Eunice (with Rose Shade). *Marilyn: The Last Months.* New York: Pyramid Books, 1975. Print.
Newsweek. *Marilyn Monroe The Lost Scrapbook.* United States: Newsweek, 2014. Print.
Noguchi, Thomas T., M.D. *Coroner.* New York: Simon and Schuster, 1983. Print.
Ricci, Mark and Conway, Michael. *The Complete Films of Marilyn Monroe.* New Jersey: Citadel Press, 1964. Print.
Riese, Randall and Hitchens, Neal. *The Unabridged Marilyn: Her Life From A to Z.* New York: Congdon & Weed, 1987. Print.
Russell, Jane. *My Path & My Detours, Jane Russell: An Autobiography.* New York: Franklin Watts Inc. 1985. Print.
Schwarz, Ted. *Marilyn Revealed: The Ambitious Life of an American Icon.* Maryland: Taylor Trade Publishing, 2009. Print.
Spoto, Donald. *Marilyn Monroe The Biography.* New York: Harper Collins, 1993. Print.
Stapleton, Maureen and Scovell, Jean. *A Hell of a Life An Autobiography.* New York: Simon & Schuster, 1995. Print.
Staff of Beckett Publications. *Joe DiMaggio: The Yankee Clipper.* Dallas: Beckett Publications. 1999. Print.
Strasberg, Lee. *A Dream of Passion.* United States: Little, Brown and Company, 1987. Print.
Strasberg, Susan. *Bittersweet.* New York: G.P. Putnam's Sons, 1980. Print.
Strasberg, Susan. *Marilyn And Me: Sisters, Rivals, Friends.* New York: Warner Books, 1992. Print.
Vaccaro, Mike. *1941 -- The Greatest Year In Sports.* New York: Doubleday, 2007. Print.
Vincent, Fay. *We Would Have Played For Nothing.* New York: Simon & Schuster, 2008. Print.
Whitehorn, Chester. *The Marilyn Monroe Story.* New York: Screen Publications, Inc., 1955. Print.
Winters, Shelley. *Shelley II.* New York: Pocket Books, 1989. Print.
Winters, Shelley. *Shelley Also Known As Shirley.* New York: Ballantine Books, 1980. Print.
Woodard, Eric Monroe. *Hometown Girl.* United States: HG Press: 2004. Print.
Young-Breuhl, Elisabeth. *Anna Freud.* United States: Sheridan Books. 2008. Print.
Zolotow, Maurice. *Marilyn Monroe.* New York: Harcourt, Brace & Company, 1960. Print.

Articles

"Actress, Joe Not Married." *Greensburg Daily Tribune*: Jan 6, 1954. Online.
Adams, Jane Meredith. "Joe DiMaggio's Funeral Features Quiet Dignity Yankee Star Cherished." *Chicago Tribune*: Mar. 12, 1999. Online.
"All GIs Want In Korea Is Marilyn Monroe." *Palm Beach Post:* Nov. 10, 1952. Online.
"Along Came Joe." Marilyn's Life Story. *DELL:* 1962. Print.
Anderson, Dave. Behind the Mystique, DiMaggio Lives a Quiet, Private Life." *The New York Times*: Sept. 13, 1998. Online.
Bacon, James. "Coroner Investigates. Did Marilyn Deliberately End Her Life?" *Gastonia Gazette*: Aug. 6, 1962. Online.
Bailey, Judson. "DiMaggio's Home Run Tops Keeler's Record." *Ottawa Citizen*: Jul. 3, 1941. Online.
Barbour, William. "The very private life of MM." *Modern Screen:* Oct, 1955. Print.
Barnes, Bart. "American Icon Joe DiMaggio Dies at 84."*The Washington Post*: Mar. 8, 1999. Online.
"Birth of Marilyn Monroe Shown to Be Legitimate." *The New York Times:* Feb. 13, 1981. Online.
Bony, Bill. "DiMaggio Runs Hitting Streak To 50 Straight." *Times Daily*: Jul 12, 1941. Online.
"Bouquet-Laden DiMaggio Again Calls on Marilyn." *St. Joseph Gazette*: Feb. 13, 1961. Online.
"Braves' Pitching 'Worries' McHale." *The Milwaukee Sentinel:* Mar 23, 1961. Online.
Bumbler, Elisabeth. "Late to DiMaggio Orbit, but Staging Send-Off. *New York Times*: Apr. 23, 1999. Online.
Caruso, Michelle, Moritz, Owen, and Rush, George. "Joe D's Estranged Son In Key Role At Funeral." *Daily News*: Mar. 11, 1999. Online.
Cummings, John. "Yankee Luck: When the Old Clipper Plucked the Queen of Glamour a Million Guys Sighed and Waited." PIC, June 1954. Print.
"DiMaggio's Ex-Wife Asks More Support." *Oxnard Press-Courier:* Nov. 6, 1952. Online.
"DiMaggio stops sending roses to Marilyn Monroe's grave." *Lakeland Ledger*: Oct. 1, 1982. Online.
"DiMaggio to Fight Custody Suit." *Lewiston Evening Journal:* May 31, 1952. Online.
"Do A Dead Man's Files Finally End Marilyn Monroe's Search For Her Dad?" *People*: Mar. 1981. Print.
Derringer, John. "The Streak Still Stands." *The New York Times*: Jul. 17, 1941. Online.

Doors, Joseph. "Clipper and Gripper And Gorbachev, Too." *The New York Times*: May 30, 1988. Online.
Doors, Joseph. "Staff Sergeant Joe DiMaggio, The Yankee Clipper, Dies at 84." *The New York Times*: Mar. 8, 1999. Online.
"Excitement Upsets Marilyn's Tummy." *The Miami News:* Feb 5, 1954. Online.
Evans, Harry. "What caused Marilyn Monroe? (Part I)" *Family Circle*. May 1953. Print.
Evans, Harry. "What caused Marilyn Monroe? (Part II)" *Family Circle*. June 1953. Print.
"Flowers Taken From Cemetery – Souvenir Hunters Rob Crypt of Jean Harlow; Body May Be Cremated." *Tuscaloosa News*: Jun 10, 1937. Online.
"Friends, He Said Friends, She Said." *The Windsor Star*: Mar 23, 1961. Online.
Gelb, Barbara. "Actor George Scott Suffering Virtuoso." *Star-News*: Jan. 31, 1977. Online.
"GI Trampled In Rush But Marilyn Escapes." *Ottawa Citizen*: Feb 18, 1954. Online.
Handsacker, Gene. "Fireworks Fail to Materialize When Russell, Monroe Meet." *The Free Lance-Star*: Jan. 19, 1953. Online.
Hauck, Larry. "Two Ordinary Hurlers End DiMaggio's Streak." *The Calgary Herald*: Jul. 18, 1941. Online.
Heffernan, Harold. "Marilyn May Find Joe has Last Laugh." *The Miami News:* Oct. 9, 1954. Online.
Hengan, Jim. "Marilyn Monroe...lovable fake." *Motion Picture and Television Magazine*: Nov. 1953. Print.
"Japanese Mob Marilyn, Joe." *Lodi News-Sentinel:* Feb 2, 1954. Online.
"Jo (sic) DiMaggio Bids Fond Farewell To Marilyn At Funeral." *Bennington Banners*: Aug 9, 1962. Print.
"Joe And Bride Are Home: Wife Is Ill." *Gettysburg Times:* Feb 25, 1954. Online.
"Joe Cancels Trip To Stay With Marilyn." *The Deseret News*: Mar 27, 1961. Online.
"Joe DiMaggio 7 Games Away From Batting Record." *St. Petersburg Times*: Jun. 22, 1941. Online.
"Joe DiMaggio Jr. Dies at 57." *Titusville Herald*: Aug. 9, 1999. Online.
"Joe DiMaggio Jr.: Son of Yankees Baseball Legend Led Troubled Life." *Los Angeles Times*: Aug 8, 1999. Online.
"Joe, Marilyn Continue Honeymoon; Go To Japan." *Prescott Evening Courier*: Jan 29, 1954. Online.
"Joe, Marilyn Make Yanks Popular Team." *Herald-Journal*: Mar 28, 1961. Online.
"Joe To Nurse Ulcer Alone." *News-Dispatch*: Nov. 22, 1954. Online.
"Joe Will Fight To Keep His Son." *Spokane Daily Chronicle:* May 29, 1952. Online.
"'Just Friends,' Says DiMaggio. *Daytona Beach Morning Journal*: Mar 23, 1961. Online.
Koppel, Nathan. "BLONDE AMBITIONS A Battle Erupts Over the Right To Market Marilyn: Ms. Strasberg Seeks to Keep Control Over Licensing; Photographers Have a Beef." *The Wall Street Journal*: Apr. 10, 2006. Online.
"Korean Road Like Marilyn." *Toledo Blade:* Jan. 11, 1953. Online.
Cuter, Nanette. "Don't Blame Yourself, Marilyn." *Photoplay*. Jan 1955. Print.
Éclair, J.E. "The Real Reason for Marilyn's Divorce. *Confidential*. Sept. 1955. Print.
Lee, Matt and Lee, Ted. "Marilyn Monroe's Stuffing Recipe Stars in a Remake." *The New York Times*: Nov. 9, 2010. Online.
Leopold, Todd. "Richard Ben Cramer, influential campaign biographer, dies at 62." *CNN*: Mar. 7, 2013. Online.
Madden, Bill, Ciphers, Luke, and O'Keeffe, Michael. "Joe D & Morris: The Final Days How Lawyer Crony Isolated The Dying DiMaggio." *Daily News*: Apr. 25, 1999. Online.
Margolick, David. "THE LAW; A battle over who cashes in on the legacy of Marilyn Monroe." *The New York Times*: Jul. 21, 1989. Online.
"Marilyn Ailing On Return Home." *Spokane Daily Chronicle*: Feb 25, 1954. Online.
"Marilyn And Joe Leave On Trip To Japan." *Sarasota Herald-Tribune*: Jan 30, 1954. Online.
"Marilyn And Joe To Honeymoon In Japan." *Times-Daily:* Feb 1, 1954. Online.
"Marilyn And DiMaggio Missing, Wedding This Week Is Expected." *Miami News*: Jan 5, 1954. Online.
"Marilyn Cause Of Near-Riot." *Middlesboro Daily News*: Feb 17, 1954. Online.
"Marilyn Ends Tour of Korea." *Eugene Register Guard:* Feb 19, 1954. Online.
"Marilyn Entertains Marines in Tight Dress." *Oxnard Press-Courier*: Feb 16, 1954. Online.
"Marilyn Feuding With Greene Over Management of Company." *Chester Times*: Apr. 12, 1957. Online.
"Marilyn Is Cheered By Troops In Korea." *Miami Daily News:* Feb 16, 1954. Online.
"Marilyn In Florida." *St. Joseph News-Press*: Mar 22, 1961. Online.
"Marilyn In St. Pete For Sun, Rest And To Visit With Joe." *Ocala Star-Banner*; Mar 23, 1961. Online.
"Marilyn Gets Army 'Shots' Before Tour." *Sarasota Herald-Tribune:* Feb 6, 1954. Online.
"Marilyn, Greene Feud Over Terms of Their Contract." *The Free Lance-Star*: Apr. 12, 1957. Online.
"Marilyn Graced Sun coast For Twelve Hectic Days." *The Evening Independent*: Dec. 12, 1966. Online.
"Marilyn, Joe Off on Japan Honeymoon." *Pittsburgh Post Gazette:* Jan 30, 1954. Online.

"Marilyn, Joe Receive Gala Hawaii Welcome." *Reading Eagle:* Jan 30, 1954. Online.
"Marilyn, Joe Return Home." *Eugene Register Guard*: Feb 24, 1954. Online.
"Marilyn's Big Problem." *Tempo & Quick*: July 4, 1955. Print.
"Marilyn's Company Sees Rocky Weather. *Chester Times*: Apr. 12, 1957. Print.
"Marilyn Monroe Admitted to Hospital." *Albany NY Knickerbockers News*: Feb. 9, 1961. Online.
"Marilyn Monroe Shatters Quiet on Korean Front." *Herald-Journal*: Feb 18, 1954. Online.
"Marilyn Monroe Show In Korea Defended." *Pittsburgh Post Gazette*: Mar. 24, 1954. Online.
"Marilyn Monroe Suspended; May Elope With DiMaggio." *Reading Eagle:* Jan 5, 1954. Online.
"Marilyn Monroe To Appear In Divorce Court." *Ocala Star Banner:* Oct. 27, 1954. Online.
"Marilyn Monroe To Be Discharged." *The News and Courier*: Mar 5, 1961. Online.
"Marilyn Monroe Weds Blushing DiMaggio." *The News and Courier*: Jan 15, 1954. Online.
"Marilyn Monroe Wows Servicemen in Korea." *The Deseret News:* Feb 16, 1954. Online.
"Marilyn Moves In, Takes Corporation." *Spokane Daily Chronicle:* Apr. 17, 1957. Online.
"Marilyn Rests Up For Korea Trip." *Sarasota Herald-Tribune:* Feb 4, 1954. Online.
"Marilyn Stirs Korean Front To Wild Action." *Pittsburgh Post-Gazette:* Feb 17, 1954. Online.
'Marilyn Takes to Bed With a Tummy Ache." *Ellensburg Daily Record:* Feb 6, 1954. Online.
"Marilyn Taking Psychiatric Treatments." *Daytona Beach Morning Journal*: Feb. 9, 1961. Online.
"Marilyn to Spend 4 Days in Korea." *The Deseret News:* Feb 3, 1954. Online.
"Marilyn Upsets Japan Industry." *Palm Beach Post:* Feb 5, 1954. Online.
"Marilyn Walks In, DiMaggio Forgotten." *St. Petersburg Times:* Feb. 15, 1954. Online.
"Marilyn Works; Joe Plays Golf." *Oxnard Press-Courier:* Oct. 8, 1954. Online.
"Marines in Korea Happy With Marilyn's Party Dress." *Eugene Register-Guard:* Feb 16, 1954. Online.
Martello, Scott. "Suit Alleges Monroe Exhibit Mostly Bogus. *Los Angeles Times*: May 31, 2006. Online.
"Merger Of Two Worlds: Marilyn and Joe find a secret wedding is not for them." *LIFE:* Jan. 25, 1954. Print.
Meryman, Richard. "A Last Long Talk With A Lonely Girl." *LIFE*: Aug. 17, 1962. Print.
Meryman, Richard. "Marilyn lets her hair down about being famous." *LIFE*: Aug. 3, 1962. Print.
Miller, Jennifer Jean. Celebrating Marilyn and Jane in Color Sixty Years Later and the Artist Behind the Hand and Footprint Traditions. *InsideScene.LA*: Jun. 26, 1953. Online.
Miller, Jennifer Jean. "Was Phenergan Marilyn Monroe's Silent Killer, and Was She a Victim of Psychological Abuse, Medical Malpractice and Wrongful Death? New Possible Theories Regarding the Death of Marilyn Monroe." *TheAlternativePress.com*: Aug. 2, 2012. Online.
"MM Gets Out Of Hospital; Nerves 'Fine'. *The Times-News*: Mar 6, 1961. Online.
"MM's Mexican Pal Is in Beverly Hills." Daily News: Aug. 9, 1962. Print.
Monroe Exhausts Korea Film Supply." *Southeast Missourian:* Feb 19, 1954. Online.
Monroe, Marilyn. "My trip to Korea." *St. Petersburg Times:* Jul 22, 1956. Online.
"Monroe Reported 'Feeling Better.'" *Meriden Record*: Feb 26, 1954. Online.
"Mrs. DiMaggio to Relax Demands on Famous Joe." *Sarasota Journal:* June 3, 1952. Online.
"Mrs. DiMaggio To Visit Troops in Korea." *Victoria Advocate:* Feb 2, 1954. Online.
Muir, Florabel. "Joe to Marilyn at Rites: 'I Love You.'" *Daily News:* Aug 9, 1962. Print.
"Mystery Illness Hits Star After 'Near Collapse.'" *Ottawa Citizen*: Feb. 9, 1961. Online.
"'Never Seen A Ball Game,' Says Marilyn." *Daily Reporter:* Feb 3, 1954. Online.
"No Bathing Suits." *Greensburg Daily Tribune:* Feb 3, 1954. Online.
Ocker, Lisa. "Bitter Clash Over Wills Ends Dollmaker's Daughter To Takeover Estate." *SunSentinel*. Apr. 28, 1991. Online.
"O'Doul to Aid Baseball in Japan." *Spokane Daily Chronicle*: Jan 26, 1954. Online.
"One Casualty As GIs Surge To Monroe." *Lewiston Evening Journal*: Feb 18, 1954. Online.
Roger, George. "Does Sinatra Make Bushwhacking a Hobby?" *On the QT:* Nov. 1957.
Ross, Sid. "You Won't Believe This About Marilyn Monroe." *Compact…For Young People*: Oct. 1953. Print.
"School for Stars." *Colliers:* Mar. 16, 1956. Print.
Skolsky, Sidney. *"Marilyn."* Dell: 1954. Print.
"Soldier Hurt As Marilyn Appears On Korea Stage." *Times-News:* Feb 18, 1954. Online.
"Soldiers, Not 'Cowboys.'" *Pittsburgh Post Gazette*: Feb. 25, 1954. Online.
"Soldiers Riot Over Marilyn." *Windsor Daily Star:* Feb 18, 1954. Online.
"So They Say." (Tom DiMaggio Comments). *Oakland Tribune*: Oct. 29, 1954. Online.
"Star Poses For Airmen." *Reading Eagle:* Feb 19, 1954. Online.
"Stars Barred at Rites -- Lawford's Shocked." *Daily News*: Aug. 9, 1962. Print.
"Stolen Marilyn Monroe Items Recovered, Mostly. *The New York Times*: Mar. 30, 1994. Online.

"Studio Grants Marilyn, Joe An Extension." *Reading Eagle*: Jan 21, 1954. Online.
"Support Of Soldiers Abroad Gave Her Breaks In Films, Says Marilyn On Tour Of Korea Area." *Times-News*: Feb 19, 1954. Online.
Talbot, Gayle. "Yankees Keep Pace With Joe In Homer Derby." *The Miami-News*, Jun. 30, 1941. Online.
"There's no joy in St. Pete as Mets prepare to leave town." *Gainesville Sun*: Mar 20, 1987. Online.
"The Psychiatrists Look at Marilyn Monroe." *Focus*: Sept. 1952. Print.
Thomas, Bob. "Death of Actress Stuns Film World." *Corpus Christi Times*: Aug. 6, 1962. Online.
"Tokyo Mobs Joe, Marilyn." *Middlesboro Daily News:* Feb 1, 1954. Online.
"To Visit Korea." *Ottawa Citizen:* Feb 4, 1954. Online.
"The Mentor and the Movie Star." *Vanity Fair:* June 2003. Print.
Vescey, George. "DiMaggio's Last Call: It's About Famiglia." *The New York Times*: Mar. 12, 1999. Online.
Wallace, David. "He Makes Sure DiMaggio's Roses Are Always There." People: August 1982. Print.
Wender, Susan. "Marilyn enters a Jewish family." *Modern Screen*. Nov. 1957. Print.
"'We Want To Be Left Alone,' Reunited Joe, Marilyn Say." *The Evening Independent*: Mar 23, 1961. Online.
"Where to put Joe DiMaggio Highway?" *Syracuse Post Standard*: Mar. 11, 1999. Online.
"Whistles Greet Marilyn On Tour Of Korea Front." *Sarasota Herald Tribune*: Feb 15, 1954. Online.
Wilson, Earl. "Inger On Buttermilk Binge." *Galveston Daily News*: Feb. 23, 1962. Online.
"Women In Japan Shed Underwear." *Ottawa Citizen:* Feb 5, 1954. Online.
"Yank Clipper, Marilyn Monroe Wed." *Long Beach Press-Telegram*, Jan. 15, 1954. Online.
Zinoman, Jason. "Arthur Miller's life had its own lost act: A son placed out of sight." *The New York Times*: Aug. 30, 2007. Online.
Zolotow, Maurice. "Who Runs Marilyn Monroe?" *The Milwaukee Sentinel*: Dec. 16, 1956. Online.

Online Sources

America's Queen: The Life of Jacqueline Kennedy Onassis: http://books.google.com/books?id=quSGedVr4ZEC&printsec=frontcover&dq=Kennedy+Americas+queen&hl=en&sa=X&ei=FtW6Ury1CdSosASQwoDAAg&ved=0CDoQ6AEwAA - v=onepage&q=Kennedy Americas queen&f
Argenta Images – Jacqueline: https://www.argentaimages.com/media/image/q/Jacqueline/page/26
Augusta Chronicle – "DiMaggio's great-grandchildren remember 'Big Joe:' http://chronicle.augusta.com/stories/1999/03/27/bas_257357.shtml
Barry Halper Obituary: http://www.nytimes.com/2005/12/20/sports/baseball/20halper.html?_r=0
Baseball in Wartime: http://www.baseballinwartime.com/player_biographies/dimaggio_joe.htm
Behind The Picture: Rare Photos From the Night Marilyn Sang to JFK, 1962: http://life.time.com/history/marilyn-monroe-john-kennedy-happy-birthday-may-1962/ - 1
Bill Clinton Receives Award in S. Fla: http://miami.cbslocal.com/2014/01/24/bill-clinton-to-receive-award-in-s-fla/
The Boston Globe Obituaries – Dominic Paul DiMaggio: http://www.legacy.com/obituaries/BostonGlobe/obituary.aspx?n=Dominic-Paul-Dimaggio&pid=127086769
Carl Anthony Online: Other Protos & Stars from Marilyn Monroe's Happy Birthday Night to JFK & His Reaction: http://carlanthonyonline.com/2012/05/19/other-photos-stars-from-marilyn-monroes-happy-birthday-night-to-jfk-his-reaction/
Carl Anthony Online – The Most Shocking Truth About JFK & Marilyn Monroe: http://carlanthonyonline.com/2012/05/18/the-most-shocking-truth-about-jfk-marilyn-monroe/
Carmody McKnight Estate Wines http://www.carmodymcknight.com/more-information/16/
CNN: Forged Monroe-JFK letters sought: http://www.cnn.com/2004/US/03/09/fake.monroe.letters/
CNN: One last standing ovation: http://sportsillustrated.cnn.com/baseball/mlb/news/1999/04/23/dimaggio_cathedral/
CNN: "Richard Ben Cramer chats about his book, 'Joe DiMaggio: 'The Hero's Life:"http://www.cnn.com/chat/transcripts/2000/10/25/cramer/
Daily News: Joe D., Sinatra were on the outs: http://www.nydailynews.com/archives/gossip/joe-sinatra-outs-article-1.825048
Daily News: Joltless Joe Diary: http://www.nydailynews.com/entertainment/gossip/joltless-joe-diary-article-1.270662 - ixzz2ots8UJkr

"Dead-Celebrity Dealmaker Salter Buys Marilyn Monroe Name." Bloomberg: http://www.bloomberg.com/news/2011-01-13/dead-celebrity-dealmaker-salter-buys-marilyn-monroe-name.html

"Did The Devil's Disciple Successfully Summon the Spirit of Marilyn Monroe on the Eleventh Anniversary of Her Death?: http://www.redicecreations.com/specialreports/2006/08aug/monroe.html

Dorothy Kilgallen's Voice of Broadway: http://news.google.com/newspapers?nid=1946&dat=19621006&id=vJMuAAAAIBAJ&sjid=zJ0FAAAAIBAJ&pg=7142,1277049

ESPN: "Engelberg sued by former law partner Thursday": http://a.espncdn.com/mlb/columns/misc/1480351.html

ESPN: "I'll never forget my honeymoon – with the 45th Division": http://static.espn.go.com/mlb/s/dimaggiobook7.html

ESPN: "Joe DiMaggio dies at 84:" http://espn.go.com/sportscentury/features/00014156.html

ESPN: "There was no counterbalance to Joe's will": http://static.espn.go.com/mlb/s/dimaggiobook6th.html

East Bay Regional Park District: http://www.ebparks.org/parks/martinez.htm

Everlasting Star: Drew's Fantasy Dinner Guest: http://blog.everlasting-star.net/2010/08/celebrities/drews-fantasy-dinner-guest/

Fedo, Michael. "Joe DiMaggio Turns His Lonely Eyes Toward the Girl at 2833 West Third Street." http://www.whistlingshade.com/0301/dimaggio.html

FindLaw: Milton Greene Archives v. Marilyn Monroe LLC: http://caselaw.findlaw.com/us-9th-circuit/1610741.html

Freudians Prefer Blondes: http://www.salon.com/1999/11/10/marilyn_2/

Gay Talese, "The Silent Season of a Hero:" http://www.randomhouse.com/kvpa/talese/essays/dimaggio.html

Gus Zernial obituary: http://mlb.mlb.com/news/article.jsp?ymd=20110123&content_id=16486118&c_id=mlb

Hauls of Shame: http://haulsofshame.com/blog/?p=1862

"Hello Normal Jeane: http://www.fearandloafing.com/features/marilyn.txt

Hospital Birth Trauma – Appears Planned As Trauma Based Mind Control: http://beforeitsnews.com/power-elite/2013/05/hospital-birth-trauma-appears-planned-as-trauma-based-mind-control-2442144.html

IMDb – Joe DiMaggio: http://www.imdb.com/name/nm0227154/?ref_=nv_sr_1

IMDb – Marilyn Monroe: http://www.imdb.com/name/nm0000054/?ref_=nv_sr_1

Itami Air Force Base: http://www2.osk.3web.ne.jp/~aranishi/itmbase2.htm

Joe DiMaggio Playground: http://sfrecpark.org/project/joe-dimaggio-playground/

Joe DiMaggio Sports Complex: https://www.myclearwater.com/gov/depts/parksrec/facilities/jdsc.asp

Joe DiMaggio Official Site: http://joedimaggio.com/

Joe Dobson article - Lakeland Ledger
http://news.google.com/newspapers?nid=1346&dat=19760521&id=BG5NAAAAIBAJ&sjid=r_oDAAAAIBAJ&pg=6726,5416014

Jordan, Elisa and Woodard, Eric: Marilyn Monroe and 'Rain,' the project that never came to be, part 1: http://www.examiner.com/article/marilyn-monroe-and-rain-the-project-that-never-came-to-be-part-1

Julien's Auction 2010 Online Catalog: http://www.juliensauctions.com/auctions/2010/hollywood-legends/icatalog.html

Last Will and Testament of Joe DiMaggio: http://livingtrustnetwork.com/estate-planning-center/last-will-and-testament/wills-of-the-rich-and-famous/last-will-and-testament-of-joseph-p-dimaggio.html

LA Times: Chasing Marilyn: http://latimesblogs.latimes.com/thedailymirror/2007/06/marilyn_monroe.html

Laist: X-Rays Proving Marilyn Monroe Had Plastic Surgery Sold For $25,600 At Auction: http://laist.com/2013/11/14/x-rays_proving_marilyn_monroe_had_p.php

LinkedIn – Jennifer Strasberg: http://www.linkedin.com/pub/jennifer-strasberg/34/79/832

Mail Online: Marilyn Monroe's last weekend: Told for the first time, an eyewitness's account of the row with Frank Sinatra that friends fear signed her death warrant: http://www.dailymail.co.uk/femail/article-1299496/Marilyn-Monroes-weekend--told-time-eyewitnesss-account-row-Frank-Sinatra-friends-fear-signed-death-warrant.html

Mamie Van Doren: "Joltin' Joe DiMaggio:" http://www.mamievandoren.com/insideout/insideout/2012/04/joltin-joe-dimaggio.html

Marian McKnight, Miss American Pageant Results, 1957: http://pageantcenter.com/pageant%20results/Miss_America_Pageant/1957_miss_america_pageant.html#.Uq5IomRDvss

Marilyn Monroe Estate Loses Tax Case: http://vqrginc.com/1/post/2012/09/marilyn-monroes-estate-loses-tax-case.html

"Marilyn Monroe honoured on 40th anniversary of her death:"
http://www.theage.com.au/articles/2002/08/06/1028157932093.html

Maurice Zolotow Milwaukee Journal article:
http://news.google.com/newspapers?nid=1499&dat=19790414&id=WlMaAAAAIBAJ&sjid=oSkEAAAAIBAJ&pg=4869,3417961

MK-Ultra/Payne Whitney/Tavistock: http://permalink.gmane.org/gmane.culture.discuss.cia-drugs/22897

Monroe Family Assessment Service: http://www.tavistockandportman.nhs.uk/monroefamilyassessmentservice

"Monroe's Legacy Is Making Fortune, But For Whom?" NPR:
http://www.npr.org/2012/08/03/157483945/monroes-legacy-is-making-fortune-but-for-whom

Newsweek Return to Print: http://www.nytimes.com/2013/12/04/business/media/newsweek-plans-return-to-print.html

New York Daily News: Amy Greene, close friend of Marilyn Monroe, recalls the star as new documentary airs on HBO," http://www.nydailynews.com/entertainment/tv-movies/marilyn-monroe-words-fill-love-marilyn-article-1.1370579

PDN: In Bankruptcy, Photo Archive Cuts Deal with Marilyn Monroe Estate: http://pdnpulse.pdnonline.com/2012/01/in-bankruptcy-photo-archive-cuts-deal-with-marilyn-monroe-estate.html

"President Bill Clinton to Receive Inaugural Joe DiMaggio American Icon Award, January 24, 2014: http://www.marketwired.com/press-release/president-bill-clinton-receive-inaugural-joe-dimaggio-american-icon-award-january-24-1864261.htm

Restore Paper – Dear John Letter from Marilyn Monroe to Elia Kazan: http://restorepaper.com/services/stain-reduction/.

Rossmoor Realty – Sue DiMaggio Adams: http://www.sue-dimaggio-adams.com/

Seeing Huston's Freud: http://www.clas.ufl.edu/users/nholland/huston.htm

SF Gate – Obituary for Daniel Greenson:
http://www.legacy.com/obituaries/sfgate/obituary.aspx?pid=158048249

Stella Adler in People, originally published 7/17/89:
http://www.people.com/people/article/0,,20120772,00.html

"Tax Maneuvers Cost Marilyn Monroe's Estate:" http://www.courthousenews.com/2012/08/30/49818.htm

The Loudon Hunt: http://www.loudounhunt.com/

Salon .com: "Marilyn Monroe, baby sitter:"
http://www.salon.com/2013/09/26/marilyn_monroe_baby_sitter/

The Daily Mirror – Black-Foxe Military Institute: http://ladailymirror.com/2013/07/29/mary-mallory-hollywood-heights-hats-off-to-black-foxe-military-institute/

The Downfall of Barry Halper, Baseball Collecting's Bernie Madoff: http://deadspin.com/5818225/the-downfall-of-barry-halper-baseball-collectings-bernie-madoff

The Faces We Live – "DiMaggio, Joseph Paul Jr.: His Love for MM:
http://thefaceswelive.com/2011/12/27/dimaggio-joseph-paul-jr-his-love-for-mm/

The Free Dictionary – Pentobarbital: http://medical-dictionary.thefreedictionary.com/Nembutal+Sodium

Shaw Monroe: http://www.scribd.com/doc/79378387/Shaw-Monroe

The Smoking Gun – "Actually, He should Have Been Nicknamed 'The Yankee Clapper.'"
http://www.thesmokinggun.com/buster/psychoneurosis/did-joe-dimaggio-give-marilyn-monroe-clap

The Smoking Gun –Monroe's Last Will And Testament: http://www.thesmokinggun.com/file/monroes-last-will-and-testament?page=0

The Smoking Gun – "Say It Ain't So, Sergeant Joe:"
http://www.thesmokinggun.com/documents/celebrity/say-it-aint-so-sergeant-joe

The Swellesely Report: "Red Sox star Dom DiMaggio's wake, funeral to be in Wellesley:
http://theswellesleyreport.com/2009/05/red-sox-star-dom-dimaggios-wake-funeral-to-be-in-wellesley

Transcript Bob Hope from CNN: "Thanks For The Memories," 2003:
http://edition.cnn.com/TRANSCRIPTS/0308/01/lkl.00.html

Vanity Fair: For Love of DiMaggio: http://www.vanityfair.com/society/features/2000/09/dimaggio-200009

Vanity Fair: The Hollywood Blog: X-Rays from Marilyn Monroe's Doctor's Visit, Taken Two Months Before Her Death: http://www.vanityfair.com/online/oscars/2013/10/marilyn-monroe-plastic-surgery-x-rays

Wicked Local Wellesley – "Goodbye to baseball great Dom DiMaggio at Wellesley's St. Paul:
http://www.wickedlocal.com/wellesley/news/x1194166174/Goodbye-to-a-baseball-great-at-Wellesleys-St-Paul

Cursum Perficio: www.cursumperficio.net
Marilyn Monroe Family Facebook Page: www.facebook.com/MarilynMonroeFamily
Marilyn Monroe Family Website: www.marilynmonroefamily.com
"The Surgeon Story" Website: www.surgeonstory.com
YouTube: www.youtube.com
When Jackie O and JFK Called Middleburg Home: http://www.visitloudounblog.com/2010/05/19/when-jackie-o-jfk-called-middleburg-home/
Yale University – Class of 1964 – "In Memoriam, Joe DiMaggio, Jr.:" http://yale64.org/remembrances/dimaggio.htm

Photo by One Red Tree Photography

Jennifer Jean Miller has held a love of writing her entire life, and kicked off her professional career in 2006. She began her tenure with local news publications in 2008 and has worked as a journalist, photojournalist, columnist, marketing consultant and editor within the industry. She was a freelance reporter and photographer for *Straus News, The AlternativePress.com*, and *LH! Weekly*. She spent a segment of her career, as a local editor and reporter for *TheAlternativePress.com* in Sussex County New Jersey before she branched out on her own with her local news site *NJInsideScene.com* and Hollywood entertainment site *InsideScene.LA*. Along with these publications, she launched her media, public relations, and publishing company J.J. Avenue Productions in 2013. Jennifer has garnered award nominations, for her business achievements through the Sussex County Chamber of Commerce and its Economic Development Partnership. She additionally received a nomination for her photography while at Straus News. Jennifer received the Media and Entertainment Award from the New Jersey Governor's Council on Mental Health Stigma in 2010 for her sensitivity in reporting on mental health subjects.

Among some of Jennifer's other journalistic accolades, Jennifer was also the New Jersey State Director in 2014 for the Reuters Ipsos Election Reporting Project. As an author, she was interviewed in 2014 for the documentary, *What Ever Happened to Norma Jeane?* She was also interviewed in 2015 for a segment of *Snapped: Killer Couples*, for the Oxygen Network as an investigative reporter.

Jennifer has been an admirer of Marilyn Monroe's since childhood and hopes to share more of her knowledge about the star with the public, as well as her collection. She owns a collection of Marilyn Monroe and Joe DiMaggio items and photos -- some unpublished -- and some are now featured in this book. Several items from her collection are also highlights of *Marilyn Monroe & Joe DiMaggio - Love In Japan, Korea & Beyond*. Her collection has been on exhibit with the Ted Stampfer Marilyn Monroe Collection and she has assisted Mr. Stampfer with writing and translation aspects of several of his exhibition catalogs.

Jennifer is the personal press representative for the "Marilyn Monroe Family" website and Facebook Page, representing the descendants of Marilyn's great-uncle, William Marion Hogan.

Marilyn Monroe & Joe DiMaggio - Love In Japan, Korea & Beyond is her first book. Her second is Arcadia Publishing's *Stanhope and Byram* from the Images of America series. Her third is with Jason Edward Kennedy (they married in July 2015), her spouse, with whom she runs MarilynMonroeFamily.com, *Marilyn Monroe Unveiled: A Family History*. She has other books in the works about other historical figures and events.

Her book is the first in a series endorsed by "Marilyn Monroe Family" at MarilynMonroeFamily.com. Stay tuned for one of the next upcoming book releases in the series, *Surgeon Story*.

www.ingramcontent.com/pod-product-compliance
Lightning Source LLC
Chambersburg PA
CBHW040903020526
44114CB00037B/47